PRAISE FOR GERALD ASTOR'S
THE MIGHTY EIGHTH

"No one does oral history better than Gerald Astor . . . here the men of the mightiest air force ever built tell their story in their own words—of trials, tribulations, triumphs, terror, and tedium." —Stephen Ambrose

"FASCINATING . . . invaluable in terms of understanding both the process of protracted war and its effect on the human spirit. Excellent in weaving these stories into a broader analysis of the Eighth's role in the air war with Germany, Astor demonstrates once again that he's one of the most accomplished oral historians at work today." —*Publishers Weekly*

"Revealing and vivid . . . His many interviews of American airmen turn up some fascinating anecdotes, catching the grim realities of air combat in a way that more conventional histories cannot." —*Kirkus Reviews*

"GERALD ASTOR HAS PROVEN HIMSELF A MASTER. Here, World War II is brought to life through the hammer blows of their airborne triumphs and fears. This book should be of interest to anyone who fought that war—or any war—in the air, and those who want to understand what combat was like for the airmen and their leaders." —J. Robert Moskin

Please turn the page for more extraordinary acclaim. . . .

A BLOOD-DIMMED TIDE

"Original . . . evocative . . . brilliant." —*Publishers Weekly*

"Consistently gripping . . . a vivid vision of warfare from the foxhole." —*Daily Press* (Newport News, Va.)

"A gripping story . . . will no doubt take its place as a classic." —*The Record* (Troy, N.Y.)

"The immediacy and clarity of enlisted men's accounts form the core reality here, giving a palpable sense of infantry and tank warfare. Strong narrative, sound history and a good read." —*Kirkus Reviews*

"*A Blood-Dimmed Tide* is an important contribution to the history of World War II." —*Cleveland Jewish News*

"An absorbing book, fascinating for its first-person detail." —*Richmond Times-Dispatch*

"A compelling, effective contribution to World War II history." —*Booklist*

GERALD ASTOR

BATTLING
BUZZARDS

THE ODYSSEY OF THE 517TH
PARACHUTE REGIMENTAL
COMBAT TEAM 1943–1945

A DELL BOOK

Published by
Dell Publishing
a division of
Random House, Inc.
1540 Broadway
New York, New York 10036

Dell books may be purchased for business or promotional use or
for special sales. For information please write to: Special Markets
Department, Random House, Inc., 1540 Broadway,
New York, NY 10036.

Dell® is a registered trademark of Random House, Inc., and the
colophon is a trademark of Random House, Inc.

ISBN: 0-440-23693-2

Reprinted by arrangement with Donald I. Fine, Inc.

PRINTED IN THE UNITED STATES OF AMERICA

PUBLISHED SIMULTANEOUSLY IN CANADA

October 2001

10   9   8   7   6   5   4   3   2   1
OPM

To all who fought the good war

CONTENTS

ACKNOWLEDGMENTS

My thanks to the staff at the U.S. Army Military History Institute at Carlisle, Pennsylvania, for the opportunity to research materials concerning Melvin Zais, Louis Walsh, James Gavin and the operations of the 517th Parachute Regimental Combat Team.

I also want to express gratitude to my agent Henry Dunow of Harold Ober Associates for his support during some difficult moments.

PREFACE

BATTLING BUZZARDS GREW out of my previous book dealing with World War II, *A Blood-Dimmed Tide: The Battle of the Bulge by the Men Who Fought It*. In the Battle of the Bulge, the watchwords of military effectiveness, command and control, all but vanished as the Germans unleashed a strong, surprise onslaught over inhospitable terrain during the depths of winter. American forces, some of whom were inexperienced, poorly led and perhaps inadequately schooled, disintegrated. The enemy advance halted as the Allies brought to bear massive resources plus a number of what military reporters like to describe as "crack" units.

The question of what makes one group of soldiers superior started a search for an examplar of the breed. As an infantry replacement myself, during World War II, I am keenly aware of my own deficiencies as a soldier with weaknesses due to training, personal character and motivation or lack of same. The achievements and record of the 517th Parachute Regimental Combat Team made it a vehicle for discovery of what elements form a highly effective combat unit, as well as outlining my own lacks.

My approach in the earlier book, as in this one, has been in the nature of an oral history infused with enough narrative to furnish a context for the voices of the GIs. It is inevitable, of course, that memories may alter facts and gloss accounts with what one prefers to believe. Eyewitnesses during moments of great trauma often honestly disagree on what happened. Furthermore, the temptation to self-serve always lies in wait for the recorder of oral history. While admitting to these potential distorters, I have sought more than one source for what might be questionable.

In presenting the material I have retained the words of the troopers as faithfully as possible. The only significant deletions are names in a few instances where one man denigrated another for behavior under fire. One man's cowardice is another's better judgment of the situation.

Ordinarily, a book of this nature carries a list of acknowledgments by individuals. In this instance, however, the text itself indicates the contributions made by others.

CHAPTER I

AIRBORNE

FROM THE DARKENING mists of their memories, men who served in the armies of America during World War II may recall the nearly ineffable aura that enveloped the label of "Airborne." To be sure, there were some tangible trappings to envy or relish. Highly burnished leather boots and a silver badge marked a "trooper"—even that designation distinguished him from the common "soldier." Only fliers and the tiny elite Ranger units competed in glamour.

While recognizing the glory attached to parachutists, some with long military experience, as well as raw draftees, perceived them as harboring a death wish. More sensible people hesitated to hurl themselves from an altitude of several thousand feet, dependent only upon yards of silk or nylon to prevent a fatal plunge. While troopers drifted helplessly towards the ground, unable to unlimber their weapons, the enemy could slaughter them.

Still, the airborne never lacked recruits. Mel Trenary was one. "I volunteered for the paratroopers because I wanted to prove to myself that I had the ability to build my body into something worthwhile and at the same time I could do something that the average person wouldn't want to do.

"My first jump was a surprise. We put on our chutes,

sat on benches until finally we walked to the plane. The harness was so tight I could hardly stand up straight. As the last person on board, I sat right next to the door, looking out. This was my first time in an airplane and I was fascinated. It was hard to believe, at that time, that a heavy machine like this could go up into the air. I had, of course, seen planes but it was different being inside one as it went up.

"They had trained me right. It was all automatic. When the red light went on, I got up and stood at the door. I didn't look down, but I could see the horizon because of the plane's movements. When the green light came on, I felt a tap on my leg and I jumped out, just like they had taught me. I had my eyes closed, but I could feel my body going upside down. When the chute opened, it flipped me right side up and I knew everything was working right. I opened my eyes and watched others come out of the plane.

"I was the first one out and I had felt that if I didn't go then some of the others might chicken out. Later, one of the guys told me that as he saw me get ready by the door, he thought, if Trenary can do it, so can I."

Mel Trenary served his country as part of the 517th Parachute Regimental Combat Team. The outfit began its thirty-three-month life in March of 1943 as an element in the 17th Airborne Division. Eventually nicknamed "The Battling Buzzards," because of a singular emblem displaying an irate vulture against a parachute backdrop with appropriate numerals, the 517th went to war as a regimental combat team little more than a year later. It fought through five campaigns in Europe, collecting more than 1,500 Purple Hearts for wounds, and earned a multitude of medals.

From its roster the 517th produced eight general officers, including a pair who began as eighteen-year-old, lowly privates. Further evidence of the organization's élan lies in the many who chose to make a career of the army after V–E Day. Unlike most men who considered military life onerous, the parachute combat team, in spite of its grim months of combat, gave these soldiers a home.

Kinfolks of the 517th during World War II, like the 17th, 82nd and 101st Airborne Divisions in Europe, as well as the 6th and 11th Airborne Divisions in the South Pacific, fought bravely and effectively, but there were some unique features to the 517th which gave it a special quality and therein lie some truths about military effectiveness and military elites.

Commanders of great military organizations yearn for fighting forces that surpass the efforts of the ordinary soldiers although some of the very qualities that invest crack troops with super power create conflicts. In the U.S. even before Pearl Harbor, while the notion of airborne units barely existed beyond the paper stage, U.S. paratroopers already bore the status and the stigma almost inevitably stamped on an elite outfit.

James M. Gavin, who led four combat jumps in Europe and finished the war as commanding general of the 82nd Airborne Division, was part of the tiny group that created the paratrooper role. "We had an idea. We wanted to tell these guys that they were the most capable guys on earth. And when they land, it doesn't matter who they meet; they can really lick them under any circumstances. And any parachute squad is worth a platoon of anybody else. We wanted these guys to find out that there's nothing too good for them; no bed too soft, no food too good, no conditions too good for them to live. But, by God, when combat comes, then there's not too much to ask from them. We really expected to ask anything of them and we expected them to come through.

"We tried to give a whole dimension of how to train human beings and how to get them committed, dedicated and believing in what they were doing and how to make them very combat effective, consistent with trying to find the kind of leadership that could lead these guys. You had to be as good at anything as they, and often better, and be willing to do anything you asked them to do."

In fact, the airborne units carrying American colors into battle during World War II fielded superior soldiers and officers. In the U.S. Army, no other form of fighting man, with the possible exception of the Rangers, earned such well deserved praise. The 517th exemplified the training, spirit and record of paratroopers.

The parachute itself wasn't that new: Leonardo da Vinci, along with his designs for manned flight, in his fifteenth century *Codex Atlanticus,* noted the possibility for safe passage from the skies. "If a man have a tent of linen of which the apertures have all been stopped up . . . he will be able to throw himself down from any great height without sustaining any injury." Alongside of his comment, da Vinci sketched four triangular panels jointed at the top from which a human figure dangled.

The concept languished until the hot air balloon of the eighteenth century lifted humans above the earth. In 1785, French balloonist Jean-Pierre Blanchard put together a crude approximation of the device designed by da Vinci. However, rather than experiment with his own person, M. Blanchard bestowed the honor for the first parachute descent on his dog. Carnival and circus gasbag shows, forced by audiences to add more derring-do, first employed trapeze-type aerialists and then finally added the ultimate thrill, parachutists. Indeed, when baseball magnate Albert Goodwill Spalding collected a gang of all-star players for a round-the-world tour in 1888, he hired one "Professor Bartholomew" to add some show biz with a balloon ascent, trapeze act and climax of a parachute leap. Unfortunately, during one performance, the Professor bounced off a building cornice in Australia, forcing Spalding to leave Bartholomew in a hospital for repairs.

During World War I, only the Germans, in the waning days of the fighting, equipped some of their pilots with parachutes although both sides outfitted the balloon-borne observers with chutes. However, in October 1918, Col. Billy Mitchell, chief of the American Expeditionary Forces airmen, approached Gen. John "Black Jack" Pershing, the U.S. commander in France, with a daring plan.

". . . he should assign one of the infantry divisions permanently to the Air Service . . . we should arm the men with a great number of machine guns and train them to go over the front in our large airplanes which would carry ten or fifteen of these soldiers. We would equip each man with a parachute, so that when we desired to make a rear attack on the enemy, we could carry these men over the lines and drop them off in parachutes behind the German position."

Before any serious discussion of the tactic, the November armistice quashed further consideration. Still, under Mitchell's prodding, shortly after hostilities ended, a standard, practical parachute was developed for use at least by pilots.

During the 1930s, Soviet, French and Italian forces embarked on parachute programs in varying degrees. Nazi Germany, forbidden to rearm by the Versailles Treaty, sponsored glider clubs whose craft showed an obvious potential in warfare and secretly started to build a paratroop corps.

The notion of airborne fighting men, "a sword of silk" in the rhetoric of one advocate, languished in the U.S. But in 1939, Gen. George Catlett Marshall, U.S. Army Chief of Staff, enlightened by intelligence reports of the European interest in airborne and parachute soldiers, ordered a feasibility study. The hastily done research, while it supported an experimental program to develop infantry traveling by air, remarked that combat groups dropped behind enemy lines could well be on suicide missions.

Not until fighting broke out in Europe was there an American effort to create paratroop units. The entire project received a boost with the news of the German successes, using parachutists to overwhelm the Netherlands and Belgium on the way to overrunning France in the spring of 1940. On June 25 of that year, the very day the French admitted their defeat to Adolf Hitler in the same railroad car that witnessed the German surrender in 1918, the commandant at Fort Benning, Georgia, received orders for a platoon of recruits to undergo parachute training.

In 1940, jumping out of an airplane, in spite of Leonardo da Vinci's theoretical assurance that given enough canopy one could throw oneself down from a great height without fear of injury, seemed a highly dangerous business. The offhand suggestion by those who first investigated the tactics that their roles could become *kamikaze* style missions added to the sense of risk.

Sensitive perhaps to excessive demands upon men while the country was not yet at war, the brass decided that no one should be forced to be a paratrooper. Those first candidates for the new type of soldier were thus asked to break the cliché First Commandment of the enlisted man, "Never volunteer!" The tradition, begun in 1940, has served as standard procedure for assignment to airborne forces ever since.

Those in charge of those first volunteers screened for both attitude and athletic ability. It seemed obvious that the physical demands upon a parachutist demanded intensive conditioning. The original 1940 platoon exercised, marched and ran beyond the norm. In the absence of towers[1] to learn how to cushion the impact with the ground, the would-be troopers jumped off the backs of trucks and for more advanced practice leaped off the vehicles while they were moving.

The art of tumbling to avoid injury seemed critical. Anyone who failed to roll in the prescribed manner immediately received a critique that ended with a command of "Gimme ten!" on the basis that extra pushups cured carelessness. Well before behavioral scientists publicly proclaimed the virtues of "aversive training," those running the infant paratroop program employed punishment as a way to instill an instinctive resort to the right techniques. This system to build in automatic responses is another legacy that endured.

Those first volunteers spent days learning how to pack their silk. Not until well into World War II did the art of parachute rigging become a responsibility of specialists while the troopers themselves concentrated on their roles as airborne fighters.

The gear issued to the first would-be paratroopers consisted mostly of hand-me-downs. Each volunteer for that original platoon received two pairs of air corps mechanics' coveralls, a leather flying cap like those sported by World War I aces and a pair of boots with a strap across the instep designed to give support to ankles stressed by that first contact with the earth. One genuine innovation made at the very start of the program was the reserve chute carried on a man's chest. Throughout

---

[1]Maj. William Lee, who commanded this first detachment, discovered that the makers of the grand parachute tower installed at the New York World's Fair in 1939 had a pair of towers in Hightstown, New Jersey. He arranged for his unit to spend ten days at nearby Fort Dix and train on the two high platforms. Eventually, similar but higher towers were erected at the major paratroop training sites, Fort Benning and Camp Mackall, North Carolina, with a mini-size one at Toccoa.

World War II, American troopers were the only ones afforded a second chance if the main chute failed to deploy. Members of the 517th would eventually see gruesome evidence of the reserve's value.

The instructors placed great stress upon the way in which a man exited the airplane door over the drop zone. However, in a mass jump, only the first man had an opportunity to follow the manual. The rest were lucky if they went out feet first, many wound up diving head down. Any delays upon leaving the aircraft, even if counted in seconds, meant the stick of twelve to fifteen troopers would be strung out over a considerable distance, reducing effectiveness.

After the first successful jumps of the test platoon, the brass scheduled a mass demonstration to indicate the tactical power of airborne soldiers. Several members of the platoon, on their way to the barracks after watching a Western film at the Fort Benning post theater, discussed the added dangers of such an untried maneuver. One man teased Pvt. Aubrey Eberhardt that he would be so scared he wouldn't remember his own name. Eberhardt retorted with typical bravado. In a sudden inspiration he said he would shout the name of the Indian warrior bedeviled by the U.S. cavalry in the movie. True to his word, Eberhardt, as he exited the door of the C–47 the next day, yelled, "Geronimo!"

Although celebrated in the popular media, the invocation of Geronimo actually was a short-lived tradition. Experts soon taught men to forget about the chief and count, "One thousand, two thousand, three thousand . . ." and if the main chute had failed to open, it was time to yank the ripcord of the reserve. Furthermore, succeeding classes of paratroopers considered the cry juvenile. Russel Brami, a member of the 517th and who made a lifetime career of being a paratrooper, says, "I never heard anyone yell 'Geronimo!' We used to claim the translation of Geronimo was, 'Who pushed me?' The usual comment, if any, when a guy jumped was, 'Oh, shit.' "

The tangible morale builders for paratroopers followed soon after the graduation of these initial recruits. In January of 1941, the men received authorization to wear their boots with trouser legs tucked into the tops while in dress uniforms. The patch with the white parachute against a blue background for the soft overseas cap followed. Airborne artillery used a red backdrop. The silvery badge with the wings curving up from the base of a chute to meet the canopy added an adornment. A two-piece jumpsuit with plenty of pockets replaced the mechanics' coveralls. Redesign of the boot improved its function and style; the leather's potential for burnishing gave new meaning to spit and polish.

Even as the American and the British enthusiasm for airborne units swelled, the German version staggered from a near fatal blow. The Nazi war machine, rushing to the rescue of its ally Benito Mussolini's Italian army floundering in its invasion of Greece, drove the British to a last-ditch defense on Crete, the largest island of the Mediterranean Sea and a strategic block to the Aegean Sea.

Gen. Kurt Student, the German airborne commander, convinced Hitler he could conquer the British forces—mainly New Zealanders—with his glider soldiers and paratroopers descending on Crete's three major airfields. The battle demonstrated the vulnerability of such units. The initial error lay in sending gliders without being preceded by paratroopers. As the first fragile sailplanes swooped to the tarmac, the heavily entrenched defenders slaughtered the occupants almost before they could tumble from their bullet-riddled craft. When the paratroopers arrived at the airdromes the Brits wreaked heavy casualties while many invaders still hung in their harnesses. However, a handful of the airborne gained a toehold. A withdrawal by the New Zealanders due to poor communications allowed the Germans to bring up massive reinforcements. The battle tide ebbed for the British, who performed a mini-Dunkirk to rescue many of their forces.

The victory notwithstanding, Hitler, because of the enormous casualties, lost faith in airborne assaults. Of the 13,000 jumpers and gliders, 5,140 had been killed or wounded. The cost to the Luftwaffe in planes was also horrific: 350 aircraft were destroyed, including many transports that would be desperately missed when the Nazi armies headed east into the Soviet Union.

Both the British and the Americans, however, concentrated upon the success. They saw that a heavily defended position fell against a determined airborne operation which numbered less than half its foe. Furthermore, strategists perceived the tactical mistakes of the paratroopers and glider forces which landed directly on well-entrenched opposition rather than to their relatively weaker rear.

The decision to build up U.S. airborne outfits received a final boost with Pearl Harbor, December 7, 1941. By the summer of 1942, airborne outfits had grown from the original platoon-size unit up to 3,000-man regiments. Now the powers at the top decided operations of full divisions were feasible and chose the 82nd and 101st Infantry Divisions to be the forerunners of the new breed.

In the spring of 1943, with the first U.S. paratroopers already bloodied in the North Africa fighting and members of the 82nd preparing for operations in Sicily, the 17th Airborne was activated on March 15. A major component given life that day was the 517th Parachute Infantry Regiment. Also created as part of the 17th Airborne were two other units, the 460th Parachute Field Artillery and the 139th Airborne Engineer Battalion. Men from both of these would become vital elements in the 517th Parachute Combat Team. But for all of these newly formed organizations, the immediate needs were a cadre and then recruits for training.

The system was in place but making it produce the desired product depended upon the right human touch, the leadership cited by James Gavin. For new outfits like the 517th the quality of its superior officers was a prerequisite for success. The top brass would cue the cadre and the junior leaders charged with turning the raw recruits into the kinds of fighting men envisioned by Gavin.

CHAPTER II

THE BRASS

CHOSEN TO COMMAND the newly formed 517th Parachute Infantry Regiment was Louis A. Walsh, Jr., a South Brooklyn boy who graduated from West Point in 1934. The first of his class to wear the silver eagles of a full colonel, Walsh graduated from one of the early airborne classes. He barely survived an accident early in his paratroop career, when his plane "ran out of air," and at 150 miles per hour rammed into some Fort Bragg treetops. According to Walsh, when the first rescuers reached the scene, they figured him as a candidate for the morgue, attaching a toe tag that listed, "male, about thirty." Walsh, however, recovered from what he insisted added up to thirty-seven separate fractures.

In 1942 he shipped out to the South Pacific as an observer with some of the first American combat soldiers, U.S. marines and army units engaging the Japanese in the brutal warfare on tropical jungle islands. Upon his return from the South Pacific, after ten weeks of on-scene research, Walsh filed an eighteen-page report with his findings. What he saw and wrote about became a kind of bible for the creation of the 517th.

Under a section headed "Training," Walsh wrote: "Company officers must be made to understand how important they are to their men and how suddenly this becomes true when the shooting starts. Officers that have simply been tolerated by their men previously suddenly find themselves expected to know everything on every subject by their men."

Walsh referred to several instances of officer blunders which might have been avoided either through improved screening of the commanders or better guidance . . . "Corrections and instruction must be continuous but the battlefield is not the place to start."

When Walsh received his command of the newly activated 517th Parachute Regiment, he practiced as he preached. His officers were expected to lead their men in their activities, rather than watch them. Those who would not or could not meet these standards transferred out.

His memorandum noted: "Men must be exposed to prolonged hardships without food, water and *conveniences*. All maneuvers must be *two-sided* and the value of blank ammunition in training cannot be overemphasized. Troops must learn night sounds, animal noises, not to disclose their position, where to sleep, when to sleep—how to protect themselves from men, insects and nature; the simplest of sanitary hygiene measures and water discipline, and they must learn these things *in addition* to a thorough knowledge of *all* their weapons and how to employ them." These became standard lessons for his outfit.

The colonel noticed details that might be overlooked in favor of urges for tactics and firepower. "There have been many instances where men in foxholes or slit trenches have relieved their bowels or bladders and, during a lull, moved to a new position. Later, during a bombing or shelling some other person has thrown himself in the same hole and found it despoiled. He has then jumped out 'cussing' his predecessor only to be killed . . ." He commented to his subordinates that the Marines had been deficient in instructing their men on the vital matter of field sanitation.

He iterated his fealty to the Queen of Battles, the infantry. "It is . . . essential that every man in *every type of organization* be trained basically as an infantryman before he receives his specialized training as a field artilleryman, quartermaster, mechanic, etc. . . . Further, it is not sufficient that each man in the unit be trained with one weapon. He must be proficient in all weapons with which his unit is armed."

Walsh lectured on the need for weapons discipline, noting the high casualties from trigger-happy soldiers. He dwelt on tactics, citing instances where failure to move up immediately after the softening up from an artillery barrage allowed the enemy to regroup and inflict heavy damage.

He made a particular point of the need to weed out the incompetents or emotionally unfit with a quotation from a marine officer. "About ten percent of a unit do all the fighting and will never cause you any trouble—they are the backbone. About eighty percent are half-trained, scared to death and waiting to see what someone else is going to do. The other ten percent never were and never will be any good."

Before the first recruits came to Toccoa, Walsh determined to build what he called "a will to win" into his regiment. He intensified efforts to shift the percentages drastically toward the portion of troops prepared to fight without waiting to see what others did. He intended not to have anyone in the last, and useless, ten percent category.

When the troopers of the 517th qualified on target ranges with their assigned weapons, Walsh initially demanded that every man achieve the top designation of "expert" with his piece and, in keeping with his belief that all should be familiar with other armament, required the next highest rating of "sharp-shooter" with a second weapon and the minimum of "marksman" with the crew-served guns and mortars. Weeks of instruction and practice still left a number of "bolos"—the contemptuous term originated during the Philippine insurrection where those who couldn't qualify with a rifle were relegated to the machete or bolo—confined to the ranges, trying to improve their aim. Eventually, men who otherwise seemed assets rejoined their comrades even though their range scores fell below Walsh's standards.

Walsh appears to have combined some of the qualities described by Gavin along with the more conventional attitudes of a 1930s West Point product, including a tendency to bombast. Even though the U.S. was now at war, Walsh clung to some ancient prerogatives. He was a devout believer in spit and polish. Obsessed with his own appearance, Walsh, according to 1st Battalion-surgeon Ben Sullivan, insisted on wearing a very narrow boot that inflicted a case of trench foot during Tennessee maneuvers.

Capt. Herbert Bowlby, who carried himself with the stiffness of the drill fields of West Point, showed up in a floppy airborne cap and a riding crop, carry-over from his cavalry background. Walsh chewed him out. Walsh demanded his officers receive permission to marry and anyone who broke the rule could expect a transfer. Under Walsh's stewardship, about half of the captains, lieutenants and noncoms originally assigned to the 517th as cadre did not survive the training period. Junior officers and enlisted men regarded him as a strict disciplinarian and, well out of official earshot, GIs referred to him as "Cockatoo Lou."

Along with his zeal for militarily correct appearance and behavior, Walsh installed an intensive regimen bent on developing physical strength and infantry tactics. Immediately after reveille, the entire outfit, from colonel to newest rookie, broke into a trot for a two-mile, in step and in formation, run around the camp. In the afternoons, following lectures and field exercises, the men usually formed up for the assault on the outstanding topographical feature of Toccoa, Mt. Currahee, in the mountains of northeastern Georgia, about three and a half miles from the huts housing the 517th. Walsh and the others, incidentally, drew inspiration from the supposed Indian meaning of Curahee—"stands alone."

For all of his apparent stiffness, Walsh recognized the value of distinctly nonregulation morale builders. Lt. John "Tiger" Rohr, who insisted his civilian occupation had been con man and frequently demonstrated the skills of that profession while a soldier, decided B Company lacked spirit. He prevailed upon the St. Louis zoo to supply the 1st Battalion with a lion cub as a mascot. Walsh tolerated the presence of the beast, its destruction of mattresses and pillows and general threat to the health of its handlers, until it scored its first casualty. When a group of officers, led by 1st Battalion commander Maj. William J. Boyle, decided to drive into town for a celebratory party, someone thought the mascot should accompany the group. Apparently unhappy with its car ride, the cub swung a paw in the direction of Boyle, raking him across the head. On the following morning, Boyle showed up at the rifle range with his steel helmet perched high upon a turbanlike bandage. Walsh learned the source of the damage and suckered the 515th Parachute Infantry into accepting a gift of a mascot.

In fact, the party at which Boyle incurred his wounds was part of the paratrooper tradition, the Prop Blast. In December of 1940, a group of paratroop officers, with their wives in attendance, concocted a drink consisting of vodka (for strength), champagne (to add sparkle) and sugared lemon juice (for potability). In theory, the kick from the mixture was to stimulate the shock of the prop wash on leaping from a plane. The audience would count "One thousand, two thousand, three thousand . . ." as the celebrant chug-a-lugged the drink. Then, while leaping off a table, he shouted the first things that came to his mind.

At the initial Prop Blast, during the infancy of the airborne forces, Lt. Carl Buechner provided the casing from a 75 mm shell with handles manufactured from rip cord handles. Later, the names of the thirteen officers on hand were engraved on the chalice which became known as "Miley's Mug" in honor of the major who commanded the first paratroop battalion formed.

Prop Blasts became a favored recreation among paratroop units which soon had their own mugs—"Gavin Goblet," "The Sink Grail" [for Robert O. Sink] and in the 517th, the "Walsh Wassail." The last bore an inscription: "The metal pieces on this cup were taken from the parachute of a dead Jap on Guadalcanal and presented to this regiment upon its activation, March 15, 1943, by Lt. Col. Louis A. Walsh, Jr., its first CO."

When it came to matters that involved the mustering of his forces, Walsh even attempted to enlist the support of the loved ones back home. Before his men went on leave he dispatched a form letter to parents or wives: "Your ——— is a member of my Regiment. As his Regimental commander, I want to take this means of telling you of his progress and my responsibility to you and to him. I am charged with his spiritual and moral welfare, his health, his preparation for combat and finally his successful completion of his battle mission." [There is not much evidence of Walsh's actual concern with the first of these enumerated responsibilities but undoubtedly they made good reading to the civilians at home.]

Walsh then slathered his missive with flattery. "You have much of which to be proud. He, like all other men of the Five Seventeen, was carefully selected for his intelligence, physique and fighting heart. Ours is the Army's only volunteer unit. . . . He by his diligence and aptitude is, today, not only a qualified parachutist but a ruggedly trained, outstanding soldier."

Now Walsh skillfully sought to prevent the natural inclination of many soldiers to extend their time at home. "It means much for him to be with you. I ask your help to help him. His time is limited and all means of travel are restricted. He is due to report back for duty on the date indicated on his furlough and it is my sincere hope that you will see him off on time and with a feeling of confidence in those he leaves behind. He is going to war that you may be safe. Write to him often and cheerfully. . . . know that I live for no purpose but to win our war and bring him home to you, stronger and sounder than he is today."

The battalion commanders under Walsh also penned notes of this nature. Men did go AWOL but no one can accuse Walsh of not having used all means available to reduce such actions.

Walsh's three immediate subordinates, the battalion commanders, were strikingly different individuals but, like Walsh, they brought similar convictions on the way to building a superior fighting force. Col. Robert O. Sink of the 506th Parachute Regiment, a friend of Walsh's, dispatched the loser in the tangle with the lion cub, another Brooklyn boy, Maj. William J. Boyle, a 1939 graduate of the Military Academy and twenty-six years old when he reported to Toccoa.

Despite their similar backgrounds, Walsh and Boyle on the surface seemed almost incompatible. Boyle grew up in one of Brooklyn's less affluent neighborhoods. The sports and games consisted mainly of punchball and stickball on the streets, with an occasional sandlot football game at the Parade Grounds of Prospect Park. The parochial schools he attended offered little in the way of athletic facilites. "St. Augustine's on Park Place between 5th and 6th Avenues had a very small gym, barely enough for a basketball court and a one-wall handball court. In my senior year I lettered in cross-country and track. I was probably better than average in sports but not exceptional."

He secured an appointment to West Point, not because of a childhood dream of a military career, but because it was an opportunity for higher education which otherwise seemed unlikely. Not studious in high school, he managed good grades on all exams.

"Prior to West Point, physical fitness was incidental in my life. I did not know how to swim and from my high school experience I recognized no piece of gym apparatus beyond a climbing rope. In my plebe year I was on corrective exercises in swimming and gymnastics. However, I had the highest score in my company in the five track-and-field events. Nevertheless, when I volunteered for the parachute duty I was behind the others in arm strength. I didn't reach par until I started serving with the 506th Parachute Regiment."

As 1st Battalion CO, under Walsh's direction, Boyle personally interviewed the recruits. "The one question that I always asked was, 'Why do you want to be a parachutist?' The stock answer was, 'Because they are the best.' My second question would follow up: 'What makes them the best?' That's where the answers might be interesting. It was necessary to hear what was not said as well as what was expressed. My questions would then vary according to the responses but they were all designed to tell me about physical fortitude or guts, mental determination or guts.

"When they came to us they were given a physical and the AGCT [an intelligence test used by the U.S. Army]. The regimental policy was that standards set for physical qualification would be strictly enforced and no one who scored below 90 on the AGCT would be accepted. [Minimum for an applicant to Officer Candidate School was 110.] Policy, however, is a guide, not an absolute law. The surgeon would make known his opinion on

marginal cases and let them come to me. The officer in
charge of recruits would also inform me of individuals
who barely missed the 90 score. These people would be
questioned at greater length.

"My approach may have reflected the fact that I had
serious discussions with the assistant surgeon of the
506th when I checked in there. I had suffered a fractured skull in 1940. It was on the record and I was questioned intensively about it. I had been treated for a
sprained ankle a few weeks before I reported to the
506th. I had broken a finger in 1938 or '39 and one
joint was a little misshapen. The doctor made quite a
fuss over the leg and skull fracture, and while I saw his
point, I gave more weight to just plain guts and re-
sourcefulness. I accepted several marginal cases and I
don't recall any failures among them."

Intestinal fortitude, or "guts" in Boyle's word,
marked his own personality. On his very first jump while
in the course for parachutists, Boyle landed hard enough
to injure a knee. Two hours later, on his second effort,
he damaged the other knee. The surgeon observing the
drill summoned Boyle. Gritting his teeth, Boyle casually
walked to the medic without a limp. "There was no way
he was going to put me back."

Unlike his CO, Boyle admittedly was "not a spit-and-
polish officer." While a ferociously hard worker, Boyle
threw himself into the roistering with equal abandon,
and his apparent willingness to shed his insignia and
duke it out with anyone earned him the nickname of
"Wild Bill." Indeed, one of his junior officers, Charles
La Chaussee, described him as anything but the model
of military primness. "Wild Bill Boyle was a large man,
more than six feet. Boyle usually looked as though he
had just gotten out of bed, where he'd slept in his
clothes."

"I had opinions about discipline," says Boyle, "but
my emphasis was on combat training, combat reliability

and ability to rely on one another, not spit-shined boots. I was not casual. I trained intensively and expected the same of officers and men. Truth and accuracy in one's word were essential."

However, he did not totally dismiss the standard forms for turning civilians into soldiers. "Saluting is an exchange of greetings; the subordinate acknowledges the authority of the senior. Grooming in garrison should be neat. Close order drill is a disciplinary exercise designed to get us in the habit of obeying orders without question. These are necessary but they must be kept in perspective. One should hardly expect a man to look as if he is going to a dance when he is living out of a knapsack in the field." He eschewed the sort of petty tyranny known and loathed by all enlisted men under the label of "chicken shit."

A former company commander of his, Carl Herndon, had inculcated in Boyle the maxim, "You take care of the men and they will take care of you." If anything, Boyle seems to have taken extraordinary pains to know his men. John Forrest, a trooper who would earn a battlefield commission in France, remembers, "He learned our names very quickly and could recognize some of us even in the dark. On one occasion, during a night exercise, a soldier silhouetted himself against the moonlight on a ridge. Boyle yelled, 'Dammit, Stallins, get off that ridge!' I was nearby and Red Stallins was a close friend of mine but I could not have recognized that it was him on the ridge. The episode gave me the impression that Boyle had an uncanny extrasensory power exceeding anything I had ever known."

Forrest was also present on an occasion when Boyle exerted his own unique form of discipline. "We had a rash of AWOLs at Camp Mackall. To cure the problem, all officers and noncoms were restricted if they had AWOL soldiers in their command. Two men from my company, George Talarico and Dick Larson, returned from being AWOL. Boyle had me bring them to his office. He chewed them out and then chewed them out some more. Finally, he challenged, 'Do either of you think you can kick my ass?' (A formidable task for anyone and certainly impossible for me even though I stood 6′3″ and weighed more than 200 pounds.)

"Talarico affected a cherubic look and said, 'Colonel Boyle, I know I can't but Larson thinks he can.' Larson's hair almost stood on end. 'Shut up, Talarico! Do you want to get me killed?' Boyle burst out laughing."

Phil Di Stanislao, a recruit serving with Boyle's A Company, remembered a jump in North Carolina where immediately after he struck the ground, he looked up and saw a C–47 dropping men from only a few hundred feet above ground. "You had time for maybe one oscillation to control your chute and then you landed," says Di Stanislao. He saw Bill Boyle come down nearby and immediately board a jeep. "Word was that Boyle got to the airstrip just when that plane landed. He then beat hell out of the pilot for jeopardizing the safety of the men." Whether or not this actually occurred, Boyle's soldiers regarded him as a commander who held their interests closest to his heart and was not shy of using his fists on their behalf. Yet, by his own evaluation, although he joined the revelries of Prop Blasts, Boyle considered himself an introvert. And in truth, he rarely opened up on his feelings to his comrades.

From Bob Sink, one of the most effective leaders during World War II, Boyle drew the conviction that leadership through example inspires troops. When one of Boyle's captains demurred at the prospect of soldiers toting machine guns during speed marches, Boyle instantly seized the opportunity to make a point. "I ordered him to have a machine gun at his formation for the speed march that afternoon. I arrived with full individual equipment one minute early, and picked up the machine gun. I traveled beside this company commander all the way. He marched faster than usual, five miles in fifty minutes. I carried the machine gun the full distance. When he dismissed the company, I threw the machine gun at him, saying, 'Don't ever tell me anything is impossible again.'

"That demonstrates the best way to imbue troops with the proper spirit. Let them know you can and will do everything that you ask them to do, and the best way to get that across is to let the men see you do it, not just tell them." Boyle thus encapsulated the philosophy of Gavin.

He did not lecture his junior officers on this idea, being content to have them also learn by example. "When the men ran up Currahee, they ran in companies. I would usually start after the last company and run past them. One day I ran by and found two newly assigned officers lagging behind their company. I spoke to them both, arranged a schedule and progress for them so they would be able to run with their units.

"Colonel Walsh made it easy for me in this area. He decreed that no officer would do administrative duties or be in his office at any time that his troops were training. That made it simple to avoid being distracted from training."

Unlike many organizations, when in the field, the 517th officers did not mess in separate tents where enlisted men brought them their food. Instead, the commissioned personnel were expected to take a position at the ends of the chow lines.

"Boyle," wrote his subordinate, Capt. Charles La Chaussee, "was completely honest and painfully direct. The men of the battalion loved him and would cheerfully have followed him into hell. His officers trod very warily in his presence [La Chaussee himself withered under Boyle's glower on more than one occasion] and only God could help the captain or lieutenant who tried to be less than honest with him."

On one occasion, Lou Walsh summoned Boyle and demanded the name of the person responsible for some wrongful activity. Says Boyle, "I answered, 'I am.' Walsh acknowledged, 'I know you as CO are responsible but who actually did it?' I knew the guilty party was an NCO and when I first learned of the problem I had spoken to the company commander, told him to straighten it out and let me know when it was corrected. That had been done. Now as Walsh kept asking me who did it, I continued to reply that I was responsible. Finally, he accepted my approach, that my subordinates were my problem, not his, and if he had a complaint it was with me. I think the men knew my attitude and they knew that my loyalty to them was every bit as great as what I asked of them."

In another instance, Boyle dismissed a company commander. "Colonel Walsh asked why I did not consult him and I replied, 'I didn't need to.' He then inquired, 'Suppose I did not agree?' I responded, 'Sir, then you will need to relieve me.' "

Walsh obviously had great confidence in Boyle. One day, after a general criticized a problem run by Boyle's battalion, Boyle "gave Walsh a piece of my mind over the remarks." Walsh, furious already because a unit of his command had been censured, in his frustration, turned on his subordinate and chewed Boyle out. Subsequently, Boyle learned that Walsh, later that same day, had submitted his name for promotion to lieutenant colonel.

Indeed, Boyle was somewhat more forgiving with his enlisted men than with his officers. He relied mainly on company punishment, through the company commanders, to handle any problems with GIs. But with officers he was sterner. He relieved one man of rank for inveigling a GI to lie for him; another got the boot because of a mixture of inefficiency and improper use of authority.

Tough as he was on his subordinates, Boyle did not back down from what he believed when confronted by his superiors. During the invasion of Southern France his worst suspicions of an officer who put his troops at risk were confirmed and he replaced him. "After a few days, he returned and I advised him there was no place for him in my battalion. The next day the executive officer of the regiment called and said I couldn't do this. I replied simply and directly. 'I already have.' I was directed to see Colonel Graves [Rupert Graves had taken over the 517th from Lou Walsh]. Graves said he was sending the officer back to me. I said he should not do this. In fact, I said I'd shoot him when I got a chance. I doubt I would have if Graves had put me to the test but I did say it. When I told Graves I would rather shoot the man than lose a hundred or more killed because of his stupidity, Graves relented."

Although the episode with the lion cub indicates Boyle was an enthusiastic participant in Prop Blasts, in retrospect and perhaps with the sensitivities of the 1990s on alcoholic revels, he questions their function. "To some degree they may have brought officers together as a group. But as I look back, Prop Blasts were a sort of means to puff up our egos. What really brings people together is intensive training together, the bearing of hardship and discomfort together."

The 2nd Battalion commander came from an entirely different background than either Walsh or Boyle. Richard J. Seitz, roughly the same age as Boyle, grew up in Leavenworth, Kansas. His father owned a wholesale milk and ice cream company.

As a grammar-school student, Seitz occasionally ran afoul of the authorities. "The nuns would crack my head. I'd run home to complain to my mother and she'd give me a belt. I weighed about ninety pounds in high school when I tried out for the basketball team but didn't make it. I did tinker with cars and I took a discarded Model T truck from the dairy and turned it into a tin lizzie I could drive.

"My father had been the mayor of Leavenworth and was active in local and state politics. This stimulated an interest in politics and world affairs among the Seitz family. Like all Midwesterners, I was concerned about Germany and Japan. I was appalled by Hitler. I didn't have any great intellectual understanding of what was happening but, influenced by my family, I felt very strongly about the persecution of Catholics. While I was in high school, my older brother was a reserve captain and that made us even more aware of the situations with Germany and Japan.

"I entered Kansas State and majored in Agriculture and Dairy Husbandry. Within two years I had completed my senior ROTC work, received a commission as a second lieutenant in the infantry. The students and faculty respected the military instructors. The courses were tough, with three hours of drill and three hours of class work a week, each semester, but you received only half a credit. I layed out of school to work and save enough money to finish college. Even while at KSU I had held two jobs, working at the college dairy and as a houseboy at the Chi Omega house.

"Although I had done well in ROTC, I had no plans for a military career and only joined ROTC to have a reserve commission in the event the country became involved in a war. From my early days I had always expected to take over my father's business. Even during World War II, I intended to return to the business."

Whatever Dick Seitz's notions to further his education and become an entrepreneur, the world situation drastically changed his situation. In February 1940, as the United States belatedly started to rev up its military engines, he was called to active duty with the 38th Infantry in Texas. In the rapidly growing army, Seitz, still a second lieutenant, found himself a company commander, a job normally filled by a captain.

While attending an advanced course at the Fort Benning Infantry School, Seitz saw the original Parachute Test Platoon in training. He decided to become a paratrooper. "In February of '41 I put in my request. My battalion commander disapproved with some negative comments. However, shortly after this, the battalion exec was transferred to Washington. Before he departed he took me aside and asked, 'Seitz, do you really want to take parachute training?' I answered, 'Of course I do.' About four weeks later I received orders assigning me to the Provisional Parachute Group, commanded by Col. William Lee. I was assigned to the 503rd Parachute Infantry Battalion under Maj. Bob Sink. My company commander was Capt. James Gavin."

With those headliners—Lee became the first head of the parachute forces, Sink went on to lead a regiment through combat in Europe and Gavin eventually commanded the 82nd Airborne—Seitz started his four-week course that included the requisite jumps plus intensive work in weapons training and physical fitness. Seitz then took a detour to the Air Corps Technical School at Chanute Field, Illinois, where he studied the art of parachute rigging.

Because of his work at Chanute Field, when Seitz received assignment to the newly formed 503rd Parachute Regiment, he found himself part of Service Company, detailed to supervise the packing of chutes. "I was really disappointed and wanted a rifle company but I got turned down. But after a few months, they recognized my lack of enthusiasm for my job and I was given command of I Company. However, I did institute a system where the packing section in Service Company would pack all chutes for the regiment, which allowed more time in the schedule for training. The system became standard in parachute units, and the Table of Organization and Equipment [T/O & T/E] was modified to include additional riggers."

His tour with the 503rd brought him in contact with

a battalion commander named Lou Walsh. Subsequently, Walsh and Seitz reported to the 1st Parachute Brigade, with the former as executive officer and the latter in the role of S–3, in charge of operations for what was a training organization. When Walsh received command of the 517th he chose Seitz to run his 2nd Battalion.

"Lou Walsh was a great and tough trainer. His idea of a schedule was six full days, Saturday and holidays included, of hard, rough training. On Christmas and New Year's Eve, 1943, we held Battalion Commander and Regimental Staff Training Conferences. When one of my officers, Loren James, requested time off to get married, I told him, 'Great. Take off early Saturday afternoon but be back for the run on Monday.' Each evening after supper, Lou conducted officer and NCO classes. *All* administration, including courts-martial, was conducted after supper.

"Walsh was hell on weapons and physical training and high on squad and platoon training. The men of my battalion, and I'm sure the other ones, fired every infantry weapon in the inventory. Not just to fire, but to learn everything about the weapon. The troopers got a good deal of self-confidence from this knowledge. Lou was marvelous on combat courses and designed the ones we used. These included crawling under barbed wire with live fire over your head, making your way through mud, lots of obstacle courses designed by the regiment.

"Our squad and section work consisted of typical fire and movement exercises with an emphasis on aggressiveness and control by the small unit leaders. We did a lot of stuff that gave the squad leader the opportunity to lead and control his men. The attention to squad and section training was considered important because when the squad or jump stick hit the ground after the jump they would be the first and only group with immediate tactical or unit integrity. They would be required to fight on their own during the initial phase of action. This doctrine was accepted by all parachute units and is equally valid today, although the jump stick today consists of thirty or forty instead of the twelve to fifteen of World War II.

"The recruits came to us directly from the reception centers after they enlisted or were drafted. This was a unique arrangement. When the men arrived at Toccoa, they received orientation and then had to jump out of the thirty-four-foot tower. Anyone who even hesitated was immediately assigned to the 'Out Platoon,' for shipment to some nonparachute unit. I then personally interviewed every man initially assigned to the 2nd Battalion.

"If I didn't like his looks, or didn't think his background suitable, I dismissed him and he joined the 'Out Platoon.' Some of the questions I asked were, 'Did you volunteer because of the fifty bucks? [The hazard pay approved by Congress for paratroopers.] Do you think you are good enough to make a paratrooper? How many times have you been arrested? What sports did you play? Did you box? What was your best subject in school? What church do you attend?' No single answer was a reason for disqualification; the total picture determined acceptance.

"Occasionally, I asked, 'Can you ram your fist through that wall?' Everyone I challenged reared back and drove his hand through the Celotex wall of my tarpaper office. As best I can remember, no one was unlucky enough to hit one of the two-by-four studs. At reunions of the 517th it's amusing to hear the large number of guys claim they punched the wall. In reality, only a small number were asked to perform this exercise.

"The result of this selection process and the programs installed by Walsh was an outfit composed of physically fit, intelligent, motivated men with a helluva lot of confidence."

While he could pick and choose among the recruits, Seitz had no discretion when it came to the officers sent to the 2nd Battalion. "Most of them came to us right out of jump school. I was able to get rid of any who didn't measure up to my standards. But there was not great turnover from those who originally joined the battalion through our first combat in Italy.

"I was single, and only three or four officers were married. Off duty we would get together for fun—a little drinking and singing. I don't consider we were hell raisers. Some of the officers may have raised a little hell off duty but never were they so out of line that I felt it necessary to discipline them. At most I might have given them a good blast, a tongue-lashing, but that was the limit. We stuck together as a battalion group but we had a lot of respect for the total 517th officer corps. I had and continued to have the greatest respect for Bill Boyle, a superb human being and fine soldier. To mention a few others, I had and have similar emotions towards Ray Cato [CO for the 517th's artillery battalion], Bob Dalrymple, who was a damn fine engineer commander, and Ben Sullivan, a soldier's doctor and a great soldier as well."

Seitz, who made the army his career, rising to the three-star rank of lieutenant general, almost fifty years later insists, "In all my service, most of it with troops and airborne at that, I have not seen a finer group than the 517th. They were outstanding in every respect. Their appearance and spirit often caused some problems with my superiors but I admired them in and out of the battalion. They were so damn much better than the nonairborne soldier and officers that I served with prior to becoming a parachutist."

The third member of the triumvirate under Walsh was Melvin Zais, a few months shy of his twenty-seventh birthday when he arrived at Toccoa. His father, a refugee from Russia who came to the States as a twelve-year-old, was struggling to develop a meat business in Fall River, Massachusetts, when Zais was born in 1916.

"We lived near the mills on Quequechar Street near the river. Most of the families were of French or Portuguese background. It was a tough area and I had plenty of street fights as a kid. I played football on a field behind the billboards.

"Then the family fortunes improved and we moved to a seventeen-room house in an affluent section. But we lost everything during the Depression and went back to a poor neighborhood. I remember the tough, rough days of being brought up with children who didn't have much, whose parents were not well educated, and whose code of ethics and code of conduct were based on survival. But I also went to school with Yankees—the Bordens, the Braxtons and the Durfees—families that could trace their ancestry back to the Mayflower.

"Because of this background, I always had a great deal of compassion for people who didn't have much. I've understood rough language and I've been equally at home with truck drivers as with managers and owners. I've found a certain joy when I am with soldiers and exposed to the rougher elements of soldier life, and I've found great joy in the nicer elements of an officer's life. I am literally the product of two environments and both had a great deal of influence on me.

"When I was seventeen, I hitchhiked to Louisiana to attend college. My ambition was to major in journalism since I enjoyed English. I selected LSU because the out-of-state tuition was quite cheap and it would take me away from Fall River."

Thus, in the summer of 1933, Zais sought a football scholarship and performed well enough to win a slot as an end on the second-string freshman squad. Ahead of him on the charts, however, was Gaynel Tinsley, twice an all-American.

To fill in his educational program at LSU, Zais

enrolled in the ROTC unit. "It was my first exposure to the military and I hated it. I wasn't ready for this. The uniform was gray wool which itched and irritated me in the hot sun. I dreaded drill periods. I just raised hell. My grades were good but I was walking punishment every Saturday. I had problems with the cadet noncom and I fought him. I was ready to ship out on a boat headed around the world.

"Troy Middleton was a major, the CO for the ROTC. [During World War II, as a major general, Middleton ran the VIII Corps in Europe.] He interceded for me. He put me on strict discipline, which cost me my football scholarship. That eliminated eating at the training table, which was a serious problem. Middleton, however, got me a job dusting books in the offices.

"Because of what Middleton did for me, I've always had a tolerance for wild, young soldiers who are not inherently bad but just not amenable to discipline in the beginning. I developed compassion for a young soldier who sort of bowed his neck and got into a little trouble as a result."

At this point, Zais's brother Larry offered additional help. Their mother was lonely and if Zais would enroll closer to home, Larry would provide some funds to augment scholarship loans. Zais transferred to the University of New Hampshire. Along with football at his new school, and in spite of his previous experience, Zais again opted for ROTC. "Most of the ball players took it, not for any patriotic reasons but because that was the way to make a little extra money. And it also was the most important activity on campus."

The students in the reserve summered at Fort Devens, Massachusetts. Zais discovered he enjoyed the physical challenges, the sports program and company of men. He was further stimulated by a visit to the home of a girlfriend whose father was a major. The furniture, the bric-a-brac collected from postings around the world and the demeanor of the officer impressed him.

Still, as a prelaw student, he intended to enter the law school at Cornell. And he won a one-year scholarship only to discover that New Hampshire expected him to repay the loans it had granted him. In spite of a variety of extracurricular sales jobs vending ice cream, candy, hot dogs and even crepe-soled shoes, he could not afford to accept Cornell's offer. Zais solved his financial problems by accepting a reserve commission as a second lieutenant for $125 a month with an extra $143 to cover rations albeit he would have to pay for his uniforms.

"On a small army post, Fort Adams at Newport, Rhode Island, that smoldering rag pile of uncertain aspirations burst into flame. I liked the men I came in contact with. I enjoyed living in tents, marching. I was in heaven on maneuvers at Fort Devens. It was my first exposure to the ideas of duty, honor, country and that a man's word was gold. I loved it! Just loved it!"

Initially, Zais admits he was captivated by the appearance of a uniform. "I liked the pinks and green, the Sam Browne belt and the boots. There were yellow knit gloves, pink riding breeches, sabres. I spent an inordinate amount of time looking as well as I could. I was very vain about the uniform.

"The noncoms taught me how to handle men. They told me to knock off the cheerleader stuff. And they taught me how to take care of the men first, without becoming too chummy with them."

His, however, was a commission in the reserves. And when Zais attempted to convert it to the regular army he failed the physical because of a tiny cyst detected at the base of his spine. Still hankering for military life, Zais grabbed an offer as an assistant coach at Tennessee Military Institute where he also acted as tactical officer, drove the school bus and taught high-school courses in

English and biology. "I was one lesson ahead of the students."

As the country expanded its military forces in 1940, Zais applied for active duty and was accepted. While at Fort Benning he put in his papers for the paratroops but his colonel disapproved the request with the comment that these were "suicide troops." Zais persisted and in March 1941 started jump school.

"I looked on it as a big adventure. I saw others do it and my feeling was if they can do that, so can I. And after you made your one jump, you were off for the remainder of the day.

"There is a great feeling upon completing a jump. There is a tremendous release from within. You've faced fear and you've overcome it. There had been an inherent danger in jumping but suddenly the danger passed. One of the greatest morale builders in a parachute unit is participation in a jump. When things are low in an outfit and men are becoming restless, it is good to have a jump. They may not like the idea. They may not look forward to it. But once having done it, the release and the feeling are just great."

Zais started his parachuting while the specialty was in its infancy. The uniform consisted of the one-piece silk jumpsuit and cloth helmet. He and his contemporaries had learned to remove rings, officer's metal insignia or any item that might snag a line. The first chutists had armed themselves only with a knife in their boot before adding a pistol fastened by a thong around the leg. Until they were adequately secured, canteens inflicted severe bruises.

Zais happened to be aboard a plane when one jumper's shroud caught on the tail of the aircraft. From the open door, Zais and the others could see the hapless trooper whirling around "like the spinner on a fishing line." There was no way to free the soldier and it meant certain death for him if the pilot tried to land. Finally, the dangling man pulled the rip cord of his reserve chute. The shock of its opening blasted him free, although at considerable risk of severe damage to the tail.

Zais suggested a solution for future situations: a jump knife, somewhat akin to a switchblade, to be carried in a zippered compartment on the chest. Should a similar problem develop, the trooper could whip out the blade and cut away the lines of the main chute. Many years later Zais remarked that the innovation probably caused more casualties than it prevented.

"Every paratrooper, every time he got three drinks and sat at a bar, would take out his switchblade knife and flip it open. A lot of cutting went on, all over the world. I never knew of one occasion when the knife was used to cut a man free from the tail of a plane."

On the other hand, Zais made real contributions to the art. Even as the troopers began to carry rifles or carbines slung over the shoulder with the condom-covered muzzle down, or broke the M–1 rifle into two parts which fitted into a bag across the chest (designed by parachute maintenance officer, Lt. George Griswold), the heavier stuff of radios, machine guns, mortars and other equipment was dropped in bundles attached to chutes. On the ground, troopers had difficulty finding the bags which belonged to their units or held components for crew-served weapons. Zais sneaked a load of fabric-marking ink out of a supply depot and arranged with a chemist friend to use food color dyes that would distinguish parachutes bearing different bundles. His experiment worked well enough for the method to be adopted as standard procedure. He also led experiments with night and freestyle jumps and wrote the first airborne operations manual.

In April of 1943, about a month after activation of the 517th, Zais punched in at Toccoa to command the 3rd Battalion. Under the policy established by Lou Walsh, Zais, like Boyle and Seitz, screened volunteers for his outfit, but in a shift from the previous recruitment, Zais drew men already part of the paratroop program at Fort Benning. "I personally interviewed about a hundred, and had accepted sixty or seventy when the commander of the airborne at Benning protested." Indeed, there was growing resentment in military circles over the 517th's finicky approach. Walsh and Zais were summarily advised by higher-ups that parachute graduates who had already completed basic training would fill out the ranks of the 3rd Battalion.

CHAPTER III

THE TOCCOA CADRE

THE FIRST HOME for the newly activated 517th was a scrubby installation originally erected for National Guardsmen in the mountains of northeastern Georgia, close to the South Carolina border and about 100 miles from Atlanta. Originally, it had been dubbed Camp Toombs in honor of a soldier son of the Old South. A casket factory just beyond the gate added a further note of gloom. Bob Sink, one of the first parachute commanders, prevailed upon the authorities in Washington, D.C., to provide a new name, and in the absence of inspiration, the place had become Camp Toccoa, derived from a nearby village.

Walsh had confidence in the high quality of his three battalion commanders. Much of the remainder of the cadre, however, was foisted on Walsh. He claimed that in the usual fashion of large organizations, the request for experienced people from other units enabled commanders to dump ineffectives. Walsh discovered the "castoffs," in his word, had actually made the rounds, passing through a series of older, established battalions and regiments over the years until they arrived on his doorstep.

To the newly appointed commandant's utter dismay, a number of the noncoms ordered to assist him demonstrated their lack of commitment by showing up at Toccoa at such a desultory pace that the small band of officers on hand were forced to meet the first trainload of grist for Walsh's mill. The officers not only escorted these initial recruits to the camp but also issued them bedding and cooked their first meal served in the mess hall.

The junior officers designated for the 517th were themselves a mixed bag. Some would ship out almost immediately for openly failing to measure up to the standards of Walsh and his three battalion heads. One who survived was Tom Cross. He was a typical army brat, born in Amsterdam, New York, in 1919 while his father, Thomas J. Cross, Sr., was overseas with the World War I army of occupation.

The younger Cross, following the nomadic wanderings of pre-World War II military families, bounced around educational institutions in New York, Georgia, Arkansas, Panama, Kansas, Washington, Maryland and California. A souvenir from his days as a high-school student is a memorandum dated January 7, 1935. Addressed to his father, ironically serving as Assistant Provost Marshal, Prison and Police, it states:

"1. Thomas Cross, Jr. your son, has been reported for misconduct (throwing apple cores and other missiles at children on the bus, and failing to cease such practice when so instructed by the guard on the bus) on a Fort Benning-Columbus school Bus . . .
"2. Request that report of action taken be indorsed hereon to complete our files."

The document bears the signature of the elder Cross's superior officer in the provost marshal office and the indorsement requested tersely responds:

"My son, Thomas J. Cross, Jr. has been punished for this offense by being deprived of all customary week-end privileges for three weeks."

The future paratrooper admits he was never a "goody-goody-two-shoes," as a youth. He was "semi-studious" and left his final year of high school to attend a military academy, "due to a misunderstanding with a teacher."

He was always oriented towards a service career. As early as 1931–32, Cross participated in the Citizens Military Training Camp at Vancouver Barracks, Washington, even though he was barely beyond puberty. Subsequently, Cross graduated from Fishburne Military School and then enlisted in the Wyoming National Guard while seeking appointment to West Point. He flunked the physical exam for the academy twice, however, and only through an ROTC program did he obtain a reserve commission.

Because of his father's role, Cross, more than most kids his age, says he paid attention to world events, particularly in pre-Pearl Harbor Europe. Indeed, he investigated the possibility of enlistment in the Royal Canadian Air Force in 1940 but abandoned the move upon learning it could cost him his U.S. citizenship. On February 20, 1941, Thomas J. Cross, Jr., went on active duty at Fort Benning, a junior officer of Company M of the 29th Infantry Regiment. The company commander was one Lou Walsh.

"Walsh's school for second lieutenants sent them to the basement of the company headquarters building," remembers Cross. "You couldn't come out until the NCOs said you qualified with the 81 mm mortar, the .50 caliber antitank machine gun and the .30 caliber machine gun. The criteria was that you couldn't show your face if you might embarrass Walsh."

Having "graduated" the Walsh academy, Cross received a regular-army commission within a year. Meanwhile, Walsh, who had become somewhat of an idol to Cross, volunteered for the paratroops. "It was new and adventuresome," says Cross, who tried to follow his

mentor. But twice he was rejected, the second time at
the instigation of his father. "I was actually on orders to
go but while I was a student at the Basic Officers'
Course of the Infantry School, my father, through then
Lieutenant Colonel Miley, cancelled my orders. My
father thought the paratroopers were exotic, and Miley,
as a good friend of my father, indulged his wishes."

Nor was his future wife Bette, herself an army brat,
enamored of paratroopers. She told Cross she would
never marry him if he joined the airborne. She had
formed an unfavorable impression of the breed from the
cockiness and overall behavior exhibited by paratroopers
at the local officers' club.

Cross persisted. "When Lou Walsh became scheduled
to take over the newly formed 517th, he knew of my at-
tempts to become a paratrooper and he knew why I had
been turned down. I asked him to get me into jump
school and within less than a week, I was on my way.
From there I moved to the 517th, initially as exec officer
for Dick Seitz at the 2nd Battalion."

Cross sat in on the interviews Seitz conducted with
potential members of his battalion. He confirms Seitz's
occasional challenge to a man for a punch at the office
wall. "If they didn't hesitate, answered you in a positive
way, looked you straight in the eye we tended to accept
them, even those with prison records."

In fact, there was a *sub rosa* policy in some states
where officials would release a convicted man if he
would enlist in the military service. That sort of arrangement led, according to Lou Walsh, to the 517th being
charged with an excessive number of AWOLs. Walsh
claimed that the governor of a Western state approved
the release of some fifty miscreants who volunteered to
be paratroopers and were assigned to the 517th. However, when the train allegedly arrived at Toccoa, none of
them were aboard.

Tom Cross straddled the line between the top brass

and their juniors. He had come in as a company commander but quickly progressed to become executive officer under Seitz. The lower echelons continued to enjoy his company during occasional off-duty sprees. Two of the foremost revelers, John Lissner and Carl Starkey of D and F Companies, were known as *Les Enfants*. "If there was trouble," says Cross, "you knew that Lissner and Starkey would be in the middle of it."

Seitz employed a military version of the police technique, "good cop, bad cop." Says Cross, "The men would run a pool on who would do the inspection, Seitz or me. When he did one and spotted something out of line, he would not chew anyone out. Instead, preferring to be the good guy, he would tell me to handle that 'goddamn problem.' As a result I picked up the nickname of 'Black Tom' while he was only 'Dangerous Dick.' "

Another early member of the 517th was Don Fraser, who would become the CO of A Company for the 1st Battalion under Bill Boyle. He actually arrived at Toccoa even before Boyle officially received his command. "Ike Walton picked several of us for the 1st Battalion before he moved up to be the regimental exec for Walsh.

"I grew up in Blue Island, Illinois, and I was a pretty ornery kid, very independent. In 1927, when I was nine years old, I started caddying at a golf course. At sixteen I was a substitute clerk carrier for the Blue Island post office until I entered military service in April of 1941 as an infantry private."

After OCS and assignment to the 84th Division in Texas, Fraser concluded his outfit did not appear bound for overseas duty. He volunteered for paratroop training and upon graduation from jump school joined the newly created 517th.

He became an enthusiastic adherent of the regimen established by Boyle. "One time Wild Bill took us up the back side of Currahee with full field equipment. To look at it you would say it could not be done. But we climbed the mountain and the experience paid off later in combat. We stuck together like a family. When we jogged for five miles without a break, we would pass the light machine guns, the 60 and 81 mm mortars from man to man on the move. Boyle took his turn like all the rest."

Like Walsh and Boyle, one half of what Tom Cross labeled *Les Enfants,* John Lissner, called New York City home. "I was born in 1914," says Lissner. "My mother was Theresa Quigley from Ireland. My father Julius Lissner, of Germanic stock, had a Hungarian and Polish background. At 105 pounds, he was a New York State boxing champion.

"I wasn't much of a student and I dropped out of Roosevelt High. But James A. 'Buck' Freeman, who previously coached the Wonder Five basketball team in the late 1920s, early '30s, saw me playing ball. He was coaching at Iona in New Rochelle [a suburb of New York City] and he asked me, 'Kid, what school do you go to?' I had to confess I wasn't in school. He said, 'How would you like to go back to high school?' I jumped at the chance.

"Iona was nicknamed the Irish of North Avenue [for its address in New Rochelle]. We had great football, basketball and baseball teams, people like myself coming from other high schools or kids with great athletic ability just entering. I had four great years at Iona where I was maybe the only freshman to receive a star sweater with a stripe. In 1935 I was captain of the football team. After I graduated in 1936 I became the backfield coach and then later assistant coach. In July 1941, I was drafted."

Still exploiting his athletic talents and interests, Lissner started a boxing team at Camp Lee, Virginia, and coached the base football squad. The Japanese attacked Pearl Harbor while Lissner pursued a commission at OCS. Subsequently, he enrolled at the Camp Holabird Automotive School. "I picked up a newspaper with an ad, 'Be a man, be a paratrooper.' I typed a request and sent it to the chief of army ground forces. Three days later, I had orders to report to Benning and finished jump school in November 1942. I met Bill Boyle and Carl Starkey there. Starkey and I were having a few beers in the officers' club when a discussion arose at another table. A fellow I later learned was Bill Boyle picked up a wooden chair and threw it at the ceiling fan, disintegrating the chair while forcefully making his point."

Posted to the 513th Parachute Regiment, Lissner attended a lecture by a newly returned officer from the South Pacific, Lou Walsh. Greatly impressed, Lissner was delighted to join the newly formed 517th as a platoon leader in the 2nd Battalion. He sat in on many of the interviews Seitz and his staff conducted with the volunteers fresh from induction centers.

"We asked them why they wanted to serve with the paratroopers, a Godforsaken unit to many. They would say they wanted to fight for our country and if they traveled by airplane that would be the quickest way possible to participate. The kids we got were just fabulous. The running we did was great for the body, soul and mind. While they were running we would prepare them to instantly react to commands by shouting such things as, 'Fall out, climb those trees!' 'Fall out, pick up stones and throw them as far as you can!' 'Hit the ground!' 'Stop! Stand, stare, listen! Throw a jab and recover!' 'Sit down!' 'Look skyward!' 'Look low!'

"While there was a separation between officers and enlisted men, we were still like brothers. We spent all our duty hours thinking about and training people for combat. We planned night operations, loading the men into two-and-a-half-ton trucks, driving across an open field where each man jumped out every twenty or thirty yards while the vehicle was going five to seven miles an hour. It simulated putting a stick of troopers across a drop zone. They would hit the ground, simulate the time it would require to get free of the chute and take the prone position prepared to fire. We used luminous tape on the backs of helmets and uniforms and the crickets [the childrens' small metal toy whose clicking sound was employed by parachutists during World War II to find and identify one another] for night movement practice. We couldn't put people on stringent rations in an attempt to make them aware of what it was like to go for long periods without food or water, but we sure as hell talked about that a lot."

Lissner played a lead role in creating *esprit* among his contemporaries. "Before I entered the service, I frequented a bar on Seventh Street, between Second and Third Avenue, McSorley's. There was sawdust on the floor, ale sold for a dime a mug, with three for a quarter, no women allowed and the clientele was mostly Irish. They would break into a song, about the Mulligan Guards. On Sundays at Toccoa, officers either attended Catholic mass or the Protestant services, had dinner and then spent the afternoon at the officers' club, a beat-up old shack, drinking beer and singing. The Mulligan Guards song had the power to generate great enthusiasm. The sessions became known as the airborne unit of the Mulligan Guards, 517. We had cards printed and held a general meeting every Sunday. Everyone learned the words and we'd tell jokes, drink and sing together with the result we became more united."

Lissner, to this day, believes in the efficacy of the Prop Blast ceremony as a means of creating camaraderie. "The idea was not to get someone sick or drunk but it was like a fraternity rite, announcing the acceptance of a new jumper into the family."

Lissner remembers that with all of the closeness, on a Monday morning, an officer might have disappeared, quietly, without any talk, and with no remorse expressed. "It was a purification period, that touched all battalions, officers, noncoms and enlisted men."

While Walsh and his associates subsequently rid themselves of those who deserved the label of castoff, one prominent member of the initial trainers remained. John Aloysius Alicki quickly became known to his charges as "Boom Boom." He was, like Walsh and Boyle, bred in Brooklyn, New York. His parents were Polish immigrants, and Alicki had hardly been born in 1917 before his mother succumbed to an influenza epidemic.

As an eighteen-year-old apprentice die maker, Alicki gave up the hunt for a job during the Great Depression to salve an itch to travel and see the world. "I began by hitchhiking, riding the rails and visiting many places in the United States. Finally, with about thirty-five cents in my pocket, hungry and underweight, I reached El Paso, Texas. I decided to join the U.S. Army. With my thirty-five cents, I bought thirty-five bananas—they sold then for a penny apiece—to put on some weight. I was accepted and sworn in, June 1936, and assigned to 8th U.S. Cavalry Regiment. The training was rugged and grueling and it qualified me as a proficient horse rider."

Alicki sought to satisfy his urge to explore the globe, applying for foreign service. Because of the growing tension with Japan, the authorities rejected his choice of the Philippines and shipped him to Hawaii. He was a sergeant with the 53rd Antiaircraft Brigade on December 7, 1941, about to sail for the mainland and quit the army. But this final Sunday he had made arrangements to attend church services with some local friends.

"On that Sunday morning, they got me up a little early and held me to my promise to go to church. We were entering the church just before 8:00 A.M. when we heard something in the distance like firecrackers. As we went into the church the sound became more audible. When I stepped outside, I saw the red disk emblem on the sides of the planes."

Alicki came through the raid unscathed. Promoted to the rank of first sergeant shortly thereafter, he was accepted by the Officer Candidate School at Fort Benning and then earned his wings as a paratrooper. "I was directed to speak to all incoming volunteers, in what became known as 'Boom Boom Alicki's initial 517 Survival School.' "

Lieutenant Alicki, at the ripe old age of twenty-six, his face splayed with the marks of a boxer, presented the rumpled teenagers, some of whom still were in civvies, with the kind of truculent "blood and guts" military posture calculated to intimidate anyone with a shred of timidity. He bellowed at the anxiety-ridden groups, "Awright, ya volunteered for parachute duty, and now's your chance to prove ya meant it!" Still wondering what they had gotten themselves into, the volunteers shuffled to the thirty-four-foot tower. Under Alicki's orders they climbed up, strapped on a parachute harness and then stepped off into space for the short but often terrifying fall. Those who hesitated after a slap on the rump signaled go marched off to the barracks of the Out Platoon.

In addition to this initiation ceremony for all of the candidates, Alicki also sifted through the records that accompanied each man. "In terms of the type of men to be accepted, the instructions given me called for those who were daring, athletic, aggressive and willing to take risks."

In spite of Walsh's rigorous standards, and perhaps in some measure because the demands for excellence brought so much turnover in personnel, the early days of the 517th seem to have bordered on chaos. Certainly, that is how it struck one newcomer, a freshly minted paratroop lieutenant named Charles La Chaussee. He had been a federalized National Guard sergeant laboring on engineering projects. Bored with building machine-gun revetments, faced with a prospect of grading roads and digging ditches, he heeded the siren call for paratroop volunteers. Acceptance cost him his stripes but after he completed his four weeks at Benning and spent a number of months with the 82nd Airborne, La Chaussee attended OCS.

Nattily clad in his newly acquired pinks and jump boots, Lieutenant La Chaussee reported for his new assignment at Toccoa. "After a short wait," recalled La Chaussee, "a stocky individual in a basketball warmup suit trotted up, breathing hard. This was the regimental CO returning from his daily jog. His exec officer was close behind. I saluted and reported."

"Who the hell sent you here!" demanded Walsh. "I handpick my officers for this regiment." In fact, the statement was actually becoming increasingly less the case.

After the lieutenant doggedly stated that he was following his orders, Walsh growled, "All right, you're assigned to Company A."

Walsh and George "Ike" Walton, his exec, disappeared into their offices. La Chaussee waited for a few minutes, working up the courage to ask someone where he could find Company A. Walton emerged from his room and, on seeing the lieutenant, snapped, "What the hell are you waiting for! You're assigned to Company A!"

La Chaussee scurried off and eventually located the 1st Battalion area. "The only person in evidence was a large major in one-piece coveralls. I saluted and said I had been assigned to Company A. The major stared at me for a full minute, then said, 'I'm the battalion CO. How far can you broad jump?'

"I had not thought about that very much but guessed about six feet."

Boyle drew a line in the dirt and said, "Let's see you do it." La Chaussee dutifully toed the mark, bent his knees and jumped. "Six-and-a-quarter feet," announced Boyle.

"The major," as La Chaussee recalled in a memoir,

"drew a kitchen type alarm clock from a pocket of his coveralls and announced it was time to be getting on. I smiled at the alarm clock, which struck me as funny. This was a mistake."

" 'What the hell are you laughing at?' Major Boyle glowered at me. 'Watches are hard to get these days.' " The clock bedeviled La Chaussee on at least one future occasion. He had a habit of approaching the battalion commander and saying, "A minute of your time, Major Boyle?"

With an entire company of officers and enlisted men looking on, Boyle reached into the always bulging pockets of his jumpsuit and pulled out the kitchen clock. He set it and announced, "All right, you've got one minute." When the alarm went off, even though La Chaussee still had more on his mind, he knew he was finished talking.

Following his bizarre reception, La Chaussee threw himself into his work as part of the training program. After one field exercise, his fatigues were soaked with sweat, a result of a metabolic condition that caused him to perspire effusively after any sustained exertion. He was among the platoon leaders assembled for a critique. Suddenly, Lou Walsh told him to stand up.

"I rose, expecting to hear how I screwed up. Instead, Colonel Walsh said, 'Look at this man! That's the way you all should look. He's covered with sweat because he has been working every inch of the way.' In fact my performance had been no better and no worse than most of the others', but if the colonel chose to believe my appearance was the result of hard work, rather than a glandular malfunction, that was all right with me."

La Chaussee obviously must have been doing something right for he was soon assigned to replace the CO of Company C, whose performance would seem to have negated whatever screening Walsh employed. When La Chaussee first entered the Company C area he observed a mob scene around the supply hut. As La Chaussee watched, the supply sergeant held up a pair of boots and yelled out, "Size nine and a half." Several of the soldiers yelled, "Here!" and the noncom tossed the footgear to one of them.

The newly appointed CO called a halt to the proceedings and then questioned the sergeant about the system. "Did you ever hear of a Form 32?" (It listed the clothing and equipment issued to each soldier.)

"Yes, sir," answered the supply sergeant. "But that takes too much time." La Chaussee assigned the man to other duties and appointed another GI to handle the quartermaster tasks according to regulations.

He discovered that this was only one symptom of disarray. Ten soldiers from the company were AWOL and seven were already doing time in the stockade. "I made the squad leaders responsible for missing men. I gave squad leaders leave with instructions to bring back the AWOLs. Eight of them were back in two weeks."

Instead of courts-martial that would have put the offenders in the stockade or removed them from the outfit, La Chaussee disciplined them in his own way. They marched around the orderly room, lugging musette bags filled with sand, or they dug six-by-six-by-six-foot holes using the small entrenching tools given infantrymen. "The punishment was illegal but it worked."

John "Buck" Miller, who eventually became a sergeant and squad leader of Company C, recalls some rather unique incidents while serving under La Chaussee. "Several of us were given a sort of secret mission. We were to write a letter to a given post office box number. We were to report on the morale and any subversive activities or anyone talking of going AWOL. I sent letters until I went to jump school. No one ever acknowledged them and when I quit no one ever said anything about it."

After Miller received his stripes one of his men went AWOL. La Chaussee instructed him to "Bring him back and make him look like he had fallen down a flight of stairs." Miller traveled to Charlotte, North Carolina, and the home of the missing man's girlfriend. But the soldier had already returned to camp.

"I got back," says Miller, "after 12:00 P.M. and took him outside under a street light where I straightened him out. The next day I heard he had reported to the hospital." Then nothing was heard or said until La Chaussee summoned Miller while they were on maneuvers and informed the sergeant that the miscreant would receive a medical discharge. La Chaussee asked whether Miller knew anything about it. Miller denied knowledge and that closed the matter.

Throughout the training period, and until both of them fell under enemy fire, Boyle and La Chaussee seem to have had an uncertain relationship. The junior officer, regarded by his underlings as a parade-ground martinet with a penchant for punishment for the most minor failings, at the same time demonstrated, both in his preparation of his men for war and in combat, a talent and personality well suited for these occupations.

The shuttle that shipped out substandard cadre (by the definition of Walsh and associates) brought to Toccoa, as a replacement, William J. Lewis. Born in Cleveland in 1921, Lewis ranks himself as "semistudious" and a sandlot football, baseball and ice hockey player. However, most afternoons he labored in his father's bakery.

"I was interested in current events and my favorite subject in junior and senior high was social studies. We did follow the Spanish revolt and paid close attention to what Hitler and Mussolini were up to. In 1941, I tried to enter the U.S. Army Air Corps. I imagined myself as a pilot flying fighter planes. I passed the mental test but later, when called, I flunked the physical because of color blindness. I tried the Royal Canadian Air Force, thinking Britain was hard up for pilots and they would give me a waiver. No luck there, either. I also tried to enter the

Army, Marine Corps, Navy and Coast Guard, but all but the Coast Guard believed color blindness would hamper my service. The Coast Guard would accept me but stipulated that I would be restricted to the job of baker. I had that at home.

"Finally, in June 1942, I was drafted. Again, I believe because of my color blindness, I was shipped to Camp Grant, Illinois, for medical training. It was a far cry from combat but I had no choice. During basic training I entered the boxing tournament and won the championship in my class. [Lewis was a middleweight, at about 150 pounds.] I became a member of the camp boxing team. The CO at Camp Grant wanted to have a good team, so he gave one boxer to each battalion commander and instructed him, 'I want a good boxing team. I want your charge to eat, sleep, train and fight.' It was a good deal. But of course the general told us there would be no promotions while we were on the team.

"All of this didn't make me popular with my first sergeant. He was waiting for the boxing season to end so he could sink his hooks into me. I overheard him gloating to the staff about the details he had planned for me once I stopped boxing. A month before the season ended, I applied for parachute training.

"Again, color blindness almost stopped me. But this time, instead of the Isihari dot test, they used colored disks. I noticed immediately when I said 'red,' the tester had a funny look on his face. I hurriedly said 'green.' When he showed green, I said 'red' and we went through the same little tap dance. I remarked, 'The light in this building is too poor for you to be giving these tests.' He agreed and passed me."

Fort Benning demanded far more than Lewis had anticipated. "That first week, A-Stage, was tough. I doubt if I ate more than breakfast that week. And although I was an athlete, all my training aimed at two-minute rounds. A-Stage was a brutal, body-building process.

After breakfast in the morning we went on a five-mile run. Then it was judo, followed by an hour with Indian clubs to develop arm muscles. Pushups were a major item. Anytime we slacked off, the punishment was, 'Give me ten!' [Pushups.]

"At first I couldn't do ten so the sergeant would grab me by the collar and the seat of the pants and pick me up and set me down to finish the count. By the end of the week I was able to do 100 and not sweat. The run was no problem but I never enjoyed it and never took up jogging as a hobby. When we reached the barracks around 5:30 P.M. I flopped down on the bunk and slept until reveille. Only then was I up to showering, putting on clean clothes, eating breakfast and mentally prepared for another grueling day. At the close of the week, I had enough confidence to take on the entire German Army."

B-Stage for would-be troopers like Lewis meant jumping from Benning's forty-foot tower, tumbling exercises, practicing the falls that accompany a touchdown and the inexorable five-mile runs. The third week, C-Stage, involved not only the forty-foot tower but the huge 250-foot ones as well. As in the previous days, the men were not allowed to walk if it were possible to have them run. They ran to formations, ran to the mess hall, ran to the latrines. The final week, D-Stage, culminated the primary education of a paratrooper, five jumps that qualified him to tuck his trousers into his jump boots and pin on the silver-winged breast insignia.

When Lewis checked in at the 517th, the 2nd Battalion was being formed. Dick Seitz, along with Lt. Col. George Walton, regimental executive officer, and Capt. John McKinley, CO of F Company, interviewed the newcomer. Lewis recalls, "Colonel Walton said, 'Welcome, we do need medics.' I retorted, 'Sir, I didn't join this outfit to be a medic.' Walton asked, 'What else are you trained to do?' I boldly said, 'You can strap a mortar

on my back and I can carry it.' " Many questions and responses later, Lewis became part of F Company in the
job of mortar-squad leader.

In his role as mortar-squad leader, Lewis helped supervise the daily program for the trainees while learning
his own trades. One particularly grueling piece of business occurred at an area formerly used by a sawmill. "We
would double-time to the sawdust pit," remembers
Lewis, "and there we practiced what was called judo but
mostly we just plain mutilated one another. In one
'game' the sergeant drew a ten-foot circle and stood in
the center while the squad lined up in a column. One at
a time, a trooper entered the ring and tried to throw the
sergeant out. The sergeant usually bested at least three
or four of his opponents."

Another delight for the aggressively inclined was a
homemade game called "screwball." The object was to
move a basketball over an open field across a distant goal
line. Players joined in or quit as the urge or opportunity
seized them. There was no referee, no huddles, no time-
outs. The only rule was a ban on any weapons. No one
kept score, and according to one participant, the activity
fell just shy of murder.

The selection and toughening process for the first two
battalions paid off handsomely when the men, led by
their officers, left Toccoa for their jump training at Fort
Benning. "When they got off the train at Fort Benning," notes Tom Cross, "instead of the usual shouted
orders, we used whistles to form them up and marched
them to the barracks without a single verbal command.
The general watching us was amazed at the discipline
shown."

The jump-school instructors were similarly surprised
by the ease with which the candidates from Toccoa
breezed through the initial stages of the program that
had been such a trial to even a boxer like Bill Lewis.
Feeling themselves challenged by these neophytes, the

veteran cadre at Benning piled on extra miles of running and raised pushup counts but their charges remained unfazed. The strenuous program instituted by Walsh surpassed the most extreme demands of jump school.

The initial screening, designed, according to Cross, to "keep the best and shelve the rest," eliminated all of the fainthearted. Not a single man from the 517th balked when the moment to leap from an aircraft came, and the absence of any washouts established a record. There were no exceptions among the personnel as the 517th adhered to the general philosophy of airborne that every man was a potential combat soldier; cooks, bakers, clerks, supply specialists all completed jump training and had learned to handle weapons. The 517th troopers also became the first jumpers in training to wear their steel helmets rather than the modified leather football headgear previously prescribed.

The 1st and 2nd Battalions left Benning for their new home, Camp Mackall[1], North Carolina, while the 3rd Battalion hung around the installation, waiting to swell its ranks with regular products of Benning's parachute school. At Mackall, the 517th turned its attention to honing the skills of its riflemen and developing the special needs within the regiment.

According to Tom Cross, while the day ended for recruits shortly after the evening meal, the officers and noncoms attended evening classes. Here the instructors received lessons on what they should teach the following day, everything from intensive study of all of the available weapons through tactics, particularly those aimed at small unit operations. Walsh, with his brain trust, constantly created exercises that would enhance the outfit's knowledge and capabilities.

Other officers at company level took their places in

[1]Tommy Mackall was among the first paratroopers KIA, during the assault in North Africa.

the 517th. They were a mixed bag of men. Lt. Sidney "Mickey" Marks, another "hellraiser" according to Cross, and extremely popular with the troops, assumed leadership of a platoon under La Chaussee. George Giuchici stood 6'4" and started as a lieutenant in F Company where he amused his contemporaries by swinging a bullwhip and a streak of wildness off duty. Dave Armstrong, a West Pointer, had been declared excess and mustered out during the 1930s, had enlisted, won back a commission and become one of Seitz's best junior officers. Joe McGeever, a Montana football star, first a company commander and eventually the exec for the 3rd Battalion, was regarded as outstanding by both his superiors and the troopers.

While the officers and cadre commanding the line companies sought to make combat troops of their men, at the same time the staff began to assemble people for the specialties designated by the Table of Organization. A vital item was the medical unit. The regimental surgeon, Paul D. Vella, who like everyone else had been through the Benning mill, supervised the sixty-nine-man contingent. One of the first permanent assets who reported to Vella was a Floridian, would-be neurosurgeon, Benjamin Sullivan.

At the peak of the Great Depression in 1932, Sullivan finished high school. It was a desperate time. His father had been diagnosed, erroneously, with tuberculosis and for six months lay abed while the family struggled to survive. The son prowled the area in search of employment. "I literally wore out the soles of two pairs of shoes, looking for work." Through a raffle he won a job at seventeen and a half cents an hour as janitor in a junior college, where he also enrolled in academic courses. What had been known as Tampa Junior College transformed itself into the University of Tampa.

Sullivan now considered his future career. "I played the violin well enough to enter one of the conservatories and in fact I was offered a scholarship to Juilliard. But the money covered only tuition, not room and board. I saw too many poor musicians in Tampa and decided I wanted a more lucrative profession. My father was not successful enough moneywise to inspire a desire to be a civil engineer. I knew nothing about medicine but reading *The Magnificent Obsession* by Lloyd Douglass filled me with visions of the glamour of the profession."

On the profits of a slum-clearing project awarded to his father, toward which Sullivan had contributed a summerlong survey of the area, he entered Emory University for further study and eventually medical school. Upon graduation, Sullivan chose an internship at far-off Kings County Hospital in Brooklyn, New York. There, Sullivan had ample opportunity to treat "the gladiator type injuries where there was a suspicion of head trauma. Saturday night was a busy time. I could have a dozen or more belligerent and totally uncooperative drunks to sew up."

While applying for a residency in neurosurgery, Sullivan, who had previously joined the army reserve, decided in June 1941 to fulfill his commitment for a year of active service. His first duties included physical exams of potential soldiers at 90 Church Street in Manhattan. He also was dispatched, with a chauffeur, to investigate soldiers whose families reported the GIs could not return from furloughs because of illness. "I would examine the man, tell the mother, 'Yes, he certainly is sick. He needs to be hospitalized.' I would take them to Halloran Hospital on Staten Island where they'd spend one night and the next day be shipped back to their units."

Successive postings brought his talents to dispensaries where Sullivan treated a steady stream of soldiers on sick call, mostly suffering from "colds, athlete's foot, gonorrhea and homesickness. I found my medical knowledge was entirely adequate but my understanding of the army and its ways was less so." He had written to the Adjutant

General directly for a piece of equipment. For his failure to apply through the appropriate channels, Sullivan incurred a tongue-lashing from the colonel in charge. The experience led Sullivan to think out carefully future moves that might conflict with the army's established procedures.

"The army was falling short of my expectations for excitement," says Sullivan. By 1943, he found himself at the Carlisle Barracks in Pennsylvania, in a course given by the Medical Field Service. Sullivan remembers, "It was excellent as far as it went, although I realized they were teaching tactics as if this war were being fought in the trenches like World War I. I had read enough of the *Infantry Journal* to know that tactics were different and so were evacuation problems. Still, I learned many valuable things about training plowhands, truck drivers and the like to serve as medics."

While browsing through a manual, he had read a passage that specified two doctors with the rank of captain should be assigned to each parachute battalion. The book remarked that any medical officer who desired that kind of duty could volunteer directly to the Adjutant General. Having been chewed out for failing to work through channels before, Sullivan hesitated to apply. But eventually he submitted the appropriate papers.

Two sets of orders directed Sullivan to present himself at the Fort Benning parachute school during his final weeks in the field-service course. Flushed with anticipation, Sullivan sought out the brigadier general in charge at Carlisle, to request a leave for a visit home before reporting to Benning.

Sullivan describes the scene with the general: "Captain, you volunteered for this?"

"Yes sir," I replied.

"You are a cadre for a new division which is more important than your being a paratrooper. Just forget these orders."

" 'General,' I said with all the respect I could muster. 'You are giving me verbal orders to forget about some very impressive orders direct from the War Department Adjutant General's office.'

"He turned a little red in the face, and his voice went up about ten decibels. '*I SAID FORGET ABOUT THESE ORDERS!*' "

Unwilling to surrender what he considered his rights, Sullivan politely requested the return of his official orders. The general imperiously rebuffed him and Sullivan could do nothing more than salute and retreat, stewing with anger.

He completed his Carlisle course, received a furlough with instructions to report to a camp in the Arizona desert. But with the retained second set of original papers to jump school still in his possession, Sullivan headed for Fort Benning to check in as a parachute candidate. A sergeant there obligingly made a certified copy.

Sullivan was midway through Stage-C, descending from the 250-foot towers, sharpening his tumbling techniques and in a class devoted to manipulating himself to land with the wind, when he suddenly received a summons to school headquarters. A somewhat embarrassed first lieutenant asked, "Captain, what the hell is this all about? According to these papers, you are supposed to be in Arizona but you reported here with War Department Special Orders. Did you forge them?"

Sullivan innocently answered that he had not and pointed out that the sergeant at headquarters had copied the original documents which Sullivan kept. The noncom backed Sullivan up. After Sullivan retrieved the originals for inspection, the lieutenant studied them and then said, "Every class at this school contains a few enlisted men who show up without orders and we find they were AWOL from their units. We straighten out the problem by just sending for service records and pretending that they do have orders. We need good, determined men in parachute units. You came here with orders, but you are listed as AWOL from Fort Huachuca. You are not some unsophisticated, plowhand Pfc. and I think you know more than you are volunteering."

Says Sullivan, "He appeared to be a man who was anxious to help win the war rather than to preserve hallowed World War I traditions. I decided I had better level with him and told the whole story, including my frustrations.

"He stared at the ceiling for a minute or so. Then he looked at me and said, 'Go on back to your class.' "

Sullivan heard no more of the affair and after the five jumps of Stage-D received his orders to join the 517th at Toccoa. Lou Walsh greeted him with a snarly, "Where have you been? We expected you last week."

Paul Vella was far more affable and Sullivan quickly plunged into the business at hand. "Our problem was that sick call alone was a full-time job, and added was the training of new medics, examinations of trainloads of new volunteers, training the entire regiment in military sanitation, conducting inspections of the barracks and mess halls as well as the periodic monthly physicals [basically 'short arm' inspections for detection of venereal diseases]. Fortunately, extra manpower for the tasks came from supernumerary dental officers."

The instructions to Sullivan when he checked out the new recruits were "be selective." Sullivan claims he and his associates rejected more than half of the candidates. "This was a mistake," he says. "For relatively minor defects I turned down recruits who would have been fine parachutists."

He was amused when in his examination of one candidate he saw a tattoo on the man's penis which read, "Hi, Doc!" That was familiar to Sullivan, who asked the soldier whether he had been at Camp Livingston in

1941. Indeed, he had, as a member of the regular army. Sullivan rejected him, not for his dubious decoration but because "he was entirely too decrepit-looking."

The T/O dictated a medical section with a total of eight medical-corps officers and one dentist. The sixty enlisted men were divided into twenty men per battalion with the remainder assigned to a headquarters section that handled supply, medical records and reports to upper echelons. Within the battalion medical sections, two aid men were detailed to each company. There a pair of litter teams contained four paratroopers, and the rest of the section worked at the battalion aid station.

Vella, according to Sullivan, won Walsh's approval for culling the best and brightest to serve as aid men because they would often be called upon to work independently without direct supervision. Vella, Sullivan and their associates kept their eyes out for those with either college educations or some experience in the health field.

"Our medics," says Sullivan, "trained for about two months with the infantry soldiers. Then they came to us to receive the remainder of their basic training program as medical department soldiers. As might be expected, many protested at becoming 'pill rollers' instead of 'real troopers.' They all wanted to shoot guns or fire mortars. In addition, some friendships had already been formed and these couldn't be maintained as closely once we separated them from the rifle unit. To develop some sense of unity within the medical detachment, we went on long hikes together.

"Meanwhile, there was a whole book of basic knowledge we had to impart: first aid, bandaging, treatment of shock, splinting of fractures and, very important, field sanitation." Walsh, based on his observations in the South Pacific, was highly supportive of this aspect.

CHAPTER IV

THE BOYS OF TOCCOA

REDHEADED CHARLIE KEEN, a 1922 baby born in the small coastal village of Ocean View, Delaware, sprang from a family with a tradition of seafaring. "Taking orders was part of my upbringing but there was also a sense of one hand for the ship and one hand for yourself. During World War II, a local bar in town would start a letter to some lad from the area in the service every day. They would ask anyone who came in to write something on a very long letter that would keep some GI or sailor up half the night reading. The only time I ever heard from my father was the note he put on one of these letters."

On the other hand, Keen's mother firmly insisted that everyone should seek to better himself. "In high school," says Keen, "I played all sports and loved them all. My mother came to all events but my father showed up only when I boxed.

"I was president of the student government when my class graduated in 1940 and did my thing like all Keens. I went to sea for a year on a salvage ship. Our crew in the engine room were mostly waterfront bums. One night our ship ran aground and got sand in the condenser. Someone, the last to arrive—me—would have to climb a hot, steamy bulkhead and with a ten-pound, three-foot wrench remove about three hundred hot nuts in order to get rid of the sand.

"Our chief engineer was a wizened SOB with a short fuse. He yelled, 'Tell that redheaded kid to get his ass moving or I'll come down and tell the SOB how!' I threw the wrench down on the main engine deck and told him to go piss up a rope. I went ashore with the mail boat in Wilmington."

Back home, Keen bumped into a former high-school classmate intent on enrolling at Randolph-Macon, a small men's college partially endowed by the Methodists. Keen entered Randolph-Macon with eighty-seven dollars in his pocket from his wages as a seaman and toting a seabag, to the amusement of others on the campus.

"The first week was a gasser. As a pulling guard weighing 187 pounds, I got my ass knocked off every day in football. As a premed, my classes were unbelievable. They talked another language. My year out of high school left me far behind. Tuition was fifty dollars and my room thirty-five dollars. To eat I had to rake leaves, keep score at intramurals and other odd jobs.

"My first year went by and I came back to school for early football practice with twenty-seven dollars in my pocket but at least a chance for free tuition. After the first of the two-a-day practices I went to the local beer joint and ordered a ten-cent brew. When I reached for my billfold, it was empty. Someone had cleaned me out during football practice. That night I called home for help and I can still hear my father, 'Jesus H. Christ. He ships out with thieves, rummys, murderers for a year and then goes to a Methodist college and gets rolled.'"

Struggling with his academic program and battered by football, Keen started to think seriously about entering the service. With a clutch of his best friends, Keen tried to join the Marine paratroops about to be established. The Marine Corps refused to let the volunteers choose their trade before coming aboard. Keen and his colleagues then elected the army paratroops. The authorities allowed them to finish their semester at school.

"George Talarico, his brother Julius and I were all inducted at Fort Dix, New Jersey, on March 16, 1943. We went to Toccoa on the same Pullman, took basic and went to jump school together." However, the brothers received assignment to B Company and its machine-gun platoon while Keen, with his year of college and premed aspirations, was chosen for the medics. "When Julius got hit by a mortar blast in his back in the Ardennes, I bandaged him. A few weeks later George was hit and I did the same for him."

But before Keen could minister to wounded comrades he went through the Toccoa mill. "I remember a loud, screaming, bull-necked lieutenant [Alicki]. They ran us into trucks and they ran us to the barracks. We ran to the latrine and I mean if one had to go we all went. Every bastard on the post knew we were recruits and the ones doing KP or similar stuff had washed out. They would shake their heads and say, 'You'll never make it.' "

To his delight, Keen, although slotted as a medic, remained close to the Talarico brothers. "If possible, it was arranged that the medics took their basic with the same platoon they would serve in combat. You became part of the platoon and in turn the company and on up to the battalion, making one part of a family of brothers. The men of B Company are the brothers I never had. We learned to respect each other and each became aware of what to expect in the way of help when needed. At first it was only blisters, burns in the field, and crabs and the clap, treated on the Q.T. Many a case of gonorrhea never went further than the platoon because some person located an unsecured bottle of sulfathiazole. There weren't that many cases but there were some.

"Part of our medic's training was how to give shots. We spent hours in hot tar-paper barracks, sticking needles into an orange over and over again. We didn't have disposable needles so we were trained in how to autoclave, boil to sterilize both needles and syringes. More time was spent on what were to be our most immediate problems in combat, stopping bleeding, splinting, giving plasma and above all proper bandaging. There was a great source of pride in seeing how neatly you could apply a bandage, making certain it wouldn't fall off.

"I developed a tremendous amount of respect for the medical officers. Getting a damn fool to jump out of an airplane is one thing but getting an intelligent person like a physician is another. There just weren't many men of this caliber around. Captain Sullivan knew no fear and he was damned competent. He was not without a sense of humor even though he was a real stickler for military manners and discipline. I remember a man, from another battalion, who came on sick call and when asked what his trouble was said, 'Doc, I got a cold in my dick.'

"Sullivan ripped into him like a bear. 'Stand up straight, soldier. Don't you ever call me Doc and until your dick sneezes, we'll call it the clap.' "

Another of the 517th's medics, John Warren Chism, grew up in Broken Arrow, Oklahoma, a Tulsa suburb of about 1,200 when Chism was born in 1923. In Broken Arrow the local newspaper annually boasted of the summer heat by frying an egg on the surface of the main drag. Chism remarks, "I don't recall anyone ever eating the egg, perhaps due to the number of animals sharing the open spaces."

His devout Southern Baptist father was a skilled operator of machines like steam shovels but he rode out the Depression serving as the town's water commissioner while Chism's seamstress mother earned extra money. The senior Chisms tried to live by their religious principles. In those parlous times, while feeding and housing seven children, they offered room for stray passersby, servicemen and itinerant Baptist clergymen.

Attendance at church, mandated by his parents,

exposed Chism to fire-and-brimstone sermons and the hard shell intolerance of some religionists who heaped damnation upon the heads of Jews and Roman Catholics while predicting vile eternity for those who refused to accept these views. Prayers were offered *for* as well as against Adolf Hitler.

Young John Chism developed second thoughts about what he heard in church after he discovered that his Sunday school teachers used the same profanity that he had begun to learn from his contemporaries. His mother, alerted to his offensive tongue by members of a local network of prayer groups, sewing circles and quilting bees, put a switch to his backside in preparation for a more severe thrashing from his father.

On the other hand, Chism's parents accepted the need to fight "if I had a just cause." However, while the cuts and bruises of fisticuffs drew no sympathy—God would take care of the healing—a bloody shirt with buttons ripped off meant a mending effort from his mother.

Chism rates his public-school education as mediocre although he read any book he could lay hands on. When he and his chums discovered Edgar Rice Burroughs's tales of Tarzan with his vine-assisted aerial transport they experimented on a grove of giant elm trees. "First we swung with holds provided by tying a gunnysack stuffed with straw on the bottom end. We tried automobile tires and then finally plain overhand knots. We put one or two ropes in each tree and it wasn't long before we could traverse the entire grove, jumping from thirty to forty feet, making an equal arc throughout the whole stand of elms. When our mothers first laid eyes on these Lord Greystoke disciples, they realized that to forbid our fun would invite revolt. They warned us not to break our necks and marched off to pray for us. Not one of us incurred more than a rope burn."

Football largely eliminated the urge to ape Tarzan. "It was the core of sports activities around Broken Arrow.

While we were undefeated or nearly so each year I played, too much emphasis is placed on a game which causes too much pain. Besides two lost teeth, a broken collarbone and sprains, I suffered no injuries, while inflicting a great deal. Our coaches then, as now, were practically canonized. They were the highest paid faculty, often functional illiterates, honored above true heroes, intellectuals, artists and academics, and forgiven sins for which others are ruined."

Chism mistook an offhand remark by a coach hired as an assistant on the West Coast as an offer of a scholarship and traveled to California. When he discovered no free ride in return for his gridiron skills, he enrolled at the University of California in Berkeley. Chism worked harder than ever, holding down two jobs between semesters.

His brother-in-law obtained Chism the post of sole attendant and head of a dispensary for a shipyard in Oakland. Chism learned to treat men and women for everything from lack of sleep through traumatic wounds. "I was exposed to bloody injuries and got over the initial squeamishness usual when one first sees gore. I learned how drugs were accounted for. My training included at least three courses in vertebrate anatomy, Boy Scout-level first aid that emphasized restoration of breathing, through artificial respiration, control of bleeding and transportation in cases of broken bones."

Chism spent all of 1942 and the first weeks of the following year in his dual role of shipyard medic and college student. Increasingly, he fretted over his civilian status as two brothers and countless friends had entered military service. When he dropped in upon the local draft board to ascertain his status, his record could not be found. "It is amazing how fast a system can work when prodded by the innocence of a volunteer. Within a week I was notified to appear for induction."

The first night of service at the Presidio, near San

Francisco, Chism and his new associates discussed their options. "Five of the group, along with myself, were leaning towards the airborne. I'm sure I wasn't the dumbest one there but I had no idea what that would mean. The first appeal involved a vague notion we would not have to do much walking. There was also an idea that I might be able to make up for lost time in the paratroopers since they were supposed to be a new branch. There wasn't any talk about saving the world, beating Mr. Hitler, and there was no fear of jumping from an airplane or sense of adventure."

First came a long, dreary train ride. "We passed one town in Nebraska in the middle of the night just when our homesickness was becoming acute. The conductor announced there would be a thirty-minute stop and invited us all to debark and walk about. To our great surprise we found what seemed to be every female and old man in town there to pass out hot soup, homemade sandwiches and hot drinks." An appreciative bunch of young men, no longer quite as lonely, reboarded the train.

The arrival at Toccoa was a shock. "The falling-in drill and command to secure baggage which followed our detraining was an invitation to pratfalls, chaos, mayhem. In very short order we were made to feel how low caste we were and how quickly we might perish. After a questionable meal we marched to a meeting. There our schedule for entrance or rather acceptance into the 517th was spelled out. Everything now was to be done together at double time, no falling out or visiting. Since it was now between eight and nine o'clock at night, our final orders were that if there were any visits to the latrine by one, then all would go. We did not have to go to the latrine en masse that first night. Bedwetters, discovered the next few nights, were dispatched elsewhere."

Chism, having jumped from the thirty-four-foot tower and passed his interviews, received assignment to

B Company, supposedly to learn the skills of a machine gunner. He felt relieved he would not be a medic and began his basic training.

"I had my first encounter with William J. Boyle on the first pre-breakfast run around the encampment. In the darkness, queasy from inoculations, I was questioning myself about my decision to go airborne. I realized the parachute was only a means of transportation to the battle area. There was plenty of walking to do on both ends of the airborne trip. Suffering along on the run, and being fairly close to the tail of the column, I took what was a sure opportunity and slowed my pace to an easier one. Dropping my speed even more, I fell farther behind. I was luxuriating, wallowing in my scheme. Glancing over my shoulder, cautiously, I saw a great grizzly of a man bearing down on me. His intentions were quite clear. I was to catch up or end my life in the mud beside the road we were on. In instances like this decisions can be reached rapidly. Sprinting at a record pace to escape the dire threats being flung my way, I overtook my fellow runners. To be absolutely safe, I continued to move faster until I became part of the head of the column."

To his dismay, Chism learned that although he was tutored in the art of the machine gun while in the basic stage of training, the brass, aware of his background, had ticketed him as a medic. An ill-advised appeal to Bill Boyle for a reprieve sent Chism fleeing back to the safety of his platoon. One final escape route lay open, an interview with the board of doctors chaired by Vella, who asked a single question of all candidates: "Confronted by a choice of bringing up ammunition from the rear or evacuating all the wounded, in the face of savage resistance by the enemy which threatened the outfit's mission, which course would you take?"

Chism says he leaped at the chance for rejection as a medic. "I quickly answered, apologetically, that I would have to transport the ammo. Major Vella could not hide his approval of my answer. Before the day was over I was notified of my selection to be a medic."

Paul Smith, raised in Scottsboro, Alabama, and then Birmingham, sprang from more affluent circumstances than Keen or Chism. Coming from a well-educated family, Smith, as a high-school student, says he was very much aware of events in Nazi Germany, particularly in regard to its expansionism and repressive nature, less so in its persecution of the Jews.

"I owned a small crystal radio set that worked only with earphones. I used it several times to listen at three and four in the morning to actual speeches of Hitler in Germany. I was appalled at the *crazy* delivery, the short simple sentence diatribe, the anger and the apparent delight of the audience."

As an adolescent, Smith aimed his high-school courses and his two years of college towards a career in medicine. "Because of the plan to become a physician, I was inducted into the Army Reserve and allowed to remain in school. I was at the University of Alabama when the Japs attacked Pearl Harbor. Everyone was excited; with the exception of one or two, there was great anticipation over the prospect of getting into the war. No draft-card burners here, and a flag burner would have been torched himself.

"During my sophomore year, desire to get into the war led me to ask for active duty and assignment to the parachute troops. I was inducted on March 17, 1943, at Fort McPherson, Atlanta, and three days later was deposited in the north Georgia pine trees at Camp Toccoa to become part of the 3rd Platoon, Company A, 517th Parachute Regiment."

As in the cases of Keen and Chism, the medical interests of Smith caught the attention of Paul Vella. But first, like the others, Smith endured basic training as an infantryman. Along with Joe A.C. Williams, Smith was chosen for advance training as a surgical technician. Eventually, Smith was named aid station squad leader, working directly under the two battalion surgeons.

Smith describes his superior, Sullivan, as "one of the most practical and intelligent men I have ever known. His manner was somewhat brusque but knowing him as I did, I am sure this was his practical, no-nonsense personality showing, rather than any lack of sympathy towards patients. Sullivan's bedside manner was pure medicine and not fatherly."

In fact, Smith found all of the people involved with the treatment of disease, injury and wounds highly capable, from the surgeons like James McNamara and Sidney Samis through the enlisted aid men, Joe A.C. Williams, Harold Seegar, Hoyt Kelly, David Haight and John Chism. Of the last, Smith remarks, "Probably the outstanding medic in the regiment, among enlisted men. Even temperament, intelligent, capable, stoic, brave, dependable." According to Smith, Joe A.C. Williams possessed the ideal attitude for a soldier—"I can't be killed." "He was smart, practical, happy, could keep everybody happy!"

Russel Brami, like Keen and Chism, grew up in circumstances near the bottom of the economic scale. Born in Ironwood, Michigan, in 1924 of Finnish background, he lost his father at age four. "There were three boys and my mother was tough," says Brami. "She worked as the postmaster in Ramsay and taught school. I never had time for athletics while in school, I was too busy working.

"I was in Detroit, learning to be a pattern maker in a foundry, when it was obvious I would soon be drafted. I enlisted and went to Fort Custer, Michigan. Dick Seitz came through asking for volunteers to be paratroopers. It was still winter in Michigan and I had one question, "Is it snowing in Georgia?" When he said no, that did it for me. I got off the train in Georgia, wearing a heavy woolen overcoat while a hot sun was shining."

He handled the tower leap with aplomb and then went before Dick Seitz. "I don't even remember what he asked me," says Brami. "I was scared stiff. I just stood there and said 'Yes, sir, no, sir.' Paul Quigley, who joined the same time as me and eventually got a battlefield commission, said he told Seitz he did volunteer because of the money." Both men were accepted.

Brami did not find the physical demands onerous. He saw companions on the run up Currahee pass out and then revive to finish. "After a while, as we all became more fit and cockier, if someone ordered us to do pushups our answers would be, 'How many?' and 'Which arm?' We were farm boys, city boys, Southerners, Westerners and Easterners. Some from the South were still fighting the Civil War but everyone could read and write. [A number of World War II GIs were illiterates.] Tom Cross tried to build some spirit by having us sing when we marched. We thought that was bullshit and it never went over. Later, Colonel Graves [who replaced Lou Walsh] wanted us to chant 'True as steel,' the paratroop motto, but that didn't make it either.

"We didn't love our officers but we respected them. Most of us were eighteen or nineteen and they were only a few years older. Their life wasn't any easier than ours, except for their officers' club where they could get a drink. We would slip out of camp and head for Cornelia, Georgia, visit with the local girls and down a beer but get back in time before bed check."

Dick Jones, a Californian, signed up for parachute training after having been turned down by the navy, in spite of his growing up around boats, and rejected by the marines although his marine brother captured on Corregidor died in a Manchurian prison. "If I couldn't choose my branch of the service then I was going to pick where I'd serve in the army."

He survived his interview with Dick Seitz but almost came a cropper with his initiation into the workouts designed to strengthen his body. "The calisthenics, the long, long runs, then going back to the barracks so stiff and sore that it even hurt to think and was agony just to lie down. You hurt so bad you wished you could faint but didn't dare because you would be out." Water discipline meant extended, hot, dry hikes where the canteen was inspected to make sure it was at least half-filled with water.

Nolan Powell was the quintessential farm boy. "I grew up on a 100-acre general farm, mostly fruit, in upstate New York, between Oswego and Rochester. We had horses, cows, pigs, chickens. I was strong from pitching hay, plowing with a team of horses, and could pick 100 bushels of apples a day. I attended a small rural school with twenty-three in my graduating class. I played varsity basketball, baseball and soccer. I did not drink alcohol or smoke and was interested in the daily news and history. My dream was to travel and see the world.

"I was drafted in March of 1943 and volunteered for the paratroopers during my first five days at the induction center at Fort Niagara. I volunteered because from my sophomore year in high school I had gone steady with an attractive, intelligent blonde. After graduation, she went to work in a defense plant while I enrolled in the State College for Teachers at Albany. She met a University of Pennsylvania graduate whom she later married. I was a heartbroken farm boy and the paratroopers was my attempt to prove I was somebody to my lost love.

"After being raised on a farm where we had no electricity until I was twelve, used an outhouse, worked a sixty-hour week at twenty cents an hour, I was used to the rugged life. The paratrooper life was not a cultural

shock. I had accepted parental, teacher and boss authority so the military represented just another authority to
be accepted. The physical conditioning was tough, but
no tougher than farming. Whether you pitch hay or load
manure, push-ups, running and digging foxholes are no
harder."

Like Russ Brami, Ed Johnson enlisted to beat the
draft. Son of an Indianapolis brewery truck driver, Johnson, "as a Depression kid," toiled as many hours a week
in a meat market as he spent in high school. Like so
many his age he fantasized about World War II, even
considered running off to Canada to get to war. At his
reception center he volunteered for the paratroops along
with three others. He was the only one of the bunch
accepted.

After John Alicki administered his unique brand of
culture shock, Johnson faced Bill Boyle. "By then I was
determined not to let the bastards grind me down, but
this bull of a man who seemed nine feet tall could have
stopped me. After he asked a few gruff questions why I
thought I could 'belong,' I regained my voice and my
bravado and convinced him I sure as Hell could."

Johnson entered C Company, the domain ruled by
Charles La Chaussee. "He and Boyle came to be the two
officers for whom I had the utmost respect as combat
leaders. I developed great confidence in their judgment
and was inspired by the examples they set for us under
fire. La Chaussee could have been described as a chicken
shit barracks commander when we were out of combat.
That didn't lessen our regard for him in battle. But there
were times when we felt he was volunteering the members of the company for missions that were better left to
others or at least to the luck of the draw. Boyle's lack of
spit and polish and his personal physical prowess en-
deared him and enhanced his combat leadership."

John Forrest arrived at Toccoa from Texas as a
nineteen-year-old, self-confessed hellraiser. In fact, Forrest

had been expelled from Texas A & M for disciplinary reasons. "My father worked for Phillips Petroleum. Several of the British tankers were torpedoed by German subs as they entered the Gulf of Mexico after loading at the Phillips terminal on the Houston Ship Channel."

The ship sinkings and the family interests kept Forrest aware of world affairs. "Several of my cousins had served overseas in World War I and were suspicious of the Germans in general. Actually I initially had some sympathy for the Germans' desire to rearm and reassert themselves after what I perceived as mistakes made in the Treaty of Versailles. My attitude towards the Japanese was based on prejudice. I resented the railway gondolas of scrap metal that filled trains passing through our town. Many people expressed the opinion that the Japanese would one day shoot it back at us. The Japanese-American 442nd Combat Team which I saw in Italy and France changed my opinions about Japanese people."

Forrest enlisted toward the end of March 1943, intent upon entering the parachute infantry. "Some of my classmates and I while at Texas A & M had discussed the role of parachute troops. Obviously, we really didn't understand it. I was attracted by the prospect of excitement, the extra jump pay and the mistaken notion that being a paratrooper would somehow be different from soldiering in the straight leg infantry.

"The discipline seemed to me fair and equitable. Minor infractions resulted in push-ups. More substantial forms of company punishment involved digging holes. Neither was excessive and I don't believe anyone was punished unjustly. The most severe company punishment was reserved for being AWOL or missing a fatigue detail. Actually, most of the soldiers in my company liked KP because of the extra food and fresh milk they could get.

"After all of that training at Toccoa, it never entered my mind that any one of us would refuse to jump. And no one from the 1st Battalion did balk. I had never been in an airplane prior to my first jump and I never landed in one until after the war.

"The caliber of the enlisted men was excellent. They were intelligent and many had one or more years of college. They were upbeat, fun-loving and conscientious. Any one of them could have been an officer if OCS were open to them. Several came into the 517th from my hometown. Jimmy Slatn in Company B was killed in Italy while Bob Smathers survived. I made some great friends; Danny Coleman, who had prior military training at Porter Military Academy, was a model soldier. Red Stallins and Shorty Atkins were special. Red, a bulldozer operator from California before the war, and Shorty, an oil pipeliner from Louisiana, were both the happy-go-lucky types, strong, cantankerous and liked to fight each other even though they were close friends. Every evening after retreat formation, they'd go behind the barracks and scuffle for too long a time. During Tennessee maneuvers both were too exhausted to fight so they each wrote down every real or imagined irritant with an eye to settling accounts later. And they did, page by page."

The personality of Phil Di Stanislao resembled that of Forrest. Di Stanislao, who was among the very first would-be parachutists to come to Toccoa, grew up in a comfortable middle-class family. His hometown was a small village, Tuckahoe, a few miles beyond the outlying precincts of New York City.

"I was of Italian descent, a big family. Eventually, between my brother and ten cousins, there were a dozen of us in service during World War II. My father was an executive with Armour and Co. and he'd been commissioned a second lieutenant in World War I, after serving as the platoon sergeant with Alvin York [that conflict's most celebrated U.S. hero]."

At six foot two and 180 pounds, Di Stanislao played

football for Tuckahoe High. Di Stanislao was good enough on the field to receive a scholarship offer from William and Mary and achieved sufficiently in his academic work to pass the entrance exams for the Ivy League's Columbia.

"I don't remember any awareness of what was going on in Europe or the Far East except perhaps the shots of the crying baby in the Shanghai railroad station after the Japanese bombed it. We were very patriotic, always flew the flag on July 4th and what was then called Armistice Day. [November 11.] At the Bronxville Theater I saw a recruiting movie on the paratroopers and it really stirred me. It seemed the right way to go, be in battle with small units for two or three days and then back to clean sheets and good food.

"Shortly after I graduated from high school, I enlisted. My father walked me to the railroad station when it was time for me to report. He put his hand on my shoulder and offered me advice. 'Phil, there are two kinds of girls.' He never told me the differences. His other counsel was, 'Don't go into the infantry.' I assured him I wouldn't but I didn't tell him I was going in the paratroops."

After a few days at Fort Dix, New Jersey, Di Stanislao, along with other would-be parachutists, including Charlie Keen, rode the rails on his first sleeper. "We left the train in the yards rather than the station at Toccoa. There was a truck there for us with an officer. I didn't know who he was at the time but it was Boom Boom Alicki. He chose to come up to me, nose to nose, I felt at the time, although he was six inches shorter. He glared at me, literally spitting out his words, told me if I didn't think I was tough enough to be a paratrooper to get back on that goddamn train. I was impressed, intimidated."

Assigned to A Company of the 1st Battalion, Di Stanislao now underwent his basic training under the eyes of his immediate CO, Capt. Herbert Bowlby, and an omnipresent Bill Boyle. The cadre, so far as the new recruit was concerned, were a mixed bag, with some well qualified and others obvious incompetents posted to the 517th by commanders delighted to be rid of them.

Di Stanislao learned early on that Bowlby was a stickler for the rules. "One time he walked into the barracks and since I saw him first, I was supposed to yell, 'Attention!' But he seemed to feel I didn't notice him soon enough or yell loud enough. He made me wear a barracks bag over my head, shouting 'Attention!' until I satisfied him. He made a big deal of the correct military stance and formed a 'piss-poor posture platoon' of those he thought didn't measure up. That was ironic. Although he was a West Pointer, he carried himself like a spavined mule."

However, Di Stanislao regarded the actual training as excellent. "It was almost never company-wide but mostly small unit operations, on a platoon or even squad level. That made us very close-knit; I made friends who've lasted all my life. Physical fitness was of course a primary thing. We ran and we ran. The trek up Mt. Currahee was quite a trek but I was in splendid shape and I enjoyed it. There was another exercise, five miles with full field equipment including heavy weapons and the musette bags carrying stuff, at a pretty fast pace. We called it the Bunion Derby, traveling quick time or double time. Push-ups were a standard paratrooper thing.

"At first we sang when we ran, bawdy songs. We were all privates and thought we were being sharp and slick. We probably would have sung 'Deutschland Über Alles' if ordered. But after a while we became more sophisticated and cut that out. When someone fell out on the run up Currahee, we were told to step around him, step over him, step on him but keep going. But we would help the man out if we could. Most of us felt we could outrun a billy goat.

"We had courses in compass reading and maps. We practiced knife fighting, hand-to-hand combat. The competition was very keen. Every platoon competed with one another, the companies against each other and, when the other battalions were formed, against them. It was a wonderful life for a young guy. There were shortcomings. We were very regimented, very disciplined. There were stupid punishments. We had one man whom the company commander didn't think had his hair cut short enough. Bowlby took him into the supply room, shaved his head with a razor so closely the soldier was bleeding from all the nicks. When he put on his steel helmet and stood on the parade grounds in the hot sun he didn't last long before falling flat on his face."

Not everything went smoothly in the tar-paper barracks either. "Fist fights were common. Here were a bunch of guys in top-notch condition, locked up together. It got to the point where if someone said 'boo' the wrong way he'd be invited to the bloody pit. We had some nifty fights and I had several myself."

According to John Lissner, punch-ups involved all ranks, officers, noncoms and the lowest of the enlisted. "Things would be settled behind the barracks. No charges would be brought and nothing further said once the confrontation ended."

In fact, the prospective troopers were encouraged to stand up for themselves if provoked. Lissner recalls a pair of his men who traveled to Atlanta on their first weekend pass and, after finding two agreeable female companions, fed them and then invited them to their hotel rooms. "The house dick broke in and accused them of all sorts of offenses. They were booted out of the hotel and were not even given a refund. When they came back to Toccoa, Lt. Murrey Jones, demolition officer for the first platoon, listened to their tale of woe and said, 'If that ever happened to me, I would get my hands on a smoke grenade, find my way to the air-conditioning unit and fix their asses.' A few weeks later we read in the newspaper about the occupants of that hotel being forced to flee their rooms after some colored air suddenly was released through the ventilating system."

Murrey Jones, according to Lissner, acted as a kind of counselor in explosive revenge techniques. GIs fleeced into buying a dummy radio returned to the scene of the crime with a satchel charge, a baglike pack of explosives, and placed it beneath the shack. No one was killed or injured but the structure collapsed. On another occasion, a saloon whose barkeep abused troopers was rattled by a pole charge, a device which resembled a broom handle with dynamite mounted on a plywood slab.

"Our kids," says Lissner, "advised everyone to leave because the place was about to blow up. As soon as they cleared out the joint, the pole charge was set off and it changed what was an outhouse into an inhouse. They weren't out to kill or maim, just to say that they would not be taken."

Di Stanislao, like most of his companions, developed a reverence and respect for Bill Boyle. "I was in awe of his wonderful leadership skills. I can't say I was frightened of him because he was something of a father figure [although Boyle was at most only seven or eight years older than the youngest of the troops]. We sensed in him the personification of the way we would like to be. He was tough and would do anything he asked us to do. He had a unique feeling of when to press us and when to pull us back. He was ubiquitous. At the damndest times, we looked over our shoulders, wondering if this phantom was right behind us.

"One time, while on KP, the first cook ordered me to clean the grease trap [the filthiest job in the mess]. I refused. He was a staff sergeant and gave me some lip. I popped him and was reported. I was ordered to see

Boyle. He was sitting at his desk with his leather jacket, the officer's insignia on it. He said, 'Di Stanislao, you think you're a real tough paratrooper?'

"I said, 'No, sir.' He then announced, 'I'm going to take this jacket off and beat the shit out of you.' I just took off and ran to the barracks and hid under them. There was no way I was going to fight him. Of course, he didn't follow me."

Clark Archer, a college student from a small town in southeastern Ohio, son of a bank officer, tried to enlist over the Thanksgiving break in 1942 but a minor knee problem, perhaps due to his cross-country track career, brought rejection. Instead he began his military career three months later as a draftee and as a member of the air corps.

"I successfully recanted this assignment," says Archer, "and volunteered for the paratroops. I asked for this kind of duty for two reasons. First, and foremost, there was the uniform. Second, the recruiter commented, 'If you can run, you can make it in the troops.' I was transferred from Fort Hays with fourteen other volunteers to Camp Toccoa. Only three reached jump school."

Archer became a member of B Company and his high regard for the battalion commander, Bill Boyle, matches that of others. He was aware of the "organized effort to build esprit." While the intensity varied among units, Archer says, "The focus was placed on, 'be the best.' Be the best squad, be the best platoon, be the best company, etc. Very few recruits knew the full extent of their capability. An objective of the training was to build confidence, not only self-confidence but trust in others upon whom you would depend in matters of life or death. The physical hardening routine did most to build self-confidence. Training in extended order tactics developed a reliance on others. Ultimately, there developed a sense of, I can do it; we can do it."

The moment the would-be parachutists all impatiently anticipated actually arrived in August 1943. They traveled to Fort Benning for jump school. The 1st and 2nd Battalions, whose raw recruits had been honed to a physical peak, were excused from A-Stage at the jump school in Fort Benning, the week ordinarily spent getting the men into the condition deemed necessary for parachutists.

"We jumped from the mock towers and then the tall towers," says Di Stanislao. "Learning to pack our chutes in the sheds was traumatic. We knew that our lives would depend on doing this properly. We packed and repacked them. Later, we became a little more cavalier about the task.

"Then we were assigned to our planes and sat waiting in the 'sweat sheds'—it was hot and we were sweating. On one hand the jump didn't seem that much of a deal. We had been carefully led up to it. However, I wouldn't minimize it, either. We did all the things they had taught us. When the time came we stood up, hooked up to the static line [the connection would yank open the main chute after a trooper left the airplane], stood in the door and when the jump master patted us on the rump, out we went.

"It was a beautiful day. We were about twelve hundred feet up and after the canopy opened and I had my initial shock, I sat back in the seat sling and just enjoyed it. The experience was exhilarating, watching the geography. The landing was a bump. They told us many times to come down with feet spread and to tumble. All my landings were four point, my two feet, my head and my ass.

"They had kept us in what was called 'The Frying Pan,' tarpaper shacks thirty-six inches off the sand with screened windows propped open with batons. The food had been horrible. I'm sure it was goat and I believe I saw hair on some of the meat. We would visit the small PX nearby and live on donuts and cokes. Immediately after the ceremony when they pinned the wings on us, the usual bunch of us that hung together went down to the main part of Benning. Instead of heading for Phenix City, battling the tankers, arguing with taxi drivers, getting drunk on as much booze as we could swallow, we drank milkshakes until I was sick."

Ed Johnson remembers his most critical test. "I really did not know if I would be capable of making my first parachute jump, but a deep breath and a hard slap on the butt got me out. I cannot describe the relief of seeing that chute open over my head, after an opening shock that brought many stars to my eyes. An officer with a bullhorn talked me down. He was so pleased with my maneuvers and landing that he drove his jeep over to exclaim, 'Great jump, great landing, trooper!' I'm glad he wasn't around for my two ass-over-appetite landings on my next pair of jumps."

Paul Smith harbored similar doubts. "My feelings on jumping from an airplane: Am I crazy? Is this really me? Answer, No! Scared to death!" The moment before landing evoked, "Oh, shit!" But after touching down it was "I can whip the world, including Hitler himself! This is wonderful, I am in total control."

Clark Archer remarks, "Generally speaking, it was the magnificent obsession of earning jump wings that kept the dropout rate at Benning's jump school to zero for my battalion. I found jumping from an airplane an absolute joy. Being a skinny kid of 125 pounds, I paid the penalty of shoulder bruises from the chute's opening shock. The most common complaint at the school was the limited number of jumps."

Even before they departed from Toccoa, however, the men had received their cherished jump boots. But these prized accoutrements for the moment were only to be burnished with saddle soap and brown polish to a spit-shine brightness and adored while stored beneath their bunks. The GIs had not yet earned the right to actually wear them as part of their uniform. Now, having completed jump training, the cherished boots would be worn as a visible sign of achievement.

As the recruits evolved from raw volunteers into qualified paratroopers, the 517th continued to stock its junior officer pool. Still in his teens, younger than Charlie Keen and less than a year older than many of the men he would lead was a diminutive second lieutenant, Ben Renton. Like Di Stanislao he spent his early years in Tuckahoe under middle-class circumstances. As a grammar-school kid, he acted as water boy for the same Iona College football teams that starred John Lissner.

Although five foot six and less than 120 pounds, Renton played intramural football and baseball, swam on the varsity team at the New York Military School and boxed in the Golden Gloves for two years. He spent a summer with the ROTC at Plattsburgh, New York.

Immediately after the bombing of Pearl Harbor, the eighteen-year-old Renton, with his military school background, applied for an infantry commission. However, the War Department at this stage required officers to be twenty-one. He hit the books, intent on entering West Point in 1942. The appointment went to another youth but manpower demands dropped the mandatory age for officers to eighteen. Renton pinned on his second lieutenant's gold bars.

"I was assigned to the 35th Division as a rifle platoon leader but since my ROTC all involved World War I weapons and tactics, I was sent with others for the basic officers' course." By the time he completed this instruction, he had volunteered and been approved for parachute school. Once qualified, Renton attended demolition school for three weeks. His orders now dispatched him to Mel Zais's 3rd Battalion.

"As an eighteen-year-old in the army I was used to being called 'junior,' 'kid' and the like. I was the butt of many jokes but I regarded it as good clean fun and didn't feel hurt. When Zais picked radio code names for his officers, someone remarked that I was as small as the baby in the Popeye strip, Sweet Pea. That instantly became my code name.

"Everyone was a volunteer but I think the officers were under the most pressure. You were expected to eat after your men ate, you slept after your men were bedded down. The principle was officers in front, always. When you marched you carried full equipment like everyone else. In the 81mm mortar platoon, the officers carried sand-filled ammo bags and changed over to the base plate, the Bipod and tube. Just before we left for overseas I had the tube, tripped on a root and the tube flew forward, clipping the heel of the man ahead. It was our platoon sergeant. He swore at me in Spanish; we had a number of Mexican-Americans who liked the jump pay. Then in clear English he said something on the order of, 'Pick up that damn tube, Lieutenant. Pour the sand out and get your ass moving.' "

Ludlow Gibbons, a twenty-five-year-old native of Philadelphia, had been a member of a National Guard outfit federalized in March of 1941. "The draft was on and I wanted to get the year behind me. After I became a tactical officer at the infantry school, I found one of the few ways out was through the Parachute School. My father, who had been an infantry battalion commander in France during World War I, thought I had lost my mind.

"I joined the 517th at Mackall a few months before they were to leave for overseas. I was assigned to D Company and was accepted by the people right away. Dave Armstrong was the CO. I liked and respected him immediately. He was outstanding."

The 1st and 2nd Battalions, with the exception of some cadre and officers, were composed of soldiers whose military life, except for the first few days at a reception center, began with the 517th. But the 3rd Battalion had been told to accept graduates of the jump school, troopers who had already spent considerable time wearing olive drab.

Initially, Zais retained the privilege of culling the lot. Among these was Richard B. Robb, a refugee from the horse cavalry. The son of a Butler, Pennsylvania, doctor who had served in World War I and a mother who met the senior Robb while a nurse for the U.S. Navy, Dick Robb looked forward to a military career.

"I went to Culver Military Academy for my last two years of high school and was a member of the Black Horse Troop and Culver Lancers when I graduated in 1940. Being partially color blind, I lost my certain appointment to West Point. I learned to fly the summer after finishing at Culver but because of the color blindness couldn't get a commercial license or join the Air Corps."

Robb attended Penn State for two years but in September of 1942, through a connection of his parents, he enlisted at Fort Riley, Kansas. Most of the officers at the Cavalry Replacement Training Center (CRTC) there "disgusted" Robb. "At Riley, officers and their ladies watched polo every Sunday. Two well-known polo players held commissions, with their sole responsibilities the care of the polo ponies. Three weeks of the month, classes began for mechanized cavalry, with men bound for tank destroyer units in Texas. Every fourth week they began thirteen weeks of horse cavalry tactics fresh from the Civil War. Meanwhile, Rommel with his armor was in North Africa.

"If ever there was a bunch of draft dodgers in one assemblage, it was Riley and the CRTC that held the record. The only way out of the cavalry was to volunteer for the paratroops. And if I couldn't fly, this at least was close to my greatest dreams, those of a barely twenty-year-old idealist in time of war.

"When Major Zais interviewed me for his 3rd

Battalion, he asked why my record showed 'Reduction in rank (Cpl. to Pvt.) without prejudice.' I explained that I had demanded it because I wanted to come to the paratroops with no encumbrances."

Rowdiness was encouraged, says Robb. "Jump masters at Parachute School in Benning told us one trooper was as good as five army types. The instructors, sergeants, put the fear of God in the most fearless but all boasted they had at least one piece of military police gear, an arm band, a helmet—the most prized—personally taken from an MP. Survivors of jump qualification and training led many at Benning and Mackall to go into nearby towns looking for at least two or three nontroopers to beat hell out of, just to prove the jump propaganda was right. To come back to camp with lumps and blood evident was enough. No one asked if they won. It was assumed that if they indeed lost, it must have been they took on one too many."

Echoing Phil Di Stanislao's recollections, Robb notes, "There were no restrictions about grudge fighting in camp. Any enlisted could call out anyone, rank meant nothing, noncom against noncom, privates against each other, even private vs. noncom. There were limits: bare fists only, the Marquis of Queensbury rules, no boots used and the fight had to be refereed by an officer. Word would go out quick and all gathered around. At other times it was quick without the presence of an officer.

"To maintain discipline in this atmosphere, one had to make it perfectly clear, whatever his feelings about fisticuffs as the way to solve problems, when it came to a situation, you would not hesitate to go the distance with anyone. It wasn't whether you won or lost that mattered but that you took the challenge, no matter the odds, in this game of respect. This was the reality. The notion of perceptions as reality held true."

Robb found his CO, Mel Zais, an inspiring if somewhat quixotic leader. "He had an almost fierce look, if one did not know him. He would gather the battalion and tear ass. Never call us names but point out all our frailties, faults and screw-ups. However, he always ended these tirades with a reverse type compliment that would send us away laughing and thinking we were indestructible.

"After berating us something fearful, he ended one meeting saying that he and the officers had deliberately tried to run us down to total exhaustion in order to get our attention. He ranted, 'Then, what do I find, damn it, we get back to camp and after a shower you are all lined up to get a pass to town. What the hell is it with you men!' We left that session laughing."

During this period while the 517th evolved from a collection of eager recruits shepherded by a cadre of experienced officers and noncoms, whose own ranks witnessed a high rate of turnover, it functioned as purely a parachute infantry regiment. Meanwhile, two elements of the 17th Airborne, whose lives were to become an integral part of what Lou Walsh and company had wrought, also were undergoing the combat-ready process. These additional forces included a parachute engineer company and a parachute field artillery battalion.

Because their work involved a certain amount of technological skills as well as the capacity to serve as combat soldiers, the engineers believed that their outfit received first pick of applicants for parachute training at Toccoa. For example, Hank Simpson, born on a farm in upstate New York, was an electrician for Alcoa before he joined the engineers. Robert Wilkerson had served five years in an army hitch, leaving the Philippine fortress of Corregidor on the last boat before Pearl Harbor. When he returned to the service, he had already trained as an engineer before joining the parachute version of that specialty.

Others were grabbed because of their apparent intellect. Bill Hudson, originally a native of St. Paul, spent his

teen years in Forest Hills, New York, where he was by
his account not athletic but somewhat studious. By
1942, when he was seventeen, he was already a freshman
in college.

"I was always interested in foreign affairs. I carried an
atlas in my duffel bag when I went through the European campaigns. I was very pro-British and anti-German
during the 1938–41 period. The Italians and Japanese
seemed supporting players."

After he enlisted at eighteen early in 1943, Hudson
volunteered for paratroop training. He survived the
weeding-out process at Toccoa and subsequently Camp
Mackall, although as a youth disinclined towards sports,
the initial physical testing exhausted him. However, he
believes his high IQ scores helped get him through and
accounted for his selection as an engineer.

Charles Pugh, born in 1924, grew up in Paducah,
Kentucky. His parents divorced when Pugh was six.
Both of them remarried and created new families, leaving their son to be raised by his paternal grandparents.
The male head of the household was a city firefighter
while Pugh's grandmother operated a rooming and
boarding house.

Initially, Charlie Pugh thrived in school, chalking up
straight-A grades in his studies. In spite of his five-foot-
eleven, 140-pound skinny frame, he lettered in high-
school basketball and football, then pitched during
summers for an American Legion team. To pick up
spending money he mowed lawns, delivered newspapers,
filled in as a short-order cook, toted bags as a hotel bell-
man, ushered at the local theater, hawked soft drinks at
sporting events during evening hours and over the summer recess. Armed with a .22 caliber rifle, Pugh hunted
rabbits, birds and squirrels.

The revenues derived from his various jobs supported
his hormonal drives. "Girls, dating and drinking—not to
excess—became more important to me than school, or

anything else. My grades suffered. I went from a top student to one barely passing. I was very popular with the girls and well liked by most of my male buddies but I had a short fuse and temper. That resulted in many fist fights."

As a high school senior in 1942, Pugh dropped out to enter a federal premilitary program devoted to electronics at the University of Kentucky. But he could not generate enthusiasm for the work. In January of 1943 he enlisted, reporting March 15, 1943. At the reception center, his previous studies in electronics made him a candidate for the Signal Corps.

"That made me very unhappy. I saw a poster that invited inductees to volunteer for paratroop training. I had never even heard of paratroops. When I asked if I could apply I was told it was unlikely I could make the grade and if turned down I'd be certain to go to a combat infantry training center. I volunteered anyway.

He learned the arts of the combat engineers, bridge building, road grading, mine laying, along with the standard infantry skills. "All the while there was the indoctrination that we were the best there ever was or ever would be. We were told our training was far more rigorous than for any other soldiers in the world, and because of this we were the equal of several men. We were told we should be prepared, even expect to die in combat. We were brainwashed into believing we were superior because we were handpicked. We were told, almost daily, that we could resign and walk away anytime we chose. A few did, but not many."

Pugh's faith in his fellow engineers extended to those in charge. "Our company commander, Capt. Robert Dalrymple was only about twenty-five but since most of us were eighteen or nineteen he seemed much older and more mature. We respected him and feared his wrath if we goofed up. Very few of us liked Dalrymple in the beginning but over time we came to appreciate that his martinetlike firmness and high standards were what made us such a cohesive, effective unit. Also many of us are alive today or whole because of his leadership.

"I admired others, like Sgt. Howie Jaynes for his character, leadership ability and physical prowess." Jaynes would die in combat in Southern France. "My platoon leader, Lt. George Flannery, was another man I esteemed. Flannery was KIA in Italy and his successor, Lt. Fred Zavattero, performed at the same high level. Sgts. Allan Goodman and Jim Moses and Lt. Ray Hild maintained these standards for leadership."

Rural Kentucky fed another recruit to the parachute engineers, Joe D. Miller. Like so many in the 517th he squalled into life in 1924. His father served as station agent for a small railroad while operating a farm. When the elder Miller was laid off during the Depression, only the farm kept the family solvent.

"I worked this farm starting at a very young age," says Miller. "I was up at 4:30 A.M. with chores, ate breakfast at 6:00 and was in school until 3:30 in the afternoon. Then came basketball practice for two hours, more farm chores, dinner, study and then start all over again at 4:30 A.M. We were too tired at the end of the day for any hell-raising but my senior year the basketball team won the state championship and I had good grades. Although it was a very small school, they did a good job making us conscious of the outside world. We had a weekly news-paper with information about current affairs and there was classroom discussion. What we studied seemed to me very remote but frightening. By the time of Pearl Harbor I had formed a very negative opinion about Hitler and to a lesser extent about the Japanese."

Drafted in March of 1943, Miller opted for the para-troopers because, "I always wanted to be part of an elite group. I thought this to be the best the army could offer with the air corps second." Like most of his companions, Miller at Toccoa passed an interview with Bob Dalrymple, the company commander, and underwent basic training at Camp Mackall before jump school.

"I was numb, scared as hell on my first jump. Once in the air, it became fun. I felt like a bird, until I hit the ground. That woke me up. During my time as a paratrooper I made twelve more jumps, some very difficult but none were ever like that first one.

"Our cadre took great care to make us feel special. We were challenged to be better than others in the regiment and we set records at various tasks. My closest friend then and now, Bill Cooper, became a sergeant with the 2nd platoon. Our officers were never remote. They always led by doing what they asked us to do. My favorite among the officers was Lt. Earl Dillard. He was like an older brother and father to us. He was a kind gentle man who could be tough as nails when it mattered."

Allan Goodman, a native of Oak Park near Chicago, "more interested in athletics than academics," had blown opportunities for football scholarships available to him. The University of Illinois, by state law, had to accept residents and Goodman enrolled in a civil engineering program. However, he continued to avoid the books and dropped out in November of 1942. Five months later he volunteered for call-up through the draft.

At Camp Grant he put in for paratroop instruction and promptly surfaced at Toccoa. Probably because of his brief encounter with civil engineering at college, the initial screening parties nominated Goodman as a candidate for Capt. Robert Dalrymple's company.

Ernie Kosan was not a typical recruit. His birthplace was Berlin, Germany, in 1922, and he had emigrated to Dallas in 1926 where his father plied the trade of baker. But it wasn't so much his nativity as his personality that set Kosan apart. "I was a very shy, studious kid who always followed the rules. I kept my nose clean and stayed out of trouble. When I was young, you might have described me as a sissy, today I would be called a nerd.

"We moved to Houston when I was sixteen and while I was a teenager I was apolitical and had little or no interest in either national or world affairs. Before Pearl Harbor I had no feelings, pro or con, about the Japanese. My feelings about Germany and the Nazis were ambivalent. I was 100 percent American, having been naturalized in 1939, but I was proud of my German heritage. I knew nothing of the excesses of the Nazis."

Upon completing high school, Kosan secured work in one of the local defense plants. He received several deferments because of his job before the induction notice. Hoping to choose his branch of service, Kosan applied for the Navy but to his chagrin learned one had to be a naturalized citizen for at least ten years. The same reason barred entry to the Air Corps. He began his military career at Camp Fannin, Texas.

"During one of the indoctrination sessions it was mentioned that the paratroops were looking for volunteers and as an incentive the army offered extra pay. When I heard this, I thought, 'Ernie, you have been a weakling all your life. You were miserable in sports. You were always picked on by bullies bigger than you. You are a skinny, weak kid. Let's go for it and see if you can't change your life.'

"I was certainly not in a position to criticize the type of basic training that we received except that much of it was what we called 'chicken shit.' But who were we to know or what our officers knew. Most of them were in their twenties. They were just young snots. However, I must credit them for being serious, dedicated men who took their responsibilities seriously. The troops often railed against them, and secretly cursed them, but we were unaware of the tremendous pressures they were under."

Kosan made one close friend, a youth with a background somewhat similar to his. "Henry Wikins, whose original name was Wikinsky, had been a teenager living in Danzig, the free city, created through the Treaty of Versailles, on the Baltic Sea, between western Germany and East Prussia. The Poles call it Gdansk.

"During the 1930s, Henry's parents realized the direction things were going and they planned Henry's emigration. They believed they were too old to leave but the future of their son depended on getting to the U.S.A. A family here took him in and he became a citizen. We had long conversations aboard the ship taking us to Europe. He was comfortable speaking German and I was happy for the practice. The strange thing about Henry was that he harbored absolutely no hatred against the Germans. He taught me the Nazi party song—the 'Horst Wessel Lied.' I think that he, as well as some other German Jews I had known, considered themselves as Germans first, which is the real tragedy."

On a parallel course, the combat team's artillery battalion formed. Nat Schoenberg, as a boy, lived on 125th Street, the center of Harlem, when he was born in 1923. His father was a realtor and Schoenberg attended the local public schools.

He was a reasonably good student without many opportunities to indulge his interest in sports beyond stickball games in the streets. When he graduated from De Witt Clinton High School, Schoenberg enrolled at City College of New York in a general academic course. He followed world affairs closely and, being Jewish, developed strong feelings against Hitler's Germany.

Working for a company that manufactured electronics for the Navy, Schoenberg received short term deferments but in June 1943 he succumbed to the draft. "At Fort Dix, New Jersey, I volunteered for the paratroopers. The interviewer there asked me why I wanted to become 'a clay pigeon.' I told him I wanted to do the best I could for my country. In fact, my Jewishness had something to do with it. I was looking for vengeance."

After his leap from the tower at Toccoa and some

aptitude tests, Schoenberg and about a dozen others in
his group were assigned to the 460th Parachute Field
Artillery Battalion, training at Mackall. As a member of
C Battery, the new recruit went through the physical
toughening program while learning the duties of gun
crews. Capt. Louis Vogel supervised the activities and
Schoenberg believes Vogel and his lieutenants taught
them well.

There were no vehicles detailed to haul parachute
field artillery. Instead, an air drop included wheels that
could quickly be attached to the gun carriage and a harness. "Two men hitched up in the front where there was
a crossbar and another two men pushed from the back.
Going downhill, the two guys in front could be in a lot
of trouble."

If he thought the forces contending against Adolf
Hitler on behalf of democracy would be free of prejudice, Schoenberg learned differently. He was immediately
dubbed "Abie"—just as most Native Americans were
called "Chief." But Schoenberg was resilient enough to
deflect the often unconscious bias.

Cameron Gauthier, another recruit to the 460th, was
actually Canadian-born but raised in upstate New York.
An indifferent student, except for his interest in history,
not particularly keen on sports, Gauthier spent his after-
school hours peddling milk, shining shoes or selling
newspapers.

At fifteen, underage, Gauthier enlisted in the local
National Guard unit. But when the government federalized the outfit in 1940, his mother refused to allow him
to continue. A broken hand delayed his induction after
he turned eighteen but when he arrived at Fort Niagara,
Gauthier opted for airborne.

Like so many others, Gauthier recognizes that while
the rigors, beginning with the runs up Mt. Currahee
through the entire toughening process, were to prepare
the GIs for what they would face, survival welded the

troopers together. "Once you got in with the boys, you
wanted to stay with your own people. They became
closer than your own brother because you were aware
you did not have to depend upon your brother to stay
alive."

Actually, Gautheir acknowledges he received a break.
"I was assigned to the communications section and I
had the job of the old man's batman. [Orderly for the
commanding officer.] I had it much easier than the gun
sections. They were the mules. They pulled those guns
through the sand."

CHAPTER V

GOING TO WAR

FROM JUMP SCHOOL at Fort Benning, the members of the 517th moved to Camp Mackall in North Carolina. At Mackall, the training intensified. The rifle company people checked out on all weapons, from the M–1 through the bazooka and even some of the crew-served pieces like the mortars. The brass continued to shuffle the deck, and Di Stanislao's tormentor, Capt. Herbert Bowlby, shifted to battalion headquarters. His replacement, Capt. Don Fraser, mimicked Boyle's attitude but not his manner. To the troops he became affectionately known as "Mother Fraser." Di Stanislao now benefitted from the importation of a new platoon leader, Lt. Milton "Chopper" Kienlen. Di Stanislao describes him as "a magnificent officer, big and very brave."

Having earned their parachute wings and the right to wear the boots, the frightened volunteers once intimidated by the likes of John Alicki were now self-assured troopers who found ways to relieve the tedium of some exercises. Sent into the woods around Mackall on a compass and map orientation exercise, a bunch of rifle-bearing troopers hiked five miles to nearby Pinehurst, a golfing resort. There they rented clubs, stuffed their M–1s in the golf bags and played a spirited nine holes. On another occasion they hired horses and reverted to the child's play of "cowboys and Indians," firing blank cartridges. For all of their potentially deadly toys, the troopers were still kids enjoying a rugged summer camp.

Lou Walsh unbent far enough to congratulate them after their first six months. In October of 1943 he addressed them: "Success in battle goes to the troops who can take one more step and fire one more shot than the enemy. The physical-proficiency tests just completed give us an insight on our chances. Each unit in the Army undergoes the same tests and a company per battalion is selected . . . to represent that battalion . . . Three times in one day the U.S. Army record was broken and we now hold not only first place, but second and third as well.

"Men, it took more than just physical strength to set those records—it took determination and the will to carry through—THAT wins battles—it took teamwork and that WINS battles—it took leadership—and that wins BATTLES.

"I saw one man fall near the end of the 300-yard run. He struggled up and fell again. He couldn't rise so he crawled across the line. That's determination.

"I saw another man just back from furlough and too ill to go on—too exhausted—so his company carried him and his equipment the full four miles. That's teamwork.

"I saw each company as it neared the finish line of the speed march—they look better than when they started. That's Airborne."

In February of 1944, nearly a year after activation, the 517th traveled to the boondocks of Tennessee for maneuvers conducted by the Second Army. The War Games, pitting the Blue Army against the Red, played out amid wet snow, rain and mud for nearly a month. The tactics, according to the C Company leader, Charles La Chaussee, often resembled not even World War I but the Civil War with what he called, "a sort of Pickett's charge" by one mass of men against another.

From his unique vantage point, 1st Battalion surgeon Ben Sullivan observed the constant marches from place to place, the troops, including him, being routed out of warm pup tents to travel somewhere else, "usually wetter and colder," to no apparent purpose. "I realize that commanders and staff officers must have practice moving large bodies of men around, feeding them, keeping them supplied with ammunition and even care for and evacuate the sick and wounded. However, I did not suffer silence at the discomfort. We blamed it all on the stupidity and the imagined indolence of all staff officers, our own excepted, since we knew they were as miserable as we were."

Phil Di Stanislao, through the rosy glasses of nostalgia, recalls Tennessee as "a heckuva good experience. We worked in roving bands of three or four guys, slept in haystacks amid several inches of snow. Our physical fitness enabled us to handle forced marches over a mountain at night and into the morning when there was sleet, rain, slippery roads that obliged us to push vehicles with heavy weapons out of the mud."

He remembers a confrontation with a band of infantry soldiers hunkered down behind a stone wall. "Everyone fired off blanks in a kind of bang, bang, you're dead. Then came some yells from behind the stone wall. 'You guys think you're something special because you're big, tough paratroopers. You're overpaid and you're not worth a damn.'" Insults of a more indelicate nature followed and the 517th contingent dropped their rifles and charged. "We just beat the pudding out of them."

Shortly after this engagement, a weary Di Stanislao dropped down at the base of a tree and, with his rifle between his knees, dozed off. He awakened abruptly to the outraged voice of Bill Boyle demanding what the hell he was doing, sitting there with his M–1 pointed skyward. Di Stanislao stammered he was doing antiaircraft duty.

"Boyle went beserk. 'You're confined. You are not going anywhere during these maneuvers!' "

Later came an opportunity for the troopers to visit a nearby town. Di Stanislao ignored the restrictions placed on him by the battalion CO. He visited the supply tent to retrieve his Class A uniform from his barracks bag in order to dress properly. Boyle suddenly appeared. "He sat down on a pile of barracks bags and silently watched me dress. I figured there was no backing out now so I continued. When I had knotted my tie, Boyle said, 'Di Stanislao, have a good time.' "

Charlie Keen, the medic, says, "The Tennessee maneuvers were a bitch but good training for the Bulge [the struggle in the European Ardennes Forest during the winter of 1944–45]. We were there thirty days. It rained twenty-nine and on the thirtieth it snowed. The only saving grace was that you got to meet and indeed love those kind and wonderful people of the old Vol State. Ask any 517th trooper and he will tell you the weather was just plain shitty but the people and their cooking was redeeming. One morning, after an all-night march through the mud, rain and cold, we took a fifteen-minute break, strung out through a small village around five in the morning. In less than a minute, every house had the lights on and before we knew it, out they came with steaming pots of coffee. If the Germans had invaded Tennessee, I'm sure we would have died to the last man defending these homes."

The outfit was still battling the elements and perhaps the antagonism of the war-game officials when they received a left-handed reprieve. The 517th was to pull out immediately, return to Camp Mackall where it would be transformed into a combat team through the addition of the 460th Parachute Artillery and one company from the 139th Parachute Engineer Battalion, designated as the 596th Parachute Engineer Company.

Back at Mackall there was a frantic rush to prepare the

combat team for action. Some new faces appeared. Walter Plassman was the son of a country doctor who practiced in Golden Valley, North Dakota (pop. 300 or so), where he delivered Walter in 1916 and later his two brothers. The family settled down in Centralia, Illinois, in 1922, where Walter passed through the local schools. "I was pretty much an outdoors type, hunting, fishing, Boy Scout, football, track and only occasionally on the honor roll."

The family was upper middle-income, and Plassman, with his sights on higher education, became aware of world affairs. Of German descent, Plassman says he sometimes felt sorry for the people living under the Nazi rule.

He attended the University of Chicago Medical School as a member of the class of '43. Among his contemporaries was James C. McNamara. When Plassman enlisted in September of that year, his orders took him to the Carlisle Barracks where Ben Sullivan also received an orientation. His colleague from med school, James McNamara, was already at Carlisle, one week ahead of Plassman.

"Mac and I spent much time together at Carlisle while they tried to make soldiers out of us. Mostly it was military courtesy, map reading, road marches and the like. He came to me with information about the paratroopers. The extra hundred dollars a month sounded good. [Noncommissioned troopers received half that stipend.] At Fort Benning, Plassman located McNamara, one stage ahead in jump school. Upon completion of the course, both received assignment to the 517th, reporting in February of 1944.

"I was greeted with open arms by the regimental surgeon Paul Vella and assigned as assistant 3rd Battalion surgeon under Capt. Norman C. Siebert. He had volunteered for the paratroops to get out of Alaska where he had served for more than a year. We became great pals and I learned a lot from him. He was a dandy. Meanwhile, McNamara became the assistant surgeon for Ben Sullivan in the 1st Battalion.

"Vella was tough when necessary, and demanding, but really a nice guy, compassionate and he was good to his doctors. He was not much for training us but usually kept us informed, especially when under combat conditions."

Just as the new doctors joined the medical detachment and the 517th prepared to sail for battle an upheaval shook the newly formed combat team. Lou Walsh was relieved of his command, demoted one rank to lieutenant colonel with a notation on his record that he should not be allowed a combat command in the future.

Several factors dimmed Walsh's shining star. Even in wartime, the politics and prejudices within the military establishment conspired against him. Some were jealous of his high rank at such a youthful age. Others may have been offended by his exacting standards, his rejection of so many candidates for his regiment, including men who had graduated from the parachute school. His intense focus on building a will to win, teaching his soldiers how to fight and survive, was not matched by an interest in administration. La Chaussee's experience with the supply sergeant when he took over C Company was not strictly an aberration; it was also a symptom of an attitude within the outfit. The inattention to tidy bookkeeping would plague the 517th throughout its life.

Furthermore, Walsh was not always temperate when he disagreed with others, including superiors. "He talked too much," said Mel Zais. "He got too big for his britches." Bill Boyle happened to overhear Walsh on the telephone with higher headquarters, saying, "All you people do is fart, fume and fall back." These aspects of his personality contributed to an environment that made Walsh vulnerable.

The freshly formed combat team had rushed back to

Camp Mackall with much of their equipment aboard freight cars. Upon arrival in North Carolina, Walsh directed that all individual and crew-served weapons receive proper cleaning after exposure to the Tennessee weather and ground conditions. Then he gave the troopers several days off to recover from their month in the field. The freight cars, bearing items like mess ranges encrusted with mud and rust, were to be unloaded and serviced after the weekend pass.

Unfortunately for Walsh, Second Army Headquarters directed an immediate inspection of the 517th. According to Dick Seitz, "Lt. Col. Phil Mock, who had been a classmate of Walsh at West Point, made the inspection. He got pissed off during a debriefing with Lou. The inspection was not bad, except for lack of some entries on the Form 20s [supposedly detailing what each soldier has performed in terms of standard requirements]. Walsh tried to explain, in his usual forceful manner."

Tom Cross adds, "Mock also wanted to see the condition of all of the 517th's equipment. Walsh said okay on the crew-served pieces and that of the personnel but not the locked up boxcars."

According to Seitz, "Mock, a real son of a bitch, got upset and called Second Army to say 'the regimental commander is uncooperative.'" The rocket fired at Walsh traveled through the proper channels. Gen. Thomas Miley, as CO of the 17th Airborne and Walsh's boss, sacked him with the penalty of loss of one rank and the proscription on commanding troops.

Walsh later received a combat assignment as part of the 11th Airborne Division in the South Pacific. He was serving as executive officer for the 511th Parachute Regiment which jumped on Luzon in the Philippines. When the outfit's CO was hit, Walsh effectively took charge. Mindful of the blot on his record, the brass still refused to give him permanent command.

With the departure of the 517th for Europe imminent, Col. Rupert Graves replaced Walsh. Graves had a personality about 180 degrees different from that of his predecessor. A member of the military academy's class of 1924, he was not only much older than most of his subordinates, men largely in their twenties, but also his mild appearance added an almost fatherly touch in contrast to the stocky, brush-cut, truculent look of Walsh.

"All of the officers were very bitter about Walsh's relief," says Cross. "But Graves knew and sensed our feelings and he turned out to be ideal. He never let us down or took advantage of us. You could talk to him. With Walsh there was always a certain amount of apprehension when you disagreed with him. He was not a tolerant man. Graves was like an old shoe and made you feel comfortable approaching him."

John Lissner, who admired Walsh and who developed a close relationship to him after World War II, still remains angry at the removal of Walsh but he too rates Graves an excellent leader.

While all of the battalion leaders and most junior officers considered Walsh an extremely able leader, several were not sorry to see him leave. In his journal, Howard Hensleigh, a lieutenant who joined the regiment in the autumn of 1943, noted, "I like the change and the outfit runs a lot smoother."

Ben Sullivan says, "Walsh was too much of a believer in the way the Marines did things. He would have gotten a lot more men killed than Graves, who was considerate, he had more respect for human life."

Even Cross, an ardent fan of the deposed commander, admits, "If Walsh had been in charge, we would have had a lot more medals and a lot more casualties."

The GIs at the bottom of the pecking order had minimal contact with their regimental commander. John Forrest says, "I am certain Colonel Walsh had a clear vision of what he believed a parachute regiment should be. The training program he had Maj. Forest Paxton develop was important in preparing us for combat. His brief combat experience in the South Pacific led to requirements that seemed silly but in retrospect were excellent and rational ideas. For example, no one could wear coverall fatigues. Instead we used only the two-piece fatigues. The rule was based on the problem of getting out of your clothes when you had the GIs (diarrhea). That was something we all experienced at one time or another. He also insisted that we lace our boots a certain way to make the cutting of the laces simple when necessary to remove a boot for a wound to the leg or foot.

"I think he was a good commander but not a good leader. But Walsh's little impromptu speeches about jumping together on D-Day at H-Hour and dying gloriously caused some of us to think, 'I didn't join this outfit to die. I just wanted some extra jump pay and an even chance at survival.' "

While they snickered at the bombast mouthed by Walsh, many troopers, after the fact, believe his obsession with fitness and combat training provided them with the strength to survive and reduced casualties. "I thought Walsh was a great officer," says C Company's D. W. "Deacon" Jones, at twenty-seven one of the oldest enlisted men in the entire outfit. "He looked the part and I was sorry he wasn't going to lead us into battle. When I first laid eyes on Colonel Graves I wondered if they weren't giving us a recycled officer. But I took a different attitude about him after combat. He turned out to be a helluva good leader."

Ed Johnson, a rifleman with C Company, says, "I both admired and liked Walsh as our regimental commander. I questioned his being replaced by the 'Old Man.' Later, I determined there were a lot more 517s alive today because the 'Old Man' took over. I had the personal experience of leading an escort party for Colonel Graves from our Command Post [CP] to another CP during the Battle of the Bulge. I was on the point and thought I was moving the group rather well. A hand tapped my shoulder and the 'Old Man' said, 'Sergeant, if you can't go any faster, let me lead.' "

Walter Plassman joined the 517th as Walsh departed. He never knew the original CO but Graves left a lasting impression. "I cannot say enough good about Graves. I personally never heard him yell or swear. Just a beautiful man, and a great leader."

Dick Robb had too little contact with Walsh to rate him or measure the effects of his departure. "Our destiny was controlled by Zais and our company commanders." However, over the months spent on the line in Europe, Robb developed strong feelings about Graves. "He was not an overly dapper man in terms of the appearance of his uniform. But obviously he gave a damn. Here was a leader who cared more for his men than his promotion or his Army career. He was a man who looked at the daily casualty reports as though each were his own son."

Forrest formed a similar opinion of Graves. "He seemed much more laid-back than Walsh. I'm not certain he could have formed a regiment with the same degree of gung-ho readiness. I'm not certain he would have been as ruthless as I perceived Walsh to be in selecting key officers. But he always seemed concerned for our welfare and I admired him for it, not the same way I admired Boyle or Don Fraser but I believe he had both feet on the ground."

The final weeding-out process reached down to touch Dick Robb. "Just before going overseas, I was ordered to report to Zais at Battalion Hq. Waiting outside his office, I could hear him giving someone a terrible tongue-lashing. It was his sergeant major, who held the rank of sergeant. He had failed to return on time from leave and been listed as AWOL. Zais noted he was late because he said he met some girl and stayed with her too long.

"Being AWOL, the man had let Zais down personally since he had recommended him for the job. In a loud voice Zais said, 'Here's your goddamn promotion to staff sergeant!' and I heard the tearing of paper. Apparently, he threw the pieces at him. 'Now, since you care more about some bimbo than either me or the regiment, go back to the guardhouse and await your court-martial.'

"Zais dismissed him and came to the door, beckoning me inside while a GI with an M–1 escorted the AWOL back to the stockade. As Zais sat down at his desk, he said, 'At ease, Corporal.' [Robb had earned back his two stripes.] At my feet were the torn pieces of paper. I started to bend over to retrieve them and Zais said, 'Leave them, that's where they belong. See that yours never end up there. If you heard, you know now my feelings about loyalty, if you didn't know before.'

"I thought, 'Jesus Christ, what am I into here.' Zais told me he needed a new sergeant major and did I want the job. I was only a corporal and the position was that of a staff sergeant. I got the impression that I was not there to be asked a question. It was not even an order but more like a command. I suppose I could have refused but that would let him down. He said if I performed to his satisfaction, my stripes would come swiftly. 'Yes, sir, thank you, sir, when do you want me to start?' What else could a fellow say in the presence of such a man?"

Something of a similar if less dramatic change shook the command of the 460th Parachute Artillery Battalion, numbering twenty-nine officers and 534 enlisted men, now committed as part of the regimental combat team. The CO throughout the training period and Tennessee maneuvers, along with his staff, departed. Col. Raymond Cato, West Point '36, with eight other officers took charge.

The son of a farmer in the Midwest, Raymond Cato

attended DePauw University in 1930–31. After two years at DePauw, Cato entered the Military Academy. "I was well acquainted with world affairs," remembers Cato. "DePauw's President Oxam was on a national committee that sought to settle the war between Japan and China over Manchuria. President Oxam kept the student body informed. I also played volleyball with my professor of German, who'd emigrated from Hitler's Germany."

Serving with the U.S. Army in the Philippines from 1937, Cato encountered American soldiers, including Joseph Stilwell [the famed general who worked with the Chinese during World War II], who were evacuated to the island because of the Japanese invasion. Cato became further aware of Japanese intentions while a member of a small detail assigned to observe a Nipponese lumber company opening up trails deep in the jungle interior.

Some time after Pearl Harbor, Cato arranged a transfer from a job of schooling soldiers to one more likely to get him into action. He qualified as a paratrooper in 1943 and received an assignment to the 466th Parachute Field Artillery Battalion, a component of the 17th Airborne Division. "The powers that be in Washington made the decision to replace those in command at the 460th. I selected the other seven officers who accompanied me."

Serving as exec under Cato was a University of Florida graduate in agriculture, John "Jack" Kinzer. "I was born in Jenkins, Kentucky," says Kinzer, "a coal-mining town with tough kids as my peers. They taught me a lot beyond what I learned as the grandson of two Methodist ministers and the son of God-fearing parents." Kinzer's father, in obedience to his religious vows, forsook his job as an accountant with a coal-mining company rather than drink and gamble with his new boss. The family moved to Pittsburgh, where, after considering application to either the U.S. Military Academy or the U.S. Naval Academy, Jack, at age sixteen, hied himself to Florida to labor in the citrus fields. His employer helped finance him through college.

Along with his labor in the citrus and academic groves, Kinzer also invested sufficient time with the military to earn a regular-army commission. In 1940, orders posted him for duty with a horse-drawn cavalry unit at Fort Benning. Kinzer became discouraged with a career that saw him training newly drafted African-Americans to handle the big guns and then watching them relegated to truck drivers and ordnance handlers. "I volunteered for parachute training to get into duty more useful in the war."

Another officer chosen by Cato for his new command was Worthington J. "Tommy" Thompson, who held the dubious honor of the oldest lieutenant in the 517th. Born on his maternal grandfather's Maryland farm in 1911, Thompson's sire lent his skills as a mechanical engineer to the building of the Panama Canal.

"I grew up in New York City," says Thompson, "went to the public schools including Stuyvesant High School. I played football and was very active in the Boy Scouts. In 1929, when I was 18, the stock market crash occurred and my father died. I went to Panama, took a job in a mahogany concession which was followed by two years in the oil fields of Colombia before coming back to New York to face the Depression. I partially supported my mother and kid brother who changed his name to John Dall, then made it big as an actor on Broadway and in Hollywood.

"When Pearl Harbor began World War II on December 7, 1941, I was an assistant to the president of the J. W. Wilson Glass Co. I found a replacement for myself, as I had promised my boss, and enlisted. The Army accepted me, although I was not 1–A but 1–H in the draft, healthy but too old."

Thompson's earliest military training was at a barrage balloon training center, after which he attended OCS. While with an antiaircraft outfit, Thompson volunteered for paratroop school. Five times the post commander refused to endorse the request. Thompson then filed an application directly to Gen. George C. Marshall, the U.S. Army Chief of Staff. Nine days after he sent in the papers, his orders to Fort Benning came.

He was at a base near Atlanta learning how to pack his battalion for overseas movement when a telegram directed him to join Cato and the others as part of the 460th in the newly created 517th combat team. "Cato made a very smart move by retaining the four existing battery commanders and the exec, Ed Frank, in place. He used his former 466th people as battalion staff. That brought him profound respect from the start."

For its overseas assignment, the 460th mustered a headquarters and four firing batteries, each of which employed four 75 mm pack howitzers. Originally designed for transport by mules over mountainous terrain, the pack 75 broke into seven pieces for a parachute drop with two more bundles bearing ammunition.

The men of the 460th, once on the ground and having recovered the bundles, could within minutes set up a gun that hurled a 13.9-pound shell a maximum of 9,650 yards, almost six miles. It was not a high-velocity missile and ineffective as an antitank weapon. To compensate for that weakness, one battery was designated to handle tanks. Instead of futilely seeking to penetrate the heavy German armor, the battery would lay down white phosphorus explosives which could ignite oil on the tracks of a tank, rendering it useless.

Unlike standard artillery battalions which would operate usually as a single unit with all batteries directed out of a single CP, the 460th batteries often split up for support of the separate battalions and companies from the 517th infantry. In those instances the battery commander formed a fire direction center to coordinate his operations with the foot soldiers.

The organization of the 517th Parachute Combat Team also included what had been C Company of the 139th Airborne Engineer Battalion. In its new capacity, it became the 596th Airborne Engineer Company with a complement of eight officers and 137 enlisted men. Because it was designed for deployment by parachute, the 539th bore no engineer heavy gear but relied basically on "pioneer tools"—picks, shovels and axes. Airdrop bundles contained mines, mine detectors and demolition materials.

The 517th, as a parachute unit, could be characterized as "light infantry" in comparison to the standard foot-soldier regiments. The T/O was based on a triangular structure. That dictated three rifle companies plus a headquarters unit for each battalion while ordinary infantry outfits numbered four such companies along with a headquarters company.

The backbone of each parachute company was the rifle squad, two per platoon. Seven in each squad bore rifles, three manned a machine gun and a leader with his assistant filled out the twelve-man contingent. A third squad included a 60 mm mortar crew. A lieutenant led each platoon, with a second officer as his deputy, and a sergeant held the third highest rank. The officers had several runners to carry messages as well as radio equipment or field telephones where available. There were three platoons to each company as opposed to four in a straight leg outfit. A regular infantry platoon contained four squads, three of which were riflemen while the fourth toted machine guns and mortars. The table of organization complement for one of the 517th's line companies added up to 127 enlisted men and officers, and battalion strength, including headquarters and the three companies, amounted to 530 troopers, augmented by a handful of people drawn from regiment including the medical personnel. In contrast, a battalion from a regular infantry regiment with four line companies plus a battalion headquarters company totaled close to 1,000.

Mobility determined the weaponry. The M–1 rifle with its eight-bullet clip was the primary piece. The .30 caliber carbine gradually replaced the highly ineffective .45 caliber pistol, issued usually to officers and some noncoms. The pistol's one value lay in the ability to bring it into play immediately upon touching down, even before one freed oneself from the chute. Even the M–1 when packed for a jump required a few seconds for assembly. Light machine guns, the Browning Automatic Rifle (BAR) and the .45 caliber Thompson submachine gun bolstered the firepower. A battalion normally faced tanks with the 2.36″ rocket launcher, known as a bazooka. It was not nearly as effective as the larger, better designed German *Panzerfausts,* derived from the original American version. Backing up the 60 mm mortars were 81 mm mortars assigned from battalion headquarters on an as-needed basis.

The same principles of organization that governed the line platoons extended upward. Three companies added up to a parachute infantry battalion with a headquarters unit serving as the command and control center over the three companies in its jurisdiction and maintaining liaison with the regimental headquarters. Unlike their groundbound contemporaries, the parachute companies dispensed with such amenities as kitchens. The only cooks and bakers, for example, operated at the battalion level instead of being attached to individual companies. Because they were intended to arrive by air and fight with what they could tote on their backs or recover from bundles, all parachute outfits operated with a minimum number of vehicles. The absence of jeeps and small trucks became an issue after the 517th went to battle.

As a net result of the configuration, parachute

infantry regiments, battalions and companies all carried
fewer men on their rolls than the regular line organizations. That in turn reduced the total firepower, although
the use of hand-held tommy guns compensated somewhat.

In theory, the artillery and engineers supported the rifle companies of the combat team. That called for close
cooperation. Unfortunately, according to the memories
of those involved, the three elements of the combat
team while learning their trades in Georgia and North
Carolina rarely worked at coordinating actions.

The three prongs of the 517th assembled at Camp
Patrick Henry in Virginia. There they saw some of the
recent POWs, members of the elite German *Afrika
Korps*. "They were big, strong, arrogant guys," says Tom
Cross. "We decided to show them what we looked like.
We ran our battalion past them, all dressed in shorts,
T-shirts, boots, bodies tanned, and chanting in unison."

The demonstration, intended as much to impress the
Americans that they were not up against supermen, was
followed by embarkation at Newport News. Sympto-
matic of the separation, even when they shipped out for
Europe, the 460th and 596th personnel boarded the
Panama Canal ship *Cristóbal,* while the troopers from
the three line battalions and regimental headquarters
trundled up the gangplanks of a former cruise ship, the
Santa Rosa.

It was not a matter of insufficient space to accommodate the entire combat team, for the troopers on the
Santa Rosa shared their boat with a number of airmen
and members of the Women's Army Corps, many of
whom were to operate telephone switchboards in Italy.

The idylls of gangway and deckside romances ended
after a two-week voyage as the ships docked at Naples on
May 31, 1944. Fourteen months of intensive preparation had shaped the 517th into a potentially crack, although untried, organization. To be sure, for all the

meticulous screening that covered admittance for the vast majority of the regimental team, and the sifting of personnel during training, some less than perfect specimens remained members. And, however superbly schooled, the ultimate test for the 517th lay ahead.

Almost immediately, commanders in the Italian theater scheduled the 517th forces to engage the enemy. The mission was abruptly canceled when Rupert Graves advised the higher authorities that his men had only their rifles; all of the crew-served weapons, including artillery, and the few vehicles used in support were still unavailable. The Regimental Combat Team bivouacked in the crater of a long-dead volcano north of Naples to await their missing firepower.

"With another trooper," says Di Stanislao, "I hitchhiked to the town of Caserta to visit a WAC I'd met on the ship. We still needed transportation to get to see the WACs. We borrowed a jeep from an engineer and while driving we saw another jeep parked on a dark street. We got it going and he took off in it. Just as I was about to start behind him, a man tore out of the building, leaped into my jeep and announced he was 'Major so-and-so,' the provost marshal of Caserta. 'Follow that jeep,' he ordered.

"I drove as slowly as I could. The provost marshal said, 'Go faster, faster!' I refused, saying, 'The speed limit here is only fifteen or twenty miles an hour. I can't go faster.' When we reached the middle of Caserta, the major jumped out. 'You are one dumb bastard,' he told me. We had set up a rendezvous point and I met my companion there. We returned the engineer's jeep and went to see the gals. They were great. Having saved rations, they put on a spread for us and even baked pies.

"We returned to our bivouac area and stashed the jeep in some brush. But when we went to retrieve it about a week later, someone had stolen it. My friend was outraged. 'We have nothing but thieves in the 517th.' I tried to remind him that we had stolen the jeep but he refused to count that as a crime."

Removed from the restraints of their American environment, under the stress of imminent danger or during the rush that accompanies survival of life-taking threats, GIs sometimes seemed excessively lustful. Among peoples exploitable by the death and destruction visited on them by war, there was little to control the sexual appetites of young soldiers.

After two weeks the troopers struck their tents, and from a Naples beach boarded LSTs, detailed to bear them to Anzio where U.S. forces had clung to a bloody toehold for five months. But even as the 517th sailed, the strategy changed as the Allied Armies advanced well beyond Rome and relieved pressure on Anzio. A quick change in orders dispatched the LSTs to the port of Civitavecchia from where the troopers marched inland to organize for combined operations with the veteran 36th Infantry Division.

For the only time in its history, the 517th became overstrength as the outfit received a number of replacement paratroopers. Among them was nineteen-year-old Howard Ruppel who actually had arrived with a contingent of jump-school graduates almost two months earlier than the 517th. A Wisconsin native, Ruppel attended public schools in Sheboygan and then Milwaukee. "I was an eager learner with a natural thirst for knowledge. When I was younger, I enjoyed doing things, like playing baseball. But as I got older, I lost interest when I sensed the others felt winning was more important than the challenge of just playing. I picked friends with similar interests to mine, like stamp collecting, building model airplanes. I was always something of an introvert and even when I was in elementary school I was very proud when my teachers noted on my report cards that I was 'self-reliant.' "

Drafted in July 1943, Ruppel could not qualify for

the air corps so he "settled" for an opportunity at least to ride in an airplane by joining the paratroopers.

There were 600 men at the 2nd Replacement Depot a few miles from Naples. In a series of seemingly senseless assignments of manpower, half of the replacements left for Anzio. The remainder rode boxcars for several days, then took a ferry to Sicily.

While GIs in the vicinity of Rome tangled in bloody struggles to expel German soldiers from the country, the healthy, well-trained replacements in Sicily like Ruppel built an encampment, guarded supplies destined for a detachment of Free French airborne forces and taught the French unit how to exit from the door of an American C–47.

After six weeks, the authorities suddenly called upon the paratroopers performing garrison chores in Sicily for their combat talents. Ferried across to the mainland, they rode freight cars north until they detrained in Naples. Marched from there to the crater with a tent city occupied by the 517th, the additions were parceled out to various units.

Howard Ruppel remembers that while enroute to join the 517th, the word was "it was a crack outfit, having trained together. We replacements were assigned to different companies. We were outsiders and more or less ignored or excluded from regular conversations. All of 'us' sensed an animosity. Whenever time permitted, we looked each other up and socialized separately. We were viewed as extra men and sometimes placed in jeopardy with things like, 'You go first,' or 'Make a break for that tree and I'll cover you.' "

Herb Reichwald, another newcomer assigned to the 596th Engineers, remarks, "As a replacement, you don't have many close friends."

Their feelings of rejection, however, do not match other memories. Mel Biddle, an Indiana youth, had become a paratrooper on a whim. "When I was drafted, I had lunch with a girlfriend who asked me to write to her if I decided to become a paratrooper. That cinched it. When the army asked for volunteers, I said why not. I was assigned to B Company in the 1st Battalion. I was made to feel at home almost right away."

Acceptance or rejection of replacements usually rested upon individual circumstances, the personality of the newcomer and that of the squad to which he was assigned. In some instances, the troopers, particularly after they had seen combat, embraced a stranger only after he proved himself.

CHAPTER VI

SEEING THE ELEPHANT

SOME TWO WEEKS after stepping onto Italian soil, as June heat smote the hills above Rome, the 517th sailed, rode and then finally hiked towards combat. The outfit was attached to a veteran infantry division, the 36th, which had slogged its way up the Italian boot from Salerno for nine months. As the Germans slowly retreated above Rome into the mountainous region of Tuscany, the 36th with its helpers from the 517th, working along the western flank, were to encourage an accelerated exit from Italy. With the invasion of Normandy on the west coast of France ten days earlier, pressure in Italy would prevent a shift of German troops to reinforce that front.

Dick Robb, officially promoted while at sea on the *Santa Rosa,* as sergeant major for the 3rd Battalion, remembers what he'd read about the Civil War. "The largest animal ever seen by the farm boys in uniform had been a steer or a big mule. Their first visit to a circus or fair where wild animals were exhibited produced a feeling of indescribable awe as they saw an elephant. It could be compared to nothing else they had ever seen. So it was, their first day of combat was described as 'having seen the elephant.' "

Opportunity for members of the combat team to observe the elephant was at hand. "We had dug our first

The 517th, blooded a few miles north of Grossetto, Italy, flew from Frascati for the drop in Southern France.

foxholes on the night of June 15," says C Company's Ed Johnson, who was among those soon to come under fire, "in a bivouac area about five miles from Civitavecchia. The purpose was to protect against strafing or bombing from the air. A day later, following a truck trip and footwork, the 1st Battalion received a briefing on the enemy supposedly fifteen miles further north."

On the eve of the ordeal by fire, Rupert Graves admitted he was almost overwhelmed by the prospect. "After issuing the plans for the next day and moving up to assembly positions, we almost unbelievingly waited for the dawn of our first day in combat. To command a regiment in combat was an honor almost beyond my comprehension. Would we acquit ourselves well and be able to take our objective or would we run into a stone wall in the famous German army we had read and heard so much about? Perhaps somebody would call the attack off before we had a chance to get into battle and put us back in reserve somewhere."

Graves, following the drill of an infantry-school exercise, set his attack in columns of battalions. The order of march was led by the 1st Battalion under Bill Boyle with regimental command next, the 2nd and 3rd Battalions trailing. In a vision-blurring rain, the troopers under Bill Boyle climbed into the Moscona Hills. When the advance-guard Americans started down the reverse slope of the very first hill the enemy, well concealed in the brush, opened up, pinning down the attackers.

B and C Companies were at the fore. Remembers Ed Johnson, "At 7:00 A.M. we ate what proved to be our last hot meal for quite some time. Pedometers had registered just four and a half miles [supposedly the foe was still about ten miles or so off] when a series of rifle shots and machine gun fire announced our first closing with the enemy."

According to Bill Boyle, his initiation into combat arrived in a burst of machine gun fire from a distance of only seventy-five to one hundred yards off on his right flank. "I reached for my pistol and cussed a little at the inadequacy of a pistol at that range. My runner was better equipped and picked off the entire machine gun crew. I ordered C Company to move around the right flank and I went to B Company. I don't recall any special feelings about people who were trying to kill me. I believe my training adequately prepared me for this and enabled me to function under these conditions."

Deacon Jones, also with C Company, says, "The first shot fired made me realize this was for keeps. Blanks were a thing of the past. Survival became uppermost. I wasn't really aware of the dead bodies, ours and theirs, until later."

John Forrest's baptism of fire taught him a lesson for the future. "The first action revealed to me, at least, a need for more aggressive use of scouts and flank security. This was pure hindsight but I was startled when the main body of troopers came under fire almost as quickly as the forward element.

"Immediately to my front was a freshly plowed area. Mortar shells started dropping and one hit in the dirt near me. There must have been a heavy rain earlier because the earth was muddy. That shell somehow buried itself in the mud before it exploded. All I received was a mud bath, for which I was extremely grateful.

"I heard someone from my company yelling words to the effect that 'Corporal Taylor has his gun (a machine gun) in action just over the crest of the hill. But he's out of ammo.' A runner from B Company, Jimmy Slatn, my high-school classmate, came up and said, 'Give me a couple of boxes and I'll get it to him.' A sniper put a round through his helmet and Slatn never knew what hit him.

"By the time the ammo got to Taylor's gun, the same sniper had hit him with a bullet that entered just to the left of his nose. He was dead also. Dan Hershey tried to fire at the sniper with his bazooka and he received a serious wound in the chest. We finally killed the sniper.

"Although there were other casualties, these were the first that I had seen. One was a boyhood friend and the others friends with whom I had soldiered from the beginning at Toccoa. I felt some guilt about Slatn because I had influenced his decision to join the 517th. Later, I watched the graves registration people sack him in a mattress cover, throw his body into a weapons carrier and drive away with his head bouncing against the tailgate. Somehow, I felt I wanted to cushion his head.

"From that day on, I was aware of the vulnerability of my comrades. But strangely, it never occurred to me that I might be killed. I was concerned about their mortality but foolishly convinced of my own immortality."

The shooting that led to these casualties intensified. Boyle brought to bear mortar fire from his troopers. The howitzers of the 460th sprinkled some rounds on distant hills where enemy soldiers scurried about.

Johnson claims troopers from his company actually scored the 517th's first kills. "Pfc. H. B. Ford, carrying his light machine gun, opened fire on a group of six enemy soldiers from a range of about eight hundred yards. All were immediate casualties. Leslie Perkins had made his way into a small gulch and in a short, brisk firefight killed at least one German and captured three others."

At the height of the fiercely blazing battle, C Company's S. Sgt. Wilford Anderson and Pfc. Nolan Powell worked their way into a twisty ravine. Through their accurate shooting, combined with Anderson calling out in his high-school-learned German for surrender, the pair bagged four separate groups of prisoners, totaling nineteen of the enemy as well as a working mortar.

What happened is a blur to Powell. "Either from the days I played war games with my boyhood friends or because of my paratrooper training, I thought when you're in an attack, you move forward to overrun the enemy.

So I moved forward down the hill but soon realized that no one else was with me. I can't recall how Sergeant Anderson, my platoon sergeant, and I met on the side of the hill in front of the company but I recall capturing the mortar and machine gun. Later, we fired the captured mortar at the Germans retreating on the other side of the valley." Subsequently, both troopers received the Distinguished Service Cross. In all, the company would capture fifty-eight of the enemy by the end of the first day.

Clark Archer in B Company, as part of the 2nd platoon, started forward in the company of a pair of scouts. "A German came walking down in my general direction with arms extended upward in a gesture of surrender. As he approached to within twenty yards, he suddenly pulled a 'potato masher' grenade and tossed it in my direction. I dove behind a nearby tree but was hit with shrapnel in both legs. The damage was minimized because our platoon medic, Joe Williams, was on the scene within seconds. I learned don't get so smart that you assume gestures lead to a next most logical action. Lesson two was you cannot afford the luxury of holding fire until your weapon is ideally positioned. And I realized, show me a medic and I will show you a hero."

Lt. Ben "Sweet Pea" Renton, as an assistant platoon leader from the 3rd Battalion's I Company, led two squads across a field towards a farmhouse. Rifle and automatic fire dropped everyone to the dirt. "I shouted for them to stay down and I remember an assistant machine gunner named Greenberg yelling, 'I can't. My nose is in the way.'

"We moved to the next fence in spurts, hitting the ground, rolling over, just as we had been trained. I took one squad to the right and Corporal Green had his squad in a sunken road. We reached an olive grove when the side door of the farmhouse opened and three Germans appeared. I yelled I have number one, meaning the guy in front. I had my carbine and let loose with a full clip, as fast I could pull the trigger. The German still went around the corner of the building. My runner, Private Beyer, opened up with his M–1, dropping the second soldier in the doorway. The sergeant with us fired a burst from his BAR and cut down the third one. We took the farmhouse and Beyer brought me around the corner to show I'd hit the Kraut four times in the stomach area and three times in the nuts. He'd still managed to take several steps to get away. As soon as I could, I got my hands on an M–1 and threw away the carbine. The entire platoon had acted as a trained team and we lost only two men in the open field who were wounded but not seriously."

Later that day, Renton as part of a two-platoon pincer started up a hill. "Mines went off. I got a call to come down since I was the one who had run a school at Mackall for demolition. I came down from the high ground with Beyer and the medic and when we came to a stream I left them there for their safety. Beyond the creek, in a field were some troopers including a medic, Sporos Gorgos, who'd come to assist the wounded. I removed about a dozen of the Bouncing Betty heads." The German S–mine, dubbed by the Americans, Bouncing Betty, was an anti-personnel mine in a canister slightly larger than a soup can. An unwary soldier who trod on the prongs at the top activated the mine or it could be set off by trip wires. When triggered, a short delay allowed the victim to step off the mine. Then a secondary charge threw it about five feet in the air where the primary explosive flung shrapnel both horizontally and downward for maximum effect.

Even as Renton painstakingly tried to dismantle the devices, someone in the field set off a Bouncing Betty. The blast killed Gorgos and Pfc. Pedro Licano and blew Renton into a hedge. "When I came to, I found my helmet had two holes in the back but the ball shots had hit the plastic liner and traveled between the steel shell and the liner. I had about twenty-five pieces of shrapnel casing in my back and neck. I kept yelling for everyone to stay in place and not to move. I made my way to four of the troopers whom I helped along a cleared path back to the street. I found Beyer with a shot in his shoulder and Massie, the medic, dressing his own wound to his lower left arm.

"Lieutenant Feeney with the 3rd platoon directed some men upstream to remove the wounded. I was helping out a man when he tripped an S–mine. I put him down and dropped on top of him. My cheek was cut and bled but I got a few more out. The rest were dead. A sergeant from Feeney's platoon began leading me down the stream when an artillery or mortar shell struck the embankment on our right. I felt a hit on my right hip while the sergeant went down in the water. I picked him up, fireman fashion, and managed to stagger to a point on the stream where an aid station was set up. I dropped off the sergeant, then passed out."

When Renton regained consciousness, he was in the process of being evacuated to Naples and a military hospital. His tour of duty in Italy had ended in one explosive day that earned him a Silver Star for bravery and the first of his four Purple Hearts for being wounded. Aidman Gorgos, a burly youth almost overanxious to win friends, probably tripped the mine that killed him and knocked down Renton. He received a posthumous Distinguished Service Cross for his efforts to help those previously struck by the mines.

Phil Di Stanislao's A Company was in reserve, behind B and C, when they first heard shots. "We started up and the Germans fighting a rear-guard action turned and ran. I moved into a stone building, a shepherd's hut, and from the window, which had no glass, saw some of them about 100 yards away. I set my M–1 on the ledge of the window and set my sights very deliberately. I squeezed off a shot and one of the Germans went down. I squeezed off several more but did not hit anyone. Two of the Germans came back, grabbed the man I knocked down and dragged him back over a hill."

"The first day of combat," recalls Dick Robb, "I was with battalion headquarters behind a company line, abreast at the bottom of a hill. Some officer commanded in a loud voice, 'Fix bayonets!' Shades of World War I. Ridiculous bravado, but that was the most sobering thing to everyone within earshot. Reality set in like a clap of thunder.

"Later, at the top of a ridge with two or three others, we heard a series of snaps, then the sounds of firing. I felt I couldn't get any closer to the ground because my buttons were in the way. These people were trying to kill me. We quickly learned that when one is on the receiving end of firing weapons, the bullet passing by, if it doesn't hit you, gives off a 'snap' sound as it breaks the sound barrier. After that, the sound of the shot arrives.

"Someone hissed that on the flat, about three hundred yards away at a break in a stone wall, a machine gun with several Germans manning it was shooting at us. I was the only one with a .30 caliber carbine; the others had M–1s. The fellow on my right fired at the machine gun. The report was a very loud 'BLAM! BLAM!' I fired twice. My carbine sounded like 'Peep, Peep.' The trooper on my left was just a bit behind me, the muzzle of his M–1 was almost level with my head. He fired and the muzzle blast almost broke my eardrums. This BLAM-BLAM, Peep-Peep stuff did it. I vowed that I would dump the carbine and never again be without an M–1.

"Still later, I came upon a dead German. He looked so old, a few gray wisps in his hair. He was probably forty-five, old to me. My mother wasn't much older. I remember staring at his face and asking myself, 'Why are

you here in a war, old man? You are too old to be here.
You probably have a wife and family back home.'

"Just then, one of ours, whom I didn't recognize,
pointed to the body's hand. 'You want that ring,
Sergeant?' 'No,' I answered. He extracted his trench
knife from the scabbard. I walked away. I was told afterwards that instead of cutting the finger off at the
knuckle, standard practice, he cut as though sharpening
a pencil or whittling until finally cutting through the first
joint. When he pulled the ring off and shook it free of
any matter, he looked at it, then said to a witness, 'Nice.
See you around.' I was struck dumb when I heard this.
'My God, with what kind of people have I thrown my
lot.' I realize now that I had truly 'seen the elephant.'"

With the "kill-or-be-killed" credo drilled into them,
some troopers could never quite shake ambivalence
about breaking the Sixth Commandment. Buck Miller
recalls a firefight centering on an Italian house. "As we
approached, we killed a German. When we got close
enough, we took a look at him. He was lying on the
ground with his long blond hair hanging over the side of
his face. He seemed like he was about sixteen years old.
He was very young.

"Later, on patrol, the second platoon was going up a
hill. At the top we could see on the other side a line of
Germans walking along like they were going to chow
and heading our way. I said, 'Let's shoot them.' Lieutenant ——— said, 'No, we have to go back to the
company.'

"He knew the situation better than I. All I knew as a
dumb sergeant was to shoot at the Germans if they were
seen."

In the annals of military history and in the context of
World War II, the casualties inflicted upon the 517th on
this first day and in fact during its initial week of combat
could be described as "light." Statistics hardly scratch

the pain of the individuals wounded nor compensate those individuals who lost their lives, however few, nor the sorrow of their friends and families.

Sgt. Andrew Murphy of B Company, a fine heavyweight boxer and popular man, while directing mortar fire, actually became the first member of the 517th to die in battle as a sniper picked him off. Pvt. Melvin Biddle of B Company was horrified. "Blood was spurting five or six feet in the air. It's an awful thing to see nice people killed right in front of you. Two hours before he shared a package from home, including me who'd only just joined the company, and now he was dead. You also fear it could happen to you. Many of the guys were angered but I think it was accepted as a part of war."

In contrast to the sentiments of John Forrest, the casualties among his troopers destroyed any feelings of invulnerability for Charles La Chaussee, CO for C Company. "Our own mortality had become excruciatingly clear. Few of us had seen death before. But now it had joined for the duration."

Even Bill Boyle was taken aback by the first death. "It was not exactly nausea but it was close. Horror? No. But anger? Yes, although even before that I had developed anger against the enemy."

For artilleryman Cameron Gauthier, who with his mates had hidden their fright with jokes about getting one another's boots in case the "other guy got it," the grisliest sight was an American Sherman tank with its turret pierced by an 88 shell. "If you wanted to get sick, you only had to look inside."

The shock of war dead struck, as Robb indicated, even if the corpse belonged to the other side. Joe Miller, with the 596th Engineers, recalled his fright as the skies were lit by noisy explosions. "You could not tell the difference between thunder and lightning and incoming and outgoing shells. The first dead person I saw was a German soldier, whose wallet with a family picture lay beside him. The smells of death were something you never forget."

Howard Ruppel, the replacement who joined F Company in Italy, was part of the line of advancing troopers. "When the column stopped, we dispersed to the ditches, to sit, recline, wet one's whistle, whip out a K ration, chat a little. The silence was broken by a solitary rifle shot. The round was loud, clear and close. What happened? Someone accidentally shot himself in the foot, or so he said. Was this an act of cowardice or carelessness? No matter, he was not the first to take this course of action. Most of us shared the opinion that if this was an act of cowardice, better now than in the heat of battle when we may need him the most.

"On our way again, this time fanning out, stalking up a gradual rise covered with brush, low vegetation and small trees. Nearing the crown, I made a dash over the top and dove for cover behind a fair-sized tree. I didn't see any obvious movements or hear any sounds from the direction of the enemy. Peering intently, I noticed a man sitting with his back against a tree. Did I have the drop on an enemy? Did I want the drop on the enemy? Should I shoot a helpless sitting man, a human being in cold blood? I had trouble with this feeling for a long time. What kind of soldier was I going to be? Reacting in self-defense may be acceptable, but for me to strike the first blow is contrary to my nature. I chickened and just watched him. He never moved.

"Was he sleeping? Should I be brave and take my first prisoner? Cautiously, I stood up with the rifle at the ready and moved gingerly towards the enemy. There was no movement or sign of recognition on his part. I noticed his eyes were open. Something was wrong. I gently nudged him with the gun barrel. Horrified, I found he was a corpse. He was older than I and had darker skin. I thought he might have been a Turk or a Moslem. I learned later that the enemy had a policy of forcing conquered able-bodied men into their army. The enemy even had a name for this malarkey, *kanonenfutter;* translated it means cannon fodder. The corpse I stumbled upon was one of those fodders."

For much of his time in combat, artillery officer Tommy Thompson acted as a forward observer for the 2nd Battalion. "Very early in my military life I was imbued with the basic axiom, the purpose of artillery is to support the infantry. Dick Seitz was usually out front and I was usually right behind him to start a fire mission.

"On one occasion we were coming out of the mountains towards Follonica on the sea when 'tank attack' came over the radio. With my FO team we sped up our jeep to a spot where two tank destroyers lay in wait in a depression for the enemy tanks. I ran forward about two hundred yards to the only building in the area to call for the first round in adjustment of our artillery fire. I can still hear Dick Seitz calling me back.

"That first round fell into the sea, as I expected, because I did not want to make the horrible mistake of firing into friendly troops. The tank destroyers fired ineffectually and then a shell from one of the tanks hit the corner of the building, not more than ten feet above my head. Luckily, it was armor-piercing and did not explode on contact.

"Now, Nick Biddle, our intelligence officer, from the top of a nearby hill started the fire mission. It took ten minutes for me to get to his observation post and by then the tanks were retreating, almost out of range. Biddle asked for my sensing. I gave it to him instantly: '400 (yards) short, 400 (yards) right. Fire for effect!' What a beautiful sight! Rounds from one battery hit both tanks moving north at fast speed. Tom Cross verified the wreckage."

Seitz wanted to recommend a Silver Star for Thompson who insisted that his entire FO section should draw Bronze Stars. Some confusion in the paper work, as handled by the 460th, resulted in the lesser award for all hands including Thompson.

Amid the carnage, attitude in one respect shifted dramatically. All hands, whether literally or figuratively bloodied that first day in the Moscona Hills, no longer regarded the aidmen and doctors as above the fray. Instead they were recognized as their basic life-support systems, frequently required to demonstrate raw courage. "After that first day," says the 1st Battalion surgeon Ben Sullivan, "we were no longer pill rollers or chancre mechanics. We were all beloved." In fact, with only a 139-man complement, one glaring weakness in the structure of the 596th Parachute Engineer Company lay in the absence of any trained medics. The engineers, who received only rudimentary instruction in first aid, were expected to take care of one another.

The line companies of the 517th, however, received excellent medical help. After Rupert Graves pushed himself close to the scene of the action, he said, "I saw Captain Sullivan giving blood plasma to several men who had been hit. Sully had propped up a broken branch of a tree, placed a bottle of the plasma in the crotch and was really going to town."

What instantly established Sullivan's reputation were his emergency repairs of Lt. Howard Bacon, of B Company, struck down by a bullet that hit him in his side. According to the surgeon, his achievement was fortuitous. "Bacon picked a good place to be shot. He happened to be right next to me. There was a German sniper nearby. He was hidden in a tree and taking careful aim, fired only when there was a lot of shooting from our machine guns which enabled him to escape detection. He had already inflicted two casualties when I heard the bullet strike Lieutenant Bacon, who was about five feet from me. The 'wup' of the bullet was followed by a groan and that arresting sound of a man trying to breathe when his chest wall has been torn by a bullet. It caused what is known as a mediasternal shift. Because Bacon couldn't breathe he was turning blue. There was a classic treatment for that kind of injury. I acted as a kind of valve. He was conscious enough to cooperate and could breathe in and out at my command. In that fashion we pumped him up while I sutured the wound. As I worked on him I heard about a dozen shots. Someone had finally looked up, spotted the sniper and now everyone took a shot at him."

Dick Robb, still resorting to the Civil War metaphor, says, "The one fear and dread experienced by all who have seen the elephant is that of being left in 'no man's land,' 'on the mountain' or 'out there.' In France and Italy it was 'on the mountain.' Despite this fear, few openly discussed it. Medic Maurice White, bless his sad-eyed look, said, 'Robby, I will see that you are never left out on the mountain.' I was not only touched but I was embarrassed that he could read my inner thoughts."

Medic Charlie Keen says, "At Mackall, after lights were out, we used to talk and one thing that always came up was our first day in combat, what it would be like. In my barracks we had all agreed that the 1st Battalion would be on the point, with B Company the point for the battalion and the 1st Platoon the point for B. I would always end the conversation by adding that the first damn thing heard would be a cry, 'Medic!'

"We hit that right to a T. We walked into trouble and as soon as the initial firing stopped, the first words were 'Medic!', 'Doc'! and 'Smitty's been hit!' Steve Smith was a sheepherder from Utah and the first of our men to get it. I had never been so scared in my life, but that training and discipline took over. I ran about thirty yards and there was Smith on his hands and knees with blood streaming down his face. I noticed a lot of blood running down his arms. I was certain he had been shot through his lung but the bullet had entered the back part of his left shoulder and traveled across his back but did not touch his backbone."

The brief lull ended and Keen crawled about to aid the stricken amid heavy firing along with some 81 mm mortar bursts. He succored Lt. Robert Thomson after a missile from a machine pistol smashed into his leg. He lost track of whom else he treated and for what injuries. But for his efforts, Keen eventually was awarded a Silver Star.

According to Keen, his outfit recovered quickly from the trauma of being under fire. "In our initial zeal for combat, the training took over after a few minutes. We charged the enemy without even calling for artillery. Several of them, taken aback by the wild rushes, tried to surrender but unfortunately were killed even as they held white flags in their hands. But what could you expect from eighteen- or nineteen-year-olds told for months they were invincible. We soon added a more realistic attitude and although we never lost our hell-for-leather manner, through the work of 'Dog' Jordan and Tex Carpenter, our scouts, avoided nasty ambushes."

John Chism and those in his medical section also were learning the facts of combat life. "We were issued a basic medical kit. It was about the size of a Samsonite three-suiter and weighed 75–100 pounds. There was no way for this inconvenient bundle to be carried. It didn't conform to a one-man load. Our solution was to strap it onto a litter but at least four men were necessary to manhandle it while making our way through the mountains and hills. It is to the credit of my men we still had this thing when we were eventually relieved. But it was never opened during the two weeks on the line. It went into storage and I never saw it again."

Almost instinctively, Chism's medics established rules of conduct under combat situations. "When the order to dig in came, we found to our consternation that the Italian soil was almost impenetrable. We were reduced to scratching out what dirt clung to the solid rock with our fingers and mess tools. During this ordeal, Captain Siebert, a doctor of great skill but also a Teutonic motivator, was with us. He directed us to dig a foxhole for him. I was proud of the reaction. To a man, including little Joe Podlaski, they in no uncertain terms explained where he could go. From that day on, no one ever received an order to prepare a foxhole for someone else."

Russel Brami, serving with a 60 mm crew in E Company, the 2nd Battalion, was startled while passing through a draw and saw tiny waterspouts in the nearby puddles. "My God, those bastards are shooting at us! It was a sobering experience. It just hadn't occurred to us that we were being fired upon."

The wake-up continued as he and his foxhole-mate Jim Easter saw a German tank open up on them. "Our platoon sergeant was killed. We had dropped our packs and now we dug with sticks and helmets. Jim said, 'I can't get any lower, my buttons are in the way.' "

Amidst all this turmoil, some of the infantrymen from the 36th Division working on B Company's flank accosted the troopers with some suspicion. "They knew we were supposed to be there," says Charlie Keen, "but our jumpsuits looked just like the uniforms worn by the German *Afrika Korps*." Fortunately, the experienced soldiers of the infantry division possessed the savvy to hold their fire until investigating the strangers.

The following day, however, a dozen C Company troopers started to check out some buildings one thousand feet in advance of their assigned positions. When two Germans, displaying "surrender caps," began walking up a draw in front of them, someone fired at the pair. In the confusion of battle, the 1st Battalion's A Company interpreted the shots as coming from enemy lines towards them. The two companies engaged in a brief firefight, against one another. Fortunately, a cease-fire occurred with a toe the only casualty of the friendly fire.

Not everyone stood tall as the 1st Battalion grappled with the enemy. La Chaussee's former supply sergeant, dismissed from quartermaster chores because of his failure to keep records, and subsequently discovered also to be a trigamist [three wives], had dropped his rifle after the opening shots. He declared, "The Lord saith thou shalt not kill. I can't do it." The profession of conscientious objection notwithstanding, Platoon Sergeant Lester McCall yanked him from the line of skirmishers by his feet and then slammed him in the jaw with a right hook. La Chaussee dispatched him to the rear as a combat-fatigue case. He finished the war as an army stevedore in Naples.

And it was in these first days of the shooting war for the 517th that Bill Boyle detected a whiff of ineptitude in one of his staff officers. He resolved to watch him carefully in future actions. According to one trooper, Boyle managed to eavesdrop when a bunch of noncoms were sitting around discussing the performances they had personally witnessed by some of the officers. From this and other sources as well as his own observations, Boyle collected, in his mind, dossiers on his subordinates. The matter would come to a head in some subsequent adventures and bring on Boyle's insistence he would shoot the fellow if he remained in his battalion.

For some, that first day was less perilous. Tom Cross as exec of the 2nd Battalion occupied an elevated position with John Lissner, exec of F Company, as the 2nd Battalion was committed. Says Cross, "We stood on the high ground watching the entire operation unfold. Suddenly, we came under fire although it took us both a long time to accept it. We heard noises around us and I mentioned to John that it sounded like the crack of bullets when you were in the rifle butts on the known-distance range. It dawned on us that we were being fired on for real. We felt pretty dumb."

Cross learned another lesson as the adventures of the 517th entered a second day of combat. "We were on a hill and saw German tanks come off the road towards us. We asked the 460th for help. Their 75 mm pack how-itzers are not for antitank warfare but when the shells landed among the tanks, they withdrew. We backed off the hill but the liaison from the 460th, Lt. Worthington Thompson, remained there directing fire from the 460th. When the barrage ended, we waited for forty-five minutes and now the enemy walked 88s down the hill towards us. I got caught on the road and dove into a ditch. I never prayed so hard in my life. When it was over, we'd lost two men from E Company, S. Sgt. James Dipko and Sgt. Robert Farmer. I looked at their bodies. I had never experienced anything like this, our own peo-ple whom we trained. The pallor of their skins, the grotesque positions of their limbs. It was very hard to take.

"We also realized that a forty-five-minute wait after our artillery fire was a huge mistake, allowing the enemy to regroup. From then on, we would keep pushing whenever we could."

The 596th engineers also engaged the enemy for the first time. Allan Goodman, as a squad leader with the 3rd platoon, was among those acting in support of the 517th's 3rd Battalion. A few days into the advance, 1st Lt. George Flannery, the platoon leader, accompanied by two men from the 1st platoon, Francis T. Ropyak and Harry L. Springer, reconnoitered their immediate area in a jeep. A German ambush wiped out the entire patrol.

Ernie Kosan from the 596th, with his ability to speak German, remembers being asked to interrogate some of the first men taken prisoner. "I tried but got no re-sponse. Upon examining the IDs carried by all of the German soldiers, I saw they had long unpronounceable names. It was our first indication they were using Russian PWs in their army." As the 517th collected more prisoners they learned that a good many were Turcomans, Mongols from the Soviet Union, and Poles impressed into the German forces and under *Wehrmacht* officer supervision. While they were not enthusiastic about fighting, they had the weapons to kill, wound and delay the Allied advance northward.

Their reluctance to do battle may have saved many of the 517th, including Phil Di Stanislao. "I went on a patrol that for some strange reason consisted of Boyle, Don Fraser, then A Company CO, and one other trooper. We were several hundred yards beyond the outposts of the battalion when a machine gun opened up. I remember the tracers; they looked like they were heading right at me as big as a floodlight. I wanted to crawl into my helmet and pull my legs in after me. But Boyle, very alertly, yelled, 'He's got a misfire.' He had heard the German pulling back the bolt of the weapon, trying to get it to fire and cursing at it. We rushed the gun and spotted a German noncom who commanded a number of machine guns with interdicting fire. While he had remained at his post, all of the Russkis and Polskis, as they called themselves, had fled, leaving him alone. Had they stuck with the guns they could have put quite a dent in our forces. Even so, the German noncom escaped as we overran the place."

Flushed with this success, Di Stanislao says he now saw an opportunity for real glory. "Several hundred yards farther, I saw a stone cottage from where we could hear a lot of noise coming. My M–1 had a rifle-grenade adapter and I cockily told the others I'd take care of the place. I put down the best shots I have ever made with a rifle grenade. One went through the window and the other into the open doorway. A curtain in the window started burning, lighting up the place. Without waiting for the others, I rushed the building. Instead of a bunch of dead Germans all I found was blood, feathers and dead chickens splattered all over the walls."

Trekking into the steep hills, the troopers tried to lessen their burden by recruiting mules to pack the heavier items, machine guns and ammunition boxes. La Chaussee requisitioned a pair from protesting farmers with a document that said, "This is to certify that I have, this date, confiscated two mules for military use." He signed the paper, "Wuthering Heights." The beasts were only partially useful to C Company. One broke a leg while descending an embankment and artillery slew the second.

Others found the animals more helpful. "The problem," says John Forrest, "was most troopers knew nothing about managing mules. Most officers had not been around horse cavalry, horse-drawn or pack artillery. They didn't know what to do with the animals once we were engaged. You have to detail men to move the mules back and hold them during a firefight. There was a lack of knowledge of how to pack a mule for a balanced load and to secure it properly. Fortunately, in my company there were many of us who had grown up with livestock and understood their management. I was constantly amazed by the wisdom and behavior of mules in combat. Like good troopers, nothing spooked them if they were properly led."

The troopers were nonplussed by the behavior of both their British allies and their own countrymen. Phil Di Stanislao gaped in amazement as he saw long columns of lorries ferrying supplies and Brit soldiers halt in the afternoon for a tea break, wasting what he and his mates thought the most opportune time for movement.

On one occasion, Di Stanislao and several troopers were ordered to locate men from the 36th Division responsible for protecting their flank while the platoon advanced. "I went on forever and couldn't find the friendly forces where they were supposed to be. Finally, I came upon them and they were sitting down to some hot chow, Vienna sausages in a tomato sauce. We all removed our steel helmets, got in the line and loaded up the helmets with the sausages and sauce to carry back to feed the rest of our group. But it was inconceivable to me that any fighting force, particularly one with the glorious reputation of the 36th, would stop for hot chow, while leaving our flank exposed."

There were Italian partisans around but few members of the 517th had any real contact with them. Capt. Albin Dearing, the regimental intelligence officer, went with some of them on expeditions in the hills. Don Fraser remembers an attack across a canal against a village. "We had a partisan as a guide. It was slow going as we had to go single file on a narrow plank bridge over the canal. Lt. Chopper Kienlen, Phil Di Stanislao, Joe Chobot and two other men were with me as we advanced six abreast. A German machine gun cranked off a tracer round over our heads. All six of us had automatic weapons and we all blew a magazine. It sounded like a small war and the partisan took off, and we didn't see him for three days. When the echo died away, we also heard the rapid beat of boots slapping the ground on the run. The German outpost had also taken off."

The combat campaign that introduced the 517th to the nature of war lasted less than two weeks. The outfit pushed forward about seventy-five miles near the coast after having jumped off from Grosseto. Capture of Montesario, Sticcano and Follonica brought the troopers to the base of Monte Peloso, a strategic high ground overlooking a valley. The 1st Battalion attacked up the rugged terrain of Monte Peloso. Charles La Chaussee's C Company charged the enemy, a detachment of the 29th SS Panzer Grenadier Division, considerably more able and willing than the non-Germans forced to fight. Spontaneously, the troopers from C Company shouted various imprecations upon the foe and slogans of the airborne as they swept the Germans from their positions. Says Deacon Jones, "We were like kids with our cheers, like whistling as you went past the graveyard. La Chaussee in combat could be off the wall but he was a good commander. Mickey Marks, who was a platoon leader, was more cautious. He was not too sure of himself. Sgt. Willie Hogan was always in the middle of everything. He was the most deserving and most undecorated man in the entire outfit as far as I am concerned."

However, shortly before elimination of German resistance, an incoming 81 mm mortar burst among Bill Boyle and several others. Someone cried for a medic to attend to the 1st Battalion CO's wounds. Boyle growled, "Shut up! We don't need any medics hurt coming to aid me." Now, with the territorial dispute settled, Boyle allowed himself to be evacuated for treatment. His exec, Herb Bowlby, assumed command of the 1st Battalion.

Graves was delighted when his men were relieved by the famed 442nd Combat Team, the Nisei soldiers determined to demonstrate the loyalty of Americans with Japanese ancestry. The 517th withdrew to set up a base at Frascati. The casualties numbered seventeen KIA and 129 wounded, with more than forty accounted for on the very first day of fighting.

Without dismissing the dead and wounded, Dick Seitz credits the brief campaign with providing the 517th highly valuable rewards. "The enemy resistance was not real strong but we recognized in a hurry their artillery capability. More importantly, we learned that we were pretty damn good. The men and their leaders became cocky, convinced they could achieve in combat. Colonel Graves did a good job and we all gained confidence in his tactical ability."

John Lissner describes the experience in Italy as "a

golden opportunity for testing under combat conditions, for men to react under live fire. It was a great asset in the preparation for an actual airborne assault."

And indeed that sort of adventure was the reason for the 517th to be pulled out of the line. The Parachute Combat Team was designated to participate in OPERATION DRAGOON, an invasion of Southern France. The parachute component would be known as OPERATION ALBATROSS.

CHAPTER VII

DRAGOON AND ALBATROSS

WHEN THE TROOPERS of the 517th first retired to Frascati they were ignorant of what had been planned for them. The bivouac at Frascati was a welcome respite after their brief but furious exposure to battle.

The local Frascati wine, justly celebrated as one of the finer vintages, found 517th palates happy to lap it up. For fun and games, the troopers went grenade fishing at nearby Lake Albano. But as Lissner remembers, that activity came to a halt when the authorities were advised the lake belonged to the Holy See, and the men were trespassing on the property of the pope.

But while the climate, hot food and availability of showers were pleasant, the 517th engaged in nasty skirmishes with disease, confrontations with civilians and nagging shortages of certain conveniences. Although the troops lived outside of the badly battered town, the absence of sanitation there and the hordes of flies caused an epidemic of intestinal ailments including forms of dysentery that rendered victims unfit for duty. "In honor of the local bad guy," says John Chism, "we called it Mussolini's revenge. It was left to the medics to perform frequent and tough inspections, flyproof latrines and kitchens, while the troopers engaged in exercises. Repeated episodes and ever more stringent care convinced me that the problem comes with heat and poor water. Nothing short of boiling everything will do any good.

"One day after one of the inspections and during the subsequent critique to the mess personnel, I noticed a straight leg—nonjumper—leave the road and enter our area. He seemed lost and I went down to help him out. When I got close enough to distinguish his features, I wished I had stayed with the inspection team. One glance and I knew he was related to one of our medics, Bill 'Gene' Bosley, KIA. It became my chore to relate the details and offer what comfort I could.

"Bill Harvey told me that he was the medic who was sent to aid Bosley and a boy from Texas, both wounded by shrapnel. Harvey says they found the two troopers after traveling up a river. On the way, five Germans surrendered although Harvey said if they hadn't wanted to give up, he too would have been taken out. After they loaded Bosley into an ambulance, the driver became lost, even entered enemy territory before taking the right route to the aid station. On the way, Bosley whispered to Harvey, 'I'm not going to make it, Bill.' Harvey reassured him, 'Hold on, Gene, we'll be okay.' But he died before they reached the doctors. To this day, Harvey says, 'If we would have had plasma we might have saved him, because he lost so much blood.'

"When my own brother visited me shortly after for three days, I could not mention the incident with Bosley's brother to him."

The ravages of Mussolini's revenge spared no man. To his utter chagrin, battalion surgeon Ben Sullivan succumbed to a severe case of gastroenteritis that weakened him so badly he eventually was sent to a hospital in Rome.

The second serious medical matter was venereal disease. Passes and leaves to Rome and nearer towns enabled the GIs to indulge their hunger for fleshly pleasures. Abundant supplies of wine satisfied the thirst for alcohol, which as usual tended to increase the pursuit of sexual gratification and reduce caution.

"You could catch a ride into Rome," says Nat Schoenberg, "and there was a bus that left at 10:00 P.M. back to the bivouac area. I had a brand-new pair of boots and went to Rome, enjoyed myself and headed for home. But I missed that bus. A weapons carrier came along and I asked for a ride. They said sure. I got in and they were guys from the 517th; they had a woman with them and they were all cockeyed drunk.

"But this was a stolen vehicle and the MPs suddenly started to chase us. They had all their headlights on, sirens, it was a wild ride, like something you see in a movie about a police chase. We pulled off the road, down into a field, and everyone scrambled out. I crawled for miles through the brush, getting back to the barracks just before reveille. My wonderful new pair of boots were all scratched up."

Far more serious was at least one encounter with civilians. One evening, Sergeant Major Robb was at his field desk in a tent just outside Zais's headquarters while billeted among the olive trees of Frascati. "Zais came out of his tent and said to me, 'Sergeant, get McQuaid down here. Now.' There wasn't any question that Pvt. Woodrow W. McQuaid would be in the G Company area since he was confined to quarters. Ordinarily, McQuaid was a good soldier, no problems. But when he got into booze, he became Dr. Jekyll's Mr. Hyde. He became nasty, mean, literally uncontrollable. He had a very serious drinking problem.

"One night, he was in a bar in Frascati. That town, before and during the war, was a hotbed for Mussolini's Black Shirts. McQuaid apparently was the lone American in the bar and very drunk. Several patrons began making noises about the dirty Americans. Under the circumstances, even a bold paratrooper would have had enough sense to leave. What happened depends upon which witness tells the story. The upshot, however, was that unknown to the two Fascist types, McQuaid had a .25 cal. Beretta automatic in his belt beneath his shirt. It was generally accepted that at least one of the Italians had a knife with intent to use it. McQuaid, I believe, shot them both and definitely killed one. The Italian Government wanted to try McQuaid for murder and the U.S. Army had processed the papers for a general court-martial on the charge of killing a civilian.

"When Zais told me to fetch McQuaid, I sent a runner and then walked away from the tent to be out of Zais's hearing while I waited for McQuaid to come down the path. He was more contrite than I had ever seen him. 'The colonel is really mad, is he? But, Sergeant, I—' I cut him off. 'McQuaid, when I send you in there, you will give your name, rank and reporting as ordered. Continue standing at attention and under no circumstances do you take one step towards his desk until he tells you to. He'll tell you when. Nor are you to try to explain anything unless the colonel asks you for an explanation. You say "Yes, sir, Colonel. No, sir, Colonel." Do you think you can do that?' He said he thought he could.

"I announced him and got out of Zais's tent. There was a long silence. I knew the routine and could picture the scene. Zais would be looking at some papers; that could seem like forever. Then he would look up and with a piercing stare motion the soldier forward to his desk. It was a chewing-out of splendid proportions. Few could equal Zais, even when he was not greatly upset. This time he barred no holds. He began with the military problem McQuaid faced. Then he switched, in an almost fatherly tone. He spoke about McQuaid's drinking problem and how worried he was that even if he survived the war, it was certain that unless he got this drinking problem straightened out, McQuaid was doomed to a life of trouble.

"Zais continued and there were a few almost inaudible 'Yes, sirs, and no, sirs.' Zais did not raise his voice until McQuaid said something like, 'But, Colonel. He had a knife. They were . . .' I thought, 'Dammit, McQuaid. You promised to keep your mouth shut.'

"Zais slammed something on his desk, probably the court-martial papers. He told him to shut up, that he knew more about what happened that night than McQuaid and it was not a matter of his side or that of the Black Shirts. One thing absolutely sure. McQuaid was confined to quarters until the day we went on our mission and he was going with us. There was no way he would be allowed to sit safely in a stockade waiting for a court-martial while the rest of us were going into combat. He would have to face the prospect of being wounded or killed, like everyone else.

"Then Zais dropped the clincher. The court-martial papers would accompany the regiment wherever it went. The only way the charges would not be brought against him would be if he committed an act of bravery in combat that would probably earn anyone else a Congressional Medal of Honor. Then, maybe then, Zais would see that the court-martial papers were torn up or lost. And even at that McQuaid would have to remain a private with no promotion and no medals.

"McQuaid was still mumbling, 'Yes, sir, Colonel, no, sir, Colonel,' as he came out of the tent. It was impossible not to like McQuaid when he was sober. Many of us thought that he probably did all of Italy a favor when he wasted that character in the bar. However, murder of an Italian civilian would certainly mean time in Leavenworth. But certainly, Zais had uncanny insight into his men and that was proven later with McQuaid."

Even as the troopers had pulled back to Frascati, John Chism saw disturbing replications of what Howard Ruppel noted, the self-inflicted wounds. "We witnessed almost as many as we saw in the combat. Pulling off the line was conducted with loaded weapons. Those careless with the safety provision of weapons were paying the penalty. I recall ten or fifteen such incidents. It was a hard lesson but it never seemed to sink in and it plagued us through the last day of the war."

Few of the young troopers as well as their older officers had seen anything like the devastation visited upon Italy. John Lissner remembers the starving people who would line up outside the area where the troops were billeted. "We'd bring our leftover food for them; they were all either women, the elderly or children." The deprivation also led to one of the worst aspects of war, women peddling their flesh for the sake of something to eat.

Lt. Mickey Marks with C Company won the hearts of local civilians. When a child fell down a well and was trapped, Marks arranged for himself to be lowered down the well to rescue the youngster. He received the Soldier's Medal, awarded for courageous acts unconnected with a combat action. He had also scored a Bronze Star from his time under fire.

Jim Gavin, in describing the desire to heighten self-sufficiency among paratroopers, had feared that could lead to an aggressiveness that could be highly undesirable outside of the combat arena. His worst visions in that regard were manifested during the 517th's six weeks off the line in Italy. The T/O for the 517th, as indicated, decreed a minimum number of vehicles. As Phil Di Stanislao noted, the shortage of transportation was solved by old-fashioned theft. Troopers seized any unattended vehicle they could find. Those who thought they could defeat such larceny by removing the distributor cap discovered that the resourceful parachutists toted their own spare auto parts to enable them to snatch a jeep or small truck. To catch any unauthorized vehicles, fuel dumps kept a record of the registration numbers painted on the hoods. The miscreants, who included officers as well as enlisted men, maneuvered around that trap by daubing all of their ill-gotten wheels with the legitimate serials for the outfit's jeeps and trucks.

The reputation of the 517th for unparalleled buccaneering brought the nickname, "Rupert Graves and his 2,000 Thieves." A 2nd Battalion captain caught after he purloined a half-ton truck was transferred out. But in truth, the crime was only an excuse. He had failed to measure up when the troops were on the line and this was a convenient way to be rid of him. Only the departure for Southern France saved Graves from having to explain the outrageous behavior of his troopers to the fuming upper brass.

It was not all fun and games and some men stored away for future use experience gleaned during their brief exposure to the shooting war. Among these learners was John Forrest. "My table of equipment weapon was the Tommy gun. I had rejected it for a folding-stock carbine before we went overseas. After our first combat, I opted for an M–1 rifle since it had the advantage of range, tracer rounds could be fired from it and, using a simple attachment, it could launch grenades. The tracer round was useful for marking out fields of fire, to pinpoint targets and concentration of fire. I thought this was my own innovation but it was standard procedure.

"That first experience demonstrated to me the utility of fragmentation grenades. I began carrying four instead of the two I had formerly believed adequate. I also realized that no one could take anything for granted. You had to be very specific when giving orders. In the excitement of combat, orders did not always reach everyone who needed to be informed. Often the instructions were garbled. Particularly under artillery fire, runners sometimes became confused and failed to contact the appropriate units."

Both the German soldier and the superiority of some of his equipment were a revelation to Forrest. "Their machine gun barrels could be changed by hitting a single latch. Ours required complex mechanics. German entrenching equipment and rifle-cleaning gear was better than ours. Their chain-link cleaning rod with oiler could be stored in a tin a little smaller than a Prince Albert tobacco can. It was easy to carry and use and I replaced my own with one of them.

"The German soldier was resourceful and brave. The propaganda line that they were automatons who were useless without leaders was quickly disproven. I steadily gained respect for the *Wehrmacht* soldier and in some strange way even came to admire him."

Tommy Thompson had taken notice of the gear employed by forward observers in the 3rd Infantry Division. "They all wore backpacks with FO paraphernalia like batteries, radios, spares strapped on. We had to carry all this stuff in clumsy bags slung over our shoulders. I asked one of them about the backpacks and he told me they got them from the Fifth Army. Our supply officer obtained the backpacks right after we came off the line."

Di Stanislao says, "I was introduced to the bangalore torpedo [a device with several connecting poles and an explosive charge at one end] and the flamethrower. It was a brutal piece of equipment. The tank with fuel was heavy but the idea of shooting this flame at another human being was disturbing, although not enough that I wouldn't do it if the occasion arose."

John Lissner became acquainted with Composition C, a plastic explosive that could be molded to fit cracks in concrete walls and openings among the girders of bridges. "I said to Murrey Jones, 'Before we give this stuff to the kids, let's see how it works.' There was a partially completed observatory on a hill nearby. Made of concrete, it consisted of a tower about forty feet in circumference on a turntable. Murrey and I with a couple of enlisted men took forty-eight pounds of Composition C up to the place and lined it within a two-inch-wide space for six or eight feet between the turntable and base.

"We lit the fuse. The time it takes to blow depends on climatic conditions and since it was hot and dry we had only a short time. We tore down the winding road in the jeep. By the time we reached the bottom it had gone off and concrete was flying in all directions. We snuck back into camp, never said a word while people wondered if a 500-pound bomb had suddenly gone up.

"Some years later I met a young priest who had lived in the area. When I mentioned what I had done he told me that if I ever went back there, I'd be hailed as a hero by the local people. The observatory had been donated by Hitler to Mussolini and the natives always hated it."

Because of their command of the enemy's language, Ernie Kosan and Sgt. Gustav Larsson, issued a German manual for the weapon, instructed troopers in the workings of the *Panzerfaust*, the single-shot and more highly effective rocket derived from the American bazooka. Using captured documents, Kosan also lectured on the mines used by the enemy.

As D-Day for the invasion of Southern France approached, Bill Boyle, recovered from his wounds, returned to take command of his battalion. On his arrival he discovered a separate mess tent had been erected for the officers. Boyle immediately ordered it struck.

Sometime in August, the troopers learned, officially, of their next mission. "It had to have been the worst kept secret of the war," says Phil Di Stanislao. "We'd go to Rome and we would be told that we were about to jump into Southern France. Axis Sally on the radio told us that was where we were headed. Even the shoeshine boys seemed to know. On the other hand, the shoeshine boys would ask me if it was true that paratroopers ate human brains and that in order to qualify for the paratroopers you had to kill a member of your immediate family. We of course told them that was true."

Mel Zais, as head of the 3rd Battalion, had solved a major problem, replacing Norman Siebert who'd been promoted to assistant regimental surgeon under Paul Vella. An unquenchable thirst for booze had rendered Siebert's predecessor unfit to continue. Alcoholism reduced the effectiveness of a few others. Chism recalls another medic who rigged a five-gallon decanter of good wine with a catheter and drop valve. Thus equipped, he enjoyed a siesta with a continuous flow of wine into his mouth.

Visiting in an army hospital, Zais met Capt. Daniel Dickinson, a medic who'd previously seen the war up close in North Africa. Dickinson had joined the ROTC while an undergraduate. Called up after he completed medical school, Dickinson, because of his ROTC, as an undergraduate, was commissioned with the crossed rifles of an infantry lieutenant. He had actually served in that capacity in North Africa. However, when the authorities identified him as a qualified doctor, Dickinson began a fourteen- to eighteen-hour daily routine running a dispensary.

When Zais discovered him, Dickinson was ripe for recruitment into the 517th, although he had no parachute experience, and he was physically out of shape to boot. Dickinson became the assistant to Walter Plassman, bumped up to 3rd Battalion Surgeon. Dickinson had no opportunity for any practice jumps but Major Vella and Mel Zais prepped him with instructions to assume a fetal position when he exited the aircraft. Dickinson's leap into France would be his first.

From the bucolic encampment outside of Frascati, the components of the combat team moved to tents set up around separate airfields near Rome. The maps issued, according to Lissner, were inadequate but the briefings first-rate. The sand tables did not show the objectives but displayed topographical landmarks that would enable the troopers to get their bearings. Pathfinders, dropped ahead of the main body, were to guide the others in to the drop zones.

Said Zais, "We made every trooper study the sand tables. Then we would make the squad leader repeat back to us what he was supposed to do, where his squad was to assemble and what the overall objective was. We did this for platoon leaders, company commanders, battalion commanders and even members of the regimental headquarters."

In preparation for the mission, all of the troopers dressed in the clothes they expected to wear. Says Di Stanislao, "Then a guy hung a cardboard carton over your head and they sprayed the clothes with different color paints. We were issued an escape pouch which contained a silk map of the area, a compass the size of your thumbnail, a tiny metal saw to cut through the bars of a prison if you were captured and some French currency. It was laughable. We removed the money immediately and figured we'd spend it at the first opportunity. The standard joke was how we'd carefully study the map to find the quickest route to Switzerland."

Sergeant Major Robb had volunteered to be part of a pathfinder group of thirty-three enlisted men and three officers. As the ranking noncom, Robb had the responsibility for controlling his subordinates. Among them was an irrepressible member from the 1st Battalion, Sgt. Jack Burns.

"Jack Burns had attended law school at Columbia University and as a consequence he was known as 'Shyster.' He was a rogue, a charlatan, a thief. Notwithstanding, he was a charming individual. And in combat he was a squad sergeant and a good one.

"We had the usual runs, a.m. and p.m., and somehow Burns was never to be found. He always had some kind of excuse. By the time you checked one, he had three or four more that he dropped on you. But he was charming, with a soulful look, a pretended subservience to rank and promises not to make life difficult for you. 'Oh, Robbie, if I had only realized I was creating a problem for you,' was his repeated excuse.

"At our airfield were a group of British and French pathfinders who were to be responsible for their own airborne during the invasion. [The French paratroopers were those that Howard Ruppel and William Webb tried to assist in their training.] The limeys were real buddies; we played football (soccer) with them every day. The French, neither of us liked. This was partly because the Frogs (our preferred name for them) had a latrine that was nothing more than a trench with boards across. In July and August of 1944 it was usually 95 to 100 degrees. We offered the French officers a six-holer and even lime since they were lax in applying it. Apparently it mattered little to them since both we and the British were downwind. The French latrine became a matter of never-ending complaints from the British during our football game, and we felt the same.

"One day, Burns came to me and said he'd arranged for the two of us to watch the French make a jump. It sounded like fun but I couldn't believe what I saw. We stood by the C–47 waiting for the French paratroopers to load up. The security was a joke. Many had their Italian girlfriends there, even though as an advanced invasion group we had sophisticated, secret radar equipment.

"Their officer gave the order to get in the plane. Some did, some stayed there smooching their girls. Those on the plane saw this and they got out to get one more kiss also. All this with both main and reserve chutes on. With great difficulty, their officers got everyone in the airplane. The crew chief was American and Burns and I stayed with him in the tail.

"On the last leg, coming over the field, the jump master had the red light and the pilot could level off, throttle back to about 95 mph for the green light. While we watched, at the order 'Stand up and hook up' it was chaos. Since some had been in the wrong place in line, it was unhook and wiggle around each other. They couldn't get squared away in time to complete the equipment check, let alone take the red light and the command, 'Stand in the Door.'

"On the final leg over the field, the Frog lieutenant had to tell the crew chief to ask the pilot to go around again as there was no way they were going to be able to take the green light. They weren't ready. What a disgusting display of discipline and soldiering! If it hadn't been for Burns and the crew chief giggling and muttering about Laurel and Hardy, I guess I wouldn't have thought it more humorous than disgusting. As we headed back to our area, Jack said to me, 'See, Robbie, it's worse than you thought.'

"Several days later, I was told Sergeant Burns wanted me outside the tent. Why didn't I sense something instead of thinking it was pathfinder business? Before I could say anything, Burns declared, 'Come on, Robbie, there's something *we* have to do.' 'We?' He guided me to the supply tent. Inside, on seeing Burns, the sergeant put a box on the counter, jerked his head in my direction and asked Burns, 'Who's he?' Burns assured him I was okay and then this sergeant said to me, 'Listen, I don't know you and you don't know me. Keep it that way. Neither of you was ever here and I don't want to see you again, ever.'

"While we backed out of the tent, Burns kept sweet-talking him, 'I owe you, I really owe you, don't worry.' Burns took off in a trot carrying the box, heading for the ditch, actually a moat used to drain springtime floodings from the Tiber. It was twelve to fifteen feet across, up to eight feet deep. And in that ditch, just outside their tent area, was the French latrine.

"I followed Burns into the ditch and around a bend where we were out of sight of anyone using the path across it. Finally, I got him to stop and look at me. 'Jack,' I said, 'answer me. What in hell is this all about?' He opened the box he got from supply and in it were four quarter-pound blocks of TNT and one hundred feet of primacord, a Number Eight dynamite cap and timing device.

"I started to stutter in shock. 'What the hell do you think you're doing!'

"Jack replied, 'Robbie, we are going to blow up the Frogs' shithouse.' I mumbled something about this 'we' stuff as he held up the TNT and ordered, 'Okay, start wrapping the primacord around these while I hold them. Primacord was a fuse that burned so fast it literally exploded and was great for setting off dynamite. Burns was a combination of Rasputin and Svengali, with all the world serving as his Trilby. The audacity, the daring, the paradox of doing something evil while performing a Dudley-do-right act that righted a grievous wrong against the British and us inspired me. And Burns reminded me that the victims certainly deserved it after that obscene performance on the practice jump. Soon we were both giggling at the thought of what we were going to do. I realize that I was his Trilby for the moment."

The conspirators deftly placed their charge, and when Burns announced the demolition warning, "Fire in the hole," they sprinted for safety. "It was one hell of a boom. Dirt, boards, paper and the obvious flew at least fifty feet in the air, some of it coming down in the French tent area. Burns and I sat down by the Tiber, laughing ourselves almost sick. Jack offered to bet a hundred bucks that the first thing the next day, a Frog lieutenant and a couple of enlisted men would look up our officers to take that offer for a six-holer. He would have won the bet. At our afternoon football game, everyone denied knowledge of who committed the act. George VI may have sat on the throne but to the British, we Yanks were king for that day."

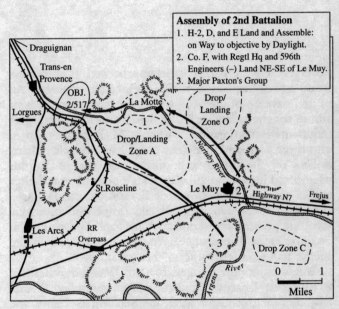

The airborne attack in Southern France as part of Operation
DRAGOON, launched at night, scattered the men of the 517th well
outside the targeted drop zones.

CHAPTER VIII

THE DROP

AS H-HOUR FOR DRAGOON approached, the troopers stood a final inspection at their respective airports. "All of us," says Di Stanislao, "were expected to carry extra ammo for the heavy weapons. I had a mortar shell, plus fragmentation grenades. With my M–1, broken down into three parts and in a Griswold, I had a couple of bandoliers of .30-caliber ammunition for the M–1, plus what fitted into my regular cartridge belt. I had a shelter half, a raincoat, two boxes of K rations, one D Bar—chocolate, a canteen, first-aid kit, escape pouch, a Mae West life preserver and entrenching tool. You could slip in some extras like a knife. We spread it all out on the shelter half while the officers checked it out."

A few troopers arranged for the 1944 equivalent of a Mohawk haircut. Almost everyone applied liberal amounts of green and black greasepaint to their faces, from tubes bearing the logo of the Lilly Daché cosmetics company. This was for camouflage and prevention of reflections that might alert the enemy to their presence. Burdened by ammunition for crew-served weapons and their parachutes, the troopers would stagger up the steps to their C–47s bearing well over 100 pounds. In fact, few of them could mount the steps without assistance.

The 3rd Platoon assembled at the Orbetello airfield where Mel Zais addressed his men. "I told them and I really meant it that I would much, much rather be in our position than that of anybody on the ground, because we knew where we were going, where we were coming in, how many of us there were. We knew what we were going to do, and we had the advantage of having the initiative.

"Meanwhile, those on the ground would have descending upon them at night, out of the heavens, innumerable people. Those on the ground had only three alternatives. They could lie still and be captured. They could run and probably be shot. Or they could shoot at us and if they got one or two, they would be lucky but they would never live after that because all of our attention would be directed toward them.

"What I said to the troopers was in direct opposition to the old fuds who used to sit down on the field, smoking their pipes, look up at paratroopers descending and say, 'sitting ducks.' They could never psychologically project themselves into the situation where paratroopers landed to the front of them, to the rear of them, to the left of them and the right of them. It is inexorable once they have exited from the airplane and are coming down, you can't stop them, no matter how much you shoot.

"I told this to all of my men. Of course they were up, high, just cheering." Some, like Allan Goodman, however, regarded Zais's declamation as just a "Knute Rockne-style pep talk."

Neither Boyle nor Seitz chose to make any long-winded addresses to their people. Nor did anyone replicate the instructions of some commanders before the airborne invasion of Normandy several months earlier when some troopers claim they were advised not to take prisoners.

Something of a special meal was served, boneless chicken from a can, and three cans of beer were issued to each trooper. There was debate about whether to drink it on the spot or carry it along. Di Stanislao opted for the bird-in-hand approach. The troopers of the 1st Battalion watched a movie, *Stage Door Canteen,* a highly improbable romance between a soldier on leave and a celebrity appearing at a stateside canteen. Before the last reel, however, the loudspeakers called upon them to report to their planes.

The pathfinders, like Dick Robb and Jack Burns, were charged with a far more serious mission than reforming the sanitary habits of their neighbors. Their responsibility was to touch down at the drop zones and guide in the planes carrying the main body of troopers.

Their gear included a medium-frequency beacon that automatically broadcast a signal with a range of twenty-five miles in the mountains. But to home in precisely, the parachutists in DRAGOON were to rely on the Eureka, a forty-pound electronic gizmo. In the mountains, its direct-line range totaled about five miles. It was a slave unit, a "eunuch" in Dick Robb's vocabulary. A Eureka transmitted back a signal received from the "Rebecca" carried by the lead planes of the invasion group.

After picking up the transmission from the aircraft, the Eureka responded with a signal on another channel that brought a blip on the scope operated by the plane's navigator. Once in contact, the two-way system punched up every thirty seconds. When the planes' engines could be heard on the ground, the Eureka coding stopped and as the lead ship flew overhead, the blip on the scope collapsed. The navigator hit the switch for the green light and troopers poured out the door.

Says Robb, "In practice and total darkness, we had jumpers landing on us, breaking the Eureka's antennae. On one drill I landed twenty feet from the Eureka operator and I was the twelfth man out."

The pathfinders also bore special lights mounted on a tripod that created a five-foot by three-foot target in the drops zone as well as luminous panels to aid a daylight glider landing. The panels also indicated wind direction. The teams took two of everything in the belief that redundancy compensated for any mechanical or electronic malfunction.

On the afternoon before the start of DRAGOON, the British and French stationed alongside the U.S. pathfinders rode off to another airfield. A ration of beer meant for all three groups, three fifty-five-gallon drums of ice and brew, arrived at the field. The Americans attacked them with gusto.

"About ten o'clock," says Robb, "Lieutenant Fuller stood up and with a slight weave and a bit of a slur said, 'Lesh go over thish one more time.' Someone said, 'Oh shit, Lieutenant, we've been doing this for a month. If we don't know it now, we never will.' He said, 'Right, so let's have another beer.'

"We gathered at the planes around 11:30 for a midnight take-off. As we started to put on our gear and chutes, I put a can of beer in each side pocket of my jacket. Jim Kitchen was ahead of me. He was laughing and fumbling with his gear and couldn't get his foot up to the first step onto the ladder. The crew chief came out and boosted him up into the plane. The air-corps types thought it a riot we were all so smashed we couldn't get into the planes without help. We were having a ball too.

"However, I can assure anyone that a flight time of three hours and thirty minutes and an altitude temperature drop of fifteen or twenty degrees did a lot to sober up all concerned. The adrenaline and fear of what was in store added much to the process. Vasoconstriction from the latter plus the beer put extra pressure on the bladder. Gearing up and flight time left almost no chance to pee. There were thirty-six fellows almost in tears begging to get out of the three planes to perform the mission. Later, I suggested to Lieutenant Fuller that beer might be one of the surest means to eliminate jump refusals."

In February of 1944, strategists had concocted ANVIL,

an operation featuring sea and airborne forces to pierce Southern France. ANVIL's desirability increased as Allied Forces struggled to break through in Normandy after the invasion of June 6.

Three infantry divisions, the 3rd, 36th and 45th, waded ashore on the French Riviera, the Mediterranean beaches between Marseilles and Italy. At the same time, the 517th, two additional U.S. airborne battalions, the 550th and 551st, plus glider units along with British and Free French parachutists, would descend inland initially to forestall any efforts to reinforce the defenders along the Mediterranean shores. As refinements to the scheme developed it had received the new code label, DRAGOON, and the parachutists' role subsequently was dubbed AL-BATROSS. The targets for the 517th, as part of the First Airborne Task Force, were towns named La Motte, Le Muy and Les Arcs which anchored crossroads through which any inland enemy forces would need to move in order to aid their comrades near the Riviera. Regimental headquarters for the combat team were to be sited at the Château Ste.-Roseline, amid the three villages.

To confuse potentially hostile reception parties, six aircraft hauled 600 rubber parachute dummies and dumped them to the north and west off Toulon, well away from the actual drop zones. Battle-noise simulators, devices that exploded upon hitting the ground with a sound resembling rifle fire, accompanied the dummies to further convince the enemy. Planes also scattered tons of metal strips to deceive enemy radar. The official Allied report claims that German radio transmissions indicate the tricks fooled the enemy but the subsequent messiness of ALBATROSS inevitably confused all sides.

Altogether, 405 C–47s under the Troop Carrier Command lifted off ten Italian airfields with 5,630 paratroopers bound for Southern France. The largest single outfit was the 517th Combat Team. Not only were its three major combat components aboard but also some men not ordinarily considered as ground forces. From the Service Company, eighteen parachute riggers volunteered to accompany the combat team. They were initially assigned to assist the 460th in setting up their howitzers. In the tradition of airborne, the two chaplains, Protestant minister Charles Brown and Roman Catholic padre Alfred J. Guenette went along.

As the flights of aircraft bearing troopers from the three Rome airfields droned towards their targets, the pathfinders prepared to descend. The strategists had arranged for boats spaced thirty miles apart in the Mediterranean to provide checkpoints for the aircrews. These enabled the planes to make their landfall accurately. Unhappily, as their planes flew over the coastline, a heavy fog obscured the ground. Navigational problems due to poor visibility, shifting winds and perhaps some pilot error handicapped the Pathfinder operation.

Robb recalls, "The pathfinder pilot-commander, a lieutenant colonel who led the Normandy pathfinders, advised us that he could not locate our DZ exactly. The beer we consumed had nothing to do with the fact that we landed about six miles from the DZ. And when we were immediately discovered by a company of Germans, we got into a running firefight which gave us no chance to guide in the other planes." His conniving companion Jack Burns was wounded as he touched down but managed to free his weapon and wipe out his attackers. Without the pathfinders and the Eureka-Rebecca system to guide them, the pilots relied on their airspeed, and the navigational checks they managed to make before the fog blotted out the ground.

The entire affair was jeopardized by misplacement of the pathfinders and an inability of the pilots to navigate by visual means. Even after the results of the overall operation were recorded, the Troop Carrier Command boasted this was the most successful drop of the war with eighty-five percent accuracy. In fact, only four out of ten of the flights of planes unloaded their sticks anywhere near their DZs.

While Dick Robb and his pathfinder comrades were engaged in a firefight far from the place pinpointed to bring in parachutists, troopers of the 3rd Battalion started their journey to the earth. Without the expected help from Robb's team, the flyers could only guess when they should switch on the green light. In contrast, however, to the Normandy airdrop, the ground-to-air fire was not heavy and the airspeed of the aircraft, if not the altitude [because of ignorance of the terrain], was appropriate.

Mel Zais, who'd fallen asleep once his airplane took off, immediately sensed a problem. "I jumped as soon as the green light went on. I swung twice in my chute before I hit and I knew then we were in the wrong place because we should have been at 1,100 feet and over a vineyard. It had been nowhere near 1,100 feet and this was no vineyard that I landed in."

Zais was, in fact, twenty-five miles east of his appointed drop zone. "I started to unstrap my chute after taking my pistol out and laying it beside me in case there was any shooting. I could hear thuds from here and there as the bundles from the planes dropped. About twenty yards away I saw a yellow chute. That was one that carried a radio and I knew I must get it because I was in the wrong place.

"A soldier came out of the gloom, pressing his little cricket for identification. I said, 'Hey, trooper.' A voice answered, 'What do you want?' Then he added, 'I'm looking for a blue chute.' [The color signified a machine gun.] I told him the yellow chute had a radio. He said, 'You can't shoot no radio.' "

Zais, who claimed he knew every trooper in his battalion, believed he recognized the voice. "Is that you ——— ?"

"He said, 'Oh, is that you, sir?' " When Zais answered affirmatively, the trooper resignedly responded, "I'll get the radio right away." The battalion commander, however, reversed himself. "Never mind, go get your fucking machine gun."

Zais later explained that ———— was a soldier assigned to his battalion from the Fort Benning jump school. "He had a bad conduct discharge from the Marines but was a splendid soldier. He became a platoon sergeant and then first sergeant but he could not handle payday. He kept getting drunk and being busted. He was a natural leader, a great fighter, and the soldiers loved him. But he couldn't handle booze. Finally, we decided we had enough summary courts-martial for ————. We made him a machine gunner, let him have the rank of corporal and handled his payday incidents with company punishment while he would be fine with the machine gun."

The 3rd Battalion, according to John Chism, chief of the enlisted medics, boasted at least two specimens like ———— and the CO may have confused them. "———— was tall, perfectly proportioned, strong voice and usually without a hair or thread ever out of place. Sober, he could qualify for any military school in the world. Had he been in an army similar to the British one, he might have been able to purchase rank and hide the booze habit. He could identify the difference between good Scotch and champagne compared to rotgut. But he would never throw away the latter. Instead he would save it and serve it from the same glass as the best stuff when the rotgut was all that was left.

"The other man was a bootlegger from West Virginia. His instincts, under the influence of rum, were to take serious umbrage at any perceived slight. And when so aroused, he went for the throat. It was rumored that his father was in prison in the States and the trooper's plan was to take his favorite weapon, the BAR, home as part of a rescue plan for Dad. But while both men were afflicted with the ills of demon rum, they also had an instinctive flair for combat."

With the arrival of daylight, Zais, using his maps, located himself and determined that his troopers were spread over the landscape in three segments roughly four miles apart. He started collecting troopers and marching towards a road junction between Les Arcs and Le Muy through which the enemy would try to move its reinforcements. "My exec, Bob McMahon, had landed against a wall, ripping open his knee so badly I could see white cartilage. He insisted on walking so I carried his musette bag."

Lt. Howard Hensleigh, with G Company, was part of Zais's lost legions. Having tossed two bundles with bazookas from his plane, he also lost his dinner for the first time during a flight. But he avoided serious injury even as he caromed off a tree onto a couple of rocks. "I got the chest snap, leg straps and bellyband unbuckled, just as they taught us in jump school, pulled the M–1 out of the bag and assembled it, inserting a clip and putting her on safety."

Hensleigh started to round up men from his scattered stick. Aided by Sgts. John Podalack and Carl Boyer, Hensleigh accumulated seventy to eighty enlisted men. One of them discovered a house. "I went up, after placing five or six men behind cover. I banged the big brass knocker on the door. When I heard a female voice in French from the balcony just above, I said, 'American parachutists' in my bad French. The house seemed to shake. Soon a group of half a dozen men and women greeted us with kisses on both cheeks and strong handshakes. We went in, had a glass of wine. I asked where Le Muy, the town we should have landed near, was. They showed signs of distress and through a conglomeration of sign language, English and French told me we were thirty-three kilometers away."

The column continued to swell although the most senior officer was 1st Lt. Ludlow Gibbons of Company H. Then the Battalion Headquarters Company commander, Capt. Joseph McGeever, appeared with a number of troopers. McGeever had met up with eighty Brits and between the GIs and the Tommies, a German truck convoy bearing infantrymen had been wiped out. The union of the two American groups brought the total to 400 troopers heading for their assembly area near Le Muy.

The 2nd Battalion, led by Dick Seitz, came down closest to their drop zone. "The battalion," says Tommy Thompson, "was the lead one for the jump in France. I was with Seitz in the lead plane and he made me jump master. He wanted to be the first man out the door. But my large artillery bundle, blocking the door, had to be pushed out first by my section member, Smitty. Then came Seitz and I with the rest of the paratroopers in close order on my heels. Since it would have taken too long to hook up to the static line, I hooked up on the run to a hole in the seat beside the door. Everything went well."

Others fared more poorly. "I saw fog over the water as we approached the French coast," recalls Seitz's exec, Tom Cross. "Then I saw some islands, then more fog. When the green light came on for 'go' I really wasn't certain we were over land so I prepared for a water landing, or tried to, but I really couldn't. I had too much equipment on. I never saw the ground but unfortunately, I grazed a tree and then landed unevenly in a ditch. I thought I sprained my right leg but I broke it above the ankle. The trench knife strapped to my right boot may have helped snap the leg but now it acted like a splint. It hurt like hell when I started to walk, but the name of the game was to get going. All of us were aware of how the Germans had killed troopers whose chutes caught in trees or were wounded during the Normandy invasion. That was a highly motivating factor towards meeting up with the rest of the men.

"As I hobbled along, I saw T/5 Victor Cawthon, of Headquarters Company's communications platoon, and hailed him. He said he had to find his radio and scooted off in search of the communications bundle. I gathered everyone that I could find and we headed for where I thought would be the assembly area. It was still foggy and difficult to establish our position.

"A Frenchman on a bicycle wheeled up and I asked him for directions to La Motte in my fractured French. With the grease-paint smeared on our faces, all I did was scare him. Suddenly, a German machine gun started up. We couldn't determine the direction of fire or its location but it was too damn close for comfort.

"I had a sizable force with me, about the size of a company, when I met Dick Seitz. He took over and we marched on our initial objective. I tried to start out at the head of the column but couldn't keep up until they halted because of enemy machine gun fire. That allowed me an opportunity to hobble up to the front. When we finally reached our objective, I sat down beside a tree. Then I could not get up when it was time to move out. Someone helped me to a nearby château that became an aid station of sorts. A French family took care of us temporarily."

Seitz himself had been in the lead ship of his formation. Standing by the door, he saw the green light flash and helped dump the door-load out. He followed the bundle. "I was not surprised that I couldn't see the ground because I had been hanging out the door during the flight and knew the fog obscured the ground. Below it looked like an ocean but I knew we were over land because I had seen the coast as we made landfall.

"I carried a .45 and a carbine with a metal folding stock. I didn't use a Griswold container because I wanted the carbine readily available. It was a decision I would regret the rest of my life. I put the weapon under my reserve chute and held it with my hand, the butt of the metal stock uppermost. The opening shock of the chute brought the butt up and it struck me in the mouth. And when I hit the ground, the damn thing again slammed me in the mouth. Eventually, that forced me to wear a dental bridge to replace four front teeth.

"Immediately on landing, everything appeared calm and quiet. Then I began hearing a few crickets. About that time there was some sporadic enemy fire, some in our area but the heaviest a distance away. I got a report on Dave Armstrong, D Company commander, that on landing he had a stake rammed up his butt. While our intelligence had been good, nobody warned us about the stakes used in the grape arbors. Armstrong had to be evacuated, as was Tom Cross."

The 1st Battalion, like the 3rd, also leaped far from their drop zone. Don Fraser led his stick from A Company out into the early-morning darkness. "I had a bundle in the door with the radio equipment and shoved it out. I saw the light on the bundle and then it disappeared in the fog. Never saw it again. Looking down, I was sure the air corps had dropped us into the sea. But then I went through the fog, crashed off a tree and struck the ground next to a rock wall. As I unhooked my chute and loaded my carbine, I heard someone nearby. I challenged him and it was Chopper Kienlen.

"By daylight we had seventeen from A Company and one little British trooper. How he ever came to us I never figured out. In that first light there were white parachutes scattered over the hills as far as you could see. We picked up a Frenchman from the FFI [Free French of the Interior] on the road and headed for the Château Ste.-Roseline, designated as the regimental CP.

"On the way we engaged in several skirmishes. At the very first, the British trooper hit the ground with his finger on the trigger and by accident blew a string of bullets past Kienlen. Chopper picked him up with one hand and told him to lock the weapon on safety until he told him otherwise. That Britisher followed Chopper around all day saying he had never met anyone like him. He wanted to transfer to Kienlen's platoon and we were sorry when he went back to his own unit.

"I was leading the way down the road towards the Château Ste.-Roseline with a flanker downhill to my left and another uphill to my right. Chopper was about twenty yards behind me and the others strung out along the road behind him. I was watching my flankers when Chopper yelled and then fired a couple of shots. I had walked right by a German in a slit trench. He would have killed me but Chopper got him first.

"Kienlen jumped down in the ditch and came up with an Iron Cross and a small pistol in about ten seconds. He smiled and waved me on.

"We got to the château and then Colonel Graves came in behind us with a big lump on his nose." Graves's battered nose resulted from a hard landing. When the CO struck the ground, his carbine, which he had tucked under his reserve chute, snapped up and smacked him in the face, just as it had Seitz. Before he disconnected his harness, Graves carefully pulled out his pistol and placed it on the ground where he could seize it in an emergency. After hacking through the cords of his chute he started to feel about for his weapon. He couldn't find it. Graves searched for ten minutes and then gave up.

Among those who came across the combat team's CO was Don Saunders from the 596th engineers. "With the ground fog which I couldn't see through I thought I was over water and I couldn't swim. I was greatly relieved to land in a tree. I ran into Ennis and we stayed together until we met up with Colonel Graves." Some minutes later, Saunders and his colleagues saw a German motorcycle with a sidecar approaching and inflicted their first casualties upon the enemy.

The first troopers who came upon Rupert Graves naturally asked him where they were. In his typical fashion, Graves responded, "I feel reasonably certain that we're somewhere in France. Other than that, I haven't the faintest notion."

"Graves had a big nose anyhow," says Fraser, "and took our kidding good-naturedly. He was very cool under combat conditions and he told me the 3rd Battalion had been dropped way out and would probably take two days to come in. He instructed me to take my seventeen men and hold the 3rd Battalion's objective, the hill between the town of Les Arcs and the château."

As an anxious Fraser detected the enemy starting to move on his small body of men, some miles off, one of his platoons was contemplating the wreck of their own special mission. A Company's 2nd Platoon, under Lt. James A. Reith, had been assigned a genuine movie-style piece of heroics. Says Reith, "We were to slip into the *Wehrmacht* stronghold of Draguignan before 7:00 A.M. before the enemy realized that Southern France was under parachute attack. We were to capture Gen. Ferdinand Neuling, commander of the enemy's LXII Corps. And if we couldn't kidnap him alive, we were to kill Neuling and then get out of Draguignan any way we could.

"My platoon and I had been studying the details of the capture plot for a long time. Neuling's residence was Villa Gladys, a stately old mansion that nestled among a stand of towering pines on the outskirts of the town. From our study of the aged architectural plans, stolen for us by the French underground, and a sand table reproduction of the house we knew the site well. We were also well briefed on Neuling's daily routine and personal habits."

From his plane, Reith splashed down into a watery ditch. In the nearby darkness he heard voices speaking German. He struggled desperately to get out of his harness. He was on his back, unbuckling his reserve chute, when he heard footsteps approaching through the underbrush. "Just as I freed myself, I looked up and saw a Kraut aiming a burp gun at me. I pulled my .45 pistol and rolled over just as a burst of machine gun fire struck where I had been. I squeezed off several rounds and the German toppled over, dead from chest wounds.

"Knowing the firing would alert his comrades, I hurried away toward the main highway. A glowing red light on an equipment bundle attracted my attention. I headed towards it and saw the dim outline of a paratrooper standing near the bundle, gazing up at the C–47s in the sky. I edged closer to the figure who remained focused on the planes. Moments later, I grew suspicious of my newfound comrade because the man gave off a fishy odor. I had encountered Germans in Italy who had the same odor, apparently from their diet of smoked salmon.

"I stooped to gain a better look at the man's silhouette. My heart skipped a beat when I discerned the coal-bucket-shaped helmet. He was no American paratrooper but a German. Almost at the same time, he became aware of my presence and his hand flashed towards his P–38 pistol. I beat him to the draw, sticking the muzzle of my .45 in his stomach and firing. He let out a gurgling grunt before collapsing in a heap.

"As dawn came I saw from my watch it was 5:35. I had been in France only an hour but it seemed an eternity. But how could I hope to carry out my mission of capturing the general? I was alone and had no idea of my location and the *Wehrmacht* between me and Draguignan were certainly on full alert now that thousands of paratroopers had fallen from the sky. A short time later, I ran into Joe Blackwell, my mortar sergeant. He told me we were at least twenty miles from Draguignan."

Like Reith, Lt. John Alicki, the demolitions platoon leader for the 1st Battalion, discovered himself alone. "I figured the others should be nearby since we exited from the same plane. Then I remembered that a split second after I got the green light the plane made a sudden sharp bank. And as I learned, the result was that the remainder of my stick parachuted on top of a German bivouac. There was a violent firefight as the Germans attacked my trapped men from all sides. In the confusion and the darkness Sgt. William Brown was able to get eight men together but they were quickly surrounded by thirty Germans. Private Giner was killed by rifle fire and the uneven match resulted in the capture of Sergeant Brown and seven of my squad. They were taken to Le Muy.

"Unaware of their fate, I was walking along a country road as dawn broke. Coming towards me was a French farmer, who stared in disbelief at my blackened camouflaged face and my clothes weighted down with my war gear. He spotted the American flag, sewn on each trooper's jump jacket at the shoulder. 'Américain! Américain!' he shouted over and over, dancing with joy. With tears rolling down his wrinkled cheeks, the Frenchman grabbed me in a bear hug and planted a kiss on my sweaty, painted face. I was able to extract from him the direction of Le Muy. On the way I ran into Major Paxton and some of my demo platoon from another stick."

John Forrest had packed carefully for ALBATROSS. His musette bag held socks, underwear, a blanket, shelter half and raincoat. He stored his M–1 in a pouch behind his reserve chute. He carried a half belt of machine gun ammo, and as a demolitions trooper loaded up Composition C, caps, primacord and fuses. A canteen cover with four grenades garnished his rifle belt. He wore two bandoliers of ammunition for his M–1 along with the

clips inserted in the cartridge-belt pockets. For suste-
nance he brought several K rations and a full canteen of
water. The first-aid kit, entrenching tool, gas mask, Mae
West flotation vest, bayonet and trench knife, plus the
two chutes, completed his accoutrements.

"The plane in which I traveled had a fifteen-man
stick. We had never had much respect for the Air Corps
officers and usually didn't salute them. Now we found
ourselves at their mercy as they reminded us of our sins
starting back in North Carolina. During a night jump at
Mackall, I had noticed some red sparks outside the
plane. I had remarked to the crew chief about the little
flicks of fire coming from the engine and wondered
whether it was on fire. He told me, 'You are really stupid. Those are just from the engine exhaust.' As we
crossed the coast of France I saw some red sparks go by
and assumed they were from the engine. But soon I realized they were tracer rounds. When a shell exploded
nearby, I knew we were over France.

"In theory, a plane slows down before the jump and
raises the tail before the jump. When the red light goes
on, the troopers stand up, hook up to the static line and
check the equipment. On the green light, we'd jump. In
France, the plane slowed, the red lamp lit and we went
through the regular procedure. Suddenly the red light
went off, the tail dropped and the plane accelerated to
what seemed full throttle. After a short interval, both
red and green lights showed simultaneously and the
crew chief yelled, 'Get the hell out! Get the hell out!'

"At that speed, the opening shock was terrific, giving
me two large riser burns. Luckily I didn't blow a panel in
my chute. Before we hit the ground, the planes were out
of sight and earshot. We were also badly scattered."

Forrest landed on a terraced hillside. Within minutes
he had freed himself, assembled his M–1 and found his
company commander, then Lt. Erle Ehly. They collected

troopers and the contents of equipment bundles before heading for their objective.

Forrest recalls, "We came under small-arms fire from a barracks area where there was a small artillery piece and some gasoline drums stored. After the Germans were driven off, a thermite grenade placed on the breechblock of the artillery piece welded it useless. Somehow, the gasoline drums exploded and a fireball engulfed Pvt. C. E. Lynch. The flames were extinguished but he was badly burned. In those days it was believed oil was a proper unguent for burns. Ehly's action was great. He had us give him the oilers from our rifle butts and he spread the oil over Lynch's exposed body.

"Since there was no way to evacuate Lynch, he marched with us, eyes swollen shut, his fingers the size of frankfurters. When we reached the hill we defended, he lay there without ever complaining or groaning. He even sang, 'I've got you under my skin, ya little maggot you.'"

John Lissner found his way to the CP, where Graves informed him that F Company CO John McKinley would now serve as battalion exec since Cross was now *hors de combat*. That bumped Lieutenant Lissner up to the top slot of F Company.

As daylight pierced the morning fog, Waco gliders, carrying infantrymen, antitank and 4.2-inch chemical mortar units, and towed by C-47s, were now coming in to their landing fields. To forestall such airborne incursions, the enemy had planted a full crop of *Rommelspargel*—Rommel's asparagus, which the renowned German field marshal first used against the Normandy invasion. The anti-glider obstacles were poles imbedded in the ground at close intervals. Some asparagus had already been hacked down by paratroopers but many of them still stood. The gliders plowed into them but the saving grace was that many poles had been poorly installed. They snapped off wings but acted almost like brakes upon the careering sailplanes. Nevertheless, a total of 108 men from the more than 2,250 passengers were injured and a number were killed from collisions with the more sturdy asparagus, hedgerows and stone walls, many of which were undetected in the pre-invasion aerial photographs. Tom Cross, expecting to be driven back to a hospital, says the noise of the crashes was like artillery shells. Soon, injured glider soldiers joined Cross in waiting for medical treatment. Among them was engineer Bob Wilkerson. Riding a glider bearing mines, he was among the victims.

Troopers like Don Fraser, manning their posts in front of the Château, heard the terrible crashing noises as the wooden craft slammed into the poles, trees and thick shrubbery. But although a number of the glider borne were killed or injured, others took the field with their weapons.

To Fraser's immense relief, one of the chemical mortar outfits that came in via glider set up its 4.2s. "They put down a walking barrage through the vineyards to our front. It was beautiful to watch and chewed up the German unit attacking us. They really saved our asses."

The combat team's own artillery quickly added its resources to those of the line companies. John Kinzer, the exec of the 460th, rode in the same plane as Rupert Graves but when he jumped he touched down on the other side of a ridge from Graves. "I prepared for a tree landing," says Kinzer, "after hearing the bundles hitting trees. I ended up with my toes against a large rock on the mountainside. When I opened the Griswold container, one of my submachine-gun magazines fell out and I heard it bounce from rock to rock down the hillside. Therefore, I proceeded with caution until hooking up with other troopers below.

"Since I was not an infantryman, I led our first small

group walking in front, until the trigger-happy guy just behind me fired a shot between my legs. From that point, trigger-happy led and I guided him from behind.

"Upon arrival at our assembly areas I assisted Colonel Cato in organizing our battalion command and control. The most impressive thing about our operation was the delivery of our major artillery power in one serial of aircraft, rather than breaking it up into batteries in support of battalion combat teams. That gave us coordinated fire support in position on D-Day. Three of our four gun batteries were in action within twenty-four hours of the landing." It was a prodigious achievement considering that a quarter of the artillerymen and their pieces were dropped several miles from their designated area and everything, from the weapons through the ammunition, piled into small, hand-pulled carts, moved only by straining legs, backs and arms.

Phil Di Stanislao, one of "Mother" Fraser's troopers, although in Fraser's airplane, came to earth well out of sight and sound of his A-Company buddies. "I had decided that when the red light lit, if we had passed over the coast, I would discard my Mae West. When I went out of the plane and looked down I said 'Oh, Christ!' I wanted to climb back up the suspension lines of the canopy and retrieve the Mae West. But my landing was dry, heavy and hard.

"I didn't see anyone nearby. When I went to get my rifle out of its container, the trigger housing slipped out of my hands. I was on my hands and knees searching for it until I found it. My compass was smashed. I didn't know where north or south was. I tried to locate my position from the pattern of planes overhead but they were going every which way.

"I can't speak very well of the pilots, whatever the navigation problems. But on the other hand, maybe it was fortuitous. Berlin Sally had said before we left that they knew we were coming and where we would land.

They would have been sure to light up the DZs well. Scattered as we were presented some tactical advantages. We were all over the area, in groups as small as two or three, sometimes even as individuals.

"As my friend Joe Blackwell, who was a sergeant with a mortar crew, insisted, we all thought we were capable of being officers. We all felt we had the leadership ability. We knew what to do, as a result of both training and ego. And we believed in each other.

"I came across two or three British troopers and since I was the ranking noncom they followed me. We ran into a group of Germans entrenched behind a huge bramble patch. We killed them. The Brits went their way and I continued by myself.

"Even though my compass had been smashed, I had lots of maps. In the dark I couldn't find out anything but with daylight I came across what I could see was a small irrigation canal and I plotted a route towards my primary target where we would rendezvous or capture, whichever came first. In my travels I met up with a team from the 460th, pushing and pulling their howitzer. I stayed with them a bit, helping them move towards their target.

"I headed for where I was supposed to be and ran into Joe Chobot. We were not the best of friends. In Toccoa, one night, while I was charge of quarters, I went to his barracks and told him to turn the light out. He told me to shove it and we had at it outside. I believe I bruised him pretty badly and he was never warm towards me. But situations like this make strange bedfellows. Together, Joe and I started up the path of a wooded, not very steep hill. He ran ahead and suddenly dashed back. 'Goddamn, there are Germans up there.'

"The two of us hit the ground, preparing to fire. Then they rolled down the path concussion grenades, little black eggs. One stopped almost against my head. I did a complete flip-flop and it exploded near my boot.

My foot went temporarily numb but it wasn't a fragmentation grenade or I'd have had it. I asked Joe how many there were but he said he couldn't tell. I said, 'Let's stand up, fire into the area and then haul ass.'

"They rolled a few more grenades at us, all concussion. I could never figure out why they didn't use fragmentation ones and didn't fire. We stood up, emptied our rifles and then scrammed. I think I could have jumped high buildings; I know I leaped over some big boulders."

Di Stanislao says he gave up on reaching the primary objective and decided to head for the secondary target. During his wanderings he came across machine-gunner Frank Grbinich. "A fine soldier, Frank had landed on his back. I couldn't tell if he had fractured his spine but he was in extreme pain. I helped him take off his equipment, gave his canteen to him so he'd have water, put his grenades in front of him and got his carbine ready in case he needed to defend himself. I found another fellow with a broken ankle. I did the same for him but moved him into a barn. I couldn't move Frank because he might have a broken back. Subsequently, the two were picked up; Frank's injury was not a fracture and they both rejoined the outfit later."

Di Stanislao's day ended on a lonely note even though he finally found several dozen men at the second objective. The battalion exec, Herb Bowlby, dispatched Di Stanislao to a nearby mountaintop to serve as a "one-man listening post" if friendly troops from the seaborne landing showed. Di Stanislao could not imagine what he could do if indeed he did get an inkling of the GIs moving out from the beaches.

The 460th's C Battery with Nat Schoenberg had been designated to support the 1st Battalion. Schoenberg almost missed DRAGOON because of a severe attack of food poisoning. Hospitalized, he heard the appointed hour of the drop was near. He managed to get discharged although when he left the vehicle that took him to the bivouac area he collapsed. A day later, he recovered enough to accompany the others into Southern France.

"I watched the green lights of our bundles after I jumped. After I landed, Capt. Bob Roberts, the forward observer, saw me and he said, 'Welcome to France, Abie.' When we assembled on the ground we retrieved our bundles. We didn't know where we were and in the darkness nobody knew how close the Germans were. But the guys didn't give a damn. Putting the carts together to pull the guns, they used sledgehammers to bang the wheels into place.

"Captain Vogel, the battery commander, was very impressive. He organized us. There were some troopers from the 517th who wanted to take off but Vogel insisted they stay with us to guard our flanks." The artillery contingent sweated and strained to move their pieces to the Château Ste.-Roseline and eventually reached it. The expected extra musclepower from the eighteen parachute riggers never came as they touched down well separated from the artillerymen.

Nat Schoenberg also recalls the incoming gliders. "We had colored parachutes spread out atop trees to show areas held by friendly forces. The gliders came down right near us," says Schoenberg. "I ran over to help. We pulled bodies from the wrecks, eight or nine of them were dead. The most incredible sight was one of them landed and as soon as it stopped, this Jap, a soldier from the 442nd Battalion, tore right through the canvas side of the glider and appeared with his rifle and bayonet at the ready."

Among the gliderborne arrivals with the 442nd were five troopers from H Company who had boarded a C–47 around 4:00 A.M. at Orbetello. Assistant platoon leader Lt. Ed Athey stood in the back of the aircraft as it rolled towards its takeoff. "I really never liked jumping.

Until I went to OCS, I hated being in the blackness at the rear, then suddenly running out into nothing. It was a little better when I became an officer because then I was always first out and I was by the door, able to see.

"As the C–47 at Orbetello went down the runway, the pilot found he wasn't getting enough speed. He saw a disabled plane parked dead ahead and he did the only thing he could. He yanked back on the stick, pulling the nose up. The ship stalled and crashed nose down. The pilot and copilot scrambled out the observation window. Except for one man up front, none of us had been strapped in. On impact we all piled on top of one another. The jump door was about thirty feet off the ground and one engine was on fire; the entire plane was about to start burning. I knew that the bundles with all of the ammunition would blow.

"My platoon sergeant and I pushed open the door, pulled each trooper up the forty-five-degree incline and shoved them out the door before we jumped. Everyone survived, although seven men needed hospitalization for broken arms, legs, ribs and a head injury. The rest of us escaped with cuts and bruises; mine was a severe laceration of my hand.

"I took the other four and arranged with the officer in charge of the 442nd Antitank contingent to ride with them in one of their gliders that would get off after daylight. When we landed, we were among the few paratroopers from the 517th to come down close to the designated spot near Les Arcs."

Jim Reith had reluctantly abandoned any hopes of ever carrying out the snatch of the enemy commander. Instead, he rounded up a large band of troopers until he brought fifty to sixty soldiers to an assembly area where the party united with the band of troopers led by Forrest's CO, Erle Ehly from the 1st Battalion Headquarters Company, and C Company's top gun, Capt. Charles La Chaussee.

The latter, having glimpsed the sea and white surf pounding the beaches before the fog bank, suddenly saw the green light flash without being preceded by a red one warning of five minutes to hook up. La Chaussee yelled to his startled troopers, "Let's go." He crashed into a vineyard, injuring his right arm, slashed himself free of his chute and dumped his Mae West. But he was alone.

"I headed east until I saw a house through the vines. I rapped on the door with the barrel of my submachine gun. A young women opened it. She was terrified by my blackened face, the brush hanging to my helmet netting. In my high-school French I said, *'Bonjour, mademoiselle. Je suis* . . . parachute *américain* . . . *l'invasion commence aujourd'huis. Où est la Château Ste.-Roseline?'* "

The young woman summoned two older people and one of them said, "Papa will guide you, *pour la France.*" The aged citizen led La Chaussee into the darkened street but then the guide vanished. Subsequently, the captain accosted a teenager but he offered no help either.

Outside the village, La Chaussee detected movement and challenged, "Lafayette!" There was no proper countersign. La Chaussee drew back the slide on his machine gun, ready to fire. A voice now declared, "Ah, some fooking cowboy." It was a British Tommie busy unhooking his parachute. He happened to be a medic and he fixed a sling for the captain's arm.

The Briton soon located his mates, heating water for their tea. " 'Tis all fooked up, lak Sicily," remarked a Scotsman. La Chaussee went off on his own, dumping his gas mask and about ten pounds of maps.

He met up with some troopers from the battalion mortar platoon, participated in a brief shootout with some German laborcorps soldiers and then came upon Reith and Ehly. The group set its sights on a position that would block Highway 7, a vital artery that led to the beaches.

Along the way, Reith led a patrol into the woods after sniper fire harassed the advance. He came upon an entire stick of British paratroopers whose chutes failed to open. Reith counted eight bodies horribly battered from the impact of their falls. Apparently, some breakage in the static-line cable caused the terrible accident. The safeguard of a reserve parachute would probably have saved all of them but only U.S. troopers wore a spare.

Capt. Walter Plassman, the 3rd Battalion surgeon, with a Sergeant Harvey and six other medics traveled in a C–47 with I Company while John Chism and Daniel Dickinson, the newly recruited assistant battalion surgeon, and another half-dozen medics accompanied G Company. Says Plassman, "I carried two aid kits strapped to my legs, two canteens of water, one unit of plasma and my musette bag with medicine strapped below my reserve chute. I could hardly get in the plane. Four bundles with plasma, litters and other stuff were loaded on the para racks beneath the wings but we never found them.

"We landed far from our objective and those who could walk left to join the main forces. About six men and myself were unable to do more than hobble. One man had a fractured leg. My left knee had banged against a rock wall next to a road. With the help of two civilians, we managed to reach Montoroux, which was about one kilometer off.

"I set up a casualty station in a building that had been a TB sanitarium. There were only three cots there but people brought in mattresses. While I was there, I met a French dentist who happened to be visiting his in-laws. He was great. He managed to scrounge food and water for us. Another very helpful person was the local priest.

"Things were quiet except for a few artillery rounds

that fell quite close. That night, around 1:00 A.M. about twenty-five German soldiers came into the town. They had one old truck and they were part of an engineer company. Their captain spoke some English. He said we should stay put and later they would try to evacuate us to their hospital.

"The Germans remained all day. They had one wounded man with them, a gut shot. I examined him but explained I could do nothing except give him morphine. He died in a few hours. That night, around 2:00 A.M., they pulled out, taking their dead man."

Other lost members of the 517th improvised similarly. John Chism, temporarily immobile after slamming into a tree stump on his landing, set up shop in a couple of stone buildings. Two adolescents, fourteen- and fifteen-year-old Boy Scouts, put themselves at Chism's disposal. He had three medics, Larry Constantine, Austin Post and Maurice White, to help him with a patient list that grew to twenty-five patients, including seven Americans and a number of injured British troopers. The site at Fayence was loosely under German control but the enemy left Chism to tend his men.

Post and White scouted the nearby area, discovering other wounded and injured, some of whom were hurt so badly they could not be moved to Chism's makeshift aid station. "A Scotsman with his belly running out onto the ground was one of the bravest of the brave," recalls Chism. "He accepted the heat of August and that he would not get out. I teased him about attending my birthday party, to be held August 20, but on the fourth day, during our daily check, we found his position covered with cigarette butts and evidence that he had washed his face, straightened his clothing and then passed away."

Some of the GIs reciprocated the action of the British trooper who attached himself to Fraser's band by working with his countrymen. Others formed alliances with the French Maquis (the overall designation for the various armed resistance forces) roaming the area and even with an American OSS officer. Through their impromptu actions, Sgt. George Heckard and Cpl. Albert Deshayes received credit for the surrender of a large number of Germans, bringing each trooper a DSC.

An American patrol from B Company near Draguignan failed to return. The men had been captured by an enemy outfit. In turn, a large band of the French Maquis surrounded the Germans, who rather than surrender to the guerrillas put themselves in the custody of their former prisoner, Pfc. Doyle Gray. He promptly handed his prisoners over to the Maquis.

Medic Charlie Keen, serving with B Company of the 1st Battalion, became persuaded that the large Red Cross painted on the helmets of aidmen was a mixed blessing. "It simply did not make sense for a bright shining red and white cross to flash away our platoon position for all enemy eyes to spot, risking the lives of the platoon." Accordingly, the medics, like Keen, covered their helmets bearing the insignia with heavy netting as they readied themselves for ALBATROSS.

"We [the medics] were all shot at at one time or another. When that happened, no German dared stick his head or hand up with a white flag." Keen had taken to carrying a .45 pistol but he went further. "When I jumped in Southern France, I carried a carbine as it was a night jump behind enemy lines. That is not an occasion on which one should be without arms.

"As soon as I cleared the plane door, I heard a roar of what I took to be a fighter plane. It kept getting so loud that I thought there was no way he could miss me. I drew my legs up out of fear of this unknown.

"I thought I was coming down in a nursery as I fell in a tangle of lines and raw nerves. I landed within ten yards of a white farm building. While I was getting out of my chute, I saw a figure come out of the building and walk around it. I could not for the life of me get out my carbine. The password was 'Lafayette' and the counter was 'Democracy.' All I heard was someone ask, 'Who are you?' I was greatly relieved to discover it was Mel Biddle, a B-Company man whom I believe came through the roof of the building."

Keen and Biddle had no idea of their location and as they wandered about "trying to find where in hell we were, or someone who knew," they came across other troopers. "Near daylight, we met Captain [William] Young [the battalion's S–3]. About thirty of us started out to see just what we could tear up. First we passed under a long string of heavy, cross-country electric cables running from the coast to the interior. Young must have been out of his mind because he sent a man up the high metal towers to cut the one-inch cables with a pick mattock. The poor fellow hit once and then raised himself up and really gave it a whack. When he hit the second cable a flame or spark jumped from the overhead cable about a foot, sounding like a cannon.

"The man's body went rigid. He fell stiff as a board to the ground, bouncing off a small building and knocking off some of the tile roof. His feet were still on the metal support of the tower when he stopped falling. The next thing I heard was 'Keen, see if you can help him!'

"I knew nothing about electricity so I used a tree limb to free him. But even then I knew it was all over for him. His helmet was still on and when I removed it, it was hot and burned black. All the hair on his head was burned off. His skin was black. There was no heart or pulse beat.

"Our leader decided we should attack the cables with a rifle grenade. That failed and we also lost some of our crowd who apparently did not like the direction of our leader."

The remainder of the group pressed on until they bumped into a young Frenchman. "I was chosen to ask him where was the railroad. '*Où est la gare?*' is what I think I said. He answered with a long series of French words and hand gestures. I confessed I had no idea of what he was saying. Trooper John Garcia, a 110 percent American Indian, who learned a lot of the language at the reservation school, informed me the Frenchman wanted to know what state in America I was from. So much for my college French course."

Keen and his fellows straggled into a farmhouse, bemused by a bevy of scantily clad young women gaily waving from windows upstairs. Inside they met their first member of the FFI. Also on hand was a trooper who stubbornly insisted he belonged to the 11th Airborne Division. Says Keen, "Here we are lost and asking for help from a guy who is 10,000 miles from his unit." The 11th Airborne was fighting in the South Pacific.

Making do as best they could, Keen and company piled into the back of a flame-spouting, smoky, charcoal-burning truck. The driver headed for the village of Les Arcs. "At the edge of town we disembarked because no one knew whether the Americans, the FFI or the Germans controlled the town. In a very military manner we crossed through the streets until stopped by a man who spoke perfect English, as well he should. He had come there after World War I from his hometown of Boston.

"He explained to Captain Young that the land beyond the railroad bridge was in German hands. In the middle of the bridge sat a burning 75 mm howitzer that had belonged to our own 460th. Later we learned that a crew from the 460th had assembled the gun after their landing and were pulling it through the town when the Germans hit them.

"Our commander decided we would all climb abroad the fire-belching, charcoal-burning, slow-moving truck and storm across the bridge to carry the war to the enemy. While the fireman was stoking the burners of the lorry, I spotted an old man in the uniform of the French Foreign Legion. He had ribbons down to his belly and he was waving his arms, yelling *'Suicide!' 'Suicide!'* My French may have been poor but suicide happens to mean the same in French and English. I took one look at Captain Young, then looked at the old, decorated Legionaire. Without another moment's hesitation, I climbed over the side of the truck and down to the street. All of the other troopers followed.

"God, observing our predicament, saw fit to have Colonel Boyle appear, from God only knows where, and assume command." Keen, like Di Stanislao, Chism and others, still marvels at the omnipresence of Bill Boyle. They insist he invariably surfaced at moments of crisis and in fact, wherever he happened to be of a moment, firefights broke out.

That Boyle stepped on stage at Les Arcs at that moment was almost a miracle, considering the start of his role in DRAGOON. When the group of aircraft ferrying his troops was perhaps twenty to twenty-five minutes from the drop zone, Boyle glanced out of the open door of his C–47. The formation of some fifty planes seemed in order. He turned his attention to his stick and the equipment bundles which included the vital radio gear necessary for communications. Boyle himself was weighted down with his individual needs, plus a can of machine gun ammunition. He required every man not a member of a crew-served weapon to bear either a mortar round or the machine gun ammunition. Officers were included not only because of the value of the extra rounds but also because Boyle reasoned that if the men saw that officers bore the added weight it would maintain morale.

"When we jumped," says Boyle, "I discovered that my plane was the only one in the sky I could see. The fog bank below me looked like the sea and I started to prepare for a water landing. On the ground, Boyle realized his troops were scattered very widely. In fact, he could find only half a dozen troopers. Fortunately, a pair of French civilians provided directions to Les Arcs, his target.

There he discovered the small group that included Charlie Keen. Unfortunately, when Boyle sought to advance towards his objective, control of a rail line near Le Muy, his force of perhaps forty troopers met a strong German attack with as many as 400 soldiers. Boyle and his crew fell back to a defensive stance on the edge of Les Arcs.

Ed Johnson, the trooper in C Company, like so many others, dozed off as the engines carrying them towards France droned on and on. "There was much confusion on the flight deck. They started and stopped our stick twice, spreading us all over the landscape and far from our equipment. The low clouds strongly resembled water and I was sure they had dumped us in the ocean. But I came down through the 'water' and landed astride a rocky vineyard terrace, cutting my mouth and loosening a few teeth in the process." Unfortunately, the fears of a watery end to their drop, expressed by so many, were fulfilled by two sticks from one of the brother airborne battalions. They fell into the sea near St. Tropez.

Johnson was among eighteen troopers from C Company dug in at Les Arcs with Bill Boyle's outnumbered band. "We held the town for a day and a half," says Johnson, "although there were ten of them to every one of us. At the height of one of their attacks, Pvt. Jim Dorman spotted three Jerries coming up the railroad tracks on the left flank about fifty yards away. Depressing his rifle, he let go a muzzle-aimed antitank grenade. It caught the middle man squarely in the back and killed all three Krauts. Patrols led by Sergeant Landsom, Corporals Perkins and Lathers and Privates First Class North and Shaddoz gained vital information about the disposition of the enemy and the whereabouts of friendly troops." And in spite of casualties, Boyle's forces actually increased as 1st Battalion jumpers sifted into the Les Arcs redoubts.

The enemy took heavy casualties from a machine gun operated by Pvts. Richard Jamme and Albert Ernst. Boyle deployed Johnson as part of a machine gun team to guard one avenue leading to the embattled troopers' position. The strategy worked for a while but then German snipers infiltrated some of the taller buildings in town, making the spot untenable. Indeed, the only way to avoid death or capture lay in a retreat. Boyle skillfully extricated his troops. A major reason for the American escape lay in the courageous actions of Al Ernst.

Phil Di Stanislao remembers Ernst from his very first days in the army. "We met at Camp Upton on Long Island and when we were on our way to Toccoa, his fiancée and his mother met us at Penn Station in New York City. I was told that when the Germans overwhelmed them, Ernst told the others he would defend the others during the withdrawal by manning his machine gun. The last anyone saw of him, blood was streaming down his face while he fired the weapon. He was declared missing in action and presumed dead. I received letters from his mother, who wrote in disbelief that anything could happen to her son, Al. But in fact he was killed." Jamme, the other machine gunner, also died from wounds incurred during DRAGOON.

Battery C of the 460th with Nat Schoenberg rushed to provide artillery fire which would reduce the pressure exerted upon Boyle's force, now in danger of mimicking the last stand at the Alamo. En route, shots sent everyone diving for cover. Lt. Harry Moore and Pfc. Phil Kennamer yelled they would deal with the problem and dashed forward. Five minutes later, when the firing ceased, the gun crews started forward. "We found Moore and Kennamer," says Schoenberg, "facedown in the road, both of them dead."

E Company's Russ Brami, fortified with dexadrine

(other troopers do not recall receiving any amphetamines or other drugs) and weighted down with an extra mortar round for the 60 mm piece, a half belt of machine gun ammunition, three white phosphorus grenades and five fragmentation ones along with his carbine and pistol, landed in a tree. After he slid down, he started to seek companionship.

"Using my cricket, the first man I saw was Rupert Graves. He had banged up his nose. He made me carry a bazooka, the 2.3 inch which was a lousy weapon. As soon as we could, we started using the captured German *panzerfausts*.

"I joined up with some others from E Company and we headed for La Motte. We were on our way when the kid in front got one right between the horns. We started pushing out patrols to see what was around.

"With some others I was outposted on a hill where the gliders from the 551st were to come in. We pulled out some of the poles put in to prevent gliders. There were mines on wires between some. We shot at them but we had no real tools for removing the poles."

The immediate concerns for Dick Seitz upon the assembly of his troopers were to take over for Don Fraser in front of the Château Ste.-Roseline and to help break out Boyle's small garrison before the enemy enveloped it. On D-plus-one, Lt. Carl Starkey, the *Les Enfants*-twin to John Lissner, led a pair of D Company platoons into Les Arcs from the north. One of the units then pushed through to contact some of the embattled Boyle troopers. The still-outnumbered Americans hung on, fending off the enemy with their own small arms and aided by 4.2 mortars as well as marauding Air Corps P–51 Mustangs that dumped 500-pounders on the foe.

Bill Lewis was with a mortar section from F Company that set up shop behind a house near Le Muy. "A mortar squad leader and I went up into the attic and observed and directed fire from there. We fired all day, helping to keep the Germans from crossing the railroad tracks to our front. We made one mistake. We fired near dusk. The mortar flash outlined the house. The next round fired by the Germans missed the house. Before they could get off a second round, the observer and I were sharing the basement with the family who lived there. That second shell went right into the attic. None of us in the cellar were hurt."

For Sgt. Buck Miller, there would be one more disagreement on tactics with the lieutenant from his company. "We were watching Germans walking up and down the railroad tracks across the valley in front of us. I asked Lieutenant —— several times to let us go after them but he said, no, we would shell them when the 4.2 mortars came up. We could see the enemy very clearly, about five to eight hundred yards away which was too far for rifle fire.

"Then they started shelling and I got hit. As they were taking me off the hill back to the aid station, we passed Lieutenant —— and he was hunkered down so deep in one of the German-made foxholes, all you could see was the whites of his eyes.

"Back at the aid station, which was a farmhouse, they put me on a table. On the mantelpiece over a fireplace there sat a bottle of whiskey. I said that it sure looked good. One of the doctors asked if I wanted a drink. But then the other one said, 'Think we ought to go and take the arm off?' The first doctor answered, 'No, let them do it back at the hospital.' That's how close I came to losing my arm."

But Miller's days as a combat soldier were over. He rode an ambulance back to an evacuation center on the beach before boarding a hospital ship. He would never return to the 517th.

The orphan status continued to afflict the 596th Airborne Engineer Company even before they took off from Italy. The brass requested the CO submit his needs for DRAGOON before they ever informed Captain Dalrymple of his objectives. Unlike infantry assaults, engineer operations were supposed to determine their loads based on the types and amounts of bridges that might need to be blown, the capacity of the aircraft available and other specifics. Dalrymple could only requisition the basic materials which included approximately 6,000 pounds of explosives, 2,000 pounds of land mines, fourteen mine detectors, several bazooka bundles and a few other items.

The contingent that included Engineer Ernie Kosan had previously separated, temporarily, from the 517th PRCT. The 1st Platoon of the 596th Parachute Engineer Company was detached from the 517th RCT to work with the 509th Parachute Battalion, a veteran combat outfit that had been part of the airborne forces during the invasion of Italy in September of 1943. "I was proud to be attached to an outfit with the reputation of the 509th," says Ernie Kosan. "The objective was to secure the bridges into Le Muy for the advancing seaborne troops. It seemed like a simple, classic operation. But we were naive.

"While we waited on the tarmac to take off, we received a welcome bonus, grapefruit juice with a good, stiff shot of medicinal alcohol. Also we were given four condoms and four prophylactic kits. These had to be shown to the officers as we boarded the planes. Failure to display them would eliminate you from the jump, which would then be treated as a case of desertion.

"I wore on my left calf a knife taped to the uniform. On my right calf was a hand-held walkie-talkie. My chest had my reserve chute and my pack. On my belt was my canteen, first-aid pack, entrenching tool and ammo container. Additional ammo was in pockets inside the skirt of the jump jacket, together with the condoms and pro kits. Attached to the helmet webbing was a second first-aid kit with a couple of vials of morphine. The rifle was slung, muzzle down, on the right shoulder. And on my right side, under my arm, I carried a gas mask.

"As the platoon radio operator, I was responsible for packing in the bundle the SCR 300 radio and the spare battery, more than sixty pounds altogether. On the way to the drop zone we sat quietly on the plane, lost in our own thoughts. We were also completely bushed after the physical exertions and emotional stress prior to boarding the plane. We were discouraged from leaving our positions to look out the door because of the sheer bulk of our equipment. Anyway, because of the overcast and fog it was impossible to see anything.

"Finally the red light came on and the jump master alerted us to get ready. Then the familiar commands, one after another, 'Stand up! Hook up! Check equipment! Sound off for equipment check!' That sequence occurred almost by habit. I was third man in the stick, after our platoon leader, Lieutenant Hild, and Platoon Sergeant Roberson. We shook hands and wished one another luck.

"Then came the final command. 'Stand in the door!' The engines throttled back and the nose was dropped and the plane began to shudder. The red light continued glowing, for an eternity it seemed. Suddenly the green light came on. The jump master screamed, *'GO!'*

"The jump seemed like any other, except in this case it was a relief from tension. My chute opened and it was quiet—eerily quiet. There were no shouts, no laughter, no banter. I knew there were others out there but I couldn't see them. We were descending in a dense, cold fog. I assumed the 'prepare-to-land position' and waited. Suddenly, I heard below noises which chilled me to the marrow of my bones—these were crashing sounds. I thought, God, no, a water landing. I began saying my prayers because very few troopers can survive a water landing. The equipment is like a pair of concrete boots. Add to that the drag of the parachute and you're a goner.

"Then I hit a clump of shrubbery and the ground. It is impossible to describe the feeling of relief upon being safe on *terra firma*. All was quiet. I freed myself of the riser lines and took off the chute harness. The gas mask came off and went into the bushes.

"Abruptly, I froze. I heard a loud sound from the bushes. I couldn't remember the password or counter-sign. I crouched with my carbine and waited. Incredibly, a British paratrooper came striding through the brush. He saw me and without any preliminaries asked in a nor-mal voice, 'I say, have you seen anything of my chaps?' All I could answer was, 'No.' 'Cheerio,' he said and dis-appeared back into the woods."

Another engineer discomfited in the first hours of AL-BATROSS was Sgt. Jim Moses. "While sitting in the planes waiting to leave, an air corps colonel came by and called all the pilots to the rear. He shook hands with them and said, 'I'll see you at breakfast.' Nobody even told me I was going to have breakfast and that sort of discouraged me a little.

"I saw the coast when we passed over it and threw my Mae West back in the plane. There were three of us then trying to get a bundle out of the door when Dick Shell knocked all of us out. When I looked down, I thought I was headed for the Mediterranean without a life jacket, but when I entered the fog, I knew it wasn't the water below. I landed in a tree. The first man who came along didn't bother with the sign and countersign; he just said, 'That's a helluva place to put a chute.' He helped me down but in all of the anxiety, he went one way and I another. Never saw him again. Both Shell and Paul Roberson, who went out with me, broke bones. Rober-son, with two broken ankles, found the nerve and adren-aline to walk to an aid station."

The 596th not only did not jump as a unit into Southern France but it also was well dispersed. One group fell at Le Muy, a town designated for future assault and which lay four miles from the planned DZ. The jump brought serious injuries to two men, one of whom was Pvt. Henry Wikins, Ernie Kosan's fellow refugee from Germany. Heavy mortar fire on the Americans forced them to pull back. Because of the severity of Wikins's injury, a broken leg, he could not be removed. A day later he was found dead, apparently executed by the Germans. The murderers cut off his penis and stuffed it in his mouth, perhaps because they knew he was Jewish since he wore a Star of David on a chain around his neck.

"This had a profound effect on our attitude towards the enemy for the rest of the war," says Charles Pugh. As both a radioman and a demolition specialist, Pugh had made his jump with a forty-pound radio strapped to him, several blocks of TNT and the usual field pack, weapon and extra ammunition. With his two chutes, Pugh figures he bore between 130 and 140 pounds.

"My group," says Pugh, "missed its drop zone more than anyone else. About sixty of us landed some thirty miles off. We marched, mostly at night, and after three or four firefights with Germans trying to retreat, we contacted the main unit on D-plus-two. We ate K rations but we had all the wine we could drink, which came from the French people as we marched through their villages. We also picked up some potatoes, tomatoes and onions, even an occasional chicken, while traveling on foot."

Allan Goodman and his 3rd Platoon had been designated to support the 3rd Battalion and flew in that fifty-aircraft serial. Part of the contingent, including Goodman, came down in the foothills of the mountains a disastrous twenty to twenty-five miles off course. Goodman remembers, "We couldn't have been more than 200 to 250 feet high when we jumped at 04:00. I located a couple of men from my stick but due to the steep, rocky terrain, the rest couldn't be found. We discovered a path leading us to the village of Callian. It was beginning to get light and I knew from the study of the sand table we were nowhere near the intended area.

"As we progressed, I was much relieved to hear a challenge and meet my platoon sergeant, Corey Gibbons, with about a dozen more men, mostly 517th infantry. Gibbons had been our cadre sergeant and was very able, with six years in the Army prior to the war."

Their meeting actually occurred in a walled courtyard garden of a house. The woman there greeted them warmly and her pretty, fifteen-year-old daughter insisted upon kissing the troops, still smeared with face paint, on both cheeks.

When another civilian advised them three troopers were facing some fifty Germans down the road, Gibbons, Goodman and several others joined an infantry lieutenant with eight men to confront the enemy. The gun battle lasted fifteen minutes and left six Germans dead, thirty-seven as POWs and two of the Americans with wounds. Throughout the next few days, the engineers in Goodman's area engaged in a series of skirmishes that destroyed German transport and inflicted heavy casualties.

Engineer Joe Miller received a special assignment, collection of all equipment in the bundles dropped by one of the regimental headquarters planes. "I went into combat with a planeload of strangers, men I had never met before. The sergeant in charge screwed up the chute drop, making it impossible for me to see it on the way down.

"I landed a few hundred yards north of Highway 7N right by the Nartuby River. I touched down on the unseen edge of the river bank, and to my surprise tumbled backwards over the cliff to the edge of the water. In the process, I sustained a fractured right foot and was left hanging by my chute which caught in treetops above the bank.

"Although I was not badly hurt, my dangling position made it most difficult to get out of the harness and ready for battle. During those awful seconds which seemed like hours, I realized someone was wading the stream and approaching my position. A moment of panic occurred but then I decided to remain very silent with the only weapon I could reach, my jump knife, firmly held in my right hand. It was my intention to defend myself with the knife if this person seemed to be the enemy."

When the stranger was only inches away from Miller, he uttered the password. Miller quickly acknowledged and then, while unloosing a blue torrent of curses because of his foot pain and predicament, gratefully accepted assistance in climbing up the river bank where he could more easily discard his chute. Unhooked, Miller realized that his Samaritan carried no arms and in fact was Chaplain Charles Lynn Brown. Embarrassed by his language, Miller accompanied the chaplain toward the highway.

"We were suddenly halted by the booming voice of a British sergeant major who had already assembled his troops and was preparing to do battle in Le Muy. I was impressed that he had his act together so quickly while we still seemed in limbo."

The two Americans continued to trek in search of comrades. A Frenchman on a bicycle approached and when the paratroopers halted him he was so frightened he fell off. According to Miller, "He seemed suspended in midair for several seconds while his bike continued towards town."

Chaplain Brown interrogated him, asking where they were and whether Germans occupied the town. To Brown the terrified man jabbered responses in a loud voice. The chaplain commanded, *"Tais-toi,"* French for telling a barking dog to shut up. Brown later said, "I have regretted my un-chaplainlike language. But I was afraid of German patrols in the area. When the man got up, he started back for his village. I told him to go to his fields but not return 'this way.' "

Miller and Brown parted after meeting others from the 517th. The chaplain in fact had seriously injured himself on the jump. Major Vella diagnosed a broken ankle and arranged for him to be shipped to a hospital in Naples at the first opportunity. Miller could not function effectively. After hiking several miles, he removed his boot and then found walking further impossible. He too soon headed for the hospital in Naples.

The 1st Platoon of the 596th with Ernie Kosan had been designated to aid British troopers but Kosan never found the Tommies. However, T/5 Hal Roberts and Staff Sergeant Hoffman from the supply section, who landed near Le Muy, hooked up with the Brits after several desperate hours.

Roberts recalls the first frantic incidents as he was entangled with a bush that pierced his backpack housing. "I lay there on my back, listening to the bullets chew up the bushes, and I thought I was dead. I got out my Beretta pistol for one last shot if it was to work out that way. Finally I heard someone yell, 'Roberts!' That drew a new burst of fire. After another interval, a crashing sound and more rapid fire, I saw Staff Sergeant Hoffman. I thought he was dead but he moved, whispering, 'Are you all right?' I explained that I was pinned, so he fixed the problem by cutting through my shoulder strap."

The two noncoms discussed their plight in whispers and began to look for a route of escape from the many enemy soldiers around them. As they crawled about they came across several corpses, troopers cut down by enemy fire. "As dawn was breaking, we cut out a grapevine each, stuffed the branches and leaves into each other and sat in a row until the Germans checked out our area. I was sure they could hear my heart beat as I sat there, pistol ready for my last shot. They cruised the row to the side of me and were satisfied that there were only dead in that grape vineyard."

The pair of troopers, bloodying their hands and knees, wriggled through the orchard. They neared what was apparently a soldiers' barracks and command post behind a stone wall. "We crawled as close to the barracks as we dared and watched German soldiers play with a wounded trooper in the front yard. He was hanging in a tree there. We counted sixty men, but could have counted some twice. We watched as they talked, gestured, and mounted motorcycles to go into Le Muy and back. There was nothing we could do for the dying trooper."

Roberts and Hoffman continued to look for an escape route. A ditch alongside a road appeared promising but an enemy machine gun blocked the way. In the lead, Roberts fired twice and both of the crew slumped over. They entered a sluiceway with water shoulder deep for Roberts and up to Hoffman's chin. In an open area, they paused to let the sun dry them. After a catnap they continued their odyssey until a French boy saw them. "He kissed my dirty old arm brassard and told us 'Les Anglais were là.'" It was a forty-strong platoon of English paratroopers under a soft-spoken major.

The Americans offered the intelligence that they'd disposed of the machine gun and the British decided to attack the German quarters although they were probably outnumbered. The two engineers assisted in making plastic explosive grenades, big ones with dynamite caps. Says Roberts, "We all sneaked up to the wall, then ran the last 100–150 yards, yelling, 'Bash 'em! Bash 'em!' The grenades went over the wall. There was one hell of a lot of concussion and black smoke. Those boys fanned out on a dead run into the openings with the Tommy guns chattering away. They stitched the second floor and in five minutes had a bunch of dead and prisoners. They stopped at 3:00 P.M. and had their spot of tea which they shared with us."

Roberts and Hoffman were thus at the scene as their fellow engineer Ernie Kosan arrived with comrades for the final assault on Le Muy. Shortly after his encounter with the British trooper in search of his "chaps," Kosan had located his equipment bundle through its glowing red light. He removed the radio and assembled it but abandoned the extra battery. "I was conscientious but not so that I felt like carrying an extra thirty pounds."

His platoon slowly assembled, gathering in a gully, and luckily had no jump injuries. From the direction of incoming shells lobbed at known enemy areas by naval forces supporting the seaborne invasion, the troopers located themselves as being near the coastal road to Le Muy. There seemed to be no duties for them to perform on behalf of the 509th so they struck out for Le Muy, which was designated as an objective.

As dawn broke, Kosan was among those at the bridges of the approach to Le Muy. A British paratroop outfit pushed the enemy back but could not seize the town. Not until a day later, with U.S. gliderborne soldiers committed, did Le Muy fall.

The 517th's regimental intelligence officer, Capt. Albin Dearing, captured near the village with eight other troopers after inflicting considerable damage upon the enemy shortly after landing, actually helped negotiate the surrender of Le Muy. Freed from captivity also was John Alicki's demolitions noncom, William Brown, and others of the squad taken prisoner almost immediately after they landed.

It was about 6:30 that evening when Kosan recalls, "A tank commander who had lost his radio asked me to tune to his frequency and relay his orders. I, of course, did. Some hours later, we were officially detached from the 509th and made our way to the command post of the 517th. This is when I heard of the jump injuries in the 517th and of the terrible death of my friend Henry Wikins.

On D-Day plus one, Rupert Graves remembers he received a gift. "A soldier drove up to the CP in a big, black German car built rakishly low to the ground. It was a welcome present, as we had no transportation and needed vehicles to get around and deliver written reports to Task Force Headquarters. The back of the car was quite a mess, however, as it was about half full of blood and what looked like brains scattered on the floor. When I remarked that the car was a little untidy, the soldier said, 'Colonel, don't worry about that.' He fired a round through the floorboards, allowing the gore to drain out."

Graves's sporty transportation came from a platoon led by Lt. Harold Rearden which set up a roadblock on Highway N7. Unaware of the American presence, the German staff car, motoring along the route with two officers in the back, paused at the roadblock under the impression the soldiers were their own. While the officers started to give the Hitler salute, trooper, Steve Weirzba, let fly a rifle antitank grenade. In his excitement, however, he forgot to arm it and the missile failed to explode. But it struck the driver squarely in the back of the head, spilling human detritus over the floor. The two officers, realizing their mistake, leaped from the vehicle but small arms cut them down.

The fluid nature of the combat area caused a number of unexpected confrontations. Pvt. Richard Lynam of H Company participated in one. "Lynam," says Robb, "at times was accused of fabricating his stories. He always carried a six-shot, .45 caliber revolver, U.S. Army Model 1917. It had a left-handed holster and Lynam always wore it on the right side with the butt forward, Wild Bill Hickok style. He claimed he got the piece from a Chinese naval officer killed during a street fight in Havana before December 7, 1941. That may have been a fairy tale but the other incidents with Lynam had witnesses.

"On the morning after the drop, Lynam was walking in a town with the .45 in hand when a German captain on a bicycle rode around a corner towards him. They were so close to each other that Lynam's shot knocked the German completely off his seat but the bicycle continued the few feet between them and ran into Lynam. He removed some things from the man's body, including a picture of a French girl. Later, Lynam told someone this girl was *his* fiancée. Most of us didn't believe it. He also claimed to have pictures of a fiancée from his West Virginia home. Later, these items would muddy the mystery of Lynam."

Lt. James Reith at another roadblock provided a red roadster for his company commander but under more unfortunate circumstances. When the automobile roared down the highway, Reith says, "We shot the driver right out of his seat and the roadster careened into a ditch but wasn't badly damaged. The driver was not a German but French. What a helluva mistake!"

Lt. Ben "Sweet Pea" Renton from the 3rd Battalion organized his heavy-weapons section to deal with an antiaircraft gun mounted on a truck. Having accomplished his initial task, Renton had checked in with Zais, whose battalion at this moment consisted of Company I and a handful of Brits. "My platoon was posted in a cemetery outside the town of Callas. We were hit by a motorized patrol, three bikes and a scout car. Firing through a stone wall, we raked them with machine gun, M–1 and a bazooka fire. Platoon Sergeant Nunnery knocked out the scout car and one bike escaped. Two 9 mm bullets struck my left leg after passing through a heavy chocolate bar above the box of detonators in my pocket. The platoon medic sprinkled sulfa on it and bandaged the wounds.

"I sent a runner to town about the action and the message back was to hold the position. At dawn I dispatched another trooper to Callas. He returned telling me Company I had left. We bypassed the town until we reached a keystone type of bridge. I set off charges and dropped the bridge but a German patrol showed up and cut loose at us. We got away and when I found I Company I yelled at Colonel Zais for leaving the platoon hung out there. Major McMahon grabbed me and took me aside to calm me down. He said it was his fault, not Zais's.

"Later I reported to the regimental aid station and Major Paul Vella probed my wound. He told me he had lost a lot of medical supplies, especially the ether that was supposed to come in on gliders. To dull the pain as he poked the wound and removed the slugs, he gave me 100-proof whiskey. Hung over, with my wound pains and an artillery barrage, that was the worst night I ever spent."

On the same afternoon that Graves received his gift of a racy auto, the weary 3rd Battalion troopers, having marched more than twenty miles along mountain roads, plunked down their exhausted, sweating bodies along the slopes by Château Ste.-Roseline. Sprawling under anything that would shield them from the afternoon sun, the men expected a night to recover their strength. However, Rupert Graves believed any delay in the operations around Les Arcs might jeopardize the entire mission. He ordered the 3rd Battalion to attack.

Bereft of sleep for as much as thirty-six hours, H and I Companies led the assault with G in reserve. Ray Cato's 75 mm howitzers, bolstered by the 4.2 mortars flown in by glider, poured 1,000 rounds upon the enemy in a period of twenty minutes. To some of the 460th it seemed like a contest to see who could fire the most. Everybody assisted in the loading, including captains and lieutenants. While the guns were still in recoil after firing, another shell was being loaded for almost immediate re-firing. German prisoners later asked whether the victors had belt-fed howitzers.

The troopers jumped off a few minutes after 8:00 P.M. It seemed unlikely that anyone could have with-stood that avalanche of fire, smoke, white-hot phospho-rus and shrapnel. But Zais's forces met stiff fire. The attack bogged down as the Americans hugged the ground. Zais said, "I knew I had to get them to move up into position, to cross the line of departure. I was just breaking out into the open and I kept walking. When I walked out there and said, 'Come on, let's go. Every-body get up,' the firing for whatever reason stopped."

There were two companies up ahead which had halted in their tracks. Ludlow Gibbons says, "I got across the embankment and saw there was only one other man there. I came back to the other men. I looked up and saw Lieutenant [Harold] Freeman walking on the top of the embankment. I yelled to him to get down before he got killed. He came down. A few minutes later I heard rifle shots and saw that he had been hit. He had gone back on top."

Zais's version is slightly different. "First Sergeant Gaunce had been shot in the throat and when Lieu-tenant Freeman went to help him he was hit in the belly. Then a third man went down. I thought, 'Boy, this is bad.' I wasn't sure what to do. Every time someone tried to get up on the railroad embankment ahead they were shot. I called for mortar fire from the chemical bat-tery that had come in on gliders because the 460th with its pack 75s couldn't get the right angle.

"My S–3 had been injured and the acting S–3 was a great youngster but getting very nervous. 'Colonel, I'll do anything you want to do, but this is suicide.' I said, 'What would you suggest?' He answered, 'We can't go over the embankment. Gaunce has been killed. Freeman has been killed.' He sounded almost hysterical.

"I said, 'We'll do what we've got to do. They're not going to shoot if all of us appear at once.' The mortars put down a barrage and then we attacked. The enemy came out running, hands up. There were about eighteen of them and they all surrendered."

The citation accompanying Zais's Silver Star states that Zais, "completely disregarded the enemy fire and moved out into the open in direct observation of the enemy, shouting to his men to continue forward. Inspired and encouraged by the actions of their battalion commander, the men rose to their feet and continued the attack with vigor."

Howard Hensleigh was there. "We hadn't had rations and the attack was through a vineyard. During the attack, each man would reach up for a bunch of grapes when pinned to the ground by enemy small arms fire. We were to advance across railroad tracks. Only a few of us got over and that's when Freeman and Gaunce were killed. For some reason they missed me on the way over. Each time after firing I changed positions and saw the old spot kick up dust. Sawicki and Fenton were going to town with their BAR and bazooka on the houses and the hedgerows. That music sounded good. I went back over the tracks to get more men across, even if I had to toss them by the seat of their pants. The plan had changed and we moved down the railroad track. Caylor and I got two guys in the hedgerow and a P–38 pistol each. Mine slipped out of my pocket later that night.

"The next day, early, things were quite badly fouled up. Someone had misread the map and when we thought we were at the south end of Les Arcs we were about 800 yards from the objective. I was rather irritated at the incompetence and asked to take a squad into town to see what was there. They gave me troopers from 'H' and we took off. A few French showed us a house where they said some Jerries had American prisoners. It was early and the guards were not too alert. We took them and let fourteen 45th Division men loose, arming them with Jerry weapons. Just then, another Frenchman told us there were Jerries coming up the road. I split the boys, put them behind a stone fence a little over waist high. We let the Krauts get to point-blank range, then came up over the wall. They all dropped their weapons and yelled 'Kamerad!' Not a shot was fired. We went back and the battalion moved into Les Arcs. The patrol is the story behind my Bronze Star."

Ed Johnson from C Company and part of the original band with Bill Boyle, which almost had been destroyed at Les Arcs, was among the victory party that occupied the town. "I confess my view of the enemy changed when we took about fifty German military students prisoners. They were just kids, like us. Their small equipment bags spewed out pictures of their loved ones, just as ours would have. We turned them over to the French FFI where I am sure the sentiment was different."

All along the front the Germans died, surrendered or retreated. The 551st Parachute Battalion and British troopers captured Draguignan, bagging also Reith's intended victim, General Neuling. From out of the hills trickled several hundred members of the 517th, men who'd been listed as missing and were feared dead or prisoners but who in fact had fought small skirmishes with the enemy on their own or on some occasions tied in with scatterings of the FFI. Actually, few members of the 517th found the French helpful for much more than a rather dubious form of intelligence. "If you saw them around waving their weapons," remarks Di Stanislao, "you could be pretty sure the enemy was long gone."

The contact with armored units attached to the 45th Infantry Division in the vicinity of Le Muy, and whom Ernie Kosan assisted inside the village, marked the success of DRAGOON. The soldiers who had waded ashore on the Riviera had linked up with the airborne forces holding the interior.

John Forrest was still with the group controlling N7 when they observed armored scout cars working their way along the road. "At first we thought it was another German attack but then we recognized them as from the 45th Division. When the lead one pulled up, a red-haired soldier stuck his head out and asked, 'Does anybody here know "You Are My Sunshine"? I can sing the harmony.'"

With hostilities temporarily reduced to the occasional sniper, Howard Hensleigh requisitioned a handful of troopers to scout Montaroux. "I found Doc Plassman wearing a white uniform, just as if he were a part of the small hospital. All the boys were there and that was a relief since we heard all kinds of rumors how the Jerries had treated them. I made arrangements to have them evacuated by ambulance."

Now that the shooting had died down and DRAGOON was concluding, the 517th parachute infantry units counted the toll absorbed. It added up to nineteen dead, 126 wounded and 137 injured, which is a high fourteen percent of the complement. Furthermore, the casualties occurred in less than a week of action and do not include the losses suffered by both the 460th Parachute Field Artillery and the 596th Parachute Engineers.

Boundary Change of Sept 3, '44

Col de Turini

Lantosque

Moulinet

Peira-Cava

Utelle

St. Jean-la-Riviere

Mont Gros

Sospel

ITALY

Pont Charles Albert

Levens

Col de Braus

la Roquette

517 SSF

l'Escarene

517 SSF

INITIAL BOUNDARY

REVISED BOUNDARY

ITALY

MENTON

Var

Pont de la Manda

MONACO

MEDITERRANEAN

NICE

0   5   10
Miles

During the Champagne Campaign, the 517th drove east, across the Var River, up into the Maritime Alps towards the Italian border against strong resistance, particularly in the vicinity of Col de Braus.

CHAPTER IX

THE CHAMPAGNE CAMPAIGN

"BY D-PLUS-FOUR or -five, it was definitely over," says Phil Di Stanislao. "Rumors abounded on our next destination. We were told to deposit all our live ammo, shells, cartridges, bandoliers, hand grenades at a central spot. The word was we would return to Italy. That fantasy lasted for about six hours until we were told to retrieve everything we had put down. Our mission now was to protect the eastern flank of ground troops moving up the Rhone River Valley."

The course set for the 517th ran roughly parallel to the Riviera coastline into the Maritime Alps. Ultimately, it would pinch off the border between France and Italy, tie down German forces and protect the flank of the troops now moving up from Mediterranean ports into the belly of France. Also committed to the strategy were the 509th and 551st Parachute Battalions charged with clearing resistance between the 517th and the Mediterranean Sea in a kind of tandem move. Because of the potables produced in the region and occasional opportunities to visit the Riviera resorts, the military operations became known as the Champagne Campaign but it would be anything but a bubbly pleasure.

Rupert Graves replaced Maj. Ike Walton, his injured regimental executive officer, with Mel Zais, designating Maj. Forest Paxton, formerly his plans and operations specialist, to take over the 3rd Battalion. "Paxton was a westerner, like me," says John Chism, the noncom in charge of the 3rd Battalion medics. "He was quiet, not a professional soldier. But he was smart, brave and considerate. He usually positioned himself up front where he could get quick information and apply his personal knowledge to the situation." The musical chairs process seated the 1st Battalion's exec in the slot formerly occupied by Paxton. Bill Boyle picked his Company A CO, Don Fraser, to replace Bowlby.

With the few vehicles designated by their T/E still in transit from Italy, the troopers of the 517th were expected to hoof it. The 596th Engineers commandeered a small number of captured enemy trucks and cars to haul their heavier supplies. The 460th FA dragged their pieces by hand with an occasional lift from borrowed jeeps. The artillerymen back-packed their ammunition. Rifle units, limited to a pair of jeeps per battalion, stuffed with communications gear and reserved for medical evacuations, loaded themselves up and marched toward the enemy. A few troopers reverted to thievery of small vehicles which slightly eased the use of human beasts of burden.

Between their original positions achieved by the 517th with the success of ALBATROSS and the Maritime Alps lay an increasingly difficult series of natural obstacles. The troopers would need to ford the Siagne, Loup and Var Rivers, traverse several steep gorges and start climbing in the rugged hinterlands where distances listed on a map would stretch from thirty to fifty percent.

The bodies manufactured by the process begun at Toccoa generally stood up well under the forced-march pace towards the new objectives. Capt. Daniel Dickinson, the 3rd Battalion surgeon seduced from a soft spot running a hospital dispensary by Mel Zais, however, was not at the same high level of fitness. "Instead of killing

himself," says John Chism, "Dickinson adopted the
practice of not taking a break. Instead, he started near
the head of the column where he could be located
quickly if there was a need for his services. Gradually, he
would fall back down the column. When we reached our
destination or his services were requested, he would
keep walking until he caught up. He would be drenched
with sweat and near exhaustion. But strong-willed as he
was, there was never a complaint nor hint of pain on his
part. By the time we struggled up the Maritime Alps,
Dickinson was back in shape and gung-ho."

Dr. Ben Sullivan, recovering from his bout of dysentery in Italy, could not make the ALBATROSS jump. But
as his condition improved and he received news of the
Southern France invasion, Sullivan on his own looked
for a way to rejoin the outfit.

"I went to an airfield hoping for a ride on a bomber
headed for Southern France. Air operations refused to
check out a parachute to me. They seemed to think I intended to do a free fall from a bomber, which was indeed what I planned. Then I found an airplane that was
traveling to Corsica. I tried to convince the pilot of the
B–25 to add thirty minutes flying time and let me parachute into Southern France. He refused. In Corsica, I
met a navy medic, an old buddy who had interned with
me. Through him I located a PT boat headed for the
Riviera. I asked if they could dump me where I could get
to the 517th. But they said they were only taking stuff to
Monte Carlo which was neutral. I got off for a brief time
in Monte Carlo. It was odd to walk around and see German officers on the streets, as well as a few British and
Americans."

Back at Corsica, Sullivan discovered a British LCT, a
landing craft equipped to carry tanks but loaded with
supplies, bound for the vicinity of Cannes. "The ship
pushed right onto the white sand beach and the bow
doors opened for unloading. I went ashore and walked

up the hill away from the beach. When I was perhaps half a mile inland, I heard AA fire, both .50 caliber and 37 mm. I saw a plane, presumably German, a few miles up, and which appeared unfazed by the fire directed at it. Suddenly a loud boom and a cloud from an explosion rose from the ship I had just left. I learned later that the blast came from a guided glider bomb, used on an experimental basis in Southern France. The LCT was destroyed. I considered going back to help with the wounded but I saw an ambulance headed there and decided the 517th needed me more."

Sullivan continued his journey, hitching a ride on a truck that brought him near the front. He found a small hotel willing to accommodate him for a night and a nearby officers' mess fed him with no questions. He reasoned that the best way to find his unit was through a field hospital with wounded paratroopers. He located an installation consisting of two tents for patients, one tent for surgery and a fourth for mess. In one of the tents he saw two familiar faces. They advised him of the capture of Les Arcs a day earlier. When a jeep arrived with more wounded, Sullivan hopped in for a return trip which carried him home to the 1st Battalion. He now accompanied the troopers wearily plodding towards the enemy and the Maritime Alps.

Throughout the combat period, troopers, who like Sullivan could have delayed their exposure to the perils of battle, demonstrated time and again their loyalty to the outfit, going to extremes in order to rejoin their comrades. After the crash of their C–47 at Orbetello, Ed Athey and the four able-bodied troopers from his stick had immediately sought out transportation to the fighting. Indeed, Lt. Albert Robinson of 2nd Battalion Headquarters Co. had gone AWOL from a hospital in Italy to participate in DRAGOON and lost his life as a consequence.

Following the track that would lead into the Maritime

Alps, Dick Seitz and his 2nd Battalion struck out for their initial objective, the town of Fayence. "I sent a patrol under Lt. Walt Irwin on a patrol into the area of Fayence. Irwin brought back accurate and fairly detailed info on the enemy emplacements and particularly the locations of their 20 mm guns."

Irwin had left his patrol when they initially came under fire and on his own proceeded a mile, to infiltrate the town. On his way back to his unit, Irwin barely escaped a murderous fusillade from German automatic weapons. The sketches made by Irwin provided such precise locations that the well-concealed 20 mm installations were destroyed with a salvo of artillery. For his efforts he would receive a Silver Star.

The success of Irwin's mission prompted Seitz to call upon the foe to yield. "We sent a message to the German garrison commander that if they didn't surrender, we 'would blast them out of the town.' Initially, he replied, 'You won't do it with those peashooters,' meaning our pack 75s with which the 460th would support our attack."

From a nearby olive grove, Pfc. Bill Hudson from the 596th watched the scorned 75s toss shells into Fayence. "I noted a hit on a stone wall of a house which barely dented the plaster. Shortly thereafter, however, we saw a German ammo dump in the town explode. The fireworks were magnificent."

The ability of the building walls to resist the artillery, and his denigration of the American firepower notwithstanding, the *Wehrmacht* officer surrendered his entire force of 184 soldiers just before Seitz ordered the first shots fired in his scheduled attack.

The troopers dispatched their prisoners to the rear and slogged forward towards Grasse which had been bombarded by artillery. "We bypassed it," recalls Company F's John Lissner. "Grasse had been a center

Lou Walsh, the first CO of the 517th, did not take the outfit into battle but saw combat in the Pacific. *(Courtesy U.S. Military History Institute)*

Lt. Col. Dick Seitz headed the 2nd Battalion. *(Courtesy Gen. Richard Seitz)*

Lt. Col. Bill Boyle, center, led the 1st Battalion. Lt. Mickey Marks from C Company flanks Boyle's right, with supply officer Bill Price on Boyle's left. *(Courtesy William Boyle)*

Melvin Zais commanded the 3rd Battalion and then became executive officer for the Regimental Combat Team.

Rupert Graves succeeded Lou Walsh as the 517th's CO and led the outfit throughout its combat career.

Dick Seitz sits seventh from left; John Lissner of F Co. is third from left; Battalion exec Tom Cross is sixth from left; and Carl Starkey D Co. is second from left. Standing are Dean Robbins of B Company CO eighth from left; F Company CO George Giuchici eleventh from left; Walter Irwin Hq. Co. thirteenth from left; and demolition counselor Murrey Jones second from right. *(Courtesy Tom Cross)*

Officers of the 2nd Battalion gathered at Camp Mackall. Standing, from left to right, are Jack West (Hq. Co.), Robert Newberry (E Co.), John Lissner (F Co.), Tom Cross (Bat. exec.), Dick Seitz, Joe Kizlewicz (E Co.), Paul Quigley (E Co.). Seated, left to right, are Bill Hale (Hq. Co.) and R. Schmitt. *(Courtesy Tom Cross)*

At an officers' club table, left to right, Lt. Gail Rounds and Lt. Carl Starkey hold down the rear seats while Lt. Leonard Cooper and Lt. John Lissner occupy the front positions. *(Courtesy John Lissner)*

Lt. John Lissner congratulates enlisted men of the 2nd Battalion after they earn their parachute badge at Fort Benning. *(Courtesy John Lissner)*

Ludlow Gibbons served with the 3rd Battalion through all of the 517th's campaigns. *(Courtesy Ludlow Gibbons)*

Cameron Gauthier was a member of the 460th Parachute Artillery Battalion. *(Courtesy Cameron Gauthier)*

Nat Schoenberg, from the 460th Parachute Artillery, did KP at Camp Mackall, N.C. *(Courtesy Nat Schoenberg)*

Lt. John Forrest won a battlefield commission shortly before being seriously wounded in the Champagne Campaign. *(Courtesy John Forrest)*

Ernest Kosan, an émigré from Germany, joined the 595th Airborne Engineer Company. *(Courtesy Ernest Kosan)*

Richard Robb fled the cavalry in favor of airborne, winning a battlefield commission. *(Courtesy Richard Robb)*

Jack Burns, an irrepressible schemer, proved a redoubtable trooper. *(Courtesy Richard Robb)*

Lt. O. J. Nunnery won his bars on the battlefield. *(Courtesy Richard Robb)*

Ed Johnson, one of the early Toccoa boys, fought with C Company. *(Courtesy Ed Johnson)*

Howard Ruppel joined the 517th as a replacement just before its first time under fire in Italy. *(Courtesy Howard Ruppel)*

Harland (Bud) Lorel, Hq. 1st Bt., stands by plane a few hours before DRAGOON. *(Courtesy U.S. Military History Institute)*

ABOVE: At Toccoa, a youthful gang of would-be troopers from D Company underwent the process that would turn them into parachutists. Kneeling, from left to right, are Canziani, Stegall, Konolusci, Martin and Haney while Young, Ericson, Cohen, Simmons and Dellucci stand. *(Courtesy U.S. Military History Institute)*
BELOW, RIGHT: A stick from the 517th, lined up before their aircraft just before DRAGOON, includes (front row) Anderson, Duzinski, Hauslin, Knoechelman, Lytton, Jones, G. (standing), Forrest, Steger, Larson, Caunois, Dice, Morrow, Hunter and Finley. *(Courtesy John Forrest)*

LEFT: Cpl. Charles Keen, B Company medic, enjoys a soft landing in a North Carolina cotton field. *(Courtesy Charles Keen)*

Capt. Dean Robbins, the B Company CO, Lt. Pop Moreland and Lt. Richard B. Bridges enjoy a pause after capture of fort in Sospel. Moreland and Bridges both earned battlefield commissions. (*Courtesy Charles Keen*)

At Colle Sr. Loupe, France, 517th officers Capt. John Dugan, 1st Lt. Terry Sanford (later North Carolina Governor and Senator) and a bushy Bill Boyle take a break. (*Courtesy Charles Keen*)

BELOW: Members of C Battery of the 460th Parachute Artillery toured Rome during the summer of 1944. Seated are Joe Habetz, Cameron Gauthier and Bernard Baragree; kneeling are Joe Marko, Norbert Bergstrom, Pembroke, Bill Honston, Schneider and Junie Kawamuria. Standing are John Brunner, James Motir, Albert Gallwas, a British Tommy who joined the party, Charles Nielson, Tony Castagnaro, A. Bouchard, Pat McGraw and Joe Miller. (*Courtesy Cameron Gauthier*)

Battalion Surgeon Capt. Ben Sullivan shares a moment with Bill Boyle in southern France. *(Courtesy Charles Keen)*

William Bradley near Naples; he received a battlefield commission during the Battle of the Bulge. *(Courtesy Charles Keen)*

LEFT: A 1st Battalion inspection involves, left to right, Lt. Col. Bill Boyle, Lt. William Price (S/4) and Charles La Chaussee, C Company CO. *(Courtesy Charles Keen)*

RIGHT: Before boarding a 40 & 8 en route to Soissons, John Garcia, Billy Davis and Doc Keen lean on Sgt. Don Strange, Stan Rozwood with top hat and Steve Wierzba at left. *(Courtesy Charles Keen)*

About to head overseas, a group of 1st Battalion troopers faced the camera. From left to right in the back row are Armando Cobos, Stedman, Needham, Sgt. Andrew Murphy with rifle, the first KIA of the 517th, Davis, Hartnett and Setness. In the front row are Reese, Clark Archer, Kellogg, Stompro and Bolin. *(Courtesy Charles Keen)*

Replacement Joe Holten arrived during the Champagne Campaign. *(Courtesy Joe Holten)*

Near the stiffly resistant enemy position on Hill 1098 in the Maritime Alps, a 2nd Bat. Hq. Mortar platoon consists of Collins, Leonard, Butler, Fritz, Knee, Wold, standing left to right, while Tunstall, Kane, McDaniel and Dodd kneel. *(Courtesy U.S. Military History Institute)*

In southern France, troopers Twibell, Cyrus, Wayda, Duggan, Haynes, Goodsell and La Rochel have climbed into the Maritime Alps. *(Courtesy U.S. Military History Institute)*

LEFT: Cpl. Joe Locke loads a sled with medical supplies, M-1 and bedroll in Belgium. *(Courtesy U.S. Military History Institute) ABOVE RIGHT:* T/4 Jessie Welch, Hq. Co. 2nd Bn., cooks a steak in the Ardennes. *(Courtesy U.S. Military History Institute)*

A 1st Battalion patrol from the 517th pauses in its search for the enemy during the Battle of the Bulge. *(Courtesy U.S. Military History Institute)*

This year-old lioness acted as a mascot for the 517th until it raked 1st Battalion CO Bill Boyle with its claws.

ABOVE, AND RIGHT: Several troopers wait along a snowy Ardennes trail. *(Courtesy U.S. Military History Institute)*

At Camp Mackall, some of the medics included, standing, second from left, John Chism, and Bill Harvey on his right. In the back row at the far right is Lt. Ray Spendlove, who transferred to the 11th Airborne and was a KIA. Squatting are Lloyd Pennington at left, KIA at Bergstein and Joe Podloski. *(Courtesy John Chism)*

TOP LEFT: Nolan Powell earned a Distinguished Service Cross, the second highest honor given, for his valor in Italy. *(Courtesy Nolan Powell)* *TOP RIGHT*: Sgt. Allan Goodman of the Airborne Engineers survived several nasty jobs clearing mines. *(Courtesy Allan Goodman)* *MIDDLE LEFT*: Lt. John Saxion went AWOL in order to join the 517th while it struggled through the Champagne Campaign. *(Courtesy John Saxion)* *MIDDLE RIGHT*: Trooper Milton Johnston was a Co. B KIA near St. Jacques. *(Courtesy Charles Keen)* *BOTTOM LEFT*: Trooper George "Monk" Meyers from Thief River Falls, Minn., was killed at Coulee, Belgium. *(Courtesy Charles Keen)* *BOTTOM RIGHT*: A grave marker notes the final resting place for Ledlie R. Pace, killed Dec. 23, 1944, at Soy shortly after the 517th rushed to halt the German advance. *(Courtesy Charles Keen)*

Lt. Ben "Sweet Pea" Renton posed in a dress uniform with the shoulder patch of the 17th Airborne Division. *(Courtesy Ben Renton)*

Melvin Biddle, a replacement in Italy with B Company, receives the Congressional Medal of Honor from President Harry S. Truman in the White House Rose Garden.

At Sammy's Bowery Follies in New York City, Capt. John Lissner of F Company is third from left while the 460th Forward Observer Tommy Thompson is at extreme right. *(Courtesy John Lissner)*

Some of the 14,000 Who Flew Into Beachheads

Taking it easy before the jump, these American parachutists relax in a C-47 troop carrier as it wings toward their objective in Southern France.

The jump master (standing) gives final instructions as the 12th Air Force plane approaches the dropping zone.

There's still time for a smoke and a laugh . . . At least 14,000 airborne troops—'chutists and those landed by plane and glider—have dropped behind the beachheads.   Signal Corps Radiophotos

A now defunct New York City newspaper, *PM*, carried pictures of unidentified paratroopers flying towards their drop in southern France. "Taking it easy" in the top frame are, from left to right, Phil Di Stanislao, Barney Hekkala and Joe Chobot. At bottom left, the "jump master" is Lt. Chopper Kienlen speaking to Carl Kiefer. At bottom right are troopers Kochersberg, Donleavy (with cigarette) and Lincoln. The appearance of the newspaper startled Di Stanislao's family, who had no notion of their son's involvement in DRAGOON. *(Courtesy Phil Di Stanislao)*

Lt. Ed Athey (left) survived a plane crash on takeoff from Italy and reached France aboard a glider. He posed with platoon sergeant Fred Harmon (center) and Pvt. Walter Friebel, later killed in action. *(Courtesy Edward Athey)*

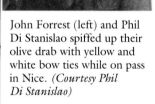

John Forrest (left) and Phil Di Stanislao spiffed up their olive drab with yellow and white bow ties while on pass in Nice. *(Courtesy Phil Di Stanislao)*

Forward observers Tommy Thompson (left) and Joe David Brown, wounded after earning a battlefield commission, celebrated at a reunion in the States.

for manufacturing perfume and the smoke from the fires carried the aromas of the scents to us." Engineer Ernie Kosan also detected the smell of flowers as he moved by Grasse.

Mel Zais actually entered the town. "I was standing on a corner watching a column pass by. Then I was alone in the town and decided I needed a haircut. While I was in the barber chair, a man approached me and spoke excitedly, pleading. I knew a little French from high school and college courses and understood more than I could speak. This fellow wanted me to accompany him for an important reason. His sincerity convinced me to go.

"We walked a short distance and then entered a perfumery with basins full of crushed flowers. He led me up five flights where two elderly women welcomed me, bringing out wine and cheese. I sat there, wondering what it was all about. Then a very old man in a wheelchair was rolled in by one of the ladies. His skin was parchment and he had the look of old people, red blotches on his skin, his eyes red-rimmed, sort of rheumy and almost tear-filled.

"When that old man saw the American flag on the shoulder of my uniform, he wheeled his chair over and burst into tears. He patted the American flag on my shoulder. He was sobbing, almost convulsive choking. The problem was obvious. The Americans had landed but he didn't believe it. So they needed to have an American in uniform with a flag on his shoulder so the old boy could see we were really there."

This sort of experience was replicated in other ways for Zais. "In a couple of French towns, one of the most poignant, touching things I saw were the little school children out on the streets singing the 'Marseillaise.' The people would present flowers and offer wine."

He continued to have contact with French forces, occasionally employing them to interpret for him. "But they weren't reliable and we learned not to depend upon them. We would never engage in an operation which would fail if they did not show up."

While the Americans may not have shown high regard for the FFI or the Maquis, the Germans treated them savagely. Several times troopers discovered fields where a number of men, still wearing their arm bands, had been executed.

Sullivan was not the only member of the 517th to enter neutral Monaco. The U.S. Navy wanted to retrieve and examine some German torpedoes seen bobbing along the shoreline. Since the pathway to the beach seemingly had been mined by the retreating enemy, the Navy requested help from the 596th engineers. Lt. Glenn Gainer led the detail with Pvt. Art Kemp at the wheel of the jeep and Ernie Kosan in the rear with a radio.

"Permission for passage through Monaco," says Kosan, "had been obtained by the Navy. Our little two-jeep convoy, the Navy in front with us behind, proceeded through the principality. It was a strange feeling because the war had not touched or affected Monaco. There was no German occupation and the people showed no visible signs of the war around them. We were gawked at as if we were aliens from another planet."

The engineers stopped at a deserted luxury hotel with an outdoor swimming pool overlooking the crashing breakers. Their binoculars spotted the torpedoes floating in the surf just beyond a very rocky shoreline. Because the path to the water was so steep and stony, minesweeping equipment could not be used. Instead, the trio very cautiously made their way down toward the sea, encountering a series of trip wires. "Each one had to be examined carefully to make sure it wasn't double-acting, that it wouldn't explode if you decreased or increased the tension. As each bomb was defused, we placed it to one side with identification to allow eventual destruction. We finally reached the shore and I taped a secure path."

Kosan and his mates were rewarded with a treat from the grateful navy officers. The two enlisted men, with their lieutenant, were invited aboard a ship for the evening mess. "What a repast! It had been months since we had a meal like that, sitting down at a table with real dishes, silverware and napkins!"

While Seitz and his troopers took Fayence and detoured around Grasse, Paxton directed his 3rd Battalion against the stronghold of St. Cezaire. The town sat on high cliffs across the Siagne River and several hundred German soldiers appeared poised for strong resistance. Supported by artillery, at 7:00 P.M. G Company swung around in an encircling move while troopers from I Company waded the Siagne and started to climb the cliffs. During the intervals between barrages from the big guns no enemy appeared. Under cover of dark, concluded the observers, the Germans had slipped away.

But as I Company reached the halfway point up the steeps, the Germans opened up with machine guns and mortars. Doggedly the troopers continued their ascent until they could bring their rifles and grenades into play. By midnight the town had fallen with twenty-one enemy dead, dozens of wounded. The assault team lost five KIA and another twenty wounded. The 596th specialists dismantled an intricate network of mines and booby traps for the unwary who might wander down narrow lanes or the pathways to the local wells.

Forest Paxton received a Silver Star for "exposing himself to intense enemy fire, and displaying great physical endurance, courage and leadership . . ." as he personally urged the troopers on in the face of the withering fire from the defenders.

A few days later and thirty miles further to the east, the combat team faced the enemy dug in across the Var River. The stream was perhaps three-quarters of a mile wide but in the drought of summer much of it seemed dry although, unknown to the Americans, in some sections, water flowed briskly. The main bridge had been damaged by demolition but the Americans believed it could be repaired. However, on the German side, a pair of sentries loitered, more than likely with instructions to blow up the shaky span once the Americans appeared. To forestall that plot, Cpl. Leslie Perkins and Pfc. Reginald Richards volunteered to overcome the German guards.

The pair stripped off their shirts, removed their helmets, tied sweatbands around their heads and pulled their pants out of their boots, to disguise themselves as native workmen. They placed weapons in the bottom of a wheelbarrow and then innocently trundled it across the bridge. When they were but a few yards away, the two enemy soldiers became suspicious and went for their firearms. But Perkins and Richards were quicker and killed both. The bridge became the property of the Americans.

Medic Charlie Keen with B Company participated in the advance to the Var River and beyond. "The fighting now was a matter of chasing the enemy eastward and always up the highest mountain in the area. The people would cheer you as you went through town after town and usually hand you some wine which you had to grab for a quick pull because we never stopped. On one occasion, as we tried to cross the Var, a firefight held us up until daylight the next morning. After dark, Don Strange, Hump Schumacher and I sneaked back to some cottages and were given wine and beer. There were about six couples there and soon they got out a mandolin, accordian and guitar, pushed back the tables and we all began to dance.

"They called for a dance they said was something like 'La Napolitan.' We went around in a circle like the Paul Jones and when an order was called, we would change and reverse direction. The highlight came when the ladies spun us around and jumped up on our backs, piggyback fashion. We all had plenty to drink but Strange's partner weighed about 225 and when she climbed on his back, Strange—who stood maybe 5′6″—started slowly sinking to the floor, yelling, 'Dammit, Doc, help me before this woman breaks my back!' They ended on the floor with a thump.

"After the dance we returned to our lines and the platoon. Each lady walked with us and their husbands brought up the rear. But there was no hanky-panky, just grateful people thanking us for liberation. Sneaking back into the bed-down area, I stepped smack dab in the middle of Lieutenant Fisher's stomach. 'What the hell?' he demanded. I just whispered as quietly as I could, 'Shoosh, I think they might still be in the area.' "

There were two citadels of resistance, the villages of Levens and La Roquette. Dick Jones with the 2nd Battalion's E Company was part of the force committed to the assault on La Roquette. "Our route was over a ridge, down the side of a gorge, across the river, up the other side of the mountain to form an attack from the rear. It had been prepared with an artillery barrage which included white phosphorus that burned off most of the vegetation.

"We were advised by our FFI guide that since it was summer, the river would be no problem, only ankle deep. Around midnight, off we went. It was absolutely pitch-black. Over the ridge, stumbling down the side of the gorge it was easy to keep track of the man in front. You kept falling on him. Finally we reached the rocky and gravelly riverbed. Have you ever tried to walk quietly on gravel on an ink-dark night, knowing that if anyone hears you, all is lost? The roar of the 'ankle deep' river got louder all the time. Finally we got to the edge and it was about thirty feet across, waist deep and running about twenty miles an hour, a regular torrent.

"As we struggled to get across, Scott got the mortar base plate crosswise to the current and was swept downstream. Someone pulled him out, less base plate and helmet. Finally we all got across, soaking wet, then began to climb the other side of the gorge. When the artillery burned off the vegetation it left soot and ashes. Combined with our soaking uniforms, this made us look like chimney sweeps after a hard day.

"We formed up and attacked in darkness. We took La Roquette house by house, room by room. In one house we captured two Germans. In another room was a woman and two children behind a mattress against a wall. We put the mattress back and told them they could stay. Finally the resistance ceased, the prisoners were put under guard and the rest of us sacked out.

"The next morning we looked over their gun positions and fields of fire. One flare at night as we crossed the river and we would have been vulnerable. It was also a good thing we came from behind them since all of their positions aimed the other way. The first emplacements we took were the mortar positions, behind the town."

Battalion commander Dick Seitz considered his E Company capture of La Roquette under Capt. Bob Newberry, "the most impressive combat operation in Southern France. It was textbook all the way."

The fall of La Roquette persuaded the Germans to abandon Levens, the second redoubt behind the Var. They retreated skillfully, employing small raiding parties to harass the Americans while they headed for more strongly fortified places in the Maritime Alps.

The 596th troopers, detailed to deactivate and remove the mines and booby traps left behind by the retreating enemy, could often depend upon French folks to tell them where they had seen the devices placed. But when they reached the Var River Valley, some of the rocky riverbed was dry.

"The Germans had set poles with wire strung between them," says Allan Goodman, "and hung 155 mm artillery shells attached by spring-loaded detonators in the shell nose. There were antiparatroop and glider landing-prevention devices. Sgt. Howard Jaynes and Ernie Coffelt, along with Leonard Mathis, were clearing a path across the road for jeeps and supply vehicles. The method was for one man to lift the shell to line up the hole for a safety pin while another man knelt below to catch the shell after the third man inserted the pin and cut the suspension wire. Something went wrong—a sophisticated secondary trap or a mistake. All three were killed in the explosion. Howie Jaynes had been my closest friend, both of us made sergeant at the same time, had gone home on leave together and had double-dated while on leave.

"When I heard of the accident I went to the site and stayed with the remains until Graves Registration showed up. The explosion was all horizontal, leaving only legs and torsos for identification. Graves would not have been able to tell which remains belonged to which man.

"There was a memorial service in Chicago for Howard Jaynes which my mother and sister attended. When the organist did not arrive, some of the family went through the congregation asking if anyone could play the organ. Mother volunteered, much to my sister's consternation. She said, 'Mom, you have never played an organ.' Mom replied, 'Yes, but I've always wanted to.' She proceeded to play her favorite hymns, as she had on her piano, by ear."

The crossing of the Var completed the first phase of the Champagne Campaign. In spite of probing thrusts from the two sides, the troopers tasted their first respite since plunging to the French earth. Howard Hensleigh and other 3rd Battalion officers, the highly esteemed Capt. Joseph McGeever, Capt. Bill Pencak and Lt.

Ludlow Gibbons took advantage of the lull for an uneventful visit sampling the pleasures of Nice.

During the first few days after he had parachuted into France, John Forrest incurred a wound, one he considered so slight that he did not believe it merited medical attention. "With the example of Lynch [the badly burned trooper] and Sergeant Ford [after a bullet passed through Ford's calf, necessitating a painful probe by a medic, he continued to fight] I just applied sulfa and a bandage and tried to forget it. But in time the wound became infected and I had to go to a field hospital for further care.

"At the hospital I was impressed by the excellent treatment of severely wounded Germans who were brought in. My infection quickly responded to penicillin, a good bunk and hot chow. But my stay was cut short when the hospital came under shell fire and it was necessary to pack up.

"Phil Di Stanislao of Company A was in the same hospital [he had contracted a high fever] and while everyone was preoccupied with moving, we decided to go AWOL from the hospital and go back to the battalion, which we did by hitching a few rides with supply convoys." The two would pair up subsequently for their own memorable visit to Nice.

The German resistance stiffened considerably as August faded. On the last day of the month, Don Fraser accompanied a patrol gathering intelligence along the roads approaching the heights of Col de Braus and Peira Cava. Says Fraser, "We got some bad information on where the Germans were. A jeep from the antitank company of the 442nd Combat team, attached to the 517th, with Lt. R. L. Emmons and three GIs rounded a bend on a mountain road. German fire knocked them out. Emmons and one man managed to crawled back to me. I was coming up on foot.

"I inched forward along the edge of the road to the disabled jeep, but machine gun fire pinned us down so much we couldn't raise our heads off the road. Then Ben Sullivan came crawling up the road, right where the machine gun was hitting the roadbed. I had to order him back around the bend until we could get the wounded back to him. Just about then I heard the cough of a mortar and one round landed just below us in the ravine. I knew the next one would drop on us. Trying to drag one badly wounded trooper around the bend we had pushed him to a place beside the back of the jeep. The mortar banged once more and the round struck right on that wounded trooper; that was the end of him.

"A Frenchman had come up over the ridge top and started a truck up the road, behind the cover of trees. He let the truck coast quietly around the bend above us, and before the Germans realized it, he was rolling by us, heading for the cover round the next curve. As he passed us, we threw the one wounded man who was still alive on the truck and ran alongside it around the bend. Doc Sullivan treated the wounded and evacuated them. They patched up Emmons and he returned to the outfit later." Fraser's role in saving the casualties brought him a Silver Star.

Both Col de Braus and Peira Cava proved to be tartars for the combat team. Actually, three strategic sites, L'Escarene, Tête de la Lavina and Col de Braus all had been abandoned in the first days of September. But the strategists at Task Force Headquarters decided to shift units about in an effort to reorganize the order of march. The change in responsibilities vacated some valuable real estate and the enemy swiftly exploited the opportunity with veteran troops brought in from northern Italy. The 517th troopers would have to recapture all three places now strongly defended.

Col de Braus, which consisted of a few buildings, blocked the high road that led to a good-sized, important town, Sospel. To Dick Seitz's 2nd Battalion went the job of pushing the enemy out of Col de Braus. D Company, whose executive officer Lt. Carl Starkey actually served as the field commander, started out for the objective. Starkey himself took a platoon up the steep slopes towards Col de Braus. Misinformed that Col de Braus was empty of enemy, the troopers learned the truth when peppered by small arms.

The platoon with Starkey had climbed perhaps a mile before they ran into a sheer, thirty-foot wall of rock. Unwilling to lose more time with a long detour, Starkey and two scouts started to make their way up the barrier. The lieutenant tripped over a wire and the explosion wounded one scout while temporarily rendering Starkey dazed and deaf. He recovered and doggedly continued using foot- and hand-holes. The remainder of the platoon followed, encouraged by Starkey's remark, "Ain't this a helluva way to make a living!"

When the D Company troopers quietly lifted themselves over the crest, they surprised a platoon-sized contingent of German soldiers, off guard because they assumed their mines and the cliff would keep them secure. The brief gun battle left seven enemy dead while eleven surrendered. However, reinforcements started to show up, and they brought both artillery and mortar fire against the Americans.

Starkey's diminishing band formed a semicircle with their wounded and the cliff behind them. Pvt. Felix Povinelli, a runner, slipped through German patrols to bring the facts of the situation to the attention of Seitz and his staff. By morning, the remainder of D Company had joined the battle, bringing in machine guns and mortars with them. The arrival of comrades allowed evacuation of the wounded who had to be passed by hand down the same precipitous wall and hill climbed by the first attackers. According to Rupert Graves, the enemy zeroed in on the Red Cross markings of aidmen seeking to remove the casualties.

The battle raged through the day and another night. Not until September 7, almost two days after Starkey and his associates began their trek towards Col de Braus and G Company from the 3rd Battalion relieved them, did the Americans firmly possess a foothold. But that only made them vulnerable to both artillery and counterattacks originating on the dominant nearby mountain, Tête de la Lavina.

Colonel Paxton charged G Company's 2nd Platoon led by Lts. Arthur Ridler and Dick Spencer to roust the nearest infestation of Germans. Like John Forrest, both officers had left hospitals treating their minor wounds without waiting for a formal discharge. The defenders occupied a series of well-constructed dugouts and pill boxes that in some instances seemed almost impervious to the projectiles launched by the 460th and the heavy mortars. The platoon encountered brutal blasts from cannons, machine guns, rifles and *panzerfausts*. Several times the enemy repulsed the American advance and a machine gun cut down Ridler as he tried to lead his men to the next crest. Two days of desperate fighting failed to increase significantly the turf, known as Ridge X, held by the 517th. The costs to the 517th at this point included Ridler, three other KIAs and ten wounded, including Lieutenant Spence who added another Purple Heart with a chunk of shrapnel in his backside.

Ben Sullivan remembers, "There was a dome-shaped pillbox atop Tête de la Lavina with a gun that produced more casualties than any other single piece of artillery. It would pop up and fire, then pop down. Colonel Cato brought one of his 75s right up to the base of Tête de la Lavina and they would bore-sight and fire as soon as that

German gun popped up. But nothing worked. They even got the Navy to blast away with their big guns. Nothing seemed to work."

Scouting the action with his binoculars, Paxton discovered that the Germans were taking refuge behind the thick stone walls of a few buildings until Ray Cato's artillery fire was lifted. Then they would sprint back to their positions where they could bring downpours of small arms and mortars upon their attackers. Paxton communicated with Cato and the American artillery halted a barrage momentarily. When the foe emerged from their hiding places to take advantage of another apparent lull, the 460th gunners blanketed the hillside.

As the remainder of G Company sought to flush out the last pockets of resistance, Paxton directed the CO of I Company to lead an attack from nearby Mount Scandeious aimed at linking up with G Company. When Paxton at his command post had heard no word from I Company, his exec, the former University of Montana football tackle, Capt. Joe McGeever, headed for Mount Scandeious with Sgt. Dan Brogdan.

McGeever discovered the captain from I Company, an officer always suspect in the eyes of his troopers, in a funk, cowering in a cave and unable to function. McGeever assumed command of the outfit and chose a platoon under Lt. Reed Terrell to lead the advance. As Joe McGeever, followed by the platoon, hiked toward the enemy, troopers from I Company who had already met considerable resistance from well dug in Germans during their patrols warned of trouble. McGeever, aware of the pressure upon G Company back at Ridge X, dismissed the intelligence.

Wilbur H. (Bill) Terrell, a distant cousin of the platoon leader, was with the group under McGeever. "I came to I Company from the guardhouse at Camp Mackall. Captain McGeever then had said, 'Just what I need, another Terrell.' I had acted in many capacities in the 517th and at the time of this assault I was serving as a medic. I was directly behind point, which consisted of Captain McGeever, Lieutenant Terrell, Sergeant Brogdan and Pvt. Willis Woodcock. We had advanced to the top of the hill without incident. The point disappeared over the crest and there was immediate gunfire, then silence.

"Everyone hit the ground, knowing full well that someone up ahead had been hit. I got up and, in a half crouch, followed the path taken by the point through the underbrush. I came into a clearing and right upon six German soldiers who surrounded Sergeant Brogdan. They were as startled as I and turned their guns on me. I did some mighty quick gesturing, explaining I was a medic. They searched me for weapons, took a pair of scissors and a scalpel. Then I was left alone while they formed their circle around Brogdan.

"I went first to Captain McGeever who was lying on his back. He was already gone. I suspect he died instantly [four machine gun bullets had pierced his chest]. He had been stripped of his personal belongings. I then went to the private, who was on his back, unconscious yet breathing. Then I went to Lieutenant Terrell who was conscious and in great pain. His right hip and buttock were practically blown away with a great loss of blood. I put a large gauze pad over the wound and injected a morphine ampule into his leg.

"The private started to breathe very hard. I knew I couldn't take care of both men. I made it known to the Germans who were about to leave with Sergeant Brogdan that I wanted to get help. They sent a young soldier with me, why I don't know.

"As I came back over the top of the hill I kept shouting, 'Don't shoot. This is Terrell. Don't shoot.' But as soon as the Jerry was spotted behind me, everybody opened fire. I hit the dirt; the German was hit in the abdomen. I put a square gauze pad on him to keep his insides from spilling out.

"Lieutenant Maciac and, I think, Lieutenant Pierce questioned me whether we should attack or hold off. I said, 'Hell, I've got to go back over there and get two men.' They pulled back from the hill.

"I went slowly back over the hill. I knew they would be waiting. But they were all gone. I went first to the private and tried to raise him up. He died in my arms. I heard a shout, looked up the hill and a Jerry had a sight on me. Someone, I never knew who, shot him. I got Lieutenant Terrell up, and halfway carried, dragged him back to our lines where John Chism and others took over."

Chism evacuated both the lieutenant and the young wounded German who had accompanied Bill Terrell before being shot. Terrell's heroics earned him distinction only among his mates. He never received any official recognition for his valor.

According to Chism, "When we started up the Col de Braus–Sospel highway, we encountered some determined folks among the opposition. They let us follow on their tail until we reached a spot in the gorge where you could almost reach both sides at the same time. It was so narrow that they selected a curve with the road hanging about fifteen or twenty feet above the river. Then the rotten bastards blew about fifty feet of the road into the river. The engineers performed another of their miracles by repairing the blocked place." Chism fails to remark that his efforts on behalf of wounded during this period brought him a Silver Star.

The enveloping action proceeded in spite of the fallen. In the week-long struggle, begun when Carl Starkey dragged himself over the edge of the cliff to open the fight for Col de Braus, the enemy had inflicted 147 casualties, including twenty-one dead, 123 wounded and three captured. The losses added up to more than the normal complement of a 517th rifle company.

During the G Company attacks, the enemy fought from behind the thick walls of French-built pillboxes. Dick Robb witnessed a remarkable episode that climaxed a drama he had seen just before the start of ALBATROSS. "In view of many of us, a GI had climbed up and was atop the one pillbox everyone was shooting at. Someone shouted, 'Cease fire, he's one of us!' Apparently oblivious to all the action, this character dropped a white phosphorus grenade down the vent pipe. As those inside came stumbling out, he jumped down and took them all prisoner."

Robb recognized the intrepid trooper. "Here comes Woodrow McQuaid down the road with eight Germans ahead of him. Word had come down that 'Whomever that man was, Colonel Zais wanted to see him.' I had no doubt that Zais had seen the whole thing and that he was told who the hero was. I watched McQuaid trot up to Zais, give him the biggest and most exaggerated parade-ground salute you could imagine. He also flashed that ear-to-ear grin he did so well. Zais was trying hard to be professional and not smile, but it was difficult for him.

"I was too far away to hear the conversation but could see it. Zais supposedly said, to the effect, 'Was that you up there, McQuaid?' McQuaid answered, 'Yes, sir, colonel. I got all the prisoners too.' Then Zais told him he had done one hell of a job and he was lucky that his own hadn't shot him.

"McQuaid said, 'Colonel, I got something for you and I want you to have it.' From underneath his blouse he pulled out a beautiful wooden piece that could be worn as a holster and also serve as a stock to be attached to a pistol. Inside, it held a Luger pistol, chrome plated with an eight-inch barrel. It was absolutely beautiful. 'I got it from a German officer. It's yours, colonel.' He handed it over to Zais, holding it in both hands as though he were presenting the king his crown.

"It's hard to say who had the biggest grin. Supposedly, Zais said, 'I guess we can forget about those court-martial papers, McQuaid. And you don't know how lucky you are to be alive. Now away with you. Go.'

"McQuaid saluted and mumbled over and over, 'Yes, sir, colonel. Thank you, colonel.' He kept grinning as though his God had truly granted him absolution. I don't know how Zais did it but I know he would not have made the promise he did in Italy if he couldn't have made good on his word. What a leader of men!

"We all knew Zais was not for sale. McQuaid had already completed his part of the bargain and even though he was the most uncomplicated of men, he was not stupid enough to think he could bribe Zais. The pistol was not that. It was his way to show his undying respect for the one man he considered if not a god, certainly the closest thing. Zais with his infallible insight into men, sensed McQuaid's reasoning and allowed him to have this day. I am certain that in McQuaid's lifetime, never again would he have a day as good as that one."

Such moments, however fraught with meaning for those immediately involved, were hard to savor at the time. The enemy retained strong positions even as the territory controlled by him shrank. The menace from the heights of Tête de la Lavina continued. Rupert Graves plotted strategy to eliminate enemy presence from that height.

Among the positions blocking achievement of Graves's strategy was a knoll designated Hill 1098. John Lissner with F Company drew the task of driving off the foe. "We had Hill 1040, with a huge dip between it and 1098. We attacked with two platoons and in a fierce fire-fight took 1098. It had a clear view into Sospel but it was most unwise to have many soldiers occupying such a small territory. We decided to rotate platoons. We would stay on top for a day or a day and a half and then the direct fire would drive us off. We'd notify battalion and the next morning, another platoon would go up and get the Germans off. But then they'd come back and take over. This went on for several days. We were sitting ducks up there and the shelling had denuded the place, leaving no tree cover. You couldn't dig in either, the ground was practically solid rock. I told Dick Seitz I'd like a bullhorn so I could yell to the Germans, it's your turn to take the hill. I was tired of getting our asses kicked.

"When we were on top, our artillery observer could direct fire right into Sospel. In peacetime, 1098 was a park for sightseeing. You could see over to Italy, even a piece of Monaco and the Mediterranean."

The positions held by both sides were tenuous. Howard Ruppel, the replacement trooper who joined F Company in Italy, held the job of wireman, responsible for maintaining the field telephone lines between outposts and the command post. On the outskirts of Sospel, Ruppel was advised one morning that the forward positions did not respond when called. It was assumed that shelling had severed the wires on the ground and Ruppel started up the pathway looking for the break.

"Unbeknownst to us in the rear echelon, the guys up front saw the enemy in large numbers scaling the hillside and nearing a crest where they would cut off their path of retreat. Seeing they were outnumbered, the GIs took a hazardous and unused route that would bring them back to the rear echelon.

"I had no idea the men from the outposts were thus headed for safety whereas I was going the other way. I meandered along, one eye on the phone line and the other on where I was going. Unexpectedly, just below the crest I saw three helmets in the underbrush. We surprised each other for none of us were in a ready firing position. They responded quicker than I did. I hit the ground as the rifle fire zinged over my head. I grabbed a grenade, pulled the pin, held it momentarily, very momentarily. The enemy being so close, I didn't want to give them time to throw the grenade back. I lobbed it and soon as it exploded I jumped up, fired my carbine in their general direction. Then I turned and ran like all get out. Fear is a great motivator for bursts of speed.

"I ran right into a patrol sent out to check on my welfare. Boy, did I greet them with enthusiasm. When I told the lieutenant what had happened I babbled on and on about my narrow escape, expressing a selfish concern for my welfare. After this incident, however, I received a three-day pass to Nice and later the Bronze Star. A newspaper story reported I killed three Germans, two with the grenade and one with my carbine."

On September 18, a Time Over Target (TOT) concentration enveloped Tête de la Lavina in a firestorm of high explosives, white phosphorus and smoke. TOT was a technique in which all artillery missiles arrive at the target simultaneously as a result of careful calculations by gunners, regardless of the size of their pieces or their distance from the site. It guaranteed maximum coverage of an area and in this instance included naval guns, big field artillery pieces as well as the 460th's pack 75s. Mortars, ranging up to the 4.2s blasted the mountain and at 8:30 A.M., half an hour after the extended bombardment began, the troopers of the 517th's 3rd Battalion, firing bazookas and tossing white phosphorus grenades into bunkers forced the Germans above ground. Sixty-one enemy soldiers surrendered—some with clothes still smoking or burning from the grenades—thirty or forty died while the U.S. had only four men slightly wounded.

German artillery retaliated when the Americans sought to press their advantage. A mortar round killed Lt. Hillard Thomas from H Company but the enemy retreated further, some holing up in the resort village Peira Cava and most strengthening the garrison at Sospel.

When B Company set out to remove the Germans from Peira Cava, medic Charlie Keen accompanied the riflemen. "We were headed down a steep path when they opened up with automatic fire on us from atop the mountain across the valley. The first burst hit Red Eberle and Fred Ellison. Fred took about ten slugs in his long legs and Red had maybe two of the same. Bullets were coming right down on us and we had little or no protection. Steve Weirzba and Stan Rozwood and myself were fortunately just behind a low rock slab when the shooting began. While I was trying to get to Fred, Steve and Stan both walked right out into the fire line and brought Red back behind the slab. I was never so proud of my platoon as that day. In less than a minute our machine gunners and every rifle in the area opened up and you could see the Germans hauling ass as our tracers told us we were on target. It also gave me some comfort while working on Fred out in the open.

"The two of them couldn't be removed after dark because the terrain was so rough. At first light the next morning we were brought up quick when they started laying 81 mm mortars on us. We pulled back to try an attack from the flank.

"Around Peira Cava our supplies came by pack mules. Grenades were at a premium as our outposts, at night, developed 'squirrel neurosis.' Any sound and we threw grenades. One night we were given the password, 'Litvinoff,' with the countersign, 'lapel.' We had a trooper from Sumter, South Carolina, and he said, 'I can't say that damn Russian word. I'm gonna say lapel and he better damn know the other word.' "

With the defenders at Peira Cava subdued, the troopers continued to patrol aggressively. One such venture featured the ancient .45 pistol toted by Pvt. Richard Lynam. Dick Robb and nearly fifty troopers from H Company set out one day through the mountain woods. "We were quite good at moving fairly large groups silently through the forests. It was close up, no equipment rattles, look sharp, no talk, mind where you step and watch for signals. We had Capt. Richard Roberts, a forward observer and his radio man for direct communication to the 460th and also our radio connection to battalion.

"One of our artillery-spotting planes had reported a German unit building log bunkers not too far from our forward positions outside Peira Cava. That couldn't be allowed. The 596th took us through our own mine field and then through Jerry's. After a while, we heard voices and noises of wood-cutting. At some distance we saw a sentry, only one it seemed. Very carefully, we moved quite close.

"The sentry, standing in front of a large bush, was reading a magazine, holding it in front of his face. His rifle leaned against a tree beside him. Lynam was closest, so word was passed, 'Hold fire until Lynam takes the sentry, then it's GO.' We could all now see a raft of Germans cutting trees and constructing bunkers. Two using a bucksaw were the most obvious. They apparently felt quite safe. Someone was whistling the tune, 'Maria Elena—You're the answer to my prayers . . .'

"Lynam stepped out from behind a tree, facing the sentry, certainly no less than forty feet away, and raised his Tommy gun. Apparently, when he pushed the magazine in, he did not slam it hard. When he pulled the trigger, the magazine fell out and the bolt, failing to strip off a cartridge, banged into the chamber with a loud, metallic clank.

"The sentry, young, hardly more than a boy, lowered his magazine and stared at Lynam, frozen in disbelief. Lynam threw down the Thompson and drew his .45 revolver. The sentry, still mesmerized, hardly moved. The .45 slug hit him in the chest; hands and magazine flew upward as he went backwards into the bush behind him. The last thing I saw was the soles of his hobnailed boots entering the bush.

"From here on it was chaos. Someone with a .45 caliber grease gun fired at the pair on the big saw, bullets twanging off the tool's steel. Others used them as a target although there was no problem of finding targets. They were all exposed and had no weapons in their hands other than axes and saws. A real turkey shoot.

"Captain Roberts signaled his radio man to join him so that as we withdrew, he could give coordinates to the 460th's 75 mm howitzers. We started our withdrawal down a steep drop into the valley, taking a different way home to give the Germans little or no targets if they could bring up reinforcements.

"Suddenly, the radio man tripped and fell. His equipment sailed out of his hands and over a ledge. We could hear it smash, tubes breaking as it bounced down the mountain. We continued down the slope while Lieutenant Hensleigh using our radio man talked to battalion which relayed the messages to the 460th. It began sending in 75 mm shells in a short time, bless them. We made it back to Peira Cava with only one casualty. Lynam, who had a broken arm. Just after he dropped the sentry, someone let go with a bazooka round. The backblast from this shot at a bunker hit Lynam, knocking him against a tree and fracturing his left arm.

"We heard that he took his .45 revolver with him to the hospital. First, they tried to take it away on the grounds it was government issue. He pointed it at a major, telling him there was no way he would let him steal it. Then they sought to use a general anesthetic to set his arm. He refused, saying they would steal the piece while he was out. So they told him he would have to have it fixed without benefit of anesthetic. Lynam said he yelled like hell because of the pain but never gave up the revolver."

Others in the 1st Battalion holding positions on Col de Braus and participating in what amounted to the siege of Sospel saw their numbers steadily depleted. Says

Phil Di Stanislao who now wore a sergeant's stripes, "Most of the skirmishes were small arms although occasionally the Germans dropped artillery shells on us. We started to realize we were suffering slow attrition, a few killed and wounded each day, enough to diminish our ranks.

"Carl Kiefer and I always dug in together. We made the hole deeper, laying logs across the top and placing sand bags around. The hole became our castle. German artillery marked our area pretty well. We felt they could see us clearly and they dropped mortars on us, fired their whiz bang, 47 mm cannon. We took a near direct hit, the acrid smell of burnt powder permeated our hole as we tried to clutch the ground while being bounced around. One day, Kiefer and I were filling sand bags and a shell hit the tree over our heads. Both of us dived for our hole. We banged heads at the entrance which was only large enough for one man. All we could do was laugh.

"At a nearby hole, Critchlow and Cammacho made their home. Cammacho went out to do his duty and while he was out there, crouched down, drawers around his ankles, they started dropping mortars on us. We saw him hobbling with his pants down, while Critchlow yelled, 'You're not going to get in here you son of a bitch until you wipe yourself.'

"At a bunker further down the line, Nailor and Stewart, when they prepared it, left a hole on top so they could stand guard. Damned if a mortar shell didn't find its way into that maybe thirty-six-inch hole and land on one of their shoulders, killing both. There wasn't much left of them." Another deadly explosion wiped out the mortar section led by Di Stanislao's friend Joe Blackwell, leaving Blackwell with a serious wound.

"Chopper Kienlen took over the company. Lieutenant C. J. Sadlo replaced one of the platoon leaders. He claimed he had been the master of ceremonies at a transvestite club and his stories to our young ears were really interesting. One day I was at platoon headquarters and Sadlo told me he was going to visit B Company down the road. There was a shelling that lasted about ten or fifteen minutes. Then a sergeant from B Company came with a .45, a pistol belt and holster. He told me these were the effects of Sadlo. When the artillery barrage began, they had all filed into a bunker. Sadlo was the next-to-last man in and when he was inside, he suddenly fell to his knees and said, 'I think I'm hit.' He was dead in a couple of minutes, a small hole in his back from a shell splinter which ruptured his pulmonary artery.

"Coming into Col de Braus there was a break in the hills and the Germans could see approaching traffic. Our vehicles learned to stop while still hidden, then suddenly speed up and go like the devil to get past the open area. Almost every time, if they could get one off, the Germans fired into the breech. One of our medics, in a jeep, was killed."

The victim was Pvt. Harold Seegar. "He was one of my most capable assistants," says Paul Smith, the 1st Battalion aid station squad leader. "Seegar asked the regular jeep driver if he could answer the call to pick up a wounded man. When he reached the area to get the trooper, he was turning the jeep about when a tree burst hit him in the back of the head, killing him instantly. He was the son of an American father and a French woman who met during World War I. Seegar's mother had died while he was a child and he had never seen his grandparents who still lived in France. He had saved all of his chocolate rations to give them when he made contact."

Among those who braved that precipitous and life-threatening stretch of road was Bill Boyle. Out to reconnoiter the area, Boyle was at the wheel of a jeep with C Company commander Charles La Chaussee as a passenger. They whizzed by that gap with nothing more than a shell whistling harmlessly overhead and proceeded to a tiny hamlet that had been the scene of a bloody engagement. Enemy dead still lay on the ground which was littered with equipment from both sides.

Suddenly mortar rounds exploded in their vicinity. As the bursts intensified, Boyle floored the pedal. He accelerated to forty or fifty miles an hour around a curve. La Chaussee flew out of the jeep and bounced off the pavement. Hauled back aboard, still wearing his overcoat, helmet and all his gear, La Chaussee was driven to an aid station. From there the medics transferred him to a field hospital near Nice. Although the doctors could find no severe injuries, he sprouted an ugly rash. La Chaussee endured several days of treatments with ointments and announced he intended to leave. The nurse notified him he could not depart without a medical discharge. La Chaussee sneaked out at night and returned to the 517th. Subsequently, a notice he was AWOL reached Boyle. Rupert Graves managed to quash disciplinary threats from the hospital commander.

Other earlier casualties trickled back to duty. Howard Bacon, saved by Ben Sullivan in Italy, showed up fit for duty. Walter Plassman, like so many others, did not wait for a formal discharge from his hospital bed in Italy. On a pass for a few days, he hitched a ride aboard an LST and joined the outfit in the Champagne Campaign. Lt. Bob Thomson, another victim from the first fighting in Italy, rejoined B Company.

CHAPTER X

SWEET AND SOUR GRAPES

DURING THE PERIOD in which the troopers held Sospel under siege, the men began to receive passes to Nice. John Forrest and Phil Di Stanislao journeyed to the Riviera city separately but joined together in a search for entertainment. "To celebrate our good fortune," says Forrest, "we broke a few rules. We bought yellow-and-white polka dot bow ties to wear while on leave. MPs halted us, of course. We explained we were out of uniform because, as alumni of Loyola University of the South in New Orleans, we were commemorating the birthday of Ignatius Loyola and the bow ties were our school colors. We added that these bow ties were the only yellow and white we could find and hoped the MPs could forgive our sudden burst of school spirit in faraway France. The MPs seemed to think the idea was splendid. Di Stanislao and I were so pleased with ourselves that we even had a picture taken of us by a local portrait photographer."

Phil Di Stanislao also recalls the pleasures of that three-day excursion. "In a square we were at a table eating ice cream. Some drunk came up to me. He wasn't a trooper and why he picked on me I don't know. He said, 'You look just like a pussy to me.' I had to get up and whip him, hard enough so he bled all over my clean shirt. After I cleaned it off, Forrest and I, while cruising the streets, saw the haberdashery with the bow ties. A middle-aged lady, an expatriate American, who spoke English asked us about the ties and I explained they were our school colors. She invited us to her apartment, served ice cream and cake. She had a phonograph and we listened to records with Sophie Tucker singing the music from the 1930s that I remembered my parents played.

"The American bar in Nice threw some good parties. Madam Regina ran a class house of ill repute where Jules Talarico, doing a stint as chute police [the need of some paratroopers to challenge the authority of regular military police continued abroad], convinced Madam Regina he was a member of the Al Capone group and a close friend of those Chicago folks, famous apparently even in France."

The steady diet of death and destruction calloused the troopers. "Some of our A Company men had killed members of a German patrol," says Don Fraser. "After a few days they were starting to smell so several of our guys dug a big shell hole a little deeper and dumped the bodies in, then covered them with dirt. Somebody remarked that maybe we should say a few words over the dead. No one spoke up until trooper Eugene Parche took off his helmet, held it over his heart. He said, 'Tough shit, amen.' Parche put his helmet back on and everyone crawled back to their dugouts."

Even Rupert Graves resorted to black humor. Coming upon another burial party for the enemy, the CO murmured, "Ashes to ashes, dust to dust. If the mortars don't get you then the M–1s must."

The grim miasma of constant death seemed to erode the last vestiges of the will to live. Di Stanislao came upon a badly wounded German. "I tried to offer him some water. He arrogantly refused. I took his canteen, set it by him and left. I never reported there was a dying German out there."

Bill Boyle continued to awe associates with his cool-ness under fire. While Company A manned positions along the trail by the ravine behind Ridge X, the 1st Bat-talion chief arrived during a quiet moment. Capt. Joe Broudy, A Company's CO, challenged Boyle to a game of cribbage. Kibbitzer Don Fraser recalls, "After Broudy won a few games, Boyle was ahead in the third contest. Then German mortars came over the ridge and ex-ploded in the ravine. Broudy dove for cover in his com-mand post. Boyle stood up and ordered him to come back and finish the game."

The introduction of the German V–2 rockets into the European theater of operations gave the troopers of the 517th, like so many soldiers as well as civilians, an addi-tional threat to fear. The upper echelons worried that the new weapon might carry poison gas. Forrest went on a patrol that captured some German gas masks which could be analyzed for any changes in their content which would give clues to what kind of gas might be employed.

"The prospect of poison gas," recalls Forrest, "was frightening. The only person in the entire battalion whom we knew had not long since thrown his gas mask away was Captain Ehly. People began to want to hover near Ehly. I often wondered what would have happened had gas been used. Ehly was a powerful man and I imag-ined a gas mask torn to bits as men struggled to take it away from Ehly. For some weird reason, the whole episode became a source of private laughter for me."

The booby traps, mines and unexploded bombs or shells plagued the troopers. Lt. Earl Dillard of the 596th Engineers received a Silver Star for meticulously placing a minefield near Col de Braus while German mortars rained down in his vicinity. Five GIs died when a booby trap blew up the house in which they had taken shelter. Allan Goodman discovered engineer George Ayling and several others removing a detonator from an unexploded 500-pound aerial bomb. "I gave them hell for risking it because it was in an open area and defusing the thing wasn't necessary."

A day later, the knowledge gained by Ayling aided Goodman. "I encountered another one of those bombs at a bridge approach. It had a timing device that seemed to have malfunctioned. I cleared the area and disarmed this one myself. I almost jumped out of my skin when at the critical moment, a local couple bicycled past and shouted, *'Bon jour!'* They had slipped by the roadblock but when they saw what I was doing and the look on my face, they pedaled away fast. Lieutenant Zavattero wrote up a citation and I received a Bronze Star. That embarrassed me some, since George and the others had disarmed a similar bomb just for the experience."

Lt. Ben Renton in the 3rd Battalion, who earned a Silver Star in Italy for his efforts to succor the wounded in a minefield, performed a similar duty near Sospel. Gingerly, Renton entered the area, marking the tripwires. He was accompanied by a battalion surgeon and they brought with them a stretcher to carry out two casualties. "As I lit up a cigar afterwards," says Renton, "Doc was shaking while trying to light his cigarette. 'Don't ever do that to me again, Sweet Pea,' he said."

Casualties depleted the commissioned ranks and in a few instances officers were transferred because of unsatisfactory performance. For example, the CO for whom Joe McGeever took over, barely escaped a court-martial. Under no circumstances would he be allowed any further combat role.

Ludlow Gibbons happened to be standing next to Zais when a truck rumbled past. "Zais said something to the effect that McGeever was in the mattress cover. He was disturbed by the loss. I liked McGeever but I guess I was getting used to people being killed."

Zais admitted the loss of men like McGeever struck him hard. "It's one of the problems in taking the cadre of an outfit into combat. You know the wives, you know the kids, you know the man. You take the deaths a lot harder than if you hadn't gone through all of this. It really bothered me when McGeever was killed. I really liked him. He was a young football player from Montana State, a good Catholic boy with high principles who was really loved by the men. I named one son Mitchell McGeever Zais and we called him Mickey Mac after McGeever."

Zais also coped with the pressure that broke some of his people. "We were near Sospel and there was a 1st lieutenant in the 3rd Battalion who ran off a hill. He was sobbing and said he couldn't go back up. Paxton reported it to me, since I was regimental exec.

"I went to see the fellow whom I knew and liked very much. He was a splendid young man. I was patient with him. I explained that we couldn't countenance this sort of thing. I warned him of his rights. I pointed out that his battalion commander was there as a witness. I pointed out that failure to comply with my orders would be direct disobedience and could be interpreted as cowardice in the face of the enemy. I said, 'I now order you to return to that hill immediately.'

" 'I can't do it,' he answered.

" 'I warn you, lieutenant, that while I am very fond of you personally, this is not a personal thing. We can't have this sort of thing go on in this regiment. We have done a lot of fighting and you have lost a lot of good friends.'

"He said, 'Colonel, I can't take artillery fire. I can take small arms fire but I can't take artillery fire. Artillery fire is coming in intermittently on that hill and I can't go up and break down in front of those men. I have done it once. I don't want to go up there and do it again.' "

Zais saw no way out. "You will be tried by a court-martial and I will prefer charges." Zais kept his word and followed through. According to Zais, the hapless lieutenant received a sentence of twenty-five years in prison but later, after the war ended, was set free. This, said Zais, was the first of "two cases when I personally was the son of a bitch who brought it to a head."

Enlisted men also cracked. Di Stanislao remembers a trooper who announced he couldn't stand it any longer and was going to take off. "By then we were all a little crazy. I told him he could take his chances. Either I'd shoot him or the Germans would get him. He obviously believed me and that if I fired I wouldn't miss."

The 517th hewed to a policy of promotion from within. Noncoms stepped up to the officer ranks. Bill Lewis, who had been one of the cadre at Toccoa, Flave Carpenter, Frank Kievit, Di Stanislao's pal Carl Kiefer, were among the many who earned gold bars. A short time after his sartorial escapade in the company of Phil Di Stanislao, John Forrest received a battlefield commission as a second lieutenant.

Replacements for riflemen began filling in the gaps. Their lack of combat experience occasionally exasperated the veteran troopers. "I was in a large bunker one time," says Di Stanislao, "with maybe a dozen men. Even though I was a sergeant, I took my turn standing guard. We had a replacement who did his two-hour tour and then woke me up. He said, 'Hold on, sergeant, I've got something here for you. It's a hand grenade.' I replied, 'There are plenty of hand grenades up on the parapet.' He answered, 'I know, but this one has the pin out.' I went a tad beserk. There we were in a dark hole with all of these men sleeping there and I wasn't about to transfer by hand a grenade with the pin out. I hauled his ass up outside and told him to throw that as far as he could and never do anything like that again. His argument was that he did it because the only way he could stay awake was by knowing he had a live grenade in his hand.

"Most of the replacements, however, turned out to be good soldiers who acquitted themselves well."

Among those who fitted in smoothly was a well-traveled newcomer, Joe Holton. As an 18-year-old Oklahoman, Holton, by his own description "kind of a wild kid," managed three months of college before he yielded to the military need for manpower in December 1942. He had worked himself up to buck sergeant with the 35th Infantry Division when the Army Specialized Training Program opened. It sent tens of thousands of soldiers to college where they studied foreign languages, science and engineering.

About the time the troopers of the 517th fell from the sky in Southern France, the army, now hungry for infantrymen, shut down the ASTP and the students put aside their books for M–1s. Says Holton, "While in ASTP, over half the fellows in my unit were from various paratrooper organizations. I got to know and really like those guys, they were my kind of people. So I volunteered for airborne training."

Upon the dissolution of the ASTP, Holton had been reduced in rank to lowly buck private. "When I got to the 517th, they were in the Maritime Alps, beautiful country. I had no trouble being accepted into Company F. I suppose because I could bullshit with the best of them. The men of F were very kind to us raw replacements. I took a liking to them right away."

Lt. John "Jack" Saxion joined the 517th under more unusual circumstances. A Pennsylvania high-school student who played a fair amount of football, he enlisted in the Army Air Corps a year before Pearl Harbor with the dream of becoming a pilot. But instead of flight school, he attended aircraft-mechanic classes at Chanute Field and then went to an airbase in Spokane. "The weather was dismal and the one B–17 we had we were not to touch."

Because he lacked the two years of college required then for pilot training, Saxion could not fulfill his dream. In November of 1940, he decided to try the Royal Canadian Air Force which did not demand advanced education. Saxion went AWOL, pausing at home before crossing the border.

His father, who'd served in the navy, learned his son was AWOL and persuaded him to turn himself in. In spite of a summary court-martial for his offense, Saxion some six months later, with the U.S. now at war, graduated from OCS with assignment to the 38th Infantry Division.

Still seeking greater satisfaction, Saxion now volunteered for paratroop instruction. "I recalled the beauty of the jumps I saw while at OCS and the pride and character of the troopers I saw at Fort Benning." But his regimental CO, instead of approving a transfer, pitched the request into the basket. "My wife had become friends with the wife of a major in division headquarters. My final request went through my wife to the major's wife to division headquarters where it was approved—the power of a woman."

Saxion sailed for Europe as a replacement paratroop lieutenant aboard the S.S. *Cristóbal* as part of the same convoy bearing the elements of the combat team to Italy. But when Saxion left the ship in Naples, he and about 100 other officers were tagged for occupation duty in Sicily. While there he received devastating news; his wife and child had been killed in an automobile accident.

Now in a holding pattern at a replacement depot ("repple depple"), Saxion, distraught over the fate of his family and impatient with the routine of the repple depple, alternated between fantasies of returning to the States to learn the details about the accident and hurling himself into combat.

Saxion went AWOL again, and on this occasion hitched a ride with two pilots to northern Italy in an observation plane. "They had only two parachutes, none for me. I joined a ragtag group of about twenty men, all AWOL. There were black Americans from service companies, some truck drivers and quite a few British, including a lieutenant who acted as CO. They had four jeeps, a weapons carrier and two 75 mm howitzers. Their self-appointed mission was to fire at targets of opportunity while avoiding the MPs.

"After five days with this group, we heard of the invasion of Southern France and I returned to the repple depple, hoping to be assigned to a combat unit. My assignment, instead, was to face a general court-martial. During the trial I offered to resign my commission and be sent to a combat unit as a private. I was told that if I gave up the commission I would be on the streets of Naples, a man without a country.

"The final decision by the army was to fine me $500 and order me to join the 517th as soon as possible. Back at the repple depple, however, the colonel confined me to quarters, in spite of my order. I had enough of this colonel. I went to a nearby air base, learned from pilots there was to be a supply drop in Southern France. I explained my situation and showed my orders.

"A C–47 pilot agreed to my request to be dropped over France. Two days later, I fell out of a plane, several miles west of the Var River. I had my carbine, backpack and a few other essential items in a duffle bag. I finally met up with a three-truck convoy for the 517th on the way to Col De Braus.

"I reported to Mel Zais, the exec of the 517th. He told me, 'Lieutenant, we can arrange to have you transferred back to the States.' I told him, respectfully, I had no desire to go home and if he couldn't use me then to assign me to another combat unit."

Zais instructed Saxion to find quarters for the night. "The next morning he ordered me to report to him. He offered an apology, explaining his concern at accepting an officer from a general court-martial. He said he now understood my situation and welcomed me to the 517th."

The Germans frequently tested the American ring around Sospel with aggressive patrols. The troopers also probed the defences, gathering intelligence, wiping out emplacements and conducting a campaign of attrition. Says Forrest, "The whole area was open to artillery fire. Shell fragments were as plentiful as gravel. [Indeed, the 596th engineers borrowed street-sweeping equipment from the city of Nice to remove the sharp particles that frequently punctured tires and an occasional unwary boot.]

"On one patrol I was on, we came upon corpses of troopers and German soldiers intermingled. We hypothesized they must have run into each other during the night and shot it out. I was struck by the way the flesh had already disappeared from the faces of the troopers while their jump suits and parachute boots remained in excellent condition. It was the reversal of what one expects—boots and clothing should wear out but not men. Later I was told that one of the dead troopers from that patrol was a classmate from Texas A & M.

"During the stalemate, I was also impressed by differences in the smells of rotting flesh. Dead animals emitted one odor while dead humans gave off a sickeningly sweet one. I thought of my cousins from World War I and trench warfare with what must have been daily encounters with that kind of stench."

Forrest had been an officer for about a week when he was part of an oversized company combat patrol that finally entered Sospel. "We met no resistance. [Seemingly the Germans had slipped away.] Mines were removed from the streets and white tape put down. But apparently, during the night, the Germans laid mines inside the tape, resulting in several casualties among troopers who believed the area within the tape safe. We discovered a route by which the enemy could come into town. I was sent to establish an ambush outpost to jump any German minelayers who might use this route.

"This trail into town had been cut into a cliff running alongside of the river. The vertical side was perhaps forty feet above the stream. It was a sheer drop and seemed unscalable. The pathway was narrow and sloped gradually, ending in a small valley. The hillside on the German side of the valley had rock walls, about eight feet high to support terraces maybe ten feet in width.

"For a couple of days, there was no action at our outpost. But on the third day, quite early in the morning, a Free French officer with four so-called Maquis from Sospel showed up at our outpost, intending to cross the valley and find German units beyond the river. I tried to explain to the officer that the Sospel Maquis were notoriously unreliable. When there was a lull in German shelling, the Sospel Maquis would break out their tricolor armbands, berets, Sten guns and parade around. When the shelling recommenced, the arm bands, berets and guns disappeared as if by magic. The officer shrugged off my warning and with his four men proceeded beyond our outpost.

"About an hour later, we heard the sounds of someone running up the pathway. We figured, at least we'd catch the minelayers. But as they neared the bend in the trail where our machine guns had zeroed in, we heard screaming, *'Allemands! Allemands!'* [Germans, Germans] Into our sight came the French. They had discarded their weapons, ripped off their armbands and were in a panic. The officer was not with them. They alleged he was dead, and there was no stopping them short of physically restraining them.

"I climbed to a point from which I could see the entire river and valley. I saw at least sixteen enemy soldiers cross the river to our side. I took my binoculars to get a clear view of what weapons they carried. In addition to riflemen they had what looked like a 60 mm mortar and a machine gun. As I watched the Germans, I saw their commander with his binoculars, searching the hillside for our position. We stared at each other for a minute, perhaps. Satisfied, he withdrew his unit from the water, taking positions around a little abandoned, shell-pocked stone farmhouse.

"I took a small number of men—there were three besides me with M–1s and a BAR. We worked our way above the Germans, using the terraces of their side of the valley for concealment. My plan was to get the enemy into a cross-fire between the restricted side of our ambush outpost and fire from our four-man group.

"Initially, the tactic worked well. But suddenly there was an explosion and two of us went down. Cpl. Cornelius T. Van Regenmorter—we called him Van Rigor Mortis—and I had our legs blown. I never found out what it was—a mortar round or a mine. If it had been the latter, the other two men who were not hurt, would probably have also been wounded.

"I tried to get back to our outpost, using my rifle for a crutch but my shattered left leg kept dragging the ground so painfully that I finally cut it off around the calf with my knife, hoping that would solve my problem. But I still couldn't make any progress. I didn't realize that my other leg was full of shrapnel, too. Van Rigor Mortis was having the same difficulty, having lost his right leg. It had been snowing and misting intermittently so we had scarves made from equipment-bundle parachutes. We sat down and used the scarves for tourniquets. We had left on this mission so hurriedly that we had stupidly left our first-aid equipment behind. We particularly missed the morphine packets we had been given before the jump into France.

"I believed the Germans would come up to finish us off, so I told Stompnell, the rifleman, and Bloom, the BARman, to take off. There was no need for all of us to die. Furthermore, Van and I had the high ground, plenty of ammo and grenades. But all of us had been together from Toccoa on. Stompnell and Bloom said they wouldn't leave us there to die. 'If we die,' they said, 'we all die together.'

"To our surprise, the Germans took off. Stompnell and Bloom tried to carry us back but we were far too heavy. Finally, we all agreed they should go back to our lines and bring an aidman and litters for us. They placed some sheet metal roofing from a blown-down building over us and reluctantly left. It was, of course, a long trip back. During the time we waited, Van and I kept our spirits up by discussing previous wounds. He had received a serious one in Italy while my earlier one was inconsequential. We also talked about the wounds of friends. I noticed a flow of blood melting the snow but since the tourniquet had largely stopped the bleeding from my stump, I couldn't account for where this blood was from. Only later did I learn of the multiple wounds in my other leg.

"Finally, Stompnell and Bloom brought back a couple of other troopers and aidman Joe A. C. Williams, another graduate of Toccoa. He smiled at us. 'You bastards, when you go out like this, why don't you just get killed. I had to get out of a warm bedroll in the basement of a bombed-out hotel, come out into the cold and treat you for little scratches like this.' His comments raised our spirits enormously as did the shots of morphine he gave both of us. Since I was the ranking man, I followed the 517th principle that rank comes last. I had them take Van first, in spite of his strong protests. Williams stayed with me and the litter bearers returned for me after a bit. I never saw Van again. He was evacuated before I reached the battalion aid station.

"At the aid station, Captain McNamara [Walter Plassman's associate from medical school, the Carlisle barracks, Jump School and Mackall], the assistant battalion surgeon, cleaned my wounds and applied more definitive first aid. He asked if I wanted more morphine. I told him I'd received some a couple of hours earlier while on the hillside but he gave me another shot anyway.

"I was taken in a litter attached to a jeep to a clearing station where a guillotine amputation was done. While awaiting this surgery, I heard hospital orderlies quarreling over who was to get my parachute jump jacket. If I'd had a gun, I would have killed them. After surgery my jacket was gone but the $490 I had in my pocket was placed in a sealed packet and the finance officer offered to send it home to my wife, which he did.

"From the clearing station they shifted me to a field hospital and finally the 43rd General Hospital in Aix-en-Provence. The hospital was staffed by physicians and nurses who graduated from Emory University in Atlanta. The executive officer, Maj. Hartwell Joiner, M.D., practiced in Gainesville, Georgia, and knew my wife. He was kind enough to write to her. Anne received his letter before she got the War Department telegram telling her I was wounded. The commanding officer, Col. J. D. Martin, M.D., a professor of surgery from Emory, asked me if I knew his nephew, a trooper named Schroeder. He was another Toccoa man, an outstanding combat rifleman and a particular friend of mine. I told him Schroeder was practically the blood of my heart. Colonel Martin laughed and said as soon as my gangrene was under control I'd be sent to the U.S. on the first available ship. I went home on the *Santa Rosa,* the same vessel that bore us to Italy."

Forrest survived his terrible wounds although he still carries tiny shards of shrapnel in his right leg, some which occasionally work themselves to the surface of his skin where he can pluck them out with tweezers. According to 1st Battalion surgeon Ben Sullivan, "Eighty percent of those with gunshot wounds would die, but only twenty percent hit with shrapnel did."

Walter Plassman notes some differences with what a physician sees in an emergency ward. "Civilian casualties are affected in their extremities perhaps a bit more. Bullets hit your guts. In the parachute infantry, we couldn't do anything fancy. Mostly patch 'em up and send them back to another station for more definitive treatment. During combat we attended the wounded to the best of our ability." Plassman also observes a difference in that those brought to a hospital under ordinary circumstances were strangers. As a military surgeon he knew the people he treated. "We didn't think about the KIAs until later, and then it did get depressing. Many good friends were lost or maimed for life."

From Tête de la Lavina, platoon-size patrols insinuated themselves into the environs of Sospel. Charlie Keen with B Company remembers, "We were told to spread fear among the Germans, make them fear the coming of the night. I don't know about them, but it sure as hell scared me. Lt. Bob Thomson was one hell of a fighter and a night combat patrol was just his meat. The mountain was very steep with jagged rocks and scrub trees everywhere, making the going slow. We had to look out for mines, theirs and our own.

"On one patrol, we had an Apache named Cammacho for lead scout. With his dark skin he put me in mind of a black panther, the four-legged kind. It was a bright, moonlit night; scattered clouds occasionally blotted out the moon. The trip took a long time because we had to contend with terraces, each one with a rock wall, every few yards.

"All the way down I thought I heard footsteps behind us and they sounded like hobnails, not our boots. I kept passing the word up but they thought I was spooked by squirrels. Finally everyone else heard them and they whispered back the command to 'freeze.' As luck would have it, I was caught with one cheek of my behind on a ledge and the other half of my backside hanging. Every time I attempted to move, some stones would fall. Everyone would go, 'Sshhhh!'

"Steve Weirzba and Stan Rozwood, both Polacks from Buffalo, New York, were on each side of me. Steve still had family in Poland and he hated the Germans with a passion. Stan felt the same. Suddenly, I realized the Germans were coming down the same path we were on and I was caught in the middle. Steve had to piss and did it on his hand so that the urine would run off his fingers and not make a loud noise. At the same time he muttered Polish under his breath. Old Dad, me, figured this old Delaware boy was in one hell of a spot.

"When they were only about ten feet back on the next terrace, they abruptly turned left and passed down about fifteen feet before they came down on our terrace. Just at this moment, the moon popped out. There was Cammacho, crouched over looking like a disciple of death with his Tommy gun cradled in his arms. The Germans stopped, froze and one of them said, 'Hottentot.'

"That was the last word he ever uttered because the Apache opened up and about thirty rifles and Tommy guns opened up and somebody even threw a hand grenade. Weirzba fired his rifle about four inches in front of my face. I thought, would my mother ever understand how I could have been killed by a friendly Polack in the south of France.

"Our G–2 figured if we caused some trouble, the enemy would bring out their artillery from behind their walls and our own 90 mms could fire so fast they would not have time to return to their protection. We were supposed to fire a parachute flare which would serve as a signal for our artillery to open up. The flare would also indicate we were a friendly patrol.

"The damn flare blew right back on top of us. The 90 mms never did fire but our own 81 mm mortars hit us with what seemed like a hundred shells. Why no one was

killed I'll never know. In the middle of all of the shooting, Dog Jordan, our scout, asked, 'Has anyone got today's *Stars and Stripes*? I didn't get to Willy and Joe
[cartoons drawn by Sgt. Bill Mauldin] today.' "

Edmund "Dog" Jordan happened to be one of the
few people outside his 3rd Battalion medical section that
John Chism knew. "He was one of the rogues of the 1st
Battalion. His closest buddy was Sgt. Andrew Murphy,
the first KIA in Italy. Dog's reaction was a 180-degree
reversal of character. He started a deadly search for Germans. If not a model soldier, his performance was a welcome change from the old Dog."

As an aidman, Keen, hugging the ground outside of
Sospel, had other concerns. "Our 81 platoon was the
best and this night they were right on their target. I'd
pray for a second, then listen for the cry of 'Medic!'
After they stopped, I decided I was the only man still
alive. No one could live through a barrage like that. Why
no one was killed I'll never understand. But the members of the Battling Bastards came through with only
two wounded, Sgt. Roy Bradley and Pfc. Doyle Gray.

"Lieutenant Thomson was furious. I thought he
might even kill those who called in the mortars. You
could see better now because the shells had ignited the
dry tinder. Thomson told me to find Gray as everyone
else had been accounted for. Gray was not the man to
run into at night or anytime when he was carrying his
Tommy gun. I believe he slept with it. At Toccoa he
seemed like a Momma's boy, dropping out of the runs in
training and just didn't seem to fit the paratrooper mold.

"But from the first day in Italy, he became a cold,
deadly killer, the likes of which you just didn't want to
meet in the dark or to get mad. He never raised his
voice. His face had a pallor, not unlike death. He never
smiled, his lips were a slit that silently commanded, leave
me be. In fact, he hardly did anything but smoke one
cigarette after another and volunteer for patrols or scout

or anything that gave him the opportunity to kill. Often
I've wondered what would have happened to him if he
hadn't later been killed in the Huertgen Forest fighting.

"After another quick prayer, I started back down the
trail, carrying a carbine just in case, and I spotted Gray
staggering up the path. I said out loud, 'Gray, it's me,
Doc Keen.' I'd rather a German hear me than for Gray
not to. Like Bradley, he'd been hit in the right rump
with a small piece of a shell. Gray was only in the hospital long enough to turn around and get some iodine on
it. Then AWOL, he returned to B Company. But the
fact that I dared or bothered to come looking for him
impressed Gray enough that although he never mentioned it, I knew woe be unto the German that fired on
this medic."

The nature of the Champagne Campaign, with the
howitzers of the 460th placed behind the rifle companies lessened the peril faced by artillerymen with the exception of the forward-observer teams. The demands
upon them required FOs to station themselves up front
with the dug-in M–1–toting troopers. "I had an FO
from the 460th," says Di Stanislao, "who came to my
position. He set up his radio and his monocular. He had
red hair and when he took off his shirt, his body was as
white as vanilla. I thought, 'Oh, my God! The sun will
shine off this character and every German will see us and
all hell will break loose.' But after he organized his paraphernalia he motioned for me to look into his scope. We
knew the Germans used a railroad tunnel to carry their
equipment and through the viewfinder I could see them
come out of the tunnel with mules loaded with supplies.
It was so clear, I thought I could read their belt buckles
with *'Gott mitt uns'* on them. The lieutenant waited until they all cleared the tunnel, called in the grids and ordered 'Fire for effect.' Whatever battery was on his radio
dropped one shell. He immediately screamed, 'When I
say for effect, I want effect!' All hell broke loose. All that

remained of that procession of Germans and animals were pieces of mules, equipment scattered everywhere and crumbled up uniforms. It was fire for effect, sure enough."

As autumn deepened, the enemy appeared to realize it could not destroy the forces arrayed against them. The Americans, in particular the 596th engineers, put down their own mines that effectively reduced counterthrusts by the Germans. At the same time, the attackers saw little gain in pressing forward into territory highly suited for defense with ever-mounting casualties. A kind of World War I type of siege ensued with sporadic patrols and intermittent mortars and artillery.

Nevertheless, the losses continued. One of the worst blows struck members of the 596th. A crew from Allan Goodman's 3rd Platoon had been detailed to destroy concrete defense installations and remove German Teller mines at the Nice airport. According to Goodman, "The fuses from the Teller mines could not be safely removed. We used the mines as explosive for the demolition job, or blew them up in the ocean. We were living very well but apparently, handling thousands of mines lowered the respect of some for the danger. Six men went up in an explosion of several hundred mines on a truck. I heard later that two men were tossing mines to a catcher on the truck bed. I was several hundred yards away, working on the wall when the explosion occurred, yet I was splattered with debris. Some men just behind an adjacent concrete wall were deafened by the blast. Lieutenant Zavattero had to assemble us to see who was left. With the three others killed [clearing the pathway across the Var riverbed earlier], one who died in the jump [Henry Wikins] and another who lost his life in a jeep accident near Sospel, the 596th had more fatalities than any company in the regiment, and eighty percent came from my platoon."

When the Germans finally retreated from Sospel the

Americans moved into a town ravaged by weeks of siege, the deprivations of a harsh occupation and still racked with artillery shells from the ousted *Wermacht*.

Dick Robb, having returned to H Company as a platoon sergeant, moved into the local Golf Hotel. The place faced north with its east end exposed to a narrow pass in the mountain, the border between France and Italy. The enemy's self-propelled 88 would get off its rounds, aim the final salvo at the east end of the Golf and then pull back. Robb had to move his quarters to the other part of the building.

Robb served as an eyewitness to the strange twists compassion follows during war. "We took a large patrol, as many as fifty, with an interpreter who spoke German, towards a peak at that pass which was still in enemy control. It was impossible to move except in single file. Word came, 'Bunker ahead, smell of bacon cooking, pass it on.'

"Soon a bazooka fired and then some rifles. We moved ahead. There were two prisoners, one wounded. Maurice White, our medic, was inside the bunker tending the wounded man. White was a corporal, one of the finest men I would ever know. While wearing a helmet with a Red Cross emblem and an armband with the same, he often carried arms. Once he had an old Spandau, a horrible-looking rifle so old and rusty no one could figure where he got it. He had one bullet for it. Colonel Graves saw him with a rifle once and ordered him disarmed, supposedly saying, 'What the hell does he think he is doing, an armed medic? Jesus, a medic carrying a blunderbuss!'

"When I looked at the German in the bunker I saw a slight wound on the left side of his face at the jaw line. I thought, 'My God! he is no more than a child, maybe fifteen or sixteen at most.'

"Then White said, 'Sergeant, you have to see this.' He pulled back a large compress he had placed on the

German's chest. The sternum and several left ribs had been blown away, probably by rock shrapnel from the bazooka round when it hit the stone bunker. The heart was fully exposed and beating. Impossible, but there it was."

Robb continues, "I told White we had no stretchers with us. Being exposed as we were, we probably would receive artillery or mortar fire soon. This place would be untenable, meaning we'd have to leave him. Meanwhile, the uninjured prisoner told our interpreter that many of his comrades wanted to surrender. He was instructed to walk down the slope to a clearing maybe 200 yards away. Halfway through the clearing he was to stop and call to those who wished to surrender. If he went beyond halfway, we would shoot him.

"When he reached the clearing, there was a lot of shouting from him to some Germans and then back to us. His chances of survival didn't look very good, either from his own or ours. I went back to the bunker.

"As I looked in, I saw White removing a silver cigarette lighter from the German's right-hand pocket. His eyes were open and his lips moved slowly. He was still breathing, moaning softly.

"I became furious, maybe because he was so young. I snapped at White, 'For Christ's sake, do you have to strip him of his possessions now! Can't you wait at least until he's gone? What the hell is the matter with you!'

"White gave me his most injured look, one only he could give when he chose to feign innocence. 'But, sergeant, I traded him for it.' I don't know why I was getting so angry but my tone of voice must have shown it. 'Come on, White. Goddammit. You can't speak a word of German and looking at him, I doubt he speaks any English. What the hell do you mean you traded him for the lighter?'

"I'll never forget the look on White's face as he said, 'This boy will be here with a long time to die. You yourself said we'll have to get out of here soon, and we can't take him back with us and it's sure as hell the Germans won't be up here soon either. I did trade him for this lighter. I just finished giving him six grains of morphine, all that I had. He won't be all alone up here in the dark now, waiting and with no one with him. It won't be too long. Morphine is a gentle way to go.'

"I was taken aback. I mumbled, 'Sorry, White' and walked back to see how things were going with the other prisoner." The incident revived memories of Robb's earlier conversations with White on the gnawing fear of "being left in no man's land, or on the mountain or simply out there."

White had emphasized to Robb, "I will see that you are never left out on the mountain," and he had done the same for the young German. Says Robb, "When I think of 'the trade' now, I wish I hadn't been so sharp with White that day on the mountain. He's gone now. Drinking took him some years ago."

But this was among the final acts in the Champagne Campaign. The strategy did not call for the 517th to pursue the enemy into Italy. Instead, increasing numbers of them cleaned themselves up, polished their boots and visited the Riviera. Russel Brami from E Company enjoyed two full weeks, "the greatest time of our lives in the army, at the time. The people were very receptive and we really got to know our company officers. It was all on a last name basis and you still knew who the officers were. But we ate and drank with them and forged lasting friendships."

Thanksgiving Day, 1944, saw the traditional turkey dinner served, albeit in mess kits for those up on the lines. Dick Seitz arranged for his officers to enjoy a Thanksgiving Day dinner at the Negresco Hotel in Nice. Maj. Dave Armstrong requisitioned the appropriate quota of turkeys for preparation at the Negresco.

Tom Cross, who had now recovered from his wound

was among the scheduled guests. "We preceded the dinner with a battalion officers' party the night before. Seitz asked me to keep an eye on things to keep them from getting out of control because he wanted to enjoy the event while serving as official host. Things seemed well in hand until later in the evening when I saw *"Les Enfants,"* well on their way to cognac poisoning, engineering an attempt to throw a grand piano over the ballroom balcony because of displeasure with the pianist. I moved to put an immediate stop to what could be not only a costly addition to party expenses but also a public-relations disaster. Then I saw a third musketeer elbow his way into the operation, to add additional leverage to the sport of piano tossing. Making certain my eyes did not deceive me, I took one more look at my leader's entry into the festivity, and then repaired to the hotel bar to contract my own case of cognac poisoning.

"I awoke sometime the next afternoon in my room at the Negresco and, not feeling up to a visit to the dining room, requested my portion of the Thanksgiving dinner be sent up. When I removed the silver cover over the plate, I discovered a piece of rather stale French bread upon which rested a single slice of tomato and a lonely canned sardine. After numerous phone calls, I caught up with Dave Armstrong. He gave me neither sympathy nor turkey, explaining that what the battalion had not consumed was polished off by the hotel kitchen staff. I feel that Dick Seitz still owes me one Thanksgiving Day dinner."

Elements of the 10th Mountain Division relieved the troopers in their positions along the French-Italian border. The men from the 517th, having now accrued more than 100 days of combat experience, retired to pup tents at La Colle, close to the beaches over which they had flown more than three months earlier. And on December 1, 1944, the entire outfit received orders to proceed to Soissons in Northern France and serve under the newly formed XVIII Airborne Corps commanded by Gen. Matthew Ridgway, who had led the 82nd Airborne Division from its first North African experiences through Sicily, Italy and on the June 6, 1944, D-Day jump into Normandy.

CHAPTER XI

THE ARDENNES

THREE TRAINLOADS OF 40-and-8s—forty men or eight horses under the French designation for their boxcars during World War I—bore the bulk of the bedraggled troopers to their new encampment at Soissons. The 500-mile, three-day trek seemed endless, with little opportunity to shave or wash, rations heated on Coleman burners and a scarcity of room to stretch out on the crowded, straw-covered boxcar floors.

At Soissons, the brass set about rehabilitating the battered combat team. About 500 replacements joined the 517th to fill out the depleted ranks and add a third rifle squad to each platoon, bringing the companies closer to the T/O of the straight leg infantry. "Many of these men," recalls Ed Johnson from C Company, "were people stuck in boring places that the war had passed, such as air force ground personnel in North Africa. I think a lot of them saw the chance to qualify for the airborne forces as an opportunity to get off 'high center.' It's fair to say they were not immediately accepted but subsequently most acquitted themselves well. Some resentment occurred because the replacements brought with them many NCO rankings which froze the T/O and kept acting NCOs from getting promoted."

As 1944 drew to a close, the Allied strategists thought in terms of a final stroke, a massive parachute and glider drop involving the newly formed XVIII Airborne Corps across the Rhine River into the heart of Germany. To officers like Charles La Chaussee even this seemed unnecessary. The enemy appeared to be falling back, in spite of the respite granted through winter weather. He spoke for many when he remarked, "It was common knowledge that the Germans had been beaten and the war was as good as over. We wondered why the silly bastards continued to fight."

Since the combat team was still committed to take the field, La Chaussee's superiors instituted a garrison style regimen to train newcomers and restore military discipline to the veterans. While some of the troopers accepted the need for a return to the atmosphere of Toccoa, others regarded orders to shave off mustaches, requirements to salute and snap to attention in the presence of officers amidst drills in the mud and rain, as oppressive. Ernie Kosan of the 596th Engineers contends, "The worst thing to do with a soldier out of combat is to try and reintroduce spit, polish and parade-formation life. It makes no sense. We recognized it as a necessary evil during training. But here we were, combat veterans who had seen death, felt fear, endured privation, all without a murmur. Suddenly to be given barracks chicken-shit was too much. It was almost a relief when we heard of the German attack in the Battle of the Bulge."

Trooper Ed Johnson of C Company says, "The initial reaction to efforts to reestablish discipline was bitch, bitch, bitch. After a few days, however, I think most saw the necessity of the actions."

Passes allowed some troopers to visit Paris. Most of the men spent their recreational hours in towns and villages closer to their quarters. With thousands of other paratroopers in the area, off-post reunions spiced with wine and beer guzzling, brawls and active pursuit of women kept the MPs and chute police busy.

Some of the upper echelons of the 517th perceived that venereal disease which had vexed the outfit in Italy and then Southern France threatened to seriously reduce the number of troopers fit for duty. The alleged solution was the creation of a place known as the Idle Hour Athletic Club.

It is Ben Sullivan's recollection that the Regimental Surgeon, Paul Vella, spoke to the local mayor, a woman, to clear the business with the town officials. Capt. Norman "Slick" Siebert, Vella's assistant regimental surgeon, accepted the task of organizing the bordello which was to be reserved for the enlisted personnel. The prostitutes, already professionals, were recruited from Paris and furnished with piece goods and sewing machines to occupy their idle hours.

The night before the official opening, according to one source, it would have been difficult to find any officers around their quarters or offices. To forestall any difficulties with soldiers detailed to police the area, the MP battalion on duty was awarded a membership. When the club began to entertain its customers, business was spotty. Ed Johnson says "other guys told me, you waited in line until the next mademoiselle became available. If she did not appeal to you, you moved back in the line. The price was five dollars."

Charlie Keen says, "The regimental cathouse was not exactly a howling success. The average GI didn't care for it. They weren't interested in anything in the form of sex that came out Government issued and inspected. Only the oversexed enjoyed the place."

There were daily medical examinations of the working women by Dr. Siebert and a blood test followed any suspicious symptoms. The troopers surrendered their passes and hats at the door. These could only be retrieved after a GI gave himself a prophylaxis treatment under the eyes of a medic.

The subterfuges notwithstanding, it was impossible to

disguise the nature of the business. The operation came to the attention of the 517th's two chaplains. They did not approve. Ben Sullivan felt that Protestant Charles Brown inveighed against the whorehouse "as if he were John Knox himself." Roman Catholic Father Alfred Guenette displayed a similar sense of outrage. When Brown threatened to bring the affair to the attention of authorities above the regimental command the Idle Hours Athletic Club closed down.

Oddly, there are former troopers and officers who question whether the alleged official den of ill repute ever actually existed. They maintain they only heard talk of such an operation and Phil Di Stanislao flatly dismisses it. "I think the sporting house is a myth."

The establishment of such an institution with quasi-official sanction was a desperate response to a serious loss of manpower because of venereal diseases. The solution offends some 1990s sensibilities but this was 1944, in the midst of a war that could bring death at any moment. Parents, schools, churches, superior officers and chaplains had failed to inculcate the virtues of abstinence. Furthermore, the women were already in the trade, unlike the victims forcibly impressed by the Japanese to satisfy their troops.

Actually, the place would have been shuttered quickly without clerical intervention anyway since the enemy chose at this very time to open its surprise offensive in the Ardennes, a rocky, hilly land traversed by steep gorges, swiftly moving streams and beset by a thoroughly vicious pattern of weather during the winter months. The breakthrough along what was the border between Germany, Belgium and Luxembourg began the epic, six-week campaign known as the Battle of the Bulge.

In the previous engagements, Italy, ALBATROSS and the Champagne Campaign, there had been a grand strategy behind the deployment of the 517th. But no effective contingency plans covered the surprise, massive penetration by the enemy in the Ardennes Forest. Like so many other outfits during the first weeks of the Bulge, the 517th acted as a fire brigade, rushing from one place to another to quell a series of dangerous blazes.

Mel Zais heard the disturbing news from the acting XVIII Airborne Corps commander, Jim Gavin, sitting in for Ridgway who was in England inspecting the 17th Airborne, scheduled to become part of his forces. "One day," remembered Zais, "Colonel Graves and I decided to see General Gavin. He was playing badminton with his staff. They asked us to stay for dinner. While at dinner, the telephone rang and Gavin was called away from the table. By the time he came back we had finished our dessert and were carrying on a conversation. Gavin seemed a little preoccupied. When he finished dinner, with a tremendous amount of composure, he said, 'Gentlemen, you better pay attention because something serious has happened. We're moving up tomorrow morning, as early as we can. There has been a breakthrough in Belgium in the Ardennes.' "

Zais and Graves hastily excused themselves and rushed back to Soissons to prepare their combat team for the unknown assignment that lay ahead. Tom Cross, with his injury from the ALBATROSS operation sufficiently healed for a limited duty assignment, had drawn the pleasant task of representing the XVIII AB Corps with the Red Cross in Paris. That cushy post vanished in the smoke and flames of the enemy attack. It became Cross's task to round up any paratroopers in Paris and pack them off to their organizations.

Dick Seitz says he did not learn of the German breakthrough until December 17. "We were not immediately aware of how serious it was. We did not expect we would be alerted for the front, and as a matter of fact had men on leave in England. We were deep in planning for a Christmas party. We had been instructed to turn over all

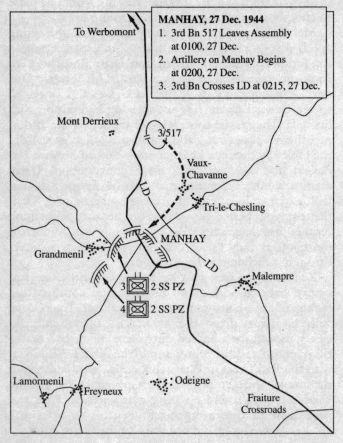

MANHAY, 27 Dec. 1944

1. 3rd Bn 517 Leaves Assembly at 0100, 27 Dec.
2. Artillery on Manhay Begins at 0200, 27 Dec.
3. 3rd Bn Crosses LD at 0215, 27 Dec.

To Werbomont

Mont Derrieux

3/517

Vaux-
Chavanne

LD

Tri-le-Chesling

MANHAY

Grandmenil

LD

Malempre

3 2 SS PZ

4 2 SS PZ

Lamormenil

Freyneux

Odeigne

Fraiture
Crossroads

Rushed into the line to halt the penetration of the Germans in the
Battle of the Bulge, the 517th met the enemy at Freyneux,
Lamormenil, Grandmenil and Manhay.

our crew-served weapons to another regiment that was alerted."

Zais spoke of a similar deficiency in the basic tools for combat. "When we were told to leave Southern France, our S-4 [regimental supply officer], Bill Hickman, had decided not to be caught short. He detoured trucks to Marseilles and picked up a good basic load of ammunition and replaced all of the weapons lost. But Graves then gave the weapons to the 508th, which had already been ordered to move. On the next day, we in the 517th scrambled to move out. We sent trucks to Paris, picked up troops who were issued rifles still covered with cosmoline. The troopers dipped the rifles into gasoline barrels and began wiping them down with oily rags as the trucks rolled."

While using gasoline eased the job of removing the preservative coating from weapons the technique ordinarily was strictly forbidden because of the high risk of an explosion from the fumes.

Bill Boyle was visiting an old chum from the 101st Airborne when Jim Gavin, as the corps commander, handed that organization its march order. The Screaming Eagles were destined for Bastogne and the celebrated siege climaxed by the acting commander Gen. Anthony McAuliffe's one word rejection of a surrender demand, "Nuts!"

Boyle hastened back to his troopers, some of whom remained unconvinced of any emergency. C Company's Charles La Chaussee said, "We had been at Soissons for ten days when it was announced that we were on a two-hour alert for possible movement. That puzzled us but it didn't worry anyone very much. We packed and stored nonessential equipment and continued our program of training and rehabilitation.

On December 21, five days after the opening salvo by German gunners and the rupture of the American lines by German armor, La Chaussee remembered, "Colonel

Boyle assembled his staff and company commanders. Boyle said, 'The Germans have made a breakthrough in the First Army area. Where and how deep we don't know. The 82nd and the 101st have been sent up and we're leaving at 6:00 P.M. We travel by the route Charleroi-Sedan-Namur to a place called Werbomont. I'm going ahead to Namur to report to someone from the XVIII Airborne Corps for further orders. One last thing. If anybody gets separated from the rest of the convoy, avoid a place called Bastogne!' "

The lack of precise information imparted by the 1st Battalion commander was not by design. The fact was the forty-mile front covering the Ardennes and the Belgian–Luxembourg border with Germany had collapsed into a chaotic jumble of units with command and control tenuous or even lost. What was already certain, as Boyle indicated, the town of Bastogne with the 101st Airborne in residence was being encircled.

Di Stanislao recalls, "The first word we got of a breakthrough was over the radio in the day room. We passed it off as minor but as time passed it became obvious this was a strong, aggressive penetration. Still, in my infinite military wisdom, I decided it would be no more than a skirmish for us after we were alerted. We were not aware of the climate in the Ardennes. I decided that since we'd be involved for only a short time, I'd wear my most comfortable footwear, shoepacks which had rubber feet and leather tops. It was one more case of doing the right thing for the wrong reason. Parachute boots are not good wet or cold weather gear.

"We didn't have overcoats which show up in some pictures of the Battle of the Bulge. I hadn't seen my overcoat since it went to the bottom of the barracks bag shortly after it was issued. I wore a combat jacket and a woolen GI sweater with the regular OD [standard issue olive drab] pants. I didn't use long underwear because it constricted my ability to move. Everyone else dressed pretty much the same, except most of the guys had on their paratrooper boots.

"We boarded the trucks about 5:30 in the afternoon while rain was spitting down. We received no intelligence on where we were going or what we were supposed to do. We remained literally and figuratively in the dark for the twenty-three hours we spent in the trucks. I vaguely remember eating a K ration, the kind I always packed, the one with cheese, on the theory that it would reduce the urge for a toilet."

When Rupert Graves and his staff reached the Werbomont XVIII Corps headquarters on the morning of December 22, the situation was so unstructured that the orders to the 517th simply specified that the first of its three battalions to appear would report to the beleaguered 3rd Armored Division under Gen. Maurice Rose at the village of Manhay.

First to arrive at Werbomont and be dispatched to Manhay for instructions by Gen. Rose was Bill Boyle with his 1st Battalion, minus Charles La Chaussee and two-thirds of C Company which had become separated from the convoy. "At the end of the briefing," says Boyle, "I asked for a map from either the G–2 or G–3 of the XVIII AB Corps. They said they had none. Since I was to report to General Rose in Manhay, I asked which road went there. They couldn't tell me. I asked an MP at the crossroads outside and he didn't know either. I went back, looked at the corps map, took distance and azimuth readings and with them found my way to Manhay."

Boyle says he reached Manhay and reported to General Rose around 1:00 A.M. "What can you learn in half an hour?" questions Boyle of his brief session with the 3rd Armored's CO and under whom Boyle's people now served. "Rose was calm and cool, although the picture painted earlier at Werbomont was not one to induce calm." The actual deployment of the 1st Battalion was spelled out for Boyle by Col. Robert L. Howze, Jr., in charge of one of the three combat commands that comprised the 3rd Armored. Howze made his headquarters in the village of Soy a few miles west of Manhay.

German armor had badly battered Rose's tanks. Task Force Hogan with some 400 of Rose's GIs were surrounded on the heights of Marcouray, about six miles southwest of Manhay. Rose committed Boyle and his troopers to a line running east from Hotton through Soy towards Manhay against the enemy's 116th Panzer Division and subsequently its 560th *Volksgrenadiers,* the major forces squeezing Task Force Hogan. Not only was the 517th, which would be joined by the freshly committed, inexperienced infantrymen of the 75th Division, trying to open an escape route for Task Force Hogan, but also the troopers and straight legs alongside them were expected to prevent the Germans from rolling up the right flank of the 3rd Armored. Enemy success here would threaten a narrow escape route for thousands of GIs trapped by the German penetration. Furthermore, an advance by the foe would envelop the 82nd Airborne, dug in along the Salm River to the east where they held open the corridor for retreating Americans.

The pattern for the 2nd Battalion duplicated that of the 1st. Seitz and the 2nd Battalion headed into the Ardennes without even minimal preparations. "A day after giving our own weapons to the 508th, we were alerted and had to draw new ones. We moved out, cleaning the cosmoline off the new weapons in the back of trucks while riding to the front. It was a helluva deal—moving up on trucks, cleaning weapons and no idea where in hell we were going."

The loss of their originally issued weapons irritated men like E Company's Dick Jones. "Our weapons were a personal thing. We cleaned them, carried 'em, slept with them, knew where they were every minute. We cussed 'em, we zeroed them in, and knew their idiosyncracies but still we had to give them away. What the hell had this other outfit done with their rifles!

"They provided us with new rifles, packed in that hated cosmoline grease. I remember cleaning the new strangers in gasoline, next to a roaring fire in the fireplace. I always wonder why we didn't burn the place down. There was no chance to zero-in the strangers."

The convoy with Mel Zais aboard hit gridlock in the Belgian city of Liège. Zais climbed fenders and hoods in search of the cause. He saw a mixture of U.S. and British vehicles, "hubcap to hubcap, nose to nose." The local citizens offered solace in the form of soup and food.

According to La Chaussee, "Trucks had been assembled by the transportation corps and the military police who simply pulled them off the highway regardless of their origin or their mission. There was no organizational control over the drivers. There were simply so many men with trucks from a variety of units." This grab-whom-you-can method obtained enough vehicles for transportation but it meant using many drivers who were unfamiliar with the road network.

"During one halt," said La Chaussee, "I walked down the line of trucks carrying C Company. At the taillight of a truck a young replacement said, 'Captain, I don't even have a rifle. What am I supposed to fight with?' I could only tell him there would be plenty of rifles where we were going."

Many of the trucks lacked even a canvas covering. Shivering in the subfreezing temperatures, as a mixture of snow, sleet and rain pelted them, the troopers huddled together for warmth. The convoy halted very briefly to permit the men to relieve bladders and bowels.

Chilled to the bone, La Chaussee, in the cab of a truck, tried to stay awake but as the procession ground into the hills, sometime after noon and already eighteen hours on the road, he dozed off. He awakened with a start, realizing the truck had stopped. They were at a fork in the road and up ahead La Chaussee could not see any sign of the convoy.

"I asked the driver, 'Where's the convoy?'

" 'I don't know, sir. They were going too fast for me and I lost them. I don't know which way they went.' " La Chaussee shuddered; it was reminiscent of a recent dream in which he had become separated from his men and then cut down "as three slugs tore into me."

The captain checked his shrunken command. He counted two platoons from C Company and a mortar section in the six trucks. Unwilling to risk further progress toward what was a rapidly changing front, La Chaussee directed his troopers to leave their vehicles and take defensive positions in the nearby brush. When a jeep with a forward-observer lieutenant aboard hove into view, La Chaussee ousted the passenger by dint of his superior rank. He retraced the convoy's route back half a mile where he located a military policeman on traffic duty. The MP supplied directions to the XVIII Airborne Corps CP at Manhay.

"I mounted up the troopers and we rode to Manhay, about seven miles south. Traffic struck me as heavy, with tanks and trucks racing in both directions. At Manhay the division [3rd Armored] staff was very jumpy. One captain drew his pistol on me. Somehow, my story of having a company of paratroops outside waiting deployment didn't seem too believable."

The pistol-waving challenger undoubtedly was responding to awareness of Operation *Greif* in which German soldiers dressed themselves in American uniforms, infiltrated the U.S. lines to destroy communications, mislead GIs and create general havoc. Ernie Kosan in a lead jeep for the engineers found himself answering a number of questions from suspicious sentries who kept their weapons trained on him before he could pass a roadblock. The fear of infiltrators disguised as Americans permeated the front.

Once La Chaussee convinced the officer of his bona fides, he was ushered in to see General Rose, the 3rd Armored CO. Bill Boyle with his contingent had not been able to wait for the lost troopers of C Company and had departed to realize the containment plan dictated by Rose. In the interval before La Chaussee reached Manhay, the strategists detected another weak point and decided to use the C Company troopers to plug the hole.

A bizarre quality suffused the circumstances surrounding the orders given La Chaussee. Instead of a staff member, General Rose himself explained the mission. "He was immaculately dressed in gray riding breeches with a Sam Browne belt and boots as befitted a cavalry officer. He was cool, self-possessed and seemed fully in control of the situation. He produced a small map, encased in plastic, and covered with red and blue arrows. He briefed me on the situation but most of what the general told me went completely over my head. I was totally disoriented. Although I knew we were in Belgium, I didn't know exactly where, or even which way the front faced.

"The gist of his briefing was that he had several task forces out and they were meeting heavy opposition. He was sending me 'to the hottest spot on the Western Front tonight' to join Task Force Kane. It wasn't the time or place to ask a lot of questions. I knew I could pick up what I needed a little further down the line. I saluted and left."

In a jeep, Task Force Kane's executive officer drove La Chaussee south two and a half miles while the half-dozen trucks with the C Company troopers trailed. Just before dark they stopped in the village of Freyneux. Darkness had fallen, twenty-four hours had passed since they left the warm, comfortable billets at Soissons. Said La Chaussee, "Now, we were God knows where with six officers and 100 men."

Trooper Ed Johnson, among those who found themselves in "God knows where," says, "When we arrived in
Freyneux, Col. Killer Kane told La Chaussee that we
were to take the village of Dochamps which was defended by ninety 'green' German troops. However, his
tankers told us we were probably facing 'a division supported by much heavy armor.' " Johnson and his comrades subsequently found themselves almost enveloped
by what was at least a battalion-strength enemy.

In Freyneux, the troopers hardly had time to stow
their bedrolls and seek cover in the village's bomb- and
shell-racked buildings before they moved out towards
Dochamps, about two miles away and linked to
Freyneux by the railroad line. From a 3rd Armored tank
unit commanded by Lt. Eldon MacDonald, La Chaussee
drew the promise of a diversionary move intended to
disguise the route of attack on Dochamps.

"It was a clear night with an exceptionally bright
moon, almost bright enough to read by," recalled La
Chaussee. "A light crust of snow crunched under our
boots. When we had cleared Freyneux, I checked the
column. One man had a cough he could not control. I
had him fall out. He was a young sergeant who was bitter about being left out of his first action. He was killed
two weeks later."

As they trudged along the narrow-gauge track, the
troopers came upon a pair of artillerymen from the 7th
Armored Division which had been badly battered trying
to hold St. Vith, one of the early objectives of the Germans. The two soldiers had taken refuge in a cluster of
wooden buildings beside the railroad. One of them, an
officer, had no useful information for La Chaussee. Instead he despairingly insisted, "The whole German army
is out there. You don't know what you're getting into."

La Chaussee said he asked them to join his contingent
but they declined. The paratroop captain could have

THE ARDENNES 275

arrested them for their behavior but decided he had more important tasks.

Suddenly, streams of tracer bullets slashed the sky and a tremendous racket from machine guns broke the silence of the night. It was the diversion promised by Eldon MacDonald but La Chaussee for one was not impressed by guns shooting almost straight up. "It surely was obvious to the Germans that we had either lost our minds or were trying to attract their attention. The firing stopped after a few minutes and I could only hope it hadn't done too much harm."

The troopers continued their advance. Everyone halted in his tracks as lead-scout Pfc. Howard L. Lee held up his hand. Lee silently went prone on the snowy ground and called out "Coleman?" It was the password with a countersign of "Burner," a simple combination based on the name of the small stoves for heating food.

There was a pause, and then Lee repeated, "Coleman?" From the underbrush ahead a voice responded, *"Vas?"* A German, confused apparently by the similarity of the password with a common Teutonic surname, had made a fatal error. Lee answered now with a burst from his Tommy gun. All of the troopers now dropped to the snow beside the railroad embankment, peering out for sign of the enemy. But all was quiet.

Sgt. Leslie Perkins, the forward squad leader, snaked ahead. He reached his scout, Lee, who said he had almost blundered right into the Germans before he saw a gun position and issued his challenge. The troopers cautiously advanced to find two corpses, members of a light machine gun crew killed by Lee's burst of fire. However, the scout also observed one of the enemy, apparently wounded, escape through the vegetation and darkness and who in all likelihood would alert his comrades.

Ed Johnson says, "On learning the situation, Captain La Chaussee sent two patrols to the flanks to ascertain the enemy strength and disposition. The patrols made little headway before automatic fire pinned them down. Concentrated fire from Lt. Tom De Coste's platoon on the railroad embankments enabled the patrols to withdraw, but not before Pfc. Bernard Coyne had the spine-chilling experience of a bullet that passed completely through his helmet, and rolled him into a mud puddle."

La Chaussee, deterred by the strong resistance, withdrew a few hundred yards to shelter by a railroad water stop and advised Col. Kane of his predicament. The response was an order to renew the thrust at 1:00 A.M.

Once again, the advancing troopers bumped up against stubborn resistance made up of rifle fire, machine guns and grenades. According to La Chaussee, "Control of more than five or six men was impossible due to the darkness and thick brush. Sergeants Jack Burns [the irrepressible companion of Dick Robb as a member of the ALBATROSS pathfinders] and Bill Delaney did most of the work with their squads, playing cat and mouse, crawling from tree to tree calling, 'Oh, Herman, where are you? Come out, Herman, where we can see you.'" The taunts drew fire, exposing enemy soldiers. When the Germans broke away, they left eight or ten dead and abandoned four machine gun nests. One trooper, Pvt. C. L. Barrett, was KIA, four wounded, including one seriously.

Following up on their success, the Americans pushed on to positions overlooking the last stretch of ground before their objective, Dochamps. Just as the first troopers appeared ready to confront defenders inside the village, a recon patrol reported a company-size enemy force seeking to outflank and cut off the troopers. La Chaussee called for another retreat to the water stop.

"We had never before failed to take an objective and never withdrawn," said La Chaussee. "But unless I was ready to throw away a hundred men, it looked as if we were going to have to start now."

From there, the remnants of C Company headed for the hamlet of Lamorménil. It was becoming obvious that rather than going on the attack, La Chaussee and his troopers would be hard pressed to even maintain themselves against a foe substantially superior in numbers. In Lamorménil, the C Company men found small elements from other units. As the senior officer, La Chaussee organized the defenses for an anticipated strong attack.

La Chaussee was still evaluating the situation as a fog-shrouded dawn crept over the small village when an apparition interrupted his concentration. "I suddenly saw a long double-column of men carrying rifles with fixed bayonets at high port, coming along the railroad track from Freyneux toward the north.

"They emerged from the fog thirty feet away. My immediate reaction was they were friendly troops coming to reinforce us. But then I noticed their ankle-length overcoats sweeping the ground. American troops did not have overcoats like those. I raised my carbine to fire. At that moment one of our machine guns opened fire in a long continuous burst from the house across the tracks. Lt. Roland Beaudoin had spotted the enemy at the same time as I and sticking a machine gun out of the window, he held the trigger down. The German column was ripped apart at point-blank range. A later count showed that Beaudoin had killed twenty-three in one burst of fire.

"The next few minutes were pandemonium as our men and the Germans, equally surprised, exchanged fire and grenades. I looked desperately for a place to deploy and make a stand. The fog was thinning fast. I saw a group of stone farm buildings a hundred yards to the northwest. Firing and running, we fell back into them. The Germans were in strength and following closely. Tactical coherence was lost as we scrambled for positions in the farmhouse. I charged into a large building in the center of the village with Sgt. Arthur Purser carrying a machine gun close behind. A family—a man, his wife and children—were calmly eating breakfast.

"Without a word," says La Chaussee, "we raced upstairs to an attic and opened fire from a window. The German attack lasted for about two hours. It was a very near thing. They seemed to be in battalion strength. They snaked along hedges and fences, using all available cover and keeping up a heavy volume of rifle and machine gun fire. A few of them made it to the center of the village before they were cut down.

"It occurred to me that Sergeant Purser would present less of a target if he were further back in the attic and I told him so. Just as he pulled his gun from the sill, a bullet ripped through, barely missing us but knocking the carbine from my hands. We smashed a hole in the roof and continued firing. When the German fire seemed to slow a little, I descended to the ground floor. The Belgian family had gone, leaving their breakfast on the table. I was drinking a cup of chicory coffee when a column of Sherman tanks roared down the street, firing their machine guns. They were from MacDonald's company, on a recon patrol from Freyneux. They were indeed the U.S. cavalry to the rescue.

"With .50 caliber machine guns they began raking the hedgerow that ran diagonally across our front. German infantry were advancing along this hedgerow, stooped over and running in short bursts. Our weapons had not been able to penetrate the earthen embankment. The .50 calibers punched through it, bowling over Germans. Enemy fire ceased altogether within half an hour of the arrival of the tanks."

After surveying the small patch of turf he defended, and adjusting some positions, La Chaussee borrowed a jeep from the tankers and checked in with Killer Kane at Freyneux. To his utter dismay, the task force commander, "impatient and critical as I made my report," directed La

Chaussee to lead another attempt upon Dochamps. "I suggested we would be doing well to hold what we had. He was adamant and repeated the order."

Back at Lamorménil, La Chaussee conferred with tanker Eldon MacDonald. They plotted tactics but the paratrooper was gloomy. "It did not look very promising and we were not enthused. But those were orders and they were to be obeyed." They were spared a potential disaster when at the ultimate moment, even as the troopers and tanks had begun to form up, new orders called off the attack. Enemy tanks had appeared upon a ridge overlooking Lamorménil. Even the higher authorities recognized that the proposed assault upon Dochamps would be suicidal. While the cancellation saved the GIs in Lamorménil for the moment, the situation in their area continued to deteriorate. Odeigne, an outpost about a mile due east of Freyneux fell to the 2nd SS Panzer Division and now General Rose with his retinue withdrew from Manhay as the enemy was poised to overrun that town. Killer Kane turned over the local command of his task force to a deputy and La Chaussee while he set off to join General Rose.

CHAPTER XII

THE CHRISTMAS SEASON

WHILE THE SITUATION facing the embattled GIs in Lamorménil hovered somewhere between hopeless and desperate, the rest of the 517th 1st Battalion with Boyle in command climbed down from the trucks a mile north of Soy, dropped their bedrolls, moved through Soy and attacked.

Di Stanislao with A Company says, "We dumped our gas masks, checked our equipment, loaded our rifles and started across an open field. The men were widely spaced out and artillery fire, probably from 88s, began falling. A piece of shrapnel bent the gas operating rod on my M–1 making it useless and then a needle shard of shrapnel stuck in my chin. I pulled it out. Fortunately, after I reached a small copse of woods, I retrieved another M–1 and loaded it.

"We had begun to receive a lot of fire. There were two or three burning tanks. I could hear cries of 'Medic!' 'Medic!' It was now pitch-black dark. The ground was frozen and it was colder than the bottom of a well. A Company received orders to come back over the field to a road. We left behind our 2nd Platoon with B Company and the 1st and 3rd Platoons mounted tanks which headed for the town of Hotton."

The key piece of territory was the high ground at

Haid-Hits from which the enemy shelled and machine gunned the Americans. Boyle, after consultation with Colonel Howze, had split his troopers into two forces, one under him and the other to be directed by Don Fraser. Force Boyle, with most of A Company and some battalion headquarters men, traveled west with the tanks towards Hotton to start an encircling move. Fraser and his GIs, A Company's 2nd Platoon, B Company and the remainder of the headquarters personnel were to act as the eastern half of the pincers.

Against intensive mortar and small arms resistance, Force Boyle broke into Hotton and a command post was established in the Fanfare Royale Cinema building. Says Di Stanislao, "We didn't see any signs of other Americans, except for a smoking tank towards the Our-the River. Carl Kiefer and I ran down to the tank and looked inside. There were two wounded Americans there. We pulled them out and brought them to the cinema building which had an aid station.

"Boyle assigned me the mission to proceed down the main street, then turn before the bridge over the Ourthe and clean the enemy out of the houses facing the river-bank. In addition to the troopers from A Company, I was able to choose some from the headquarters bunch. And there was a tank to provide support. I divided the group into two parties, sending one to the rear of those houses by the river while I kept the tank with me and led my people down the street parallel with the river. The plan was to clear the Germans, one house at a time. I figured they would try to escape out the backs of the buildings and we would have them bracketed.

"The attack did not begin auspiciously. I was on the left flank of the tank, close to the buildings and we had gone maybe twenty or thirty yards when a *Panzerfaust* hit the tank. The concussion slammed me against the stone wall of a house. I scrambled to get around the corner and just glimpsed the tank commander, a sergeant, fall off his tank. The driver put it into reverse and retreated and that's the last I saw of it.

"I crawled out into the road and saw that the sergeant was wounded, with what looked like a hole in his neck. He was making a wheezing noise, typical of a sucking wound. I dragged him through a doorway to shelter and tried to apply finger pressure to that neck wound. He started to fight me. I desperately tried to hold onto him as we rolled around on the splinters of glass and debris on the floor. I was bigger than he, but he managed to throw me off. 'You dumb son of a bitch,' he yelled at me. 'All I wanted to do was get these false teeth out of my mouth.' I almost choked with laughter, but he didn't see anything funny. I sent him back to the aid station and continued down the street.

"Without the tank to help, we ran into a lot of machine gun and small arms fire. Our army retreating from Hotton had left a lot of stuff, abandoned vans and trucks along the sides of the street. It was good cover and I dove behind one of the vehicles trying to decide the next move. The problem was we did not know the location of the machine guns which stopped firing as soon as we took cover. I rose up and hauled ass. I almost had my pistol belt shot off but firing at me pinpointed the machine guns. The men moved quickly, using small arms and grenades they wiped out the soldiers manning the guns."

The struggle continued. Di Stanislao himself accounted for another machine gun as he tossed one grenade through a window and another into a doorway. He saw an enemy soldier level his Mauser on one of the headquarters men, Ed Allington, and managed to drop the German before he could squeeze off a round. Night fell, with the block rid of the foe. Force Di Stanislao had taken some casualties including one of the replacements whose career with the 517th had begun less than two weeks earlier. "He had a bad head wound," says Di Stanislao. "I didn't think he would make it. We didn't have any litters so I sent him back to the aid station on a mattress we got from a house. But to my surprise, he survived. We prepared a defense of the house, I pulled down some chicken wire from behind the place and we rigged it across the window to prevent anyone from dropping grenades inside. The rest of the night was quiet for us. But we could hear sporadic small arms fire from where Force Fraser was trying to join us."

In the morning, Boyle directed a house-to-house attack along the river. He credits a group of tank destroyers that occupied positions covering the enemy's main routes for the movement of armor. The strategy paid off as the TDs knocked out five German tanks trying to stave off the American advance.

Force Boyle and Force Fraser ratcheted up their pressure. "We were attacking head-on, with the Germans in the middle," says Don Fraser whose opposition was substantial.

Medic Charlie Keen recalls that first night in the Ardennes. "It was cold as hell and as night closed in, the 3rd Platoon got into all kinds of firefights. They knocked out two tanks with bazookas and kept raising hell until they were called back. Pfc. Andy Foley got his Silver Star for his actions."

When morning came, with tanks from the 3rd Armored as part of the attack, the troopers gained more ground, but absorbed a number of casualties. "After we reached the woods, we could look out in the field and see burning tanks," says Keen. "From one of them, a man struggled to get out but could not make it. In an eerie silence, Ledlie Pace from B Company ran by himself, out on the battlefield and grabbing the wounded man in the fireman's carry, trotted back to cover. Not a shot was fired at Pace. Sadly, less than an hour later, Pace was killed when a trip bomb in a tree exploded, killing him and wounding a machine gunner from Headquarters Company. The latter's leg was broken by a metal ball between his knee and hip. We treated him but had to leave him for what we hoped would be our litter-bearers before the cold and shock did him in.

"I had plopped down when we heard, 'Pop! Pop!' Looking up we saw some streamers of lights from tracers. A night fighter had shot down a Nazi plane that went up in flames. We thought it would fall in our laps and it came down only a few hundred yards from us, lighting up the entire woods. Within minutes we heard shots. Apparently, in the glare of the burning plane, some trooper spotted a man in a Nazi helmet and fired. Then it was quiet and a mournful cry of *'Mutti, Mutti.'* [Mommy.] There was silence and then the same cries. I heard a series of shots and a flat country accent say, 'That ought to hold the bastard.' The fighting renewed and there were many cries, both in German and English.

"There was an acute shortage of stretcher-bearers and I went to see if Major Fraser could spare some men but everyone was busy. I noticed some men in the area formerly occupied by the 1st Platoon before the fighting started. I asked Fraser if they could handle the litters since they were not fighting. He told me they were from the 509 and not our men.

"I was heading back to the 1st Platoon when I heard someone call for a medic from the other side of the road. It turned out to be an old Toccoa man from C Company. He had the entire right cheek of his behind torn wide open. Captain Sullivan later told me it was caused by a richochet. While I was talking to him and giving him a shot of morphine, we noticed a bad odor, something burning. We both hoped it wasn't poison gas, since we'd left our masks in the trucks which had gone.

"At this moment, there was a muffled sound and phosphorus shot up about ten feet in front of us. A figure of a man sat up ahead. We were too frightened to say much more than 'what the hell!' We realized it was an American and he was burning. There was no other sound from that direction, although intense firing surrounded us."

The apparition seen by Keen was an unfortunate platoon leader, Lt. Harry Allingham. While leading his troopers, Allingham took a burst of machine gun fire. Badly, if not mortally stricken, Allingham tumbled into a ditch. He managed to tell his runner, Pfc. Nolan Powell, nominated for a DSC in Italy on the first day of combat for the 517th, to bring the other members of the platoon forward.

Another fusillade not only snuffed out Allingham's last breaths but also nicked a white phosphorus grenade in his jacket. His body burned with intermittent fury throughout the night to the horror of Keen and his wounded companion. Keen, who praises Allingham as a courageous and dedicated officer, later realized that the grenade, designed to ignite instantly upon exposure to air, periodically was contained by contact with the dead man's bodily fluids.

Powell, demonstrating the kind of initiative that qualified so many of the Toccoa graduates for battlefield commissions, placed himself in plain sight of the enemy while directing the other riflemen to appropriate positions until Lt. Carl Hornsby could assume command.

"Several times during the ensuing battle," remembers Powell, "I passed or crawled by Lieutenant Allingham's burning body. It wasn't until after I had attended 517th reunions and read some written accounts that I realized that people considered what I had done something special."

While the shooting continued, Keen recruited trooper Smiley Henderson to help him carry back the trooper with the badly gashed backside. "It was a mad dash and the three of us fell into a ditch in a pile of arms, legs and one bleeding behind. I heard a pip sound and I looked up just in time for an enemy grenade to go off right in front of us. Fortunately, it was only a concussion grenade. What I got was a closed eye, cut nose and a piece of wire in my chin. Sullivan treated me and said, 'No harm done, you still have another eye.' He picked out the wire which they apparently wrap around their concussion grenades."

On the morning of December 23, when B Company got the word to press its case, a new hero emerged. "My platoon leader said, 'Biddle, out front,'" remembers then Pfc. Melvin Biddle, an Indiana youth whose presence with the 517th stemmed from a casual conversation with a young woman when he was drafted.

Between Soy and Hotton, amid fields covered with eight inches of snow and broken by low vegetation or small stands of trees, Biddle moved out, crawling forward a few yards, then standing up for some tentative steps in the direction of the enemy.

Entering a stretch with little shelter, Biddle dropped to the ground as several Germans, concealed in a patch of brush, fired at him. Wriggling through the snow, the scout maneuvered until only about twenty yards separated him from those aiming at him. He killed three of the foe with his rifle, to begin what would be a twenty-hour cat-and-mouse game in which Biddle constantly switched roles with enemy troops.

After he had disposed of the first trio, Biddle pushed ahead for another 200 yards where he ambushed a machine gun nest, eliminating the two-man crew. He lobbed hand grenades into a second automatic-weapons emplacement and then hand-signaled to the others in B Company that they could advance.

Aware of the deadly interloper, the enemy focused on him with renewed fury, showering him with a rain of rifle and machine gun bullets. None found the mark. Biddle accounted for one of the infantry soldiers, then sprinted and rolled into another position as bullets tore up the previous spot he had occupied. Biddle and his M–1 put away a second rifleman from a short distance. A frustrated enemy grenadier slashed at him with an extended burst of his machine pistol, swinging the weapon in almost a 360-degree arc. Biddle hugged the earth until the gunner halted and then drilled him. He completed his one-man assault by flinging his last grenade at a crew of machine gunners and then charging the position. A gunner and his assistant died in the attack, only an ammunition-bearer managed to flee.

Biddle credits his achievement to his eyesight. "There was plenty of light during the day. I had great vision. I saw the faces of all of the German soldiers. I saw each of them, before they saw me and from a very short range. That was especially true in several instances when I was only about six feet away in the underbrush."

Behind Biddle B Company now rousted the enemy from their forward emplacements. The early winter darkness forestalled further action by the company. The ominous sound of armor clanking heightened the anxiety for the troopers. Biddle and three others volunteered to investigate.

In the blackness of the night the members of the patrol soon separated. Enemy gunfire quickly discouraged the others from continuing the expedition. Biddle, however, crept about the disputed territory. He made note of some enemy positions, located a pair of their tanks. During his nocturnal prowl, sentries challenged, then shot in his general direction when he failed to respond properly. But they missed him. In one terrifying moment, while he lay motionless in the snow, a German soldier looking for infiltrators, stepped squarely on Biddle's hand. He stifled an incipient cry of pain and the grenadier trudged off in another direction.

"I was out there for a very long time," says Biddle, "but I never thought about eating. I thought how cold I was, especially my fingers. I wasn't sure I could pull the trigger of my rifle. I thought I would try sticking a finger through and pull on it with my left hand. The Germans at night came extremely close. They would say 'Halt! Hottentot' which was probably the password."

Biddle brought back his information on the disposition of the enemy and Force Fraser, exploiting the intelligence, struck early in the morning of December 24. Biddle repeated his role as the point. American armor, guided by the data from Biddle, knocked out the two German tanks. When another machine gun threatened to wither the attack, Biddle approached within fifty yards of the position and then killed both the crew and two soldiers backing them up.

Force Fraser broke through the line established by the enemy and on the other side the Germans wilted under the heat of Force Boyle. Says Fraser, "I led the attack across some open ground and I knew the first man out of the woods would be Colonel Boyle. When I saw him, I walked up to him and asked if he was trying to get himself killed. He looked at me, smiled and said, 'I could ask you the same thing.' "

Shortly before Force Fraser and Force Boyle greeted one another, Phil Di Stanislao, emerged from the house in which he spent the remainder of the night. He scrounged among the wrecked vehicles strewn about Hotton. "In a huge van with tool-and-die machinery used for maintenance, I found a sack of hand grenades and a Thompson submachine gun with two clips taped together which made it easier to reload. There was also a bag of .45 caliber ammo. I took them all and they would figure later in my experience."

Di Stanislao was among the first people from Force Boyle to see their comrades coming from Soy. "Charlie Keen was leading the men from B Company as they rounded a curve near a mill. Keenie was incredible. I never met a man who could get in more trouble being nice than I could being a son of a bitch. But there he was, with his eye swollen shut from a grenade. He was like all of the medics, very brave. When things got really bad, the rest of us could hunker down. The medics would get out of their holes to tend the wounded. We always believed our medics would take care of us."

Boyle now organized a sweep to eliminate any Germans who might still menace the road between Soy and Hotton. Charged with keeping the line of skirmishers abreast, Di Stanislao saw a German walking towards him, arms raised in surrender. "He wore a smock with a large Red Cross, was bareheaded. I saw one fist was clenched like he had something in it. I waved the Thompson at him, ordering him to open his hand. He smiled arrogantly and I unlocked the safety of the Thompson. He opened his fist and dropped a candy wrapper. He'll never know how close I came to killing him.

"We found only one other live German along the way. Appleton found him, hiding under his poncho. 'Applejack' as we called him, was waving a .45 under the guy's nose, telling him he was in the hands of the meanest soldiers in the world, the paratroopers of the 517th. I don't know whether the German understood what he was saying, but he was shitting bullets. We laughed, took him alive.

"It was Christmas Eve. We had our K rations but I don't remember having eaten since we got off the trucks and went into the initial attack. It was cold and miserable, the clothing was inadequate, but our adrenal glands were working hard. Company A went into reserve. We looked for a warm dry place. Sleeping bags were issued and I found a barn with hay. I took the shoepacks off. My feet were cold and a bit wet but I did not have any dry socks. I slipped into the bag with the socks and shoepacks inside also. I didn't zip up the bag because I wanted to be fully mobile. This was my first sleep since Soissons, except for snatches while on the trucks."

The situation for the C Company troopers with Charles La Chaussee turned grimmer on the day before Christmas. Trooper Ed Johnson says, "As the first dull light of morning came, an alert TD gunner stationed at the north end of Freyneux spied four medium tanks and a company of infantry moving on the town from 400 yards off. The gunner's opening shot set the lead tank afire. Simultaneously, the Germans hit Lamorménil. Two 83rd Recon light machine gunners [from the 3rd Armored Division] had a field day, shooting up four boxes of ammo while repulsing two assaults.

"Three Mark IV tanks lumbered up the road after by-passing a roadblock and minefield. Lieutenant McDonald, from the 3rd Armored, personally led two Sherman tanks out to meet them. His skillful maneuvers soon had the enemy tanks in direct range. All three tanks were knocked out."

At 10:00 A.M. elements of German armor and infantry were only fifty yards from the town. To the rescue swooped flights of twin-tailed P–38 Lightnings and P–47 Thunderbolts. They peeled off, dumped bombs, and strafed the enemy foot soldiers with machine gun and cannon fire. The attack broke up. Ed Johnson has no doubt that the Air Corps saved that day.

Even as the troopers thought they gained a breather, disaster struck. A German light-armored car raced to the side of a building in which several troopers manned guns. Because there were Americans all about, those outside held their fire and could only sound cries of alarm. Ed Johnson watched as "fanatical SS troopers led by a captain in an ornate black uniform unloaded." They entered the building from its blind side where there were no windows for the defenders to see them or shoot at them."

La Chaussee had just returned to his command post when he heard an outburst of firing. "Everyone was committed and the only reserve available was 1st Sgt. Eldon Bolin and myself. The two of us ran down the street to find out what was happening. Troopers were firing into a cloud of smoke beside the house in which I had last seen Lt. Roland Beaudoin. The troopers told me they had seen Germans entering the house. There was smoke coming from a burning German vehicle. I ran into the house. Lieutenant Beaudoin, Sergeant Delaney and a German were all dead, sprawled out inside the doorway. Moving past them, I fired my submachine gun into the ceiling, as the Germans might be on the second floor. No return fire came and I ran up the stairway.

"Sergeant Brown was lying on his back near a window and appeared stunned. I lifted his head and my hands came away covered with blood. Aside from the dead the house was empty."

La Chaussee learned that the German jeep had driven up to the building and the SS captain with another man jumped out and started firing. Their first target had been Brown. At the doorway they confronted Beaudoin and Delaney. All were killed in the point-blank exchange while the troopers outside accounted for the enemy driver. "It was a very bad moment," said La Chaussee, "Beaudoin, Delaney and Brown were three of my best men."

That evening just before the sunset of Christmas Eve, tank-commander McDonald summoned La Chaussee to a rooftop and pointed toward a string of tiny dots about two miles off. The paratroop commander gloomily observed what looked like several battalions headed straight for the strategically important town of Manhay.

"After dark," remembered La Chaussee, "we settled down for another long night. It was Christmas Eve and our radio played appropriate music, *Stille Nacht* from a German station, and other tunes over the BBC." The embattled troopers and their armored allies learned that they were cut off.

"That night," wrote La Chaussee, "General Eisenhower came on the air with his Christmas message for the troops. As far as we were concerned, it was the wrong speech at the wrong time in the wrong place. The supreme commander used phrases such as, 'Congratulations, at last the German has come out of his fortifications to fight in the open. Good luck! Good hunting!'

"It was fatuous in view of who was doing the hunting at the moment. McDonald went out to his tank and returned with a bottle under each arm, Scotch and crème de menthe. He said, 'a helluva mixture. I was saving it for New Year's Eve. But it looks as though we might not be around come New Years.' Five of us shared it, becoming pleasantly numb, and slept."

The first real sleep savored by Phil Di Stanislao and the other A Company troopers ended abruptly. "We were told that some infantry outfit was in deep trouble which meant we were also in deep trouble." The 290th Infantry Regiment belonging to the 75th Infantry Division, in its initial exposure to battle, had been assigned to the 3rd Armored Division command and committed to a night assault upon La Roumiere, a plot of wooded high ground south of the line between Soy and Hotton.

Insufficient time to reconnoiter the terrain or study maps, inadequate supply of ammunition and inexperience brought devastating results. The men of the 75th suffered horrific losses with most of their company-grade officers victims of strong mortar, artillery and machine gun fire. In the moonlight and then as daylight came, the dark-clad Americans stood out against the snow, making them easy targets.

Capt. Ben Sullivan, who had gotten a terrible headache earlier that Christmas Eve from swigging Calvados, was called to his aid station ordinarily designated to serve troopers from the 517th's 1st Battalion. Sullivan claimed he and his crew treated 900 casualties from the 290th, close to a third of the entire complement. "None of the medics from the 75th were anywhere around," says Sullivan. "I got a hold of a major from the 75th and told him, 'We've brought out all of the wounded we can. You better bring up your own collection people.' "

In a frantic effort to achieve the objective, all three battalions from the 290th were thrown into the fray. By noon of Christmas Day, in spite of the massive number of dead and wounded, the hard-pressed infantrymen had not won the day.

Losing confidence in the brass of the 75th Division, Howze directed Boyle to assume command of all units involved in the La Roumiere battle, giving him in effect the role of a regimental commander although the casualties had reduced the fighting forces far below regiment strength, even with Boyle's own men from the 1st Battlion thrown into the struggle. The drive against the enemy resumed under Boyle's strategic and tactical leadership.

Company A and Phil Di Stanislao joined the attack up La Roumiere. He had heard that while the field-grade officers of the 275th were still in their sacks, the hapless infantrymen, bundled up in target-ripe overcoats and carrying their weapons slung, marched into the German buzz saw with as many as 112 KIA in the first few minutes.

"I saw our company commander, Capt. Joe Broudy, conferring with Boyle. As I passed them, Boyle yelled to me, 'Be careful, Di Stanislao.' Mortar fire came down on us in quantity, for as long as half an hour. We hadn't had time to dig in and we were caught in the woods. I have never felt so vulnerable. We dared not move from our prone positions, faces in the dirt. Tree limbs fell on us. I looked over and saw Mizner's eyes. He looked at me with the unspoken question, is this the end? For him it came a few days later when shell fragments killed him and 'Pop' Anderson.

"But during this barrage, by some quirk no one was killed. We continued up the hill until halted by rifle fire and a machine gun just at the crest of the hill. I felt fairly confident I knew the location of the German guns. I thought if we played it smart, one man would stand a better chance of getting up there undetected.

"I explained my plan to our platoon lieutenant. I suggested he take the rest of the men in an encircling move while I would then go directly up the hill. We agreed that at 14:15 hours, a time indelibly engraved on my brain, he would have his group rapid fire, making a lot of noise and diverting the enemy's attention. That would keep them from noticing me.

"To start the operation, I crawled up the hill towards where I thought the firing came from. I took cover behind a thick tree just below the crest. I intended to throw a grenade and hope that whoever was there—usually at least three manned a machine gun—would duck down when the grenade went off. I didn't figure I would hit them straight off. Then I would stand up spraying fire from the Thompson I had scrounged. When the lieutenant heard that, he and his group would rush up.

"At 14:15, no rapid fire. I waited until 14:30 and there was still no firing. I decided I'd waited long enough no matter what had gone wrong. I'd go ahead anyway. I picked a grenade from the bag I retrieved in Hotton. I found the grenade had the pin bent all the way back so that I could not pull it out. I took another grenade and discovered every one of them had the pin bent that way. I cursed the sons of bitches who had left grenades in this condition.

"I moved back five to ten yards, took my knife and unbent the pins on two grenades. I inched back to the tree, pulled the pin on one grenade and allowed the handle to spring. I counted slowly, figuring I wanted it to explode over the position rather than give it too long a period between throwing it and the explosion. I threw it and immediately rose up from my prone position to let off bursts from the Thompson. Suddenly I felt a tremendous whack on my helmet; I heard a loud sound and then I was unconscious.

"Those who saw me go down thought I was dead. The Germans figured that way also because that was the only shot they fired. And immediately afterwards, they picked up their machine gun and departed. When I came to, blood was coming down into my eyes and face. I was puzzled. I had no idea of what had happened. My helmet was right beside me. There was a hole right where the forehead fits and a larger, exit hole at the back. God certainly had been good to me. I was pretty punchy and started back down the hill.

"Our medic, George Lecklider, crawled towards me. I waved him back and we met halfway down the slope. He put a dressing on my head. When I reached the bottom of the hill, Carl Kiefer piggy-backed me across a stream. From there I was ambulatory. I walked most of the way until I reached an aid station. From there an ambulance carried me to Verviers. It was a long ride, with other wounded aboard. Some died on the trip."

The diagnosis for Di Stanislao was a fractured skull with a chunk missing from his head. Medical authorities shifted him to hospitals in Paris and then the United Kingdom where he underwent surgery and the opening in his head was plugged. His combat days were at an end.

"We knew," says Boyle, "that the men from Task Force Hogan who had been trapped at Marcouray were going to try to come in that night. They did not have the password. My S–1, S–3 and I undertook the job of trying to put the assorted groups of soldiers in positions and to cover any gaps with patrols. It was close to dawn when we finished. I believe I was with A Company from the 290th and as I was putting some of the troops in position a column of 200 or so marched right toward us. I challenged them but received no answer. On my third repeat, I demanded, 'Say something in English!' [Boyle was hesitant because the oncoming men could have been part of Task Force Hogan.] When there was no answer, I commanded fire. No one fired except me and my carbine jammed. I forced it clear and fired again. It jammed again. I worked it by hand and fired. The column fled and the troops around me started firing on the retreating Germans."

Boyle never saw anyone from Task Force Hogan but miraculously, the 400 GIs did pass through the U.S. lines, after crawling through the snow coming close enough to hear the enemy singing Christmas carols.

The remainder of Boyle's charges, holed up at Freyneux and Lamorménil and separated by a minimum of two miles from friendly forces, were no longer under threat of immediate attack. In a well-executed thrust, the enemy had smashed a tank-mounted defense in front of Manhay and driven Rose and the Americans off. For the moment, Freyneux and Lamorménil were relegated to the status of bypassed territory, to be reduced to submission later.

Aware of their untenable status, and no longer able to reach upper echelons in Manhay, La Chaussee with tank commander MacDonald sought a way out. Sgt. Jack Burns, the resourceful schemer, led eleven reconnaissance patrols over a two-day period. On the day after Christmas, Burns discovered a forgotten logging trail, unguarded by enemy outposts. The besieged GIs quickly piled atop the tanks and they made their way to safety, rejoining the 1st Battalion.

For its valor and effectiveness in the Soy-Hotton area, the 1st Battalion received a Presidential Distinguished

Unit Citation and Boyle won a Distinguished Service Cross.

The Ardennes, more so than any previous experiences, tested the fortitude of the most stouthearted troopers. Says Nolan Powell, "On the road back to Soy from Hotton, a grave detail was out in the fields next to the road, stacking frozen corpses in ten-wheeler trucks. The dead were from another U.S. Army unit that had made an attack on our flank and had not taken their objective. The next day we passed through a forest where several more frozen corpses lay on the ground or in slit trenches. One had his ring finger cut off. A few days later while moving from one small Belgian town to another on an icy road with sleet pelting us, tired, hungry and dejected, I hoped that I would slip and break a leg, an ankle, an arm or something to get me out of there."

A couple of members of the 517th had managed to evade the summons into the Ardennes. Bill Hudson of the 596th Engineers recalls a noncom in his platoon with a hernia. "When asked why he hadn't gone to a hospital to get it fixed, he said, 'This is neither the time nor the place.' Immediately, upon hearing we were headed for the front, he reported to the medics and we did not see him for the rest of the war."

John Chism saw another trooper avoid further combat. "While getting ready to pull out, we received word that someone had been shot. Bill Harvey and I ran to the barracks to find the mess sergeant, M–1 still in hand, with a self-inflicted wound. Without any show of sympathy, we bandaged his left toe and got him off to the dispensary at Soissons, never to see him again."

While their 1st Battalion comrades struggled through Christmas around Soy and Hotton, the 2nd and 3rd Battalions were attached to the 30th Infantry Division along a defensive line anchored to the northeast in the town of Malmédy.

John Chism recalls, "On the road to Malmédy we jammed into two-and-a-half-ton trucks. We carried basic combat loads and wore everything we possessed to prevent freezing. Despite our efforts to keep warm, the cold pressed into every fiber of our bodies. We did everything except burn the trucks to ward off the cold. The steel floors of the trucks only increased our pain, so we did our best to insulate the floors. Harvey and I commandeered the front seat to survive the long night. We shared turns with the driver, keeping the truck on the road. During one of these turns we were ushered into the jet-rocket age. We saw an irregular light pass across our line of vision. We associated a strange sound with it, like the put-put of a motorbike. The first one did not excite us because we confused it with a meteorite. After seeing one plunge earthward and witnessing the huge boom on its demise, we realized we had seen a V–1 buzz bomb headed for Liège and Antwerp. We detrucked in the heights above Malmédy, the units with us taking positions overlooking the town. Sometime during the day, the place where a number of soldiers had been murdered was pointed out to us."

Pfc. Clifton Land, a replacement with the 3rd Platoon of F Company had begun his career with the 517th in September during the Champagne Campaign. His truck bearing him to the Ardennes consisted of a flatbed with no more shelter than the railing along the side. "Eventually, we dismounted and started walking, trudging through the deep snow. We cut across a field, finding the going more strenuous in the unbroken snow. Some of the men shed their heavy coats and heavy woolen scarves, dropping them along the trail. Someone noticed nearby what appeared to be cordwood stacked at the edge of the field. He went over to investigate. He pushed away enough to see this mound was not wood, but U.S. soldiers, all dead! They were from what was called the Malmédy Massacre."

On the second day of its advance, the enemy armor had fallen upon a truck convoy bearing members of the 285th Field Artillery Observation Battery who surrendered without resistance to the superior numbers and gun-power of the German SS troops. In a field on the outskirts of Malmédy, the SS soldiers shot down about 100 prisoners, most of whom died. News of the massacre spread through all ranks in the Ardennes and invited retaliation in kind.

Dick Robb recalls the reaction after hearing about the mass murders. "We learned that men in vehicles passing by the slaughter-field pot-shotted those lying on the ground. This was done with shouts of laughter. If it was to be 'no prisoners' that was OK with us. German SS became to us, less than the lowest creatures on earth. God put every creature here, even the most vile, for a purpose. The SS were less than the bug one squashes underfoot. They had no place, no purpose on God's earth."

Trooper Land, designated as point man and thus placed in front of the main line of resistance, dug through the snow into the hard earth until he had the semblance of a foxhole. "I heard someone coming and peeped out. It was our company mailman. He dropped an envelope down to me and hurriedly left. I carefully lit a match, tore open the envelope with my cold fingers. Inside was a Christmas card from a Miss Peggy Benfield, my oldest brother's sweetheart. The inscription was 'Peace on Earth, good will to men.' And there was a picture of an angel, hovering over the manager of the Christ child.

"Some minutes later, I again hear someone approaching. He whispered my name and said, 'It's Koehler. I've got something for you for Christmas!' It was an old buddy from jump-school days who was now in my platoon. He brought me a half can of frozen creamed corn which he had saved from a meal back in Southern France."

Dick Jones, as part of E Company dug in along the same line of positions as Land, suffered through the increasingly onerous conditions. His stream-of-conscious recollection: "There is an order to move again and in the midst of a raging blizzard. The wind is blowing snow horizontally and you can't see anything. We stagger along trying to keep track of the man in front because that's all there is in the whole world. You go on and on. Finally the man in front stops and shouts, 'Spread out along the fence and dig in. Pass it on.' What fence. I pass the word, move a couple of staggers, scrape away about a foot of snow, spread out my raincoat, wrap myself in a soggy blanket, pull a shelter over me, pray a tank doesn't run over me and go to sleep.

"I remember waking up and it's absolutely silent. Not a sound. The blizzard must be over and then I realize I feel warm. I can't remember the last time I felt warm all over. I must have frozen to death during the night. Maybe just my hands and feet. Nope, they wiggle. I push on the shelter half and it opens up like a trap door. It had apparently frozen, then the snow covered it and built an igloo that kept me warm.

"Looking around, there was the fence along the road. Everything is piled over with snow, with a quietness that is almost eerie. Not having anything else to do, I opened a C ration can of hash, chipped out a bite-sized chunk, put it in my mouth to let it thaw to crunching consistency and so had breakfast."

The 30th Infantry Division had warded off a desperate attack upon Malmédy and started to eliminate pockets of German troops now resisting efforts to drive them back from the Ardennes. In fact, the high-water level of the enemy advance had been achieved by them in the first week of the breakthrough and by Christmas, nine days into the offensive, the initiative had begun to shift to the Allies. Nevertheless, as they yielded ground the Germans fought fiercely, inflicting heavy casualties.

The 3rd Battalion, transferred from the 30th Infantry Division command to that of the 7th Armored Division, was ordered to wrest Manhay from the 2nd SS Panzer Division. Two ground attacks led by armor and several air raids had failed to displace the enemy. Forest Paxton met with Rupert Graves, Ray Cato from the 460th FA and the top echelons of the 7th Armored to coordinate the assault.

Jump-off time was set for 0215 with a ten-minute blizzard of TOT shells launched by no less than eight battalions of artillery, including the guns of the 460th. The guns delivered no fewer than 5,000 rounds, dropping them inside the town and along the approaches to be used by the 517th troopers. The quantity, during a period in which there was such a shortage of ammunition, is ample evidence of the importance placed on the seizure of Manhay.

The order of advance put I Company up front with H right behind them. At 0215, the artillery ceased firing and the troopers advanced. According to Dick Robb with H Company, "Four batteries—sixteen 155 mm guns—had laid fire just in front of the town. When they stopped, we moved up. I Company entered the shelled area. The guns were to raise and then bombard the town itself. When this stopped, we would attack." The reason behind the second outburst was the opportunity for the enemy in Manhay to regroup while the troopers marched on the objective.

"Regrettably," notes Robb, "one battery of four guns did not raise. When the shelling resumed on the town, these four guns dropped their shells right on top of I Company, with H just behind it. We could hear the cries of wounded as the battery shelled them. Someone finally got the word back to 'cease fire' but when we passed I Company's position, it was an unholy mess.

"Their pleading for help caused many of us to stop. I will always remember Lieutenant [Ludlow] Gibbons from I, standing there and shouting, 'Go on! Go on! Don't stop!'

"Many years later I saw Gibby and told him of my memory of him in that field outside Manhay. He said no one can ever know what that did to him that night. To tell others not to stop and help his men, to hear them crying out and he having to say 'Go on, don't stop,' because the attack must not be delayed for even a moment. He was an extremely competent officer who truly cared for his men and he had to tell others to leave them in their pain. It was that attack and the battalion that mattered and ultimately [continuing without halting] was best both for the battalion and the other men."

Sgt. John Rupezyk, 2nd Squad, 3rd Platoon, I Company, says, "I briefed the other squad leaders, showed them where I put the map so that somebody could get it off me if anything happened to me. We proceeded to the line of departure and then stopped for a while. Then the artillery started. We didn't pay much attention but then this damn stuff is coming on us! We could hear guys screaming out there, you could smell gunpowder and blood.

"I looked around and we had mostly new guys and they were all huddled together like a bunch of babies in a blanket. I tried to get them apart because I knew if one came too close they were all going to get it. I figured, maybe if I move, these guys will separate. I started and then a shell came in, killing a guy who went overseas with me and it wounded me.

"I was still able to go and after the artillery finally lifted we come into town. I came around a house and this was the first time I saw a Royal Tiger tank, and all I had in my hand was a pistol." Another trooper, Joe Cornett, tossed a white phosphorus grenade at the tank which was immobile because it had lost a track."

As they went down the streets, the troopers flung grenades into the buildings. "We got to this one place," says Rupezyk, "and for some reason we decided not to throw any there. We went all the way through the town and on the way back, near this house we heard someone hollering. The lieutenant with us shouted for them to come out. Some soldiers backed out, begging for their lives. Two or three were in American uniforms and said they were from the 7th Armored Division. They wanted to turn around and the lieutenant said if they did, he'd kill them. They were Americans and with them were five or six Krauts."

Dick Robb was among those clearing Manhay. "Later, at first light, I came around the end of a small gully and met a German face to face. He had a Schmeisser machine pistol in one hand, arms at his side. My M–1 pointed straight ahead, my finger in the guard against the safety. We were about ten feet apart. All I could see were the two lightning bolt-insignias on his collar, SS. He started to raise both hands as though he were going to surrender, for as things were, he stood no chance.

"I shot him in the chest and again before he fell to the ground on his back. He was still armed when I shot him, which was more than his kind had allowed our GIs at Malmédy. Had he dropped his weapon before I fired, would I still have shot him? I don't know. I prefer not to behave like them but at least I need not live with that. In Belgium, after I related the incident, a business acquaintance asked me if I had any remorse or regrets for not giving the SS soldier another moment to drop his weapon? I said I had no remorse and only one regret, that I had not been given, all things being the same, the opportunity to kill 50,000 more of those less than God's lowest creatures."

John Chism occupied a ringside seat as the operation against Manhay began. "The time before the assault was properly utilized with a complete reconnaissance, rest and warm food for the troops and a rehearsal. The move to attack positions was done with special attention to

stealth. There were no vehicles or other noise-producers
to give the plan away. The medics, in anticipation of casualties, pushed forward and all units received notice of
their location. Ambulances to evacuate the wounded did
not come forward until the attack was well under way.
Even the aid station was unoccupied until the period for
deception ended.

"When the barrage began, we were impressed by the
accuracy and timeliness. My group of medics was standing on the shoulder of the road within twenty or thirty
feet of the command group. We could hear the conversations and knew instantly the moment when radio silence was officially broken. My impression is that a
request for refiring was made. We medics understood
the request as approved. At the first sign of trouble it
halted.

"If there was a time that the unit should have broken,
that was the moment. Fortunately, there were no company commanders more suited for this mission than
Capt. Jim Birder, the I Company CO, and Lt. Richard
Jackson, H Company CO. They were soldiers to the
core, fearless beyond compare and loved and appreciated
by their troops. Despite the ghastly accident, they rallied
their commands and charged Manhay. There was no failing. Objective after objective, they charged the entire
area and immediately reorganized to stop a counterattack. The Germans were repulsed when they tried."

Lt. John Saxion of the 3rd Battalion Headquarters
Company acted as a liaison with the 7th Armored Division and its CO, Gen. Robert Hasbrouck. Saxion, enroute back from Hasbrouck's headquarters in Barvaux
to report to Paxton, witnessed the artillery barrage. "I
had been told that 240 guns would be firing. It was a
clear night and I have never seen anything before or
since as spectacular and awesome as that fire mission.
When I found Paxton, he was in tears as he told me
Lieutenant Stott had been killed by the barrage.

"I left my jeep and driver and walked to Manhay. Paxton told me he expected a counterattack and I should return to the 7th and get tanks for support. Back through the mile of flat, open fields littered with debris, I passed the body of the lieutenant and several men. We returned to Barvaux and were stopped and asked for a password. There had been so many different ones in the last twelve hours I could not think of this one. The guard pointed a Tommy gun at me and my driver shouted, 'Whiskers.' I yelled 'Bristles.' I never forgot the password again."

Hasbrouck gave Saxion a bottle of Vat 69 whiskey with a few inches still in it. Saxion shared it with his driver. "I never tasted anything so satisfying. When I got back to the States, that was the first drink I ordered. I couldn't even swallow it."

A member of Hasbrouck's staff led Saxion to a tank commander and within a few minutes five Shermans were warming up. "The tank commander asked me about mines since we were going to take a paved road direct into Manhay. I told him the engineers had checked for mines. He asked about cover. I said there were trees right up to the edge of town. I was lying like hell but I had to get these tanks to Paxton. The tankers were scared shitless of mines and 88s.

"I told my driver I would drive, lead the tanks and he could stay put but he insisted it was his job so we took off. About three miles from Manhay a signal-corps jeep lay on its side, smoking. Four soldiers stood around it, their faces blackened by powder. They said they hit a mine coming out from Manhay. I was afraid this might discourage our tanks and waved them to follow me.

"As we approached Manhay, the road was straight with no trees for cover for a mile. The tanks speeded up and we charged into town. There was a heavy smell of cordite, burning buildings and the dead. Our exec was in the middle of the main street and waved us down. He wanted the tanks not to mash the dead Jerries lying around. The tanks, buttoned up by then, gunned for their positions, one facing down each one of the five roads.

"I went to sleep on a sack of potatoes in a cellar. When I awoke, the tank commander was looking for me. He said, 'You son of a bitch.' I asked what the hell was eating him, I did what I had to do. He relented and told me one of his drivers stood up in the hatch after parking his tank and was hit by an 88."

The statistics for the shootout at Manhay showed fifty dead Germans, another twenty-nine captured. The high mortality among the enemy may well have reflected the attitude taken by Robb. The 517th suffered ten dead, including Lt. Floyd Stott and another fourteen wounded. Most of the casualties were inflicted by the rain of friendly 155 mm fire.

Occupation of Manhay did not eliminate the threat to the 3rd Battalion forces. It was in easy range of German 88s and everyone sought shelter in cellars. A bemused Mel Zais watched Rupert Graves calmly sitting in one basement and cooking his meal. "He took his parachute knife, peeled a potato, sliced off strips and then held the pieces over a candle to cook them." Rank conferred no privileges against the temperature. Zais noted, "I have never been so cold in my life. The paratrooper boots were no good for the continuous cold and snow. My feet felt like two blocks of ice."

Meanwhile, several troopers dug in beyond Manhay as an outpost. The position was exposed to enemy fire but it was a friend who hammered them. A P–38 zoomed in, dumping a 500-pound bomb. The explosion killed one trooper, hurling his shredded overcoat onto a tree branch, and tore off the arm of a second man.

Later, a contingent from an infantry division relieved the troopers. Jack Walbridge, a rifleman from I Company, was astounded to see the newcomers set up a

THE CHRISTMAS SEASON 307

kitchen and mess line in the field under enemy observation. "The Germans started blasting them. It was such a waste. Why did those men have to die out there? I was only eighteen and couldn't understand it."

Joe Cornett, warily hiding himself in the wreck of a house, was confounded by a general who suddenly appeared and asked, "How is it going?" "I told him, 'You better get your ass out of here. They're firing straight down this street.' He jumped into a tank."

"The front was in almost any direction one faced," says Dick Robb. "One morning a strange lieutenant borrowed four men from our lieutenant for a patrol. Some time later, he came back and I heard him tell our lieutenant he was sorry but he had lost one of ours. He said they ran into a German patrol in the fog. In the point-blank firefight, Lynam, who'd come back to us at Soissons, was shot in the heart and he had to leave him there.

" 'You left him?' I asked. 'How do you know he was dead?' The officer said since I, a sergeant, had questioned his word, he would take me to the spot where they came back through our lines and I could see for myself. I had committed the unpardonable, not only questioning an officer's word but also implying he ran from a firefight and left one of ours wounded 'out there.'

"We reached a point on a dirt road where a cut about four feet deep served as breastworks for A Company. The men were all pointing their rifles at the woods thirty to fifty yards away in the fog. 'Go that way about 300 yards,' said the lieutenant, 'and you'll find him.'

"Jack Burns came to me and said, 'Robbie, what in the hell's the matter with you. If the Germans don't kill you, some crazy bastard here will shoot you coming back in.'

"I remember saying, 'I have no way out, Jack. I'll call

your name before I step out when I come back. Make sure none of ours shoots me.' I was already frightened witless but it was nothing to what was to come.

"About 300 yards into the woods I saw Lynam lying with his back to me. He wore a white mountain parka. I knelt behind him and placed my hand on the back of his head. I looked directly into his face. The bullet had entered just below the left eye. A large, very viscous, dark, almost black bubble, at the hole broke and the liquid slowly ran down his cheek. I took off his web belt and the .45 revolver and buckled it on me.

"The shock of seeing him that way did something to me and in addition to my fear, I started to shake. I tried to pick him up. He was so limp, no rigor even in this cold. I couldn't hold on to him, even his knees went slack as his feet came up and my arm slipped up his legs. I couldn't get a grip around his shoulders. Picking up about 180 uncooperative pounds is not an easy task.

"I knelt and tried to get him over my shoulder in a fireman's carry. I got part way up, slipped and we both fell into a pile, him on top. I did this three times with him falling on me each try. The difference between total fright and abject terror must be experienced for no words could do justice to my feelings.

"I cursed him, asking why he was doing this to me. The black liquid was all over his face and on my shoulders and both arms. If there were Germans watching this, I knew why they weren't shooting at me. It was because they were laughing so much. I pulled the hood over his face, grabbed my M–1, got up and ran as my panic overcame me. I forgot his watch, his wallet, everything. I would regret this later, for his parents did not recognize any of the effects we managed to send them. They wrote a letter to the regimental commander denying this was their son.

"In my wild flight to get away, praying I wouldn't feel a German bullet in my back, my terror almost blinded me to the fact that I was heading towards where I would soon be another target. Standing behind a big tree, I managed to control myself and after a short walk to another tree, called for Burns. He saw that I got in safely.

"I asked someone to notify the graves registration officer of the coordinates to bring Lynam in. No one commented on the black mess on my jacket, not even my lieutenant who when I informed him of where Lynam was hit—not in the heart as we had been told—said, 'You are not required to bring him back.' Lynam later was brought out to the road. Passersby took his watch, his wallet and money and anything else that was personal and of the slightest value. There were those on our side that did this with no conscience. And for that reason, Lynam's parents did not receive the items most closely connected to their son."

The 517th now passed into the control of the 82nd Airborne. Gen. Ridgway had returned to the front to lead the XVIII Corps and Gavin reverted to his role as CO of the 82nd. The 1st Battalion relieved the parachutists of the 505th starting on New Year's Day. By the time he had completed all his duties and set up the positions for those in his company, La Chaussee was exhausted. In his command post, he sat down at a table and fell asleep without even removing his boots.

"I awoke at daylight and 1st Sgt. Eldon Bolin told me that General Gavin had visited while I was asleep. Bolin started to wake me but the general insisted I be left alone. 'He needs his sleep.' We had rarely been visited by senior officers while on the line, and never by a general. I started to give Bolin hell but he said, 'Well, it was a choice between getting chewed by a general or a captain. I chose the captain.' " That shut up La Chaussee.

CHAPTER XIII

THE INVINCIBLES FALL

DICK SEITZ'S 2ND Battalion drew the responsibility for pushing the enemy out of a series of villages overrun during the first few days of the breakthrough and relieving pressure on the 82nd Airborne holding positions along the Salm River. The objective for the opening day of the drive was a line stretching from the village of Trois Ponts to Mont de Fosse, a 1,500-foot-high hill. Trois Ponts, its name derived from the three bridges across the local streams, had been the downfall of Jochen Peiper's SS armored spearhead. All three spans had been blown by retreating Americans, bottling up Peiper's tanks and armored infantry. But it was also well suited to defense and buttressed by German artillery sitting atop the Wanne Heights to the east as well as other weaponry strategically placed to the south.

Russ Brami had left his job with a mortar crew to become the operations sergeant for E Company. "I went with the company CO to the battalion briefing. There was a shortage of maps. Dick Seitz and his staff would do their own reconnaissance, come back and tell us what we were going to do."

Joe Holton, the replacement who became a member of the 517th in front of Col de Braus, went on a patrol in search of intelligence. In a clearing they spotted an apparently deserted farmhouse. There was no smoke from

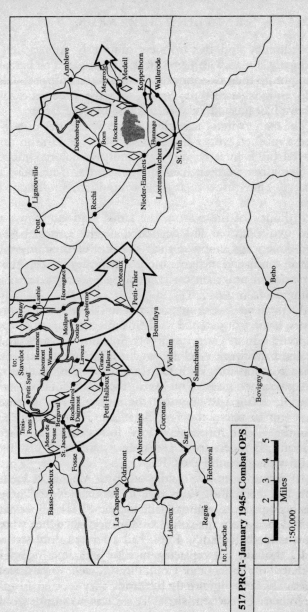

Arrows indicate the thrusts of the 517th against the Germans in the Ardennes.

517 PRCT- January 1945- Combat OPS

0 1 2 3 4 5
Miles

1:50,000

the chimney and the troopers cautiously approached. Suddenly, a man with fiery red hair emerged. The patrol brought up their weapons but to their utter surprise, half a dozen kids, aged three to ten, with the same shock of auburn hair pushed forward to stand by their father.

The man invited the soldiers inside where they discovered a mother, whose hair also was red. Joe Holton removed his helmet to display a similarly colored mop. The children were enchanted and acted as if he were a relative. They threw their arms around him and hugged him.

In honor of the season, the family had cut down a tiny, two-foot tree and decorated it with cotton balls. The Americans emptied their pockets of their instant coffee, candy and meagre rations. Then they left this tiny reminder of peace on earth, good will to men, for the killing fields.

As the 2nd Battalion prepared for its mission, Tom Cross, having dispatched to their units any paratroopers he could find in Paris, hurried to Soissons. He arranged for the paperwork to close out his assignment with the Red Cross mission. With Pvt. John Craven as his driver, and passenger Capt. Lou Rees, the regimental dental surgeon detailed to augment the medics, Cross started on a trip to rejoin the 2nd Battalion. He managed to find the XVIII Airborne Corps' forward CP at Werbomont. Troopers from G Company were performing security duty around the CP.

"A friend from my childhood days, Maj. Don Faith who had been Ridgway's aide in Normandy and now was headquarters commandant for the XVIII AB Corps invited me to join the corps' G–3 section since they were shorthanded. He knew I still had a limited-duty status and I thought he was being nice for old times' sake. I declined the offer and Faith directed me toward the 517th CP, several miles up the road.

"When I reached the CP," Cross continues, "I

dropped off Rees and a quarter-ton trailer with rations that we had towed from Soissons. Now I had Craven head the jeep for the 2nd Battalion CP. We went by a building that had been described as the CP but it did not look like one to me. Then we went into Manhay, a few miles further. There were a few tanks and trucks scattered about but I did not see any troops.

"We motored out the other side of Manhay without being hailed or spotting any signs of life. Beyond the town, I noticed a pair of tanks on the sides of the road with their guns pointing toward the front. We drove on by them but after a few hundred yards I sensed something was wrong. It was too quiet. I told Craven to turn the jeep around and to haul ass. We did."

Having almost blundered into the German lines, Cross and his driver managed to find the 2nd Battalion headquarters. "It was in an isolated farmhouse, smoke was coming out of the chimney and the German gunners had registered in on it. Dick Seitz had saved my mail and I read it." Then the battalion CO told Cross to find an assembly area from which the troopers would advance upon Trois Ponts.

Cross gathered representatives from the three companies in a courtyard behind the command post. He started briefing them. "Suddenly, a delayed-action shell passed through the roof of the farmhouse, out a window and then richocheted off the frozen ground before it exploded. Archie Brown was killed. 1st Lt. Jack West who headed a mortar section and I were among the wounded. I was hit in the left leg and head.

"They carried us into the basement where the battalion surgeon, Doc Megibow, did what he could for the wounded. Then we were evacuated. After stopping at some armored outfit's aid station, we were loaded on an ambulance bound for a hospital. The driver lost his bearings and headed the wrong way, toward the enemy lines. Fortunately, an MP stopped him at a crossroads and turned him in the right direction." Within the space of perhaps twenty-four hours, the chaotic state of the Ardennes battle had twice caused Cross to barely escape capture or worse.

Seitz and his staff abandoned the farmhouse shortly after Cross went down. The German gunners then leveled the place with highly accurate long-range blasts. That was the least of Seitz's troubles. "The problem at Trois Ponts," recalls Seitz, "was first, poor intelligence. Ben Vandervoort, the CO of the 505th Parachute Infantry whom we relieved, told me, 'Dick, we have been here a week and know there isn't anything out there but a few old men. If I was going to be here longer, I'd send a small unit out there and knock the SOBs out.' Well, the old men turned out to be a battalion-size enemy force, well dug in, fires laid and twelve hundred yards of snow-covered terrain in front of them. They had their mortars and machine guns well laid to cover all lanes."

The German infantrymen facing Seitz and his troopers were not from crack units but they held well-entrenched positions, knew how to use their weapons and were quite capable of inflicting much damage upon an attacking force.

"We were promised arty fire-support but only got a few rounds from the 460th. There was a shortage of ammo and we apparently did not have a priority. And we never had an opportunity to make a daylight reconnaissance. We arrived so late in the day we were only able to draw a map plan, after talking to the 505th. That day at Trois Ponts was the second worst day of the war for me and the 2nd Battalion."

The 2nd Battalion of the 517th as well as two companies from the 551st Parachute Infantry Battalion left the line of departure between 8:00 A.M. and 9:00 A.M. The snow by then had piled up knee-deep.

John Lissner, his captain's bars freshly minted, took F Company into the fray as the 2nd Battalion tried to advance on the Trois Ponts–Monte de Fosse line. "The Germans wore overwhites, like white sheets covering their entire bodies," says Lissner. "We were in our ODs [olive drab], and with our overcoats we stood out like little ants in the snow, easy to detect. I was hit near Trois Ponts. An 81 mm mortar shell exploded near me, knocked me off my feet. I was in shock, I tried to get up, staggered, and then realized my left knee was badly wounded. More shells and machine gun fire came in from a distance.

"I called for Murrey Jones and he crawled up. I told him I didn't think I could go on because I couldn't get up. We were lying down behind headstones in a cemetery. Around us I could hear kids screaming that they were being hit. I was carried back to a farmhouse in the rear. Murrey Jones took command.

"When I woke up the next day, here was Murrey Jones in the bed next to me. 'What the hell happened to you?' I asked him. He told me that only ten or fifteen minutes after he assumed command, machine gun fire from across the Salm River wounded him. George Giuchici took command, the third officer to lead the company within a space of just a few minutes."

Clifford Land participated in that attempt to storm Trois Ponts. "The town seemed an eternity away and that we would never reach it. Many did not, including me. Going at an angle down the hill we came to a cemetery enclosed with a cyclone fence. I heard someone yell, 'Medic!' I looked to my right and there was my company commander, Captain Lissner, with his runner in a two-man foxhole. The runner was dead and the captain wounded.

"Just before we moved out, I got the job of grenadier, carrying the antitank grenade ammunition bag slung over my head and shoulder. On the lower side of the cemetery, there was no exit gate. However, I knew I could easily vault the fence. But as I leaped the fence, the web strap to the ammo pouch snagged on the top of the wire fence. Even so, I went over, only to find myself hanging in midair on the opposite side with my M–1 crushed against my chest between me and the fence. I had reason enough to panic and I did, yelling for someone to cut me down.

"The Germans were not asleep down there in Trois Ponts. They dropped in their heavy stuff, mortars particularly but also their screaming meemies [*Nebelwerfers*, or multiple rocket launchers]. While I dangled there, a shell landed on the concrete cover on a grave just a few yards off. Fortunately, the headstone stopped most of the shrapnel. But one large sliver came my way. Suddenly I was retching on the ground in the snow. That single sliver had cut the web strap, passed on to split the stock of my rifle and stopped against my chest, leaving only a bruise."

Land recovered enough to continue his sprint down the hillside. "I made a dive for a huge ditch in which there were five others. After I recovered my breath, I sat up and leaned against a tree. Then I felt a burning in my right leg just as I heard an explosion. A mortar shell struck the fork of that tree, killing two men, injuring the others and me. One of the dead was a forward observer with our artillery."

Quiet descended and Land, who ordinarily did not smoke, retrieved a pack of cigarettes from the cartridge belt of one of the dead GIs. He lit a cigarette for himself and one companion. "That caused a big cloud of smoke to rise upward and I heard 'psst, psst' sounds above my head. I saw two tracer bullets burning out in the earth. We realized snipers were moving closer and one had seen the smoke and knew someone was under it." They doused their cigarettes and avoided further attention.

Land spent several hours in the shelter of the ditch. In midafternoon a jeep with a medic drove up. In spite of renewed sniper fire, the aidmen examined the wounded,

took the two most seriously wounded aboard, leaving
Land and a comrade, less seriously hit, instructions to
walk back under cover of darkness. Except for a visit
from some inquisitive sheep, the pair were undisturbed
and later made their way to the aid station. Subsequently, Land was evacuated, bound for a hospital in
Paris.

Dick Jones of E Company was part of the dawn onslaught at Trois Ponts. "I remember walking down the
trail, the sound of explosions of incoming mortar bursts,
close. Then the sight of my 'shelter-half' buddy,
Mitchell, lying on the trail, moaning, his right arm,
shoulder and head all bloody while a medic worked on
him. I couldn't believe it. It couldn't happen to Mitch.
Then I was lying in the snow at the bottom of the hill,
hearing mortar hits all around, shrapnel whizzing
through the snow, then a sizzle as they stopped, cooled
and sank.

"I remember raising up to look where to go, where to
shoot, then the popping sound of machine gun bullets
slicing overhead, crawling up to the ditch along the road
and firing blindly up the hill on the other side. Finally
the mortars and the guns stop firing.

"It always seemed so quiet after a firefight, not a
sound, as if you're suddenly deaf. Then the quiet noises
of people moving about, reorganizing, helping the
wounded, calling the medics over, then looking at your
friends whom you can't help anymore and the feeling
that you too have died a little. I couldn't shake my mental picture of Mitch. P.T. Harris was OK. He gave me
the mortar sight Mitch had been carrying. I didn't even
think about it.

"We set up our outposts. Across the river and up the
side of a hill is another part of the town, apparently still
occupied and looking down our throats, but unassailable
from this position. Sergeant Craig, the first man to greet
us in Toccoa and instrumental in teaching us our skills,

had received a well-deserved battlefield commission. He peeked around the corner of the building next door. A sniper fired and hit him. He died instantly. The invincibles were dying. The third squad was down to three men."

Doggedly, the 2nd Battalion struggled against the stubborn resistance. "Every time I lift my head," says Dick Jones, "shots hit the tree or blasted pieces of bark off. Small mortar shells hit the slope of the hill behind me. Then comes the realization this war has become a personal thing. They are trying to kill me personally. I can't do nor do I want to do anything. I just lie there. The mortar stops. No more rifle shots. I wonder where the rest of the patrol is. I take off my helmet and poke it above the log. No shots. Breaking the speed of sound, I get up and run back to the outpost. There's the rest of the patrol, resting and totally unconcerned. They didn't even know I was still out there."

His relaxation period was brief. The company tramped over open ground in bright sunlight. The deep snow forced a change in the point man every few minutes. Dick Jones remembers passing a burned-out German Tiger tank. He next recalls waking up in a hospital in Paris. Instead of a German bullet or shrapnel taking him down, a pneumonia organism had felled him, rendering him almost comatose for two weeks.

Although the half of Trois Ponts on the western side of the Salm now belonged to the U.S. forces, the advance bogged down in the face of murderous fire. Carl Starkey, Lissner's boon companion who commanded D Company and a dozen others, had fallen during a counterattack. Bob Newberry, the captain of E Company, one of his lieutenants and nearly two dozen troopers lay wounded in the snow.

Seitz bitterly remembers, "When Gavin came up to my observation post to see why we were stopped, it was obvious that we couldn't move because of direct, very intense, high-angle fire. I told Gavin I had used everything I had to suppress the enemy fire and needed some artillery. Gavin said, 'I'll get you some.' We got nothing. After two or three hours, he did send up four or five tanks. They were sitting ducks in the snow-covered terrain. When they came under severe enemy fire, they hauled ass."

Dispatched to locate the 551st Parachute Battalion on his outfit's right flank, Russ Brami incurred a slight wound. He discovered the other battalion also "had hell kicked out of them."

The overall plan for the operation had envisioned a sweep in which the Americans would knock the enemy off Mont de Fosse and continue on to the villages of St. Jacques and Bergeval to the south. But as night fell, Monte de Fosse remained in German hands with troopers from both the 517th and 551st burrowing in the snow. The darkness allowed the removal of casualties, which included all of the rifle company commanders and half of the platoon leaders. More than 100 GIs who had begun the day were now dead or wounded.

Bill Boyle and his headquarters company for the 1st Battalion had enjoyed their Christmas dinner late on January 2. The remainder of his troopers received their feast the following day but were forced, says Boyle, "to eat some of it on the fly." The 1st Battalion held the status of regimental reserve while their fellow troopers from the 2nd Battalion and the 551st struggled to advance. With the aid of binoculars, Boyle, in his CP at Brume, witnessed the carnage on the slopes of Mont de Fosse and the surrounding area. "Brume," says Boyle, "was on the forward slope of a large hill and provided exceptional observation of the valley below. While the 551st on the right flank had tough going, it made progress. The 551st did have considerable concealment.

The 2nd Battalion of the 517th had to go down a bare slope and then up another one against rather strong resistance in very good defensive positions."

At noon, three or four hours into the operation, Boyle told Don Fraser to prepare their men to go to the aid of their beleaguered comrades. "From where I was I saw that something would have to be done and I wanted to influence the orders I would receive."

Boyle rushed to the regimental CP. He arrived just after Gavin left, having chewed out Rupert Graves for the inability of the troopers to fulfill their mission. He had concluded his criticism by pointing his finger at St. Jacques and Bergeval on a situation map with his finger and declaring, "I want those towns by daylight tomorrow."

As soon as Gavin departed, Graves directed his staff, "Get Boyle." Having anticipated his CO's summons, Boyle immediately conferred with Graves. When the latter indicated that the 1st Battalion take the same route as the badly hammered 2nd Battalion, Boyle suggested a tactical change. "Feeling that this could only result in having two battalions chopped up, I eventually persuaded Graves to let me follow the 551st and strike from their area using the woods for cover."

Graves accepted the change and pressed Boyle to move rapidly. Boyle now led 250 troopers, including B Company and La Chaussee with C Company. Company A, minus the wounded Phil Di Stanislao, acted as the reserve. The men moved out, some still gnawing drumsticks, trying to sip hot coffee in their canteen cups.

Boyle had hoped to enter the woods and find the 551st in the last rays of daylight. But even with a guide furnished from the headquarters of the other parachute outfit, the 517th's troopers could not find the GIs of the 551st. Rather than delay his attack on St. Jacques, Boyle plunged on through the woods and underbrush. It was so dark that the men could only maintain their ranks by putting hands on the packs of those in front of them.

The timetable now off by several hours, Boyle did not close in on St. Jacques until about 11:00 P.M. He notes, "It was nearly midnight when we asked for artillery to help us in. There was no longer any possibility to surprise the defenders. The 82nd AB Division artillery advised us their quota for the day had already been fired. I could have blown up but I instructed B Company to ask for the artillery at midnight and then go on. They did as I ordered." (As soon as midnight passed, the guns could fire their ration for the new day.)

Within thirty minutes, B Company completed the capture of St. Jacques, systematically cleaning out the village house by house with rifles and grenades. According to La Chaussee, he and Boyle met in a windowless shed, lit up cigarettes and tried to locate themselves on a map using flashlights. One of the troopers announced they had an English-speaking prisoner.

According to La Chaussee, their captive was a thin, nervous corporal who said he had spent four years in England where he learned the language. Asked how many other Germans were in St. Jacques, he answered, "Fifty. We are all tired. For three days we have not eaten." He described the tracked vehicles heard by the troopers as *Sturmgeschützen*, self-propelled guns. Boyle wanted to know how many soldiers held Bergeval, the next town. "About thirty-five. They will surrender readily. For three days we have not eaten."

La Chaussee, thinking, "Goddammit, you should have thought about that when you started the fucking war," stifled his urge to bend a carbine barrel over the corporal's head.

Boyle dispatched La Chaussee and C Company who chose to exercise caution rather than gamble on the word of an enemy. La Chaussee felt the prisoner was telling them what he thought they wanted to hear.

On the approach to Bergeval, Lt. Ralph Allison's 2nd Platoon stumbled on an enemy outpost. Five shots rang out. Allison called to La Chaussee that his troopers had taken care of both sentries. More shooting erupted ahead of the 1st Platoon. According to La Chaussee, "Sergeant Deacon Jones shouted for his squad to fan out and fire. Almost all new replacements, they huddled miserably in the snow without moving. Deacon Jones said, 'All right, Goddammit, I'll do it myself.' In a few minutes he killed two Germans hiding along a fence."

There was barely an hour before daylight and while Sgt. Gerald Stark stealthily sneaked ahead to investigate what lay before them, the troopers waited uneasily. A brief mixup led Lt. Allison to scream at another platoon leader, "You son of a bitch. Throw another grenade and I'll kill you."

Upon learning from Stark that a cluster of buildings stood a few hundred feet to their front, La Chaussee requested his artillery forward observer for a bit of help. A fusillade of shells then softened up the ground before the troopers barged into the town. Instead of running up a surrender flag, the alleged small number of defenders opened up with volleys from automatic weapons. That elicited a second barrage from the big American guns.

As they had in Italy, the troopers from C Company now charged, three platoons abreast, spraying bullets and yelling. Ed Johnson was part of the assault. "It was 4:30 A.M. when we went running and yelling wildly down upon the town, tossing grenades into all the buildings and spraying them with automatic weapons. The nearest thing to resistance was an enemy machine gunner who wheeled at Cpl. D.W. Jones's approach. The 'Goat's' Tommy gun let him go no further. Pfc. V.P. Berg poured two clips of M–1 into another machine gun emplacement, silencing it for good. A huge workhorse, frightened by a grenade, charged out of a barn and into the 1st Platoon, bowling over several men on his way out of town. We captured a total of 118 enlisted men, two officers, ten more than our company strength at the time." Some twelve to fifteen enemy lay dead and perhaps twenty more fled. Remarkably, there was not a single casualty in C Company. In the street, the startled Americans spotted a pair of jeeps and a half-track bearing the insignia of the U.S. 106th Infantry Division which had absorbed the brunt of the German assault the first day of the Bulge.

Says Johnson, "What really hit the spot after laying out in foot-deep snow and freezing weather for four hours before the attack was moving all our prisoners into a barn and taking over their nice warm fires."

While Boyle and his people had provided the prizes demanded by Gavin, Lt. George Giuchici, successor to both Lissner and Jones as F Company CO, brought his troopers in a flanking movement that put them to the rear of the Germans atop Mont de Fosse just before dawn. The resistance collapsed. Many demoralized defenders not killed or wounded or who could not slip away went to ground. Afraid they would be shot down if they showed themselves, they hid in the underbrush and shellholes that pockmarked the landscape.

Shortly after the first light, a lookout reported the approach of visitors. La Chaussee, peering from a window, recalled, "I saw four men in diamond formation, carrying rifles with fixed bayonets. I stepped out to meet them and it was General Gavin with three aides. Gavin wore only a jump suit as his outer garment and carried a rifle, just like the others. He asked if I had any problems.

" 'There is some sort of tracked vehicle running around the woods. I don't know if it is a tank, but if it is these bazookas aren't much good against it.'

" 'Use these German *Panzerfausts*,' he said. 'There are plenty of them lying around.' " With that Gavin left to check out other elements of the 1st Battalion. Gavin's inspection missed Bill Boyle who was off taking his own tour of his most forward positions.

FO Tommy Thompson, supporting the 1st Battalion, was on hand as a company of enemy troops hove into range. "I called for ten rounds from the battalion. Those still able to headed for the nearest tree line where I arranged to interdict them extensively. Later, someone counted about sixty bodies on the field. Again the recommendation started out as a Silver Star but instead I added an oakleaf cluster to my Bronze Star."

With Mont de Fosse secured, the 2nd Battalion could regroup and occupy the high ground overlooking the Salm River. Boyle's B Company discouraged a counterattack and the positions appeared stable enough to set up a new aid station and resupply. Ben Sullivan says, "My system was that as soon as I had set up an aid station I would leave one doctor there and then go forward with a litter team to where Boyle was. In effect, we would have two aid stations. The chief duty of the forward aid station was to make it possible not to leave any wounded, never abandon a man." The tiny medical facility created by Sullivan at St. Jacques would prove critical for Boyle.

Meanwhile, Jack Kinzer from the 460th FA accompanied by the regimental intelligence officer, Lt. John H. Neiler, had conferred with the 1st Battalion CO to exchange information and coordinate future action. Says Kinzer, "Walking cross-country after a heavy snowfall was tiring. Neiler and I decided to return to the forward CP of the regimental combat team. We walked along the road the Germans had used to bring up reinforcements or supplies. We assumed the defenders were all gone since Boyle had outflanked them. He had sent his supply officer and a couple of riflemen with us to arrange for delivery of things the rifle companies required.

"As we approached the rear of the Mont de Fosse defenses, we saw a trio of Germans holding a discussion in the yard of a house. I had only my .45 pistol and we agreed I would try to get within range of the Germans with one of the riflemen while Neiler with the others would flank the yard on my right.

"I got close enough to use the .45 and waited for Neiler's group to get into position. The Germans went into the house. After pausing to consider my next move, I banged on the door with the butt of the pistol and yelled in Deutsch for them to come out. Germans started to file through the door and not only did our house empty out but the one near Neiler also began to empty. After making sure that all discarded their weapons, we moved them towards the regimental forward CP, about a mile or so down the road.

"I tucked my flight jacket into my pants and stuck as many Luger pistols as I could find in my jacket. While Neiler took the prisoners to a processing place, I shared the pistols with a few friends." A few days later, Kinzer, after visiting the 517th's 3rd Battalion in the company of a lieutenant colonel from an infantry division, was asked to take a pair of prisoners back with him. He paused to examine an abandoned enemy defense position and discovered two Germans still in a hole with a heavy machine gun. This time, armed with an M–1, which he stuck against the neck of one of the gunners, Kinzer and the other officer added two more captives to their bag.

Between these two expeditions involving Jack Kinzer the 1st Battalion endured another critical blood loss. While they bagged St. Jacques and Bergeval with minimal casualties, C Company was already down to little more than 100 troopers after leaving Soisson with 165 for a thirty-percent casualty rate in less than a week. The other parts of the battalion were similarly depleted.

The Germans, taking advantage of darkness and the heavy vegetation, dispatched a force of 200 across the Salm onto the heights. That move opposed the 1st

Battalion, now directed by Rupert Graves, to advance onto ridges overlooking the Salm River.

Bill Boyle remained uneasy about the lack of contact with the 551st Battalion, which should have lined up on his right flank. He dispatched a patrol led by Lt. Howard Bacon to locate the 551st. The troopers could not make contact. Boyle sent them out again only to hear the same negative findings. Convinced the missing battalion was not where he had been told, on the night of January 4–5, Boyle, accompanied by his intelligence noncom, Sgt. Bob Steele, and two other troopers, retraced the path taken by his forces towards the Bergeval area in search of the other parachute battalion.

"Although my S–3 [plans and operations officer] had said to me he thought there were Germans in the woods, I proceeded anyway. Near the bottom of the slope, out in the open, there was a bush and a lone tree about fifty feet apart. A few feet after I passed the bush, we were challenged. The field was covered with snow with bright moonlight on it and I turned toward the bush. A machine gun fired." Several bullets ripped into Boyle. While he went down, Steele and the other two troopers returned the fire. When it stopped, they checked where it had come from and then returned to their commanding officer.

"Meanwhile," says Boyle, "a heavy firefight had broken out at the two forward companies, A and C. When I was hit, I prayed, 'Do not let me die.' I was always a reasonably committed Catholic, certainly not perfect but with some weaknesses. Still, I was fairly committed, recognized sin, knew I did some and tried to truly repent. I knew that the brachial artery in my arm was severed and I was unable to stop the bleeding. This was the time when I experienced fear.

"When Steele and the others reached me, my fear was gone. I had accepted that I was dying and must do what I could for my outfit. It seemed that the brief prayer had given me peace and I was calm. I told them to report to Major Fraser that I was wounded and he was in command and that A and C Companies were in a heavy firefight. They walked away but Steele soon returned. I told him, 'I ordered you to go to Major Fraser.' He said, 'They will deliver the message. I am staying with you.' I said, 'I gave you an order. Go do it!' He again said he would stay. I told him, 'You can't do any good here. I am dying.' "

The battalion commander was much too big and heavy for the noncom to carry through the deep snow. Instead, Steele resorted to psychology. He said, "Colonel, the trouble with you is you do not have enough guts to help yourself." The comment boiled his CO's volatile juices.

"Give me a hand," said Boyle. Steele helped him to his feet. "He half carried me to Bergeval. I went first to battalion headquarters and then the aid station. In the aid station, at one point, the surgeon [Ben Sullivan] told the assistant surgeon [Capt. Sidney Samis] to quit working on me and have me evacuated while he worked on someone he could help. I knew they were right. They were unable to put plasma into me, although I needed it badly."

Sullivan actually describes the treatment of Boyle slightly differently. "I refused to have him evacuated immediately because he was suffering from such severe shock. We pumped three or four units of plasma into him." But Boyle was obviously a case whose needs demanded far more than could be offered in an aid station. Without evacuation, and there was no immediate possibility under the circumstances, his chances of survival seemed slight.

The gunfire heard by Boyle just as he went down and word of A and C Companies' involvement began with a routine placement by La Chaussee of his platoons. Fatigue threatened the captain's perceptions. "At one halt," said La Chaussee, "I looked at a firebreak and was suddenly shocked to see a German soldier standing there in full battle regalia, twenty feet away. I brought up my carbine to fire but the phantom slowly transformed itself into a small tree. While I stared at it, again, it became an enemy soldier. I moved forward and it was a tree once more."

A patrol led by Lt. Ralph Allison heard motors in the darkness of the woods and spotted the orange wire of enemy communications lines. Even as La Chaussee digested the information, something nearby moved. He turned his carbine towards the phenomenon and yelled, "Halt!"

"The movement continued," recalled La Chaussee, "and I fired. In the same split second, a voice called, *Nicht schutenzie!'* Then a bullet snarled by. I intended to fire several rounds, but the damn thing missed fire on the second trigger pull. A nearby trooper cocked his arm back to throw a grenade. He'd already pulled the pin and it would have bounced off the trees back into us. I caught his arm forcing him to roll it down the trail under-handed.

"The grenade exploded and Allison and another man ran down the trail. They returned with a German by the neck and a small sled. It was loaded with supplies and rations."

La Chaussee deduced from the sled items that an enemy force lay between his outfit and Bergeval. He hastily established a defensive line and the tired troopers reluctantly started to work with their entrenching tools. "The men were slow and apathetic digging in. I felt it was a matter of desperate urgency and as forcibly as possible told the platoon leaders to get them going. I had barely finished when a loud explosion occurred fifty yards away, followed by screams and rifle fire. Hornsby's platoon, taking its position, encountered a German antitank gun crew and put it out of action with a bazooka round."

The rumble of a half-track coming along a trail startled La Chaussee. He leveled his carbine, only to remember it was jammed. The armor passed by without receiving a single shot while the astonished troopers gaped at its large white American star, another piece of equipment seized by the enemy. The brief lull ended in a blaze of machine gun and other small-arms weaponry. A German antitank gun hurled high-velocity projectiles from as close as fifty yards off. The very first outbreak of fire killed two GIs, wounded nine others.

Pfc. Herb Loken had destroyed the antitank gun with his rocket launcher. He turned his attention to a second piece of enemy artillery and the bazooka silenced that big gun. The entire crew was shot down by Sgt. Willie Hogan and Pvt. N.A. Berry.

The enemy, however, retaliated with a swath of small-arms fire perhaps fifteen inches above the ground. The troopers could only prostrate themselves, embracing the earth while they cringed under the tracers whizzing by their heads. Ed Johnson heard La Chaussee shout, "Grab your weapons and prepare to repel the attack!" And in the classic mode, the Germans sought to follow up their small-arms firestorm with a charge. The embattled troopers fended them off and while the foe reorganized for a second attempt, the Americans deepened their holes. The attack was delayed further as Lt. Harry Covington, the forward observer from the 460th, called in their 75s.

When the Germans restarted their onslaught, the automatic weapons either froze from the weather or jammed from the intensive fire. The right-flank machine-gun crews were reduced to their .45 pistols and the position was on the verge of being overrun. Troopers Übel and Adamak, maintained the lone working light machine gun by urinating on it. They picked it up, ran the length of the perimeter to the endangered right flank and laid down enough fire to allow others to unjam weapons.

Still, C Company was nearly overrun. A messenger, Pfc. William Quinn, dispatched to get help from Boyle—C Company knew nothing of what had happened to him—fell into a foxhole occupied by Germans and became a POW. Desperate, La Chaussee, his radio shot to pieces, tried shouting a message for A Company to lend a platoon for help. Trooper Andrew Tucker, with the 1st Platoon and closest to A Company, went to guide in the reinforcements.

An impatient La Chaussee yelled, "Has the A Company platoon gotten here yet?"

From the dark, a voice questioned, "How many platoons has A Company got?"

Recognizing a Teutonic tinge to the query, La Chaussee hollered, "They've got sixteen platoons and they're all coming at you, you bastard!"

La Chaussee, C Company's CO, remembered, "Suddenly overhead, there was a blinding explosion and a streak of white light reached down and struck me just below the right knee. It was as though someone had walloped me with a baseball bat, although there was no immediate pain. Five other men around me were hit by the same shell. Aidman Hugh Webb was very busy. He reached me, cut away the pants leg, and before I knew what was happening, shot an injection of morphine into the leg. The morphine finished what fatigue and exposure had started. For an hour I was unconscious."

While La Chaussee was out, the help from A Company brought its firepower onto the scene. It was too much for the enemy and their attacks crumpled. When the fog lifted after daybreak, two shattered antitank guns, a half-track, German dead and wounded littered an acre of ground. A bevy of mortar rounds dropped upon a hitherto untouched bunker brought out more than a dozen Germans waving a white rag. The losses by the enemy included forty dead, a total of twenty prisoners, mostly wounded. The remainder of the force retreated with a number of them walking wounded.

The costs to C Company were high. Besides the two dead, cut down in the first fusillade, and the one man captured, there were twenty wounded, including La Chaussee. The 3rd Platoon could muster only seven troopers.

Like Boyle and the other casualties, La Chaussee passed through Ben Sullivan's aid station at Bergeval. "He saw that I was going to survive to the next stop and consigned me to a nearby stable. I was in shock and the morphine was taking hold. I can only remember saying, 'Sully, don't put me out here with the horseshit.' "

The captain's wound came from a shell fragment that penetrated his leg close to the shinbone. Transferred to a surgical hospital serving the 82nd Airborne, La Chaussee endured excruciating pain as the surgeons, short of anesthetic or in a hurry, relied on four men to hold him down while they probed the torn flesh. From there he traveled to a civilian hospital in Liège and finally Paris.

John Lissner, who had been struck down earlier says, "I was evacuated to the nearby hospital at Verviers. When I woke up, I saw Bill Boyle, wounded in both arms and a leg. I saw many others from the 517th there. The piece of shrapnel I picked up was behind the kneecap and difficult to extract. I was sent back first to Paris, then the coast of France and finally to England where they performed the first surgery on my knee." Tom Cross started through the chain of medical installations at an evacuation hospital near Werbomont before passing through others in Liège, Paris and finally Mansfield, England.

The losses from shot and shell were compounded by

those inflicted by the weather and climate. Paul Smith, the noncom in charge of the aid station, recalls tagging 128 men as a result of the Soy–Hotton engagements. Of these, sixty-four suffered a wound and an equal number had to be removed because of frozen or frostbitten feet. According to Ed Johnson, almost immediately after the engagement that invalided La Chaussee and more than twenty others, Ben Sullivan evacuated another fifteen troopers for frozen feet, including the acting 1st Platoon leader, S. Sgt. Tom Kerr, the seemingly indestructible Sgt. Jack Burns, and Pfc. John Adamak, one of the pair that toted their light machine gun from one end of the defensive perimeter to the other during the firefight on the ridge overlooking the Salm.

Trooper Mel Trenary, whose first ride in an airplane ended with his initial qualifying jump, had collected a Purple Heart for shell splinters in a leg hours after the start of ALBATROSS. Recovered, he rejoined A Company and in a hayloft for the night pulled off his boots and put on dry socks. When morning came his feet were so sore and swollen he could not get his boots back on. In his stocking feet, Trenary hobbled to the aid station, another victim of the cold, wet climate.

The diminishing number of available troops because of such problems apparently triggered a negative response among the brass. Medic Charlie Keen says, "Captain Dean Robbins [his company commander] really gave me hell when I sent Darvin Webb back to the hospital after St. Jacques. Webb looked like he was one of the soldiers who had wintered at Valley Forge. His feet were blue and frozen to the touch. Even after I told Robbins that, he insisted I was not to send anyone back, regardless of their condition."

Keen and Joe A. C. Williams, the medics from B Company, examined Tommy Thompson's feet and diagnosed frostbite. "I went to see the doctor from the 460th," says the forward observer. "He never liked me and he said the problem with my feet didn't amount to much. I'd just have to suffer with it. But as I left, he remarked, 'You have the right to evacuate yourself.' I went to the field hospital at Verviers. They sent me to a hospital in Paris where I stayed twelve days with a severe case of frostbite."

The frigid clime complicated the often delicate tasks of the engineers from the 596th who, because of the ebb and flow of battle, were forced to lay mines and clear those hidden by the enemy. Allan Goodman's squad received the assignment to sanitize an area strewn with the Bouncing Betty type S-mines. "The infantry was holed up in a stone structure and had some prisoners. The area to be cleared was in plain view of the woods, a few hundred yards off. I borrowed some prisoners with a couple of infantrymen to guard them and grouped them near us as we worked.

"The mines were on top of the road but under eighteen inches of snow. It was slow work checking for tripwires and the safetypin holes were packed with snow. I looked around and Gus Madison was putting his mouth over the mine part to melt the snow! The technique worked, allowing us to replace the pins. On the way back to the building, a sniper finally took a shot at us but all he accomplished was to take a finger off one of the prisoners with his arms raised."

Cheered by news that the 75th Division would now relieve some sectors held by the 82nd Airborne and its affiliated units, a bunch of 596th engineers under Lt. Ray Hild stripped to their shorts, plunged into the icy Salm River and, undeterred by an occasional mortar, constructed a trestle-style bridge across the stream to a bridgehead secured by members of the 3rd Battalion.

Other members of the engineer company busied themselves sanitizing roads and fields infested with mines. Don Saunders was among a party of engineers combing out the devices. "We happened upon a large house and found it full of German soldiers. We captured all of them without a shot and I carried a wounded radio operator out of the cellar. A little farther down the road, we saw movement in a field. We all dove for cover and a burp gun fired at us. Several of us shot back and wounded the German. Cpl. 'Pappy' Jones and I went into the field and captured three more Germans.

"We were marching them back when a bullet from behind hit Pappy and he fell to the ground. I called for a medic and held him in my arms as he died. I carried him off the field to our group of guys. It was my worst experience of the war."

From their first sighting of "the elephant" another kind of injury bedeviled troopers. Shell shock, World War I's label for emotional distress that disabled a soldier, had become "battle fatigue" in World War II. [Subsequent possible manifestations translated as "combat neurosis" and the ultimate, "post traumatic stress syndrome."] In the 517th, the phenomenon occasionally appeared. Both Ben Sullivan and Walter Plassman recall officers and enlisted men who arrived at the aid stations without visible injuries but unable to fulfill their duties. The two medics say they allowed them to make themselves useful around the area and believed most could later go back to their units. However, policy dictated, in particular, officers who showed any weakness would be shipped to the rear.

For the most part, the troopers, seeing in Dick Jones's words "the invincibles are dying," bottled up their anguish. In truth, the omnipresent perils and the miserable living conditions drained even the capacity to grieve. Newspaperman Hal Boyle filed a poignant tale about the 517th shortly after the troopers overran Trois Ponts. He wrote of a telegram that arrived at the regimental CP of the 517th. It announced that an unnamed corporal had received an appointment to the U.S. Military Academy and was to return to the United States.

The future cadet, however, had been a KIA at Trois Ponts. What makes the story more stunning is that the unlucky trooper's name is unknown. Survivors from the 2nd Battalion do not recall the man who fell into the oblivion of anonymity. Perhaps he was one of the replacements who had barely been inscribed upon a roster before death took him.

In the Battle of the Bulge, the 517th was among many outfits where the latest replacements became KIAs before anyone knew their names. Deacon Jones still wonders about the soldier who came to the company at 10:00 P.M. and by 2:00 A.M. was dead without anyone ever learning his name.

Any considerations by the Allied High Command of waiting for better weather to launch a final offensive had been demolished by the breakthrough in the Ardennes. In spite of the appalling losses on both sides, the strategy now dictated continued pressure upon the Germans as they slowly retreated through the Ardennes of Belgium and Luxembourg back to their homeland.

CHAPTER XIV

FINAL BATTLES

OVERALL COMMAND OF the elements of the 517th shifted to new authorities in mid-January. At the same time, Graves nominated Maj. Robert McMahon, the 3rd Battalion exec, to replace the wounded Boyle as CO of the 1st Battalion. The regiment, still part of Gen. Matthew Ridgway's XVIII AB Corps, took its orders from several subsidiaries. The 2nd Battalion became attached to the 7th Armored Division while the other two battalions drew the 106th Infantry Division. Actually, the 106th itself could barely field as many riflemen as the 517th since two of its three regiments had been destroyed in the first days of the enemy breakthrough. Only the 424th Infantry Regiment could muster foot soldiers in organized operations.

The 1st and 3rd Battalions of the 517th, with turf seized on the east banks of the Salm, acted in concert with the 75th Division and the 424th Regiment as the right flank of a drive towards St. Vith. On the left flank, the 2nd Battalion assigned to the 7th Armored, coordinated with the 30th Infantry Division coming down from Malmédy.

Both battalions forded the Ambleve River, another of those swift-flowing, icy streams that helped bottle up the Germans. John Saxion recalls, "Colonel Paxton assembled all of the bazookas into a single platoon and put me in command. My sergeant was an American Indian, one of the best fighting leaders I saw. When the lead company would meet resistance, the cry, 'bazookas up front' would come. Most times, I split the platoon, the sergeant taking one half and I the other. I would give him the choice of advancing through a field or a road and he would usually pick the worst of it."

The troopers marched into Stavelot and as they reached the south side, across the Ambleve, Saxion says, "The buildings were ruined, burned and windowless. Remnants of the 106th Division [from the initial thrust of the enemy almost a month before] were everywhere. Weeks-old dead were still lying where they fell. Trucks and half-tracks sat along the streets, their dead passengers inside.

"Captain Jackson [Richard]—no matter what the situation, he always seemed to be out front with the scouts—had his H Company running around in shirt-sleeves as if hunting rabbits. Colonel Paxton climbed to a barn loft to look ahead and stepped on a German soldier sleeping in the straw. He captured his first prisoner.

"I went to the aid station to get patched up from some cuts caused by tree bursts. Doc Dickinson was working on a small German lieutenant's hand. The German spoke English and was telling about his prowess as a soldier and killer. Dickinson told him if he didn't shut up he would cut his damn hand off. Lieutenant Reber of headquarters company was leaning against a post, waiting his turn. He had been severely wounded in the back."

While the 3rd Battalion savored the pause, the 1st Battalion absorbed more deadly blows as it passed through the 3rd with instructions to occupy three villages. The first two proved unoccupied but, says Ed Johnson with C Company, commanded by Mickey Marks after La Chaussee went down, "A sixth sense of foreboding told us that this was all wrong. As the 3rd

squad of the 2nd Platoon moved into the village of Logbierme, our fears were verified. Sniper fire from several
houses cut down and mortally wounded Pfc. Hubert B.
Ford, Corporal Albert J. Caraciola and Private Bruno P.
Baraglia. Pfc. Charles G. Daigh, wounded by the same
burst of fire, picked up a BAR and covered withdrawal of
the rest of the squad, shooting in all windows from his
exposed position."

Instead of falling back, C Company GIs rampaged
block by block until they reached the final structures of
Logbierme. Here, the enemy, backed by a self-propelled
cannon and machine guns laid siege to the would-be attackers. A flurry of six successive shells collapsed the roof
and walls of a building in which a number of troopers
took refuge. S. Sgt. Cecil Lockhart assigned the able-
bodied to assist the wounded in a retreat to safety. When
the sergeant discovered a pair of men had been left behind he returned. Both were dazed from the explosions
around them and needed his help to evade the continuing fire.

Others tried to outflank the enemy but small arms
pinned them down and brought further wounds. Although Lockhart directed his platoon in an attack that
secured three houses and bagged twenty-five prisoners,
the daylight exposed too many men. Company commander Marks initially settled his troopers into a defense, utilizing the buildings seized by Lockhart and his
troopers.

"We held what we had until the next day," recalls
Johnson, "while the battalion commander made
arrangements to move up tanks to assist our next try.
Snipers were rampant, mortally wounding Pvt. Walter E.
Jacobsen and injuring Pfc. Nolan L. Powell."

The latter remembers, "In the house where the CP
was located, I had picked up a case of K rations. My M–1
rifle was slung over my left shoulder, the rations were
under my right arm. While moving from the CP back to

my platoon, WHAM! It was like a baseball bat had hit the funny bone of my left arm. I looked down and saw my ring finger and my middle finger were split apart. A bullet from a German sniper had entered my left elbow, came out my left forearm and then passed through my left hand between the ring and middle finger." Sent back for first aid, Powell eventually spent a year in four different military hospitals before receiving his discharge.

When the tanks requested by McMahon rumbled up that night, C Company reverted to its hollering style and in Johnson's words, "laying down such beautiful covering fire, that the tanks did not have to be called up once. We took and held all houses, cleared the surrounding terrain of all kraut-eaters."

One unit from the 517th had not suffered either the harsh conditions or the intensive combat endured by their fellow troopers. The 3rd Battalion's G Company had pulled the enviable task of providing security for the XVIII Airborne Corps at Werbomont. Lt. Ben "Sweet Pea" Renton says, "For two weeks we had this terrific assignment, sleeping in haylofts, warm chow. We had information that a German commando, disguised as a major general, was making the rounds so the usual army ID was no good. That's when we started asking questions about Babe Ruth and Betty Grable. There was only one incident where some dummy parachutes were dropped by the Germans. We went into that area, found and killed six Germans while two of our guys were wounded. Finally, Colonel Graves asked for his attack company back. Actually we were the only full-strength one left in the 517th."

G Company advanced from Stavelot, crossing a footbridge at night. By dawn, says Renton, they had climbed a slope opposite the village of Butay. "We received machine gun fire from a building and I threw a white phosphorus grenade into it, burning down the place. Colonel Paxton earlier had picked the site for his headquarters. I moved through the settlement followed by a squad. Three Germans jumped out of a house facing us. I dropped all three with a burst of my Thompson. We cleaned out the area, accounting for six or seven dead and a dozen prisoners."

On the following day, while the 1st Battalion advanced to control Petit Thier, the 3rd on its left flank occupied Poteaux. Both towns stood along the road leading to St. Vith. Renton's company in Poteaux soon began to reel from long-range counterpunches from the enemy. "We were reinforced by two M–10 Tank Destroyers. As I was crossing the road, a barrage of screaming meemies and heavy mortars started. I heard an incoming shell that struck one of the M–10s. It broke up and took pieces out of my right thigh, kneecap, both lower legs and right shoulder. I turned my platoon over to Lt. Jerry Callahan, who'd received a battlefield commission a few weeks before. When Colonel Paxton saw me, he said, 'Again, Sweet Pea? Got any cigars left?'

"They loaded me in an ambulance bound for the regimental aid station. On the way, a shell landed nearby and one piece pierced the ambulance, killing a sergeant already hit in the lung with shrapnel. I was shipped out of Stavelot to an evacuation hospital, then Paris and finally flown to England."

Despite the casualties, the objectives had been taken, and the 424th relieved the troopers at both Petit Thier and Poteaux. The 3rd Battalion now enjoyed its rest in Stavelot. Some, drawn by lot, received passes to Paris. Saxion bunked with a bunch of junior officers in the home of a family named Jacob. "The father spoke English and was an amateur photographer. He was wanted by the Germans for partisan activity. They had two daughters and a son. Each evening the family asked two of us to dine with him. [Lt. Warren] Caufield and I would help the kids with their English. They told us how, during Peiper's attack on Stavelot, several civilians in the town, along with some GIs of the 106th, defended a bridge, too small for tanks, across the Ambleve. These people held off the Jerries with a 37 mm cannon. When the Germans finally did cross, they went from house to house along the river. They collected fifty men, women and children, dug a hole in the town square and shot the fifty."

The 1st Battalion sacked out in soft beds, showered, gobbled hot chow, read mail and put on clean uniforms at nearby Parfondruy. The number present to enjoy the luxuries was a mere ninety men. Says Ed Johnson, "Our ten days of R and R were a bit like paradise after what we'd been through. That first hot shower was a sensual experience I will never forget. The ten-in-one rations and warm billets were not taken for granted."

The 2nd Battalion was otherwise engaged. Even as the brother battalions began their R and R, Dick Seitz and his troopers joined the 7th Armored's Combat Command A with the purpose of taking back St. Vith, out of which the 7th Armored had been driven some four weeks earlier. The three combat commands—CCA, CCB and CCR—correspond roughly to the trio of regiments that composed an infantry division. Within each combat command there are battalion-size task forces which take the names of their commanders. For example, the trapped GIs of the 3rd Armored who slipped through the lines established by Bill Boyle came from Task Force Hogan.

The armored division's CCA designated Seitz to lead one of its three task forces. "Colonel William Triplet, commander of CCA, called a meeting," says Seitz. "I got the word while at my CP, about two miles away. I immediately started out on foot. The two jeeps that belonged to the 2nd Battalion were both out hauling supplies. I arrived at Triplet's CP just about the time the meeting was breaking up. Needless to say, Triplet was concerned about my tardiness, but when I told him I

had to walk to his CP, he made many comments and finished [by] saying he would take care of the problem.
The result was he gave me a half-track with radios and
other equipment to use as my CP plus another vehicle
for supply. We now had the best communication and
transportation of any time during our combat service."

Task Force Seitz included the surviving riflemen of
the 2nd Battalion augmented by a company of tankers
and a platoon of tank destroyers from the 7th Armored
under the leadership of Lt. Col. John Wemple. The task
force actually did not cross the line of departure until
January 21. The foot soldiers and the mobile armor used
the days before the offensive began to develop working
relationships and communications procedures.

The initial target for Task Force Seitz was a patch of
forest, the Auf der Hardt woods. Intelligence led Seitz
to choose an attack under the cover of darkness. He ex-
plains, "What dictated my night-attack was a German
document that my S–2 remembered. It had said, 'When
the enemy [U.S.] troops are using tanks, you can be
pretty sure that they won't attack at night.' When I
heard this, I decided we would start at 0400, without
arty prep, but with planned fire in the event we needed
it. I estimated that with the deep snow it would take us
until sunrise to reach the objective. We could then have
the tanks and TDs move rapidly through to exploit the
capture of our objective."

The troopers dropped their overcoats, and burdened
with weapons and ammunition, they plunged through
thigh-deep snow, breaking their individual paths. Russ
Brami remembers the move on the Auf der Hardt
woods. "It was 4:30 in the morning and there was a
blinding snowstorm. We couldn't see anything, but fortunately we could smell the fuel they burned. They were
asleep in bunkers along the tree line."

Surprised by the sudden appearance of the attackers,
the German outposts yielded after a brief outburst of

shooting. Six Germans were dead, thirty wounded, fifteen captured. As daylight peeked through the swirling snow, E Company overcame a force of eighty of the enemy sheltered in log huts. Fifty more Germans died. A Company D patrol under Lt. Charles Minard surprised a pair of Mark V tanks, capturing them intact. Taking the crews prisoner, the troopers disabled the armor with white phosphorus grenades.

According to Brami, the advancing troopers discovered themselves menaced by enemy soldiers to their rear, either infiltrators or bypassed pockets. Shooting erupted in every direction. During the day's melee, Lt. Paul Quigley, designated E Company commander after the previous CO, Capt. Bob Newberry, went down near Trois Ponts, was hit in the stomach. "I thought he'd die," says Brami. "But he pushed his guts back in. His messenger, Ben Adams, was also wounded. We heard a C–47 land in a cleared area at the forward aid station. When there was some question of whether to try and get Quigley back to the C–47, Adams pulled his .45 and told the medics, 'I'll shoot you bastards if you don't take him.' Quigley left on the back of a jeep litter. John Wettle took over for Quigley."

Task Force Seitz drove ahead. Brami and his companions were appalled at the sight of the old machine gun positions manned by the ill-fated 106th Division. "They were just stuck out there, nothing in front of them for protection except snow."

A patrol dispatched by John Wettle revealed, in Brami's words, "Germans all over the place." The troopers assumed defensive positions in front of Hunnange, the next-to-last hamlet on the road to St. Vith. Brami took refuge in a house. "The owner, a Belgian, pointed a finger towards the basement. I had my Tommy gun and when I went there the Germans were just milling around. I took them upstairs and, as we did with all the Krauts, pushed them in the direction of the rear."

"I think the attack on Hunnange," says Seitz, "was a textbook operation in terms of planning, coordination of fire and execution. My arty officer from the 460th was jumping up and down with the thought that he could bring in so many battalions to fire TOT. There were eighteen battalions of arty firing, a helluva lot of fire and the greatest single support we received during the war." Indeed, the massive barrage at Manhay only involved eight battalions of big guns.

Russ Brami watched the display from a ditch. "The stink of powder, the smoke, fires, was like the movies. I never saw such a thing even in Korea with the Air Force and the Navy part of the action. They chopped down every tree within 100 yards of the place."

When the artillery stopped, waves of tanks bearing troopers rumbled into the crossroads. The tankers poured cannon fire from inside their steel juggernauts while the 2nd Battalion GIs riding outside, hammered away with the .50 caliber machine guns mounted atop the armor.

Well over 100 Germans surrendered amid the litter of their dead and destroyed equipment, including three self-propelled guns. Seitz arranged that night for an outpost at Lorentswaldchen, the last crossroads on the outskirts of St. Vith. "We had a company forward on the edge of the town and could have easily taken it. We were told 'hold in your defensive position.' We sat there and watched the 7th Armored's CCB march into St. Vith with an army of newspeople."

The media had been alerted to accompany Gen. Bruce Clarke, the CO of the 7th Armored's CCB, who had been forced to flee St. Vith exactly one month earlier. Clarke wanted the satisfaction of personally capturing the site of his embarrassment.

The 7th Armored's Triplet vigorously praised the troopers of the 517th. Seitz recalls Triplet on the occasion of an attack order, commenting, "This is a job for

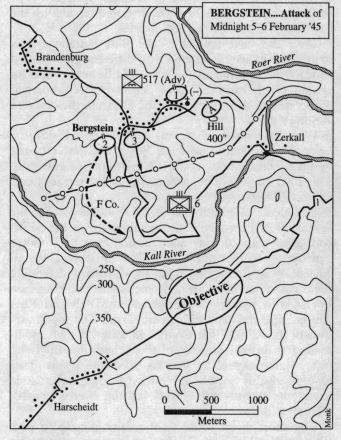

BERGSTEIN....Attack of
Midnight 5–6 February '45

Brandenburg

Roer River

517 (Adv)

Bergstein

Hill
400"

Zerkall

F Co.

Kall River

250

300

Objective

350

Harscheidt

0   500   1000

Meters

Monk

The well-entrenched enemy battered the thin ranks of the 517th as
it moved out from Bergstein for its final combat in the Huertgen
Forest.

Task Force Seitz, meaning one requiring aggressiveness and foot power." Triplet subsequently added, "I was, and still am, impressed by the quiet courage and capable, uncomplaining performance of Seitz and his crew." But the association with the 7th Armored ended as the 517th shifted to other responsibilities.

Over the next few days, the 2nd Battalion, now stripped of its armor, aligned with different units battled to retrieve the remnants of what had been the German salient. On January 27, Dick Seitz's troopers boarded trucks to join the others from the 517th in the rest area at Stavelot.

Welcome as the relief was, nothing could hide the heavy losses already incurred. Fewer and fewer of the original Toccoa boys could be mustered at roll calls. The T/O could not be maintained as the replacements fell in significant numbers.

The peaceful sojourn at Stavelot ended during the first week of February. The orphan status of the 517th continued with custody now handed over to V Corps and one of its line outfits, the 78th Infantry Division. Ahead lay confrontation with the Germans defending their native territory, most immediately the Huertgen Forest with two swollen streams—the Kall and Roer Rivers—and the Schwammenauel Dam. The top strategists of the Allied High Command feared the enemy intended to open the gates of the Schwammenauel and other water-control barriers to flood the plains. That would seriously impede any offensive toward the Rhine River, the last natural obstacle to the overrunning of Germany.

The most direct route to the dams dictated a path through the Huertgen Forest, an almost impenetrable woods fortified by extensive minefields, pillboxes and bunkers. According to Jim Gavin, he learned from later talks with German officers that they were amazed that the Americans tried to march through the Huertgen instead of outflanking it.

Americans had first invaded the Huertgen in September. Over the succeeding months four infantry divisions had incurred frightful casualties there. Indeed, part of the Ardennes breakthrough had come at the expense of the 28th Division which suffered severe losses and was still far understrength when struck by the German onslaught. Other U.S. outfits, the 4th, 8th and 9th Divisions, also traded thousands of bodies for yards of forest. The town of Bergstein, seized in an epic encounter by U.S. Rangers in December, marked the deepest penetration. Operations in the Huertgen ceased with the appearance of the Bulge.

The summons back to combat dropped morale. Charlie Keen says, "We were all dead tired and nerves were all that kept us going. It looked as if the only way out was to go through the hospital or in a mattress cover [the body bag of World War II]. Poor choice. Morale was at its lowest point and fighting without Boyle preyed on everyone's mind. Major Fraser was the only person who had the complete confidence of the men, not just the Toccoa boys but also those who had come through Italy. There was less talking and little or no joking anymore. Some spoke of it and everyone thought about it—the law of averages. It became a roar in your mind, whenever one of the old men got it. Would I be next?"

Dick Robb, as a first sergeant, saw the prospects from a different but equally dismal vantage point. "Starting back from when we were at Soissons, it had become an increasing game for some who knew we were not finished with combat. Their idea was to screw up, commit a minor offense so they would be in the guardhouse awaiting a court-martial when the call up came. Colonel Graves had issued an order that all stockade occupants would be returned to their units when we went to the front.

"Just before we were to begin our attack from Stavelot, the stockade group was brought up. It had become our practice to use them as number one and number two scouts for the lead attack unit. They would be out front and then would come the squad sergeant. These three were the most likely to take the first fire from the enemy.

"One of the stockade group, call him 'D,' said to me after learning how they would be used, 'Sergeant, you are trying to get us (the stockade bunch) killed, aren't you?' I will always remember how he looked at me. I answered, 'No, D, every squad has one and two scouts. Your chances are as good as theirs would be. You should not expect different treatment.'

"When we did attack my platoon did not have D with them. I heard later that he was killed in the first exchange of fire. That's why I cannot forget the look he had when he said we were trying to get them killed."

The 8th Division occupied the village of Bergstein by the grace of the Rangers. The higher powers decreed that the 517th relieve the foot soldiers in Bergstein and then lead an assault on the stronghold of Schmidt, across the Kall River. Dick Robb describes the infantry regiment that was relieved as "in the worst condition of morale one could imagine. The Germans had them completely cowed. At dusk, Jerry moved up close to the town into trenches and sniped at even the slightest movement. At dawn, they moved back to a wooded area and covered the GIs with rifle and mortar fire.

"Several of us entered a house overlooking the enemy positions. Outside lay a body, a GI. I asked how long he had been there. An officer told us, 'Several days.' We learned there were a number of dead that couldn't be recovered because of the situation. We were told the troops were fed only twice a day, after dark in the evening and before dawn of the next day." Indeed, Jack Kinzer at the CP for the 460th in a Bergstein basement sat down to his first hot meal in several days. "A rocket hit nearby and blew down a black soot that covered over the hot turkey and mashed potatoes which some guys had risked life and limb to bring up to the CP basement that night."

The march toward the Roer Dams began badly when Rupert Graves arrived at Bergstein and immediately sought to reconnoiter the area. Observing the activity, German gunners began dropping shells into Bergstein which led to protests from the 8th Division GIs. Their commanding general started to scold Graves who tartly responded that he could hardly be expected to launch an attack without adequate reconnaissance. The general accepted the explanation but insisted Graves should consider himself severely reprimanded.

The 2nd and 3rd Battalions were to head out at night, cross the steep ravine down to the twenty-foot-wide Kall, wade through the frigid water and seize control of the high ground overlooking the road to Schmidt. Aside from the firepower which included artillery and mortars that could be brought down upon them, the troopers knew they would contend with what was believed the biggest minefield of the war. Additionally, terrain and weather conspired to hamper operations.

Mel Zais later declared, "Warmer weather had come and the dugouts were all dripping. The outside area was like a sea of chocolate pudding, foamy and deep with mud."

According to Tom Cross, who at the time was still hospitalized but subsequently investigated the sequence of events, the strategists in charge were well aware that a frontal assault towards Schmidt invited disaster. In fact, while the 517th would be thus employed and keeping the major German forces busy, other U.S. units would swing around the defenders and envelop Schmidt. Unfortunately, instead of instructing the troopers to feint and thus distract the foe with minimum casualties to themselves, they were instructed to forcibly confront the enemy.

At headquarters of the 82nd Airborne, Rupert Graves was told by the top intelligence and operations officers of the futility of the role assigned to the 517th. The top brass of the 8th Division, having been in Bergstein for months, also knew the obstacles to a head-on assault were too formidable to challenge. Says Cross, "Mel Zais went to the 121st Infantry Regiment of the 8th Division, which was commanded by my father, Col. Thomas J. Cross. My father, who lost a lot of men trying to dislodge the Germans from Bergstein, gave Mel all the details based on his experience in the area. He told Mel that the 517th was facing an impossible task and urged him to relay that to the headquarters committing the 517th to the task. Mel said it was too late. The timetable for the operation would not permit a change."

Ludlow Gibbons, like most of the GIs in Bergstein, had burrowed in one of the cellars to escape the sniper and artillery rounds that ripped through the village. "A sergeant from the outfit that had been there before we arrived asked us what we were doing there. When I told him that we were going to take the high ground in front of us, cross the river in the valley and then take the hill on the other side, he looked at me as if I was crazy and had no chance at all. But he didn't say a word. I was a lieutenant. How right he was. The bosses should have been talking to that sergeant."

Dick Seitz critiques the operation as a classic series of errors. "High-echelon strategists can work from a map and aerial photos but it is an axiom of military operations that battalions or companies should never advance without firsthand knowledge of the terrain. We never had an opportunity to make a foot recon. The plan called for a night attack, which makes the need for good recon, enabling one to recognize terrain features, even more imperative. The plan said we were to advance with the two battalions abreast. The book calls for adequate planning, rehearsals and to proceed on a narrow front. We were unable to properly rehearse the operation. We violated all of these and jumped off right on schedule.

"I did take out my battalion in a column of companies which is a narrow front. I thought things were going well when I learned the 3rd Battalion was held up by heavy machine gun fire. They were now holding their position, waiting for artillery fire. We had started without initial arty prep to gain the element of surprise.

"My battalion, with George Giuchici in the lead, continued forward. Suddenly from the direction of the 3rd Battalion, the enemy counterattacked in force. At the same time, the Germans lit up the night with flares, it was like daylight. The enemy cut across between my command group and the 2nd Platoon of F Company. I was behind them with the 3rd Platoon. Good old George, bless his heart, a great soldier, kept going. I realized that the 3rd Battalion was not on line with me, leaving my flank exposed. I ordered a halt and to repel the counterattack."

Pfc. Myrle Traver, toting a BAR, was part of F Company. "In the early afternoon, someone brought word they had found an abandoned cabin. At last, a warm place where we could cook and eat. Joe Martin, Wayne (Willie) Hibben, Elio Masianti and I sat and talked after our meal. Word came we were to go at 10:00 P.M. Boy! We hated to leave that warm place and go out into the snow.

"I remember putting the little white strips of plastic on the backs of our helmets. The strips were fluorescent and would shine at night so we could see the man in front. We moved out and started crawling, keeping in line by following the tape strung out by engineers. Machine guns and flares kept me scared to death. Just kept crawling on the belly, flares and guns flashing, but just kept going. We finally got through the minefield and were hiking up and down mountain trails. Sometimes we would fall behind, then play catch up, so as not to lose sight of the white spot on the helmet ahead.

"After some time, I looked back. No one was following. We just kept moving. I ended up in a foxhole with Lieutenant [Warren] Caufield. He told me to keep down. About then, two German officers walked up. Caufield raised up his folding carbine and shot both Germans from about a three-foot range.

"Daylight was breaking and we began to move out again. A few hundred yards further, shells from our own artillery landed right among us. Captain Giuchici told Caufield to stay with the wounded and for George Flynn and me to follow him. We ran and ran, if you knew Giuchici, you knew he could run. He had his drum-type submachine gun in one hand like a pistol and I dragged the BAR. Flynn carried an '03 Springfield sniper rifle. We stumbled onto a young German soldier. He looked to be about thirteen years old. He begged us not to kill him and Giuchici said to bring him along.

"We reached the area where we were supposed to meet E Company but there was no one there. We hid in a large shellhole and waited, hoping the infantry would attack on schedule and pick us up. There was no attack during the day. We didn't know it had been called off. We talked about trying to get back through to our lines that night but what would our chances be, trying to pass through the minefield. We decided to wait, hoping for the attack the next morning. Again no attack. We heard troops fighting, the sounds getting closer, even heard American troopers cussing and yelling but they fell back. That night two German officers stood talking and smoking right above us. Captain Giuchici reached up and touched one of the German's boots, just to see if he could do it.

"Later that night, while Giuchici was guarding the German kid—we took turns with guard duty at night—

Giuchici woke me and said the kid was gone. We thought maybe he had crawled out to relieve himself, as we all had done. But he never came back."

Clifford Land, also from F Company says, "As soon as the flares died out, many GIs jumped up and ran. The enemy was aware this would occur so they sprayed the field the second the flares went out. Many were killed or wounded as a result.

"Concussion from a mortar shell knocked me into a shellhole. I was lying there when I heard my squad leader say, 'All right, men. Let's withdraw.' I rose from that hole and walked off in the direction I faced. It happened I was going the wrong way, into the enemy lines.

"Because of the concussion I did not know I was alone and headed in the wrong direction. Nor was I aware I was in a minefield and surrounded by the enemy. I stopped once to rest. After hearing a noise behind me, I looked and saw the unmistakable silhouette of an enemy helmet. I began to run down the hill, came to a river and took a left turn which was again the wrong direction. I wandered for three days and nights behind the German lines, laying low during the day, traveling at night, digging frozen turnips from the ground with my bayonet for food."

The troopers with Dick Robb had become infuriated by the stilettolike thrusts of the foe from its well-protected hideouts. "One of their snipers hit one of our guys carrying a plastic water bottle," recalls Robb. "That did it, those bastards were in no way going to cow us. On even a suspicion of movement in their area, every rifle of ours fired into their positions. That night we tried to attack across the open area toward them. Even with the 596th Engineers, we could not get through their mines. We lost men to mines, even those who went out to get them."

Well back in the column of the battalion marched

engineers from the 596th, carrying heavy timbers and planks to construct a crude bridge across the Kall. Allan Goodman saw the flares illuminate the sky and the incoming fire crash down on anything that moved. Even before dawn the engineers realized there was not going to be a river crossing. They discarded their timbers and planks.

"At midmorning," says Goodman, "we were asked to clear a path through the minefield. From the town plateau, the ravine, with sides at a forty-five-degree or even steeper pitch, sloped down towards the river. The path was to run halfway up on the pitched sides and mines were plentiful, Bouncing Betty and Schuh mines. They were both tripwire- and contact-type that lay buried.

"We were under constant mortar fire, but the steep slopes protected us to a degree. We laid a white tape and cleared a foot and a half path on each side as we went. The distance was several hundred yards or more. To do this, we worked all day and night, about thirty-six hours straight and I got far enough forward to receive direct fire from a machine gun emplacement. I could see German ambulances evacuating their wounded.

"On about the third day, one of the 517th's men was brought back up the path after he had slipped off and lost a foot. He actually seemed happy, and we actually envied his leaving, foot or no. That evening I was called to battalion headquarters to be briefed for a night attack. A lieutenant asked if the engineers would lead the way on the path. I interrupted to say we weren't going to be sheep. We had laid the path-line and would be close, but we were not point men and we needed both hands to clear mines when needed. The lieutenant didn't like it but the senior officer backed me up.

"That night my squad was split and my corporal, Dave Pierce, took four men and I took four to each side of the ravine. The night was chaos and the infantry never did reach the objective."

In the three days that the 517th vainly struggled to pass through the minefields and capture Schmidt, the regiment lost more than 200 troopers, about a quarter of its already depleted riflemen complement. Says John Chism, "When I finally stood in front of the side selected for our aid station and looked at the endless vista both north and south, I felt like I was looking on Dante's inferno. I did not see how anyone could survive this punishment. At night, Bergstein-Schmidt had a yellowish cast caused by the continuous use of various types of flares. Big ones from artillery discouraged troop movement. Little flares conveyed messages about attaining an objective or to fire or lift artillery. The terrain constantly absorbed projectiles of every description. It was laced with beautiful but deadly tracer ammunition from small arms. The combination of all this arcing fire provided depth to the hell washing over the pockmarked mud. The ground was chopped and chewed by round after round into a mass of growing craters. The shell-holes served as temporary cover when troops were caught in the open. It was temporary because one had to go forward or backward to survive. To stay meant certain injury.

"From Bergstein down to the river in the approach to Schmidt there were just so many paths. It was not enough to take a road with shoulders full of mines from friend and foe removed by our engineers. Security had to be provided because the Germans were adept at letting attackers pass and then sliding their own mines over a previously cleared road.

"Outside the hovel that served as the CP and aid station was a large bomb crater which had to be negotiated on entering or leaving the building. The mortar platoon had placed one of its sections behind the building and the natural berm of the crater. One of the crewmen, seeing a buddy, climbed up on the berm to talk to his friend. A sniper fired one round, hitting him in the head, tearing a huge gash and exposing the brain.

"Captain Dickinson and I happened to be at the aid station, a dozen yards away. We had to treat the man where he lay, which meant we were partially exposed. I assisted Dickinson but felt the need to take cover in case the sniper had any more ideas. Dickinson's attention was undivided. He carried on the examination with the same coolness and devotion to detail as if he were in a stateside hospital. When he finally pronounced the trooper dead, he instructed me how he would like to have him evacuated. He then secured an M–1 rifle and went after the sniper. To his dying day he believed he got that sniper. Dickinson never said anything but I believe he wanted to show any spectators that the care given the dying soldier was available to everyone." Dickinson labored under added stress since his normal associate, Doc Plassman, at the insistence of Chism, had been evacuated with a case of lobar pneumonia."

Clifford Land, after wandering through no man's land, sifted back to the 2nd Battalion. "Daylight caught us as we were coming into a clearing at the base of a mountain. A German machine gun opened up and sprayed the entire area. Men ran in every direction and I made a dive for a foxhole and landed squarely on top of the battalion commander, Lieutenant Colonel Seitz. There were maybe three other men in that hole. I will never forget how mad the lieutenant colonel was, not from me falling on him but because of the situation we were in. He arose from the foxhole and started giving orders. Standing upright, he shouted for every man to gather up all the equipment he could carry and start a withdrawal up the hillside towards our lines. And he walked as straight as any man could up that hill with a string of men following, while bullets flew and mortars fell all around."

Russel Brami with E Company of the 2nd Battalion had been directed to trail the unit's advance. "Major Dave Armstrong came to me and said, 'Brami, we're going back. You lead us.' There were thirty to fifty guys now behind me. We were all scared shitless. All I could do was walk over the thin path marked by engineer's tape. It was the scariest moment of the war for me."

The trio of Capt. George Giuchici, George Flynn and Myrle Traver of Company F, lost and out of contact with their fellows, their prisoner having vanished, spent the night futilely hoping the attacking troopers would reach them by morning. "About an hour after first light," says Traver, "we saw troops coming our way and the helmets looked like ours. We didn't realize that these were German paratrooper helmets which did not have the drop side like the regular German ones. The brush was so thick in that direction it was hard to be sure, but we believed they were ours. Six heads and guns came over the rim of the crater and then we knew.

"I asked Giuchici, 'What now?' He said, 'To hell with it.' They wanted to shoot Giuchici because they were afraid of his size. But the kid we had taken prisoner was with them and I told him we hadn't killed him. He was able to talk the others out of killing Giuchici."

Traver spent sixty-four days as a prisoner of war and his two companions a similar amount of time. Traver and Flynn, separated from the officer, tried to escape with a group of other captives but were caught. Giuchici slipped away twice only to be recaptured on both occasions.

The 1st Battalion initially had been designated as reserve for the assault upon Schmidt. After the first day of the abortive attack, the troopers under Maj. McMahon started out from Hill 400 towards Zerkall on the left flank of the line. For Charlie Keen, the days and nights after the sojourn at Stavelot had been devastating. "We would fight all day and just before total dark, the Krauts with clockwork precision would counterattack employing five tanks and a battalion of infantry. You knew exactly what they were going to do without fail. Someone overheard our officers talk about General Gavin speaking on the phone to higher headquarters. He was asked about conditions and he responded he had all five regiments committed [the 505th and 508th PR were part of the operation] and both flanks exposed for several miles but not to worry since he still had a company of military police in reserve.

"Around dark, one evening with the snow about a foot deep and still falling lightly, we were subjected to intense, heavy artillery fire, especially to our front. Slim Ford, an old Toccoa boy, came running back yelling for me to hurry as Doyle Gray had just been hit. I took off full speed as shells were still coming spasmodically and in the thick woods, a tree burst would get you whether you were in a foxhole or not. The smell of cordite or whatever the hell they put in besides powder hung over the place.

"No one was in sight since Slim and Gray were on outpost. There were no GIs and thank God no Krauts. In what you might call my free flight, I saw all the shattered trees and over to one side a paratrooper in a jumpsuit with his head stuck in the snow. It was Gray. I heard some more shells coming in and spotting a small hole near him, I grabbed for his webbing to drag him into the hole with me in one leap. Just as my hand touched his webbing, I spotted an ear on a snow-covered bush and knew instantly that the body I held did not have its head in the snow. There wasn't any head. Apparently a large piece of shell had cut or blown it off.

"The scene will go to my grave with me but I've often thought at least it was quick. Doyle was an only child always looking for some kind of spot in this life where he could find his place. He did and it was the role of a loner, utterly without fear, who would rather kill the Germans than do anything else. The success he achieved was not the vocation you could take home to civilian life and to a worshipping mother. She wrote the captain and any name she could recognize as having been with Doyle. I should have been the one to answer but I didn't."

On the night of February 6, H and I Companies were caught in the enemy guns amid the minefield. Platoon-leader Ludlow Gibbons from Company I, with a mere fifteen troopers left of his normal complement of forty, advanced until they reached a clearing.

Remembers Gibbons, "We [a scout and the lieutenant] walked twenty or thirty yards into the open field in bright moonlight. The scout and I were facing each other, squatting on our haunches, discussing whether to go right or left to skirt the clearing. I glanced up and directly behind the scout a man's figure appeared. He let out a yell while hitting the scout who went down. The German ran off to the right as I fired several rounds. I moved back to the head of the column. Moments later the scout showed up, only grazed.

"I could see the flashes from weapons when they fired. I stayed put, threw a grenade and waited. They continued to fire. I thought we'd had it. While I was trying to decide what to do next, Captain Birder showed up and decided to pull back to the nearest concealment. If we had done anything else, a lot of us wouldn't be here to tell the story and it would have been a complete waste."

As Gibbons, Birder and their people gingerly made their way back, a GI stepped off the tape and onto a mine. Birder carefully followed the wounded man's footsteps and tried to lift him from under his arms. Birder slipped in the snow and sat down on another mine, triggering a second explosion. Both of the badly

injured were carried some two miles to the nearest aid
station. But they died there.

John Saxion now served as a platoon leader for H
Company. "All morning I had sat at a tape crossing with
artillery captain Robert Woodhull and two of his observers. We watched the Germans through binoculars as
they set up mortars in the valley below us. The captain's
75s could not get enough angle to fire on them.

"About noon, H Company moved on the tape
around the hill to get a Jerry machine gun. We eliminated the gun and were digging in, eating our rations.
The point BAR man brought me two Germans, one of
average size was leading a huge soldier whose head was
bandaged along with his chest and hands. When we
interrogated the smaller prisoner, he told us that after
our third attack had been repulsed, the Germans started
to celebrate. The big guy who was arrogant and very
much a Nazi, pulled the pin of a potato masher and held
it near his head. It had gone off for a self-inflicted
wound.

"I turned the big one over to Sergeant Robb to take
to the rear. On the way back, Robb ordered him to help
carry a stretcher. He refused, citing the Geneva rules.
Robb threatened him with a .45, telling him to walk off
the tape. The prisoner then helped carry the litter up the
hill. Later I asked what became of him and was told he
died."

Robb saw firsthand the somewhat bizarre antics of the
enemy. "Beyond the end of the tape, a group of us
topped a rise at the edge of some woods looking across a
clearing to another patch of trees. A number of Germans
ran out of those woods towards us, shouting and
screaming. A turkey shoot; they had to be crazy, these
were targets less than fifty yards away. We captured one
who walked right into us and surrendered. He told us
something about his comrades using drugs. That fit their
behavior." For his deadly work, accounting for as many

as eight of the enemy, Pfc. Richard Weegar won a Silver Star.

But the Americans held an untenable place. Says Robb, "Our lieutenant requested we be allowed to withdraw unless we could have reinforcements. We were only ten or twelve and way out front with mostly wounded behind us. Permission was granted and we started back with our prisoner. I was jabbing him in the back with my left fist to move faster, my .45 pistol in my right hand, safety off, my finger very tight on the trigger. We were going by several of my friends lying off the trail. He and I were alone, no one else about. Seeing feet blown off by Schuh mines and now the dead by the trail I thought perhaps I would kill the prisoner. Why not? No one would know, just a bullet in the back. There would be no retribution for me, even if someone found out.

"I had not completely justified the act in my mind. He was a paratrooper, not an SS man. Suddenly I came on Sgt. Fred Harmon and a lieutenant. They had a stretcher and on it was one of ours, his right leg blown off at the hip, an awful sight. For an instant I cursed myself for not killing the German while I had the chance. Then I pointed to the lieutenant's end of the litter and shoved him at it. I am sure the German was pleased to take the stretcher because there lay safety for him."

Saxion watched what he describes as an endless stream of men carried back on litters. "When mortars started to pound us our position became exposed so we withdrew to our starting point. On the way back we passed the bodies of Captain Woodhull and his observers, killed by the mortars that we observed being set up that morning."

One of the wounded from I Company was Lt. Charles Casey who had been a friend of Saxion since Sicily, and through Saxion's difficult days in Rome, then the invasion of Southern France, the Bulge and now the bloody encounter between Bergstein and Schmidt.

"Casey came up from the Kall ravine," says Saxion, "blood pouring from an ear and he had another wound in his hip. He asked me for a cigarette but did not even recognize me."

Nothing demonstrated more clearly to John Chism the need to swiftly remove the wounded and begin sophisticated treatment unavailable in an aid station, than his three days on the Bergstein–Schmidt front. "Walter Frieble, who came to us fresh out of high school, and Captain Birder both should have survived, although seriously wounded. But the weather and the extra hour required to get them to the hospital was the difference that cost their lives. On the other hand, Hank Wanggrzynowicz was the most seriously wounded person I handled. He was hit by a large-caliber bullet or fragment which all but decapitated him. The missile passed completely through his chin, knocking out teeth and inflicting extreme damage. The little we could do for him was limited to removing loose debris and inserting a tube in order to prevent him from choking on blood. He could not be transported by litter and insisted on sitting up. Roy Dunne, the pint-size ambulance driver, propped him up with an extra blanket and broke all records getting him to Stavelot. Dunne surprised us when he passed the word that he had deposited a living Hank."

Even as they departed the battlefield, having been relieved by other units, the 517th suffered final losses. Charlie Keen was on his way back up the slope to safety. "We all watched as a small ball of fire came across the Roer, traveling slowly about one hundred feet in the air before it crashed right next to the only house still standing. There was a loud explosion and the concussion from the rocket caused the entire house to collapse. We didn't know it at the time but a group from B Company's 2nd Platoon was in the building. Many were injured but the one man killed was big Frank Hayes, the former heavyweight champion of the 17th AB Division.

Frank had joined the outfit at Toccoa from Painted Post, New York, and was the last man from the outfit to die in battle."

The 517th pulled out of Bergstein, in a welter of grief, bitterness and anger. The flank attack of the 78th Division brought limited casualties to its GIs. The fire-power delivered by the 517th wiped out most of the German paratroop regiment opposing it and persuaded the enemy to depart without further resistance. However, that did not prevent the Germans opening the gates to the Roer dams, flooding the ground and delaying rapid advance. The hard-hammered troopers felt betrayed as other units easily cleared what had been a killing field. Says Ed Johnson of C Company, "The Huertgen Forest campaign was truly a time when we thought our high command had taken leave of their senses. It seemed we were being asked to commit suicide for no good reason. The rationale, explained to me later, about the importance of keeping pressure on the German forces in that area so that breakthroughs could succeed elsewhere, still falls on deaf ears."

CHAPTER XV

DISSOLUTION

THE 40-AND-8S CARRIED the troopers for a week's sojourn in Laon, France. The shabby camp there provided rest, hot water, hot food and clean apparel. But the pleasure gained from such minimal creature comforts vanished with the traumatic news that the 517th RCT was assigned to become a wing of the newly-arrived 13th Airborne Division at Joigny, seventy miles south of Paris. The 517th combat team immediately lost both its artillery and engineer components which joined the appropriate organizations of the new parent. What remained of the outfit was the parachute infantry.

While in garrison at Joigny, a bitter aftertaste grated on the sensibilities of some survivors of the attack on Schmidt. Mel Zais said, "There had been a company commander down to only forty men who refused to take his men through the minefields. Some officers came to his defense [Ben Sullivan for one considered the company commander to have been properly concerned with the welfare of troopers headed for a near suicidal mission]. I wouldn't listen to them at all. I preferred charges against him and he too was found guilty."

But although the 517th was not under lethal fire, there was plenty of verbal and paper sniping. Conflict between the battle-tested troopers from the regimental combat team and the inexperienced, by-the-book staff of the 13th was almost inevitable. A difficult situation was made worse by the apparent insensitivity of some members of the 13th.

A major area of contention was the insouciant attitude of the 517th people towards paperwork. That impatience with bureaucratic niceties dated back to Lou Walsh and certainly a prolonged tour of heavy combat with only occasional periods off the line hardly stimulated any interest in filling out forms. The hierarchy of the 13th considered the absence of proper documentation evidence of careless, sloppy and unmilitary conduct.

The 13th's brass was startled to find their new addition had no battalion-level intelligence journals detailing its experiences. The survivors of combat were equally appalled that anyone would expect precise records to be kept while those involved were fighting for their lives. A good deal of inventive writing and long-after-the-fact daily accounts were created to satisfy the demand for such materials.

Recommendations for medals earned during the Bulge and before Schmidt now passed through a 13th Airborne Division Awards Board. That led to more hard feelings as some nominations were knocked down without justification in the view of those citing the individuals and groups. Several troopers, including Dick Robb, however, received battlefield commissions.

Supplies and equipment became a *cause célèbre*. From the first shooting in Italy, the troopers from Rupert Graves to the lowest private considered themselves short on tools adequate to the task, particularly since the deficiencies threatened lives. The jeep-swiping in Italy was an overt symptom of an even more systematic acquisitive urge.

Don Fraser recalls, "While in the Bulge, we recaptured an American half-track by blowing off one of its tracks and shooting the Germans using it. The battalion S–4, Bill Price, had a buddy in an armored outfit near us and he repaired the half-track. We had so few vehicles of our own that we used the half-track for running supplies, ammo and other tasks. When we were pulled out of Germany to join the 13th AB, Mel Zais saw the half-track and said it was not authorized as airborne battalion equipment. He told me to get rid of it. We drove it into the woods and abandoned it. We were sorry to lose the thing."

Zais's instructions to Fraser foreshadowed a major confrontation with the 13th AB. From transportation through weapons, those charged with supply for the 517th, designated S–4s in military parlance had scrounged, requisitioned and simply took what they believed would help the men at risk. Tom Cross says the supply officer of the regiment, Bill Hickman, believed, "Nothing is too good for the troops. His attitude was if you need it, I'll get it. He made the Sgt. Bilko of TV look like a Boy Scout. He obtained flamethrowers, shaped charges, *panzerfausts* for almost every man in the 517th.

"Hickman was a big bear of a man like Boyle but more outgoing. When the 517th went to Joigny, Hickman had squirreled away enough stuff to outfit two regiments. It was stashed in warehouses. It was all illegally obtained and well hidden. But someone from the 13th Airborne discovered the caches and they raised hell.

"They wanted to prefer charges against Hickman. Mel Zais felt terrible about it and he offered to take the rap for Hickman. But Bill refused. Rupert Graves managed to get the charges knocked down to administrative punishment but it meant that Hickman could not pursue a career in the army. Bill was not alone in his efforts to furnish the men with what they needed. Bill Price under Boyle and Joe Calder of the 3rd Battalion also were outstanding in procuring items for the troopers."

Phil Di Stanislao, following surgery in the United Kingdom, found life in the hospital "sublime" after the

Bulge experience. As he recovered, he entered a convalescent ward, delighted to discover as a bunkmate, Julius Talarico wounded at Soy. Says Di Stanislao, "An administrative officer decided we ought to stand retreat. I was senior noncom and given a platoon, all paratroopers, from my ward. When we stood retreat that first time, we thought it was chicken shit. I called the men to attention and when the administrative officer came up, I saluted him. He told me my cap was on wrong. He was a major and I said, 'Why don't you change it.' The rest of the platoon started to chant, 'Kill the son of a bitch. Kill the son of a bitch . . .' The major went on his way and there was no more retreat."

When the medical authorities diagnosed Di Stanislao as fit again for service, although on limited duty, he cajoled and begged to return to his old outfit. "I had a strong urge to get back to the 517th, my family." Dispatched to a replacement depot for reassignment, Di Stanislao tried to locate the 517th. A letter from his pal Carl Kiefer indicated the outfit was not that far from Paris. During one of several moves to different replacement camps, the 40-and-8 with Di Stanislao halted in the Paris freight yard.

"I jumped out and decided to find the 517th. I figured the best place was a sidewalk café. Sure enough, after not too long, a jeep with 517th markings showed up. I hitched a ride to headquarters, where an officer cut orders for me to pick other men at the repple depple. The orders were dated to cover the date I left the 40-and-8 and I was given a two-and-a-half-ton truck to pick up the others.

"At the repple depple, the CO said I was already listed as AWOL. When I presented him the dated orders, he became apoplectic. I thought he'd burst. When I got to the barracks and picked up the guys, you'd have thought I was liberating these guys from a POW camp."

However, Di Stanislao's elation deflated quickly when

he reached his old company. "My family wasn't there. There were only four or five left from the original 1st Platoon that went overseas. Carl Kiefer had received a field commission. It was devastating. The men from the 13th AB had absorbed a lot of noncom positions. I expected to get the platoon as mine but a man from the 13th already held the spot. I was told I could take the second position. I felt diminished and disappointed."

Di Stanislao spent very little time with his old unit. Instead he passed many days visiting with another recovering trooper, Joe Blackwell, the 2nd Platoon mortar man. Blackwell was acting as a lifeguard at a small beach by a nearby river.

"The feeling of the 517th men about joining the 13th Airborne," says Di Stanislao, "was very strong. Those who had been there before I got back and after I was there refused to wear the 13th patch on their shoulders. There were a lot of things said, but no one forced them to do it."

There had never been an official shoulder patch for the 517th. A drawing-board sketch showed a plunging eagle with a small parachute but on the eve of departure for Europe, Graves figured security needs would not permit the troopers to sport the insignia. As a consequence the only patch authorized before joining the 13th was the simple legend AIRBORNE.

Some years later, after deactivation, Dick Spencer, a former lieutenant with G Company and now a Colorado publisher, revived the idea of the insignia with a change in the bird's configuration, making it a buzzard.

Charlie Pugh, from the 596th, wounded for a second time during the Bulge says, "We were demoralized when absorbed into the 13th. Later on, when we transferred to the 82nd, as part of the 397th Engineer Battalion, morale improved since these men had been in combat."

Not every trooper felt uncomfortable with the 13th

Airborne. Engineer Jim Moses says, "When we got back to Chablis [camp for the 596th] we were in terrible shape. Colonel Harris, the aide to General Chapman, CO of the 13th, came by to see what shape we were in and every day or two as we went through the chow line, he'd be there to ask, 'Did you get enough to eat? Have you got enough clothes? Your gear all right?' Far as I am concerned, the 13th treated us well, they were fine people and I liked 'em all."

Troopers recovering from wounds continued to flow back to the regiment. Sweet Pea Renton, while recuperating in England had bumped into Di Stanislao. Renton "commissioned" Di Stanislao and took him to an officers' club for an evening in which the fraudulent lieutenant, claims Renton, charmed a young woman with his compassion for enlisted men.

Assigned to a replacement depot in France, Renton in the customary fashion of his fellows went AWOL in search of the 517th. When he located the outfit, he learned he had been listed, like Di Stanislao, for limited duty. Superiors advised him to return to the repple depple and arrange to be reclassified. Renton convinced the authorities to change his status.

The difficulties of the 517th when swallowed by the 13th Airborne Division may all be of a piece with the nature of the military structure. In a huge organization like the U.S. Army during World War II, smaller units always ran the risk of being overwhelmed by the bigger ones. Generals command divisions while only colonels boss regiments. When consigned to serve as an adjunct of a superior-size outfit, Graves and his battalion commanders could only suggest but never oppose decisions, even when they came from officers without combat experience or real understanding of the forces in opposition. And of course one cannot dismiss the element of favoritism. Some commanders, faced with a tough engagement, might well have been tempted to protect their own men and let the outsiders, the troopers of the 517th, bear the brunt.

Smallness also could be a handicap when it came to billets, supplies, weapons, ammunition and support in the field. The voice of a general demanding these accoutrements for his men sounded louder than that of a lowly colonel or a lieutenant colonel during frequent situations where the powers fragmented the combat team, separating pieces of it to work for different masters.

The 517th was at a further disadvantage in dealing with other outfits because of its reputation as an elite. Straight-leg organizations were hostile to parachutists and the animosity increased towards a separate regimental combat team. The attitude of troopers, that they were better than other soldiers, which was consciously promoted by originators of the breed like Jim Gavin and instilled in places like Toccoa, gave the members of the 517th *esprit de corps* in their eyes, but to others looked suspiciously like chips on shoulders. While the attitude served the troopers well on the battlefield, the feelings expressed toward straight-leg infantrymen, towards MPs, even the antagonism to other airborne GIs, the willingness to punch out anyone who was not a member of the elite, created alienation. The attitude may well have brought the dirty end of the stick to the 517th more often than deserved.

Unhappy as they were, the 517th's troopers prepared to return to war with the 13th Airborne. The strategists scheduled an airborne operation over the Rhine, assisting the troops under British field marshal Bernard Montgomery. When Allied ground forces leaped the Rhine more swiftly than anticipated, the High Command notified the 13th to stand down. A second plan to attack in conjunction with Gen. George S. Patton's Third Army as it bridged the Rhine also was cancelled. A third proposal would have dropped the troopers in

Bavaria where, according to rumors, die-hard Nazis intended to hold out. V–E Day, the unconditional surrender, in early May scrubbed this venture.

There was a brief period of celebration. Zais actually reached Paris on a pass in time for his birthday which happened to fall on V–E Day. "I paraded the streets and went in and out of bars. Girls kissed me. I hugged people. I went from one place to another, including a glorious all-night session of dancing in the streets, hell-raising, and had lots of fun."

Zais could indeed party with enthusiasm. Ludlow Gibbons had played a fair amount of poker with the regimental exec and in Paris on one occasion went on the town with his superior. "We took on a couple of overly aggressive lieutenants from some Ranger outfit. If we hadn't whipped them, I wouldn't mention it. But the guy that faced off with the colonel said that every time, as soon as he got up, Zais would knock him down again."

The veterans of the 517th now faced two options. They could stay with the 13th, which was scheduled for an early return to the U.S. before rotation to the war still on against Japan. Or they could choose assignment to the 82nd Airborne for occupation duty in Berlin. For example, Allan Goodman from the Engineers and Di Stanislao opted for Berlin while Ben Renton decided to continue with the 13th on to the Pacific. The majority seemed to prefer the 82nd Airborne rather than risk an early encounter with the armies of Japan.

The issue quickly became academic with the surrender of Japan early in August. A system of points based on months served, overseas duty, campaigns and medals soon qualified all of the veterans of Toccoa for shipment home and discharge.

Some of the troopers had preceded their fellows, having been sent to the U.S. for the treatment of wounds. John "Buck" Miller, the C Company sergeant struck in the arm and leg by an enemy shell shortly after the jump into Southern France, passed through a series of medical installations before being flown to Lawson General Hospital in Atlanta. He endured fourteen operations to repair his arm and leg before discharge from Oliver General Hospital in Augusta.

Newly minted Lt. John Forrest, who during the Champagne Campaign had amputated the shattered remains of his left leg with his knife, underwent a series of operations before being shipped to Halloran Hospital on Staten Island, New York, then Lawson General Hospital in Atlanta before the final institution, Letterman General Hospital at the Presidio near San Francisco. Surgeons saved his kneecap and fitted him with a prosthesis. Forrest returned to civilian life in November of 1946, a full two years after the explosion that maimed him.

Bill Boyle, having survived his brush with death near Bergeval in the Ardennes, suffered through surgery to restore function to his arms and required many months to recuperate. Nolan Powell, wracked by a bullet at Longobierne, similarly spent an extended period in hospitals before he recovered. Tom Cross was fixed up sufficiently to rejoin the 517th while still at Joigny.

John Lissner, routed to Boston and then ticketed for Halloran, read of the 517th returning to Fort Bragg at Fayetteville, North Carolina, and the 82nd Airborne command. "I was using a cane and decided if I went to Halloran I'd be taken off jump status. A leg unit was not for me. I packed a bag with all of my clothing and headed for Fayetteville. When I signed in I said it was by authority of VOCG—verbal order of the commanding general, who was Jim Gavin. I was sure he wouldn't be upset about someone coming in like me. They reassigned me to E Company and Dick Seitz welcomed me. After a week or two, however, I was called to headquarters to explain by what authority I was there. I told the truth and they explained the matter to Washington. I didn't get paid for three months."

Congressional Medal of Honor–recipient Mel Biddle traveled a different route home. Slightly wounded after his one-man onslaught, he had been prepared to rejoin the 517th for its final battles. But a directive from the top brass forbade risking the lives of any CMH nominees. In August of 1945, Biddle stood at attention in the Rose Garden of the White House while President Harry S Truman pinned the medal to his chest. "President Truman said, 'People don't believe me when I say I would rather have this medal than be president.' I wanted to say I would trade him but I was afraid to open my mouth for fear I'd be court-martialed."

Those members of the 517th who were still able to serve and had remained with the regiment sailed for the U.S. in August of 1945. Six months later, on February 25, 1946, bereft of all but those who sought to continue a military career, the 517th quietly expired in a deactivation ceremony at Fort Bragg. The casualties included the 460th and the engineer battalion that absorbed the 596th.

Beyond the official accounts and those from the troopers themselves, the most tangible evidence of the 517th's ordeal under fire can be summed up from army records. The organization participated in five major campaigns: Rome–Arno; Southern France; Rhineland; Ardennes and Central Europe. The entire combat team lost 244 men KIA. The Purple Hearts awarded totaled 1,576, an average of well over one for every two men, although in actuality some troopers added clusters to their first medal. For example, Renton and Clark Archer collected four and Dick Robb picked up three.

Biddle earned the only CMH but six, including Bill Boyle and Nolan Powell, received Distinguished Service Crosses. Three of the five Legion of Merit Medals went to Rupert Graves, Mel Zais and M. Sgt. Douglas E. Emmons. The French Government named seventeen men to wear the Croix de Guerre, including Graves, Dick Seitz, Don Fraser, Forest Paxton, John Lissner and James Birder, the captain KIA in the Huertgen. Some 131 troopers earned Silver Stars and 631 citations brought Bronze Stars. The French and Belgian Governments issued commendations covering the entire 517th.

The accumulation of medals is all the more impressive in that Rupert Graves, unlike some commanders, regarded much of what was achieved as simply doing one's duty. Furthermore, the 13th's staff had shown little inclination to boost the actions of troopers from the 517th.

When the parades and the welcome-homes petered out and the medals were stored away, the men of the 517th focused on the remainders of their lives. Both Rupert Graves and Bill Boyle, as graduates of the U.S. Military Academy, continued their careers as army officers. The quiet, self-effacing Graves may well have lost his opportunity for a general's star because of the conflict with the 13th Airborne staff, so unhappy with the absence of bureaucratic preciseness in the 517th.

In spite of the terrible wounds that left him barely able to exercise enough control to turn a doorknob, and a candidate for a full pension, Boyle rehabilitated his body until he was restored to full duty. His reward was assignment to the 187th Airborne Regimental Combat Team fighting in Korea. It was not an experience anything like that with the 517th where he had been present at the creation.

"I didn't know the men as well but the troops were good. I respected the junior officers. The battalion commanders Del Munson and Harry Wilson were very competent and some of the regimental staff were reasonable men. However, I felt the top side, the officer under whom I had to serve, was a stupid man. He wasted men, which means they were killed unnecessarily."

Boyle's conflict with his superior brought him reassignment. Like Graves, he also was denied a star for his shoulder. "I've never said I might have had one although I'm sure I would have liked it. But I also know I did not fit the mold for a peacetime army." His legion of admirers from the 517th believe it was his candor, his honesty and his devotion to those serving under him, even when it meant confronting or at least debating with superiors, that cost him a promotion. He retired as a full colonel, then began a new career, first as chief of security for a race track for trotters in upstate New York and then opening an office as an accountant. The Bill Boyle of the 1990s, with ten children and a soft-spoken voice, is sometimes hard to imagine as the fearsome commander of the 1940s.

Mel Zais, although not a West Pointer, even before World War II, had decided to make the Army his life. He succeeded brilliantly, rising to the exalted level of a four-star general. Jack Kinzer of the 460th remained in airborne units, serving in Japan, Germany and eventually as the arty CO for the 101st Airborne while posted to Fort Campbell, Kentucky. He retired as a brigadier general. Lou Walsh, redeemed in the eyes of Pentagon officials by his efforts during the fighting in the South Pacific, rose to the rank of major general.

Immediately after Japan capitulated, Dick Seitz assumed he would become a civilian, running the family dairy. However, he soon began to rethink his future. "A senior officer pointed out that I was a twenty-seven-year-old lieutenant colonel, had a good combat record and an opportunity for a highly successful career in the army." His father, whom Seitz had believed would be disappointed if he did not take over the family business, exhibited great pride in Dick's success and was enthusiastic about his continuing as an army officer. To Seitz's regret, he never saw the battlefields of Korea but instead headed the airborne section of the infantry school responsible for parachute training.

He did serve a tour in Vietnam. For two years he was chief of staff for Gen. William Westmoreland, the CO for military operations there. Subsequently, Seitz commanded the 82nd Airborne, including its tour in Detroit during the 1967 urban disorders. He completed his soldiering with several other top posts and retired as a lieutenant general.

Altogether, the 517th produced an astonishing eight generals, with four troopers who started near or at the very bottom of the military ladder clmbing to the top rungs. Mickey Marks, the Oklahoma-born lieutenant who received command of C Company after La Chaussee was hit rose to the level of major general. John Neiler, the intelligence specialist who, with Jack Kinzer, unexpectedly bagged a number of German prisoners near Bergeval, also earned two stars.

The pair who traveled the furthest were David Grange and Richard Eaton. Both of them came to Toccoa as privates. Grange acted as a runner for Dick Seitz and Eaton joined Company A. After World War II ended, Grange went through OCS for his commission while Eaton accepted one in the reserves while attending Northwestern University. Both ascended in the military hierarchy after leading riflemen in Korea and fighting in Vietnam. Grange retired as a lieutenant general, Eaton as a brigadier.

Added evidence of the thrall in which the 517th held its troopers lies in the high number who chose to become army "lifers." Russel Brami stayed on, did two tours in Korea, and continued in service even after an accident with a grenade in 1957 cost him a hand. He retired as a major and after working for Good Will Industries became the director of the chamber of commerce at Cedar Key, Florida. John Alicki, the demolitions expert and member of the original cadre, stayed with it until he too achieved the same rank as Brami. Alicki then signed up in various executive positions dealing with personnel. Tom Cross, John Lissner, Howard Hensleigh and Charles La Chaussee also were among the flocks of colonels from the eyrie of the 517th.

After Hensleigh retired, Raytheon Corp. employed him in its legal department. Tom Cross, who was made CO of the 3rd Battalion while at Joigny, went on to Korea where he actually served with his father. Terry Sanford, who as a lieutenant was a member of Bill Boyle's 1st Battalion staff, when governor of North Carolina, brought in Cross, by then retired from the army, for administrative tasks in the government. Although hired by a Democrat, Cross continued to serve the state under Republican officials.

John Lissner combined a military career in the airborne forces with courses from such institutions as Cornell, Austin Peay State University in Kentucky, and The American University (Fort Benning Branch). Upon retirement as a full colonel in 1966, Lissner accepted a job as supervisor of activities at the Westchester County (New York) Penitentiary. That was followed by the posts at Dutchess County (New York) Jail and as director of training for the Cleveland Department of Correction.

Following his retirement from active duty, La Chaussee returned to his native Maine to supervise sawmills for the lumber industry. Bill Lewis, another of the cadre, tried civilian life and rejected it in favor of the army. He too rose to lieutenant colonel. Clifton Land, who escaped unscathed from his wandering in no man's land near Schmidt, became an ordained minister and subsequently served as an army chaplain.

Ben Renton wanted desperately to continue in the army. But, although he had connived to have himself listed as fit in order to rejoin the 517th while it was in

France with the 13th Airborne, the examining physicians in the U.S. observed his limp, checked his scarred body and examined his charts. They refused to certify him as able-bodied enough for a regular-army commission. Against his will, Renton shed his uniform and became involved in construction work.

John Chism also doffed his uniform in 1945 and enrolled at the University of California in Berkeley. Among his studies was a field artillery ROTC program. In 1949, 2nd Lt. John Chism reported to the 82nd FA Battalion with the 1st Cavalry Division. Comparisons with his 517th experiences naturally ensued. He was dismayed to discover officer morale at low ebb because of reductions in force dictated by the requirements for a smaller army. He was further discomfited to find the enlisted men lacked both equipment and adequate training.

In spite of these serious deficiencies the U.S. as well as Chism engaged in the Korean War. A new commander for division artillery, Gen. Charles Day Palmer, according to Chism, whipped the organization into shape. The experience underscored the value of effective leadership that Chism had observed in the 517th. Following Korea he continued to wear the uniform and spent a period in Vietnam. "In every unit I served with, the lessons on unit training, individual training and management I either learned or polished as a result of being in the 517th."

Over a thirty-two-year life as a soldier, Chism notes, "While several units had the zing for short spurts of time, the 517th was a unique experience." In fact, it is difficult if not impossible to find anyone from the 517th who made his career in the army who does not believe the Battling Buzzards were unique and the most satisfying experience of their lives.

After mustering out, forward observer Tommy Thompson accepted the post of executive secretary for a citizens' committee promoting universal military train-

ing with emphasis upon civil defense. The conflict in
Korea and then subsequent engagement in Vietnam insured a continuation of the selective service draft
process. Thompson entered into a business involving
disposal of sewage and conversion of sludge to energy.
He also shifted the concept of universal service organization towards a youth education and training program.

None of the physicians performing as battalion or
regimental surgeons chose military medicine as their
form of practice. Ben Sullivan completed his studies in
neurosurgery and set up shop in Sarasota, Florida. Walter Plassman settled in as a general practitioner in Centralia. Paul Vella provided medicine in Georgia. Others
on the team scattered across the country.

A substantial number of the troopers charged into
civilian careers with the same vigor and tenacity that
marked their efforts with the 517th. John Forrest's loss
of the lower part of a leg disqualified him for a permanent post with the army. He moved to his wife's hometown, Gainesville, Georgia, and enrolled at North
Georgia College, essentially a military academy. Some
largely noncombat vets, indifferent to the needs of military discipline, had driven one commandant to resign
and although he was still a student, Forrest became assistant commandant to the new appointee, who quit after a
short period in office.

"I was named commandant. I applied the same 517th
principles I had been taught. Infractions of school regulations resulted in pushups and rifle calisthenics which I
performed with them. Major infractions brought tree-
stump digging. As we marched to and from details I had
them sing 'Airborne' and 'Fireball Mail.'

"One day my wife, an insightful woman, faced me
down. 'John, these boys are not paratroopers. They are
students who have come here, paying their own way to
get an education, not to be physically hardened in the
Toccoa fashion. You need to remember that!' Her

observations came as something of a shock. But I must say that the level of *esprit* among the cadets became extremely high under 517th principles and practice. Many of these young men ended up as company-grade infantry officers in Korea where they acquitted themselves heroically but the casualty rate, particularly mortalities, was extremely high. They were the victims of the downsizing of the army after World War II, the poor preparation of hastily drafted, ill-trained enlisted men."

From that position at North Georgia College, Forrest moved to the Department of Health, Education and Welfare, spending much of his time dealing with the governors from eight states in the Southeastern region. Again, says Forrest, he remembered the policy in the 517th, "to be open and frank even about things I'd like to cover up and to respect the people with whom I worked. The 517th taught me to be loyal to my superiors and staff but never to overlook the responsibility I had for seeing that our programs served the recipients well. Those principles were not always pervasive among the bureaucrats."

Don Fraser says while he did not care for the 13th AB, he nevertheless volunteered to stick with it for the coming battle with Japan. Once V–E Day signaled the end of hostilities, Fraser says, "It was enough for me. I liked the war but not peacetime service." In his hometown of Blue Island, Illinois, he acted as the local postmaster before retiring to a Florida farm where his new enterprise was raising Appaloosa horses and German shepherd dogs.

Phil Di Stanislao, spurred by Charlie Keen, applied to Randolph-Macon, where he played football and prepared himself to become an English instructor. "I thought of myself becoming a kind of Mr. Chips, coaching football and teaching literature at some prep school. Someone suggested I consider the University of Pennsylvania dental school. I applied, was accepted and became an oral surgeon." Still active as he approached his 70th birthday, Di Stanislao directs dental services in a hospital that specializes in the treatment of mentally retarded children.

His classmate at Randolph-Macon, Charlie Keen, pursued a premed course. However, according to Keen, an avid taste for whiskey and women did not mix well with the pursuit of academic excellence. "The dean at the Medical College of the University of Virginia at Richmond said how could they accept me with low grades when he had thousands of applications with A's." Keen considered dentistry when a friend interceded with the dean of the appropriate school. "One week later the dean was hit and killed by a bus. I said to hell with it and got a degree in business economics." For thirty-two years, Keen prospered as a wholesaler in pharmaceuticals.

Medic Paul Smith indulged his ambition to study sociology and anthropology, which he taught for six years. He gave up pedagogy to manage a family business and that led him into asset management and commercial real estate development. Ed Johnson of C Company used his GI Bill to obtain a degree in business and journalism from Butler University in Indianapolis. He hired on first with Kroger Co., a Midwestern food chain, and then held top executive posts with Sperry and Hutchinson Co., the premium distributor, where he specialized in advertising and marketing. Ludlow Gibbons started a Nash automobile agency but the brand went belly up fairly quickly and Gibbons embarked on a career involving contract technical services. On one of his trips to Washington, D.C., he had an opportunity to renew his acquaintance with Mel Zais. That was Gibbons's first contact with a former colleague from the 517th since he sailed home from Europe.

Age could not wither the paratrooper spirit in Gibbons. One of his friends from the 517th, Lee Hulett from regimental headquarters, had continued to jump long after he left the army. Hulett once wowed a nudist camp by floating down with a female companion, the pair wearing only their chutes. When Hulett showed up at Gibbons's home in 1993, he prevailed upon the 74-year-old Gibbons to join him for a jump. Accompanied by Gibbons's daughter they enjoyed a smooth, easy landing as a consequence of the newest gear and the absence of combat conditions. Gibbons and Hulett were not alone in their continued romance with parachutes. Russ Brami, for one, also continues to jump in spite of his missing hand.

Airborne engineer Ernie Kosan used his GI Bill benefits to study engineering at Rice University. As a member of an army reserve unit, he was called up during the Korean War, assigned as a translator. "I did not know Korean but only English, German and French." After six months of active duty, the army recognized a lack of need for his linguistic skills and returned him to civilian life. Kosan eventually became a project engineer for a chemical concern, traveling the world for the company and exploiting his talents for foreign tongues.

Ed Athey, while the 517th was recovering at Soissons after the Champagne Campaign, had been assigned to serve as PX manager. When the combat team moved out to confront the Ardennes breakthrough, Athey stayed behind to clean up the records for the PX. He thus missed much of the carnage wreaked upon the 517th over the next two months and earned a reputation as an "operator."

Demobilized with three Purple Hearts, Athey decided he was too old to finish college and took up the trade of carpenter. He became a contractor and government inspector of buildings in California.

Dick Robb returned to Penn State, graduating with a degree attesting to his knowledge of ceramics. He held onto his commission in the U.S. Army reserves and barely escaped the call-up that put Chism in Korea. "In 1950," says Robb, "I was unmarried with a combat platoon leader's classification." He was thus a prime candidate for the short-staffed forces in Korea. And he soon presented himself for processing.

"I was called aside and directed to a desk manned by a major. 'So you have nightmares? What is your problem?' I was quite taken aback, particularly his tone of voice. I said, 'Major, the question was have you ever had nightmares? Every person who answered no is a liar. Even as a child you must have had them. Hell, I'd say there was nothing wrong with me that 50,000 dollars—a lot of money at that time—wouldn't cure.'

"What I didn't know was that he was a shrink assigned to evaluate fruitcakes and their complaints. He threw down his pencil and laughed as though he'd heard the funniest joke of the year." The major then shared with Robb some of the wilder excuses he had heard from men frantically seeking exemption from the war in Korea. He also told Robb two considerations that deferred service. One was work with atomic physics and atom bombs. The second was three Purple Hearts, which appeared on Robb's record.

"I learned later that two of my friends, both married, one with a child on the way and the other with a two-year-old son, and who had the same classification as I, were shipped to combat as battlefield replacement platoon leaders. I owe my third Purple Heart to Maurice White.

"In Manhay while clearing the buildings in town, another fellow and I entered one. Inside, up a staircase there was half-open door. I took two steps up the stairs, pulled the pin on a hand grenade and let the handle fly while still holding the grenade in my hand. Dumb! Definitely *verboten* but I wanted to make sure it would not be thrown back if someone was behind that door. I bounced the grenade off the door and into the room.

The other trooper stepped out the front door and I bent over while looking up at the ceiling and started to leave.

"The grenade went off and a fragment came down through the ceiling and hit me on the jaw, knocking me flat and a little groggy. There was no one upstairs when we checked. Outside, I felt my jaw where a small lump had formed and a little blood trickled down my neck.

"I saw White and asked him, 'Does a bit of blood from a hit mean a Purple Heart, even without going to the aid station?' I told him what happened and showed him my jaw. He told me it was a dumb stunt to arm a grenade in my hand and said shrapnel had hit my jaw. He wiped off the little cut with a piece of gauze, put some sulpha on it. 'If you forget that stupid story,' said White, 'I'll see that you get the Heart. I've treated you and I've already forgotten how you got it.'

"Little did I realize that White may have saved my life from the call-up six years later. I never got the opportunity to thank him but I often quietly do when I look at my children and grandson."

Robb accepted an honorable discharge from the army reserves in 1952 with the Korean War over. Postgraduate studies in metallurgy led him to employment for U.S. Steel engaged in providing plate for nuclear subs. A colleague persuaded him to accept a direct commission in the U.S. Naval Reserves, although his old problem of color-blindness restricted promotions. Eventually, Robb retired also from the Navy, with the rank of lieutenant commander.

Clark Archer, wounded four times but with no major permanent damage, left the service in 1945. He obtained a master's degree in engineering and for twenty-five years devoted his talents and training to the development of nuclear weapons and space projects. Mel Biddle went back to Indiana to marry the young woman whose casual remark about corresponding started him toward Toccoa and the U.S.'s highest military honor.

He occupied a post with the local Veterans Administration until retirement.

Howard Ruppel, like Biddle a replacement added to the 517th roster in Italy, studied the trade of draftsman and worked twenty-seven years for the Milwaukee Bureau of Engineers. Nolan Powell, after surgery and recovery confined him to hospitals for a year, became a teacher in upstate New York.

Artilleryman Nat Schoenberg, already introduced to the world of electronics before entering the army, signed on with the RCA Electronics Institute and for thirty-five years held jobs in the manufacturing side of the industry.

Many of those in the 596th, originally selected because of their technical backgrounds or orientation, continued that interest after their honorable discharges. Allan Goodman, part of the contingent that joined the 82nd Airborne in Berlin where he played football on the division team, enrolled again at the University of Illinois. "My experience in the service, not just the 517th, convinced me I did not want to take orders from the regular-army types I had met and gave me the impetus to complete my education." He had married during the Tennessee maneuvers in 1944 and his wife bore two children while he labored towards his degree in civil engineering. He retired from a steel contract construction and supply business in 1981.

Dave Armstrong, "a man of great character, loyal, bright and imaginative," according to Seitz, tried for the second time to become regular army but was denied again. He then established a law practice in North Carolina.

Charlie Pugh attended college and then studied dentistry at Baylor University. "I went to school full time and was able to complete seven years of college and graduate school in five years." He set up practice in Fort Worth, Texas.

Deacon Jones returned to civilian life thinking of

studying physical education. But the needs of a wife and daughter detoured him to a position in photoengraving, an industry in which he then spent more than thirty years until retirement.

Joe Holton, the redheaded replacement rifleman, tried the oil fields after leaving the army in October 1945. Using the GI Bill, he obtained a degree as a petroleum engineer from Oklahoma University and became a self-employed consultant in the field.

Joe Miller, the engineer who met up with Chaplain Charles Brown in Southern France, graduated from the University of Kentucky and became a specialist in health care, taking major administrative assignments in the field. Some years after the war, Miller dug into the official records on the actions of the combat team. He discovered documentation of what he had always suspected. "Our people had a better understanding of our role as part of a combat team than did the regimental leadership. We knew it was our lot to support all elements of the RCT with our engineering capability. We also knew we could take fight as infantry if needed. They rarely took advantage of our special expertise. I was astounded to learn that our daily reports went to the Corps Headquarters for Engineers instead of to our own regimental headquarters. The operational pattern could have contributed to our stepchild status."

Miller also focused some of his time and energy on a special project. "I became concerned about graves which were improperly marked as 13th Airborne. This led to a major effort to re-mark those in Southern France. It took two years but all of our dead are now identified as members of the 517th."

Jack Saxion, whose life had been shattered by the death of his wife and child while he awaited assignment from a replacement depot in Italy, decided to begin anew with a college education. "I enrolled at Penn State but I was twenty-six and felt old among the freshman. I quit and took a job at Alleghany Ludlum Steel." Marriage in 1947 restored him to a family environment eventually graced by three daughters and five grandchildren. Retired from the post of inspector at the steelworks, Saxion and his wife, Mrs. Pennsylvania in the 1965 Mrs. America contest, operated the old family farm while breeding and training Arabian horses.

There were, of course, some individuals who did not cope well with life after the 517th. Capt. George Giuchici, celebrated by his troopers and his battalion commander as a strong combat leader, could not retain his emotional aplomb in a peacetime army. Mustered out, he lost his life in a car crash.

Another trooper who could survive only in uniform, according to Dick Robb, was Lt. Olvie J. Nunnery, his platoon leader. "He had been First Sergeant of I Company and after John Gaunce, first sergeant of H, was killed, Nunnery replaced him and later received a field commission.

"Nunnery was the only man I have ever known who seemed not to know what fear was. Herman Melville's Starbuck in *Moby-Dick* knew that true courage only comes from a thorough understanding of the danger involved in any situation, and fear becomes an integral part of courage. Nunnery's bravery seemed to lack any element of fear. I had seen him so many times where he appeared to exhibit courage with a total absence of that element.

"He was a mountain boy, from Kentucky, I believe, poorly educated and naive about much of the ways of men in society. But he was a true leader. He left the army at the war's end but like many found life on the outside with its complex, undisciplined ways too much to handle. They miss the routine, and even more the order. Nunnery tried to return to airborne with his commission but apparently he missed the time limit. He could read and write but authorities felt not at a level high enough for OCS and commissioned status through that avenue. Not even Mel Zais could help him there.

"Ultimately, he came back as a sergeant and reached the highest NCO rank attainable. When it came time for him to retire after his 30 years, the command apparently planned no special deal. Zais heard about this lack of commemoration and arranged with the general in charge for Nunnery to receive a full ceremony. But when Nunnery finally left the service civilian life was no easier for him than it had been before. Only now, there was no place to escape. Unfortunately, his wife also had some emotional problems, perhaps due to his but maybe exclusively her own. One day when he came home, his wife shot and killed him with his service pistol, then turned the weapon on herself."

There were of course those who simply disappeared into the maw of America. Some found anonymity by marking out an obscure corner of the States and others disappeared quickly through the ravages of hard living. Such was the fate of Woodrow McQuaid, believes Robb. But for the most part, the 517th's alumni acquitted themselves well in business, the professions, government as well as the military.

CHAPTER XVI

THE LEGACY OF THE 517TH

WHATEVER THE SUCCESS or failure of former 517th troopers in their post–World War II life, the organization was created not as a finishing school for young men but to manufacture combat soldiers. All of the evidence indicates that in this respect, the regimental combat team more than met the hopes of its creators as it developed into a crack fighting unit. Its actions testified to the soundness of the ideas expressed by Gavin.

The combat team's success demonstrates among other elements the value of leadership. Bill Boyle summarizes that quality as exhibited in the 517th. "As a leader, I was taught to set the example. This was particularly true in that our men knew that the officers did and would do anything we asked of our men. Exceptions were rare. Zais, Seitz and I did all we could to correct or eliminate exceptions. Also, each commander felt he had the best unit. I know I was certain I did and I'd be disappointed if Dick Seitz did not believe he had the best. Somehow, when the CO feels this way, the men think the same. My troops knew I would not waste them."

The doctrine of leadership stated by Boyle was held also by Lou Walsh. In spite of those detractors who regarded him as Napoleonic in his zeal to achieve at whatever cost, Walsh's closest associates as well as the more distant, lowest-rank troopers perceived that whatever his motives, Walsh prepared them well for what they faced. Furthermore, Walsh by skill and perhaps some luck drew three battalion commanders who inspired their troops. Every one of them demonstrated that he would literally lead, take his place up front and expose himself to whatever the men faced and did.

Under the circumstances, it seems likely that had Boyle, Seitz or Zais failed to show Walsh their mettle, they would have been gone before the outfit shipped out. Indeed, when it came to the junior officers, where the ability to pick and choose was far more limited than with the enlisted recruits, the high turnover indicates that the brass of the 517th sought company commanders and platoon leaders who also led in the fashion decreed first by Walsh and then by the battalion commanders. Says Boyle, "My first company commander after I graduated from West Point told me, 'You take care of the men and they will take care of you.' I always tried to remember and practice that. I don't recall that I ever specifically instructed officers to follow this idea but I know that I did, occasionally, speak to individuals about taking care of troops and setting an example for them."

It was either extraordinary luck or a piece of inspired selection that put Rupert Graves in charge, after Walsh's transfer, on the fields of battle. Graves, in his own style, exuded the same high caliber leadership.

The excellence included the commanders outside the three rifle battalions. Dick Seitz, drawing on thirty-two years of experience, says of Raymond Cato, "He was probably the best artillery commander I have ever met, very aggressive and keenly attuned to supporting the infantry." Seitz offers equally high praise of Robert Dalrymple, the engineers commander.

Allan Goodman says, "Many of the men idolized Dalrymple and I frankly did not. During the trek across Southern France he had people standing guard over his sleeping area, which promoted some to fire a burst from a Tommy gun at night so he would lose sleep also. But I have found that I was wrong about him in my judgment and now admire the way he trained us all. Fred Zavattero was a martinet in training but a wild man overseas. He kept us away from company headquarters."

Joe Miller, from the bottom looking up, echoes Goodman. "Our officers were an unusually good group. They made it happen. It was leadership."

From the vantage point of an enlisted man and then himself giving the orders in his later career, John Chism notes, "As a general practice the commanders who were successful were up front in the best seat in the house. While they paid a heavy price, it insured the accomplishment of missions and in the long run saved a lot of lives. In the 517th this command location was practiced up and down the line." He adds the observation, "Officers and noncoms need to show themselves to the troops. Lieutenant Colonel Paxton had his CP at Col de Braus where the troops could see him when he was out discussing the situation with them. When the Germans attempted to hit Col de Braus with artillery, Paxton would fold his hands behind his head, put his feet up and present the very picture of nonchalance and coolness under fire."

"The battalion commanders," says John Lissner, "acted like fathers to these young kids," and in that respect the junior officers behaved much like older brothers. There was a conspicuous lack of mention of anything resembling "fragging," the practice of turning weapons on one's own superiors as occurred on occasion in Vietnam.

Leadership, however, can achieve only so much. The caliber of those who take their orders eventually determines success or failure. Some of the people from the regimental combat team argue that the process of selection insured a high quality. "We kept the best and shelved the rest," insists Tom Cross. But the bulk of the

3rd Battalion drew its people from the parachute school at Fort Benning. In combat, there was no significant difference in the achievements between one battalion of the 517th and another. No less an authority than Bill Boyle remarks that the value of the screening process may have been overestimated. "It may have eliminated some with whom we would not have been happy but the single most important thing was that each man had volunteered. That in itself eliminated most who would not measure up."

Whether the 3rd Battalion chiefs, Zais and his successor Paxton, were hampered with more disciplinary problems because of the lack of a voice in selection is unknown.

But who were the volunteers? An admittedly unscientific scan of the men who supplied material for this book indicates enthusiasm for participation in the war at a high level of involvement. Not only did a sizable number enlist rather than await a summons from the draft board but also many pursued what appeared to be the most exciting or challenging forms of service. Bill Lewis, Tom Cross and John Saxion all tried to become part of the Royal Canadian Air Force before Pearl Harbor. Other thrillseekers and risktakers attempted to join the Air Corps. Charlie Keen and his friends initially tuned in the glorybound call of the Marines.

The predominant image of paratroopers as blue-collar kids more interested in fun and games, throwing punches, chasing women and hanging out in saloons when not engaged in desperate blood-and-guts combat with the enemy appears genuine. John Lissner, who admittedly did his share of the whooping it up, says, "You've got these wild, tough young kids, like pups. You've got to let the leash out sometimes for excess energy. Unfortunately, after a couple of beers, there's a fight or argument here and there, mostly when someone comes back from leave or while on a pass into Toccoa and runs into a leg. It wasn't always possible to be a perfect gent when accosted by some brazen nonjumper."

That picture reflects the notice taken of the kind of boisterous conduct that is the meat of pungent anecdotes. And in the 1940s, the ethos of the era made alcohol consumption and pursuit of women by men in uniform not only acceptable but even praiseworthy. Within the ranks there were, however, individuals with different tastes, like DSC-winner Nolan Powell. "I was a loner who was thrilled to be in far distant lands and seeing many exciting places I had read about. Many things others did—brawling, barhopping and drinking—did not appeal to me."

The backgrounds of those interviewed indicates a cross-section of the U.S. as it was during the 1940s—with the exception of nonwhites who were largely denied admittance to the ranks of combat soldiers in a segregated military. The volunteers came from the ranks of the poor as well as the middle class and even the affluent.

A substantial number of them did have athletic interests, predominantly the team games that emphasized both physical contact and skill. Even future troopers who were not enamored of the traditional sports—Howard Ruppel, Mel Trenary and Ernie Kosan—saw the vocation of paratrooper as a way to prove to themselves their physical and mental courage, the "guts" cited by Bill Boyle.

Many of those who fought under the banner of the 517th, while growing up in a U.S. afflicted by the Depression, had the initiative to find jobs even though these were scarce. And few were high-school dropouts while a number managed to squeeze in a year or so of college before the demands of war put them in uniform. To qualify as a paratrooper, a candidate also needed to score above the minimum level on the army IQ exam. The bulk of the recruits were better educated, better motivated and more intelligent than the run-of-the-mill GI.

Some had ignored world events and volunteered because they regarded fighting for their country as a duty. Others recognized from the start the threat of the European dictatorships. Once in service, most of the troopers developed a finer appreciation for freedom after they witnessed the condition and attitudes of Italian, French and Belgian citizens oppressed by the Nazi jackboots.

There were those like Doyle Gray, mentioned by Keen, who killed without compunction. Others, like Howard Ruppel, were troubled by their trade. Dick Robb with his ambivalence probably is most representative of the attitude taken by the troopers. He could shoot down SS soldiers, the most brutal of Hitler's legions, with little compunction yet he never quite lost his sense of the terrible deeds required of a combat soldier.

Dick Eaton, who went from private at Toccoa to the rank of general, adding Purple Hearts while with the Rangers in Vietnam claims, "Every military unit forges for itself a sense of identity which reflects its 'soul'—belief in its institutional self, its capacity for sacrifice and the values and attitudes which give it unity. The soul of such old-line units as the Big Red One [1st Infantry Division] rests on a tradition which needs only to be renewed with each war's performance. The 517th, like the other new parachute regiments of World War II, had to create its soul with only the traditions of the American Army and imagined myths about a new kind of warfare as a base.

"I believe what lends the 'soul' of the 517th its special enduring intensity rests not on what the combat team achieved in battle alone. After all, every good unit develops a mythology about its exploits and heroes. Nor were individual members of the 517th supermen, supremely better than all the other soldiers in the Army. I believe our distinctive character—soul—took firm root before we entered our first combat engagement."

According to Eaton, the isolation at Toccoa allowed

the organization to develop its own unique character. The long periods in the hinterlands of Georgia and North Carolina undoubtedly contributed to the *esprit* that developed. As Eaton notes, other powerful ingredients glued the 517th into a unified organism.

By nature, military units tend to be closed off. The GIs in one company often have no contact with those of another. Indeed, within the 517th, many troopers knew nothing of their fellows in the other battalions. Still, as a parachute infantry regiment with 2,200 troopers and removed from its parent organization during its first phase of life, the 517th had more of the quality of a small town. GIs in divisions that numbered as many as 15,000 men were part of a city. In the larger size units, distance from command to enlisted man and the mysteries of the military bureaucracy were greater. The opportunity for a strong sense of connection beyond the most immediate buddies was lacking.

In contrast, the smallness of the 517th enabled an intimacy to flower. The troopers knew not only those in their squad but also the others in the platoon, the company and right up to their battalion commander, who, in the exercise of leadership, made it his business to work closely with them.

The practice of company or battalion control over discipline, including offenses against regulations and punishment, maintained a sense of family. There was no higher or outside court brought into a case. While the matter was adjudicated, albeit summarily, and the penalties exacted, the trooper remained in the community. No one enjoyed extra work details or restrictions but so long as these seemed fairly implemented by the senior members of the family, resentments were minimized.

The tightness of the 517th also was a product of time and circumstances. During World War II millions of soldiers, whether draftees or enlistees, did basic training at one installation, drew an assignment for added

instruction somewhere else and then finally reported to
an operational organization. The bulk of the World War
II paratroopers volunteered for airborne status while undergoing basic infantry training. Upon completing the
preliminary course, usually of seventeen weeks duration,
those accepted left the group with whom they first
learned their rifleman trade, and reported to Fort Benning. After a four-week course there they were assigned
to one of a number of paratrooper outfits—the 82nd,
101st, 13th, 17th, 11th or as in the case of most troopers in the 3rd Battalion, to the 517th.

Unlike their fellow parachutists, the bulk of the
troopers of the 517th went directly from the induction
center to the outfit with which they then spent their entire military lives. The same raw recruits that first heard
John Alicki's opening address in Toccoa, jumped together at Fort Benning, honed their tactical skills at
Mackall together, were shipmates on the S.S. *Santa Rosa*
or S.S. *Cristóbal*, "saw the elephant" together absorbing
the first awful realization that someone was out to kill
them when they moved up on the line in Italy. Those
who did not become KIA or wounded badly enough to
spend the remainder of the war in a hospital ward, stayed
together through ALBATROSS, the Champagne Campaign, the Ardennes and the last advance on Schmidt.
They shared misery of life in combat as well as the few
moments of pleasure snatched during the intervals away
from battle. That continuity forged bonds of enormous
strength. The troopers developed a sense of their organization. They would commit themselves for others. As
Boyle notes, "When men live, eat, train, gripe and suffer
together, they stick together. These are men I loved and
protected where I could. And when I was wounded they
did the same for me." They refused to "leave him out
there."

Ed Athey credits Lou Walsh with welding the troopers together. "I hated the son of a bitch and occasionally thought about shooting him in the back when we would go into combat. When I first came to the 517th, I arrived on a train about 3:00 A.M. and after I reported in I flopped down on a bunk. I was rudely awakened a couple of hours later and brought in front of Walsh who chewed me out because three men in my platoon, which I'd not even seen yet, were AWOL. He assigned me to latrine duty. But he was so tough on everyone that those who served under him naturally banded together."

Part of the mystique of the 517th also lay in its regard for its own. "You had the feeling that the 517th would always be home for you," says Tom Cross. "When I was wounded and came back, it was clear that I would return as the exec for Seitz, even though someone else held the slot while I was being treated." When Robb and another sergeant received their battlefield commissions, Rupert Graves, as obligated by the rules, offered them the opportunity for a transfer to another outfit. Neither man would hear of it, and both requested to return to their platoons.

The combat team emphasized promotion from within. Noncoms moved up to the junior officer level (there were eighteen battlefield commissions in the 1st Battalion alone, according to Don Fraser). The system retained the best people, individuals who merited the confidence of the troopers.

The mix of excellent leadership, the training and discipline inculcated and the basic nature of the men produced the intangibles of courage and heroism under even the most horrendous circumstances. Bill Boyle offers a formula to explain how the troopers summoned up the courage to continue. "Training and discipline teach us to react to certain stresses in a certain way. I define courage as the ability to overcome fear which everyone has. Heroism is more likely to be an action taken in answer to specific situations so it is partly due to circumstances. Camaraderie contributes. Anything that enables us to have confidence in our fellows contributes."

As Di Stanislao indicated, after the 517th came off the line following its attack from Bergstein only a shell of the original outfit remained, and many of those still standing literally bore the scars of battle. The war may have been won but the 517th had taken a substantial beating in the process. While there was no great incidence of post traumatic stress syndrome, the catch-all of the ills seemingly incurred by participants in Vietnam, some troopers were bothered by nightmares and flashbacks. Jim Moses, certainly one of the more phlegmatic of the troopers, confesses to disturbing dreams decades later. Nat Schoenberg's wife says he frequently begins to weep when scenes of World War II flash on the TV screen. John Lissner still talks of "the kids" although all of the survivors are eligible for Social Security. And he remembers with regret those like Lt. John Casselman whose lives ended abruptly.

Flashbacks inevitably afflict the veterans fifty years later. Dick Robb, for example, when faced with the necessity to put down a beloved family pet suddenly recalled his terrible moments when he could not keep the body of Richard Lynam from being left out there. Robb forced himself to place the dog in a box for burial. "It was only right that this be done by someone who truly cared than by just anyone." The .45 inherited from Lynam, the notches filed off to avoid complications if Robb had been captured, has lain in his night table since he came home.

Still, the 517th emerged from World War II a victorious group and winning often irradiates a team with a warm glow of camaraderie. In the case of the 517th, however, the feelings run deeper than just the surface glow cast by triumph.

Winston Churchill once remarked on the exhilaration

of being shot at and missed. In that vein, both Ben Renton and Don Fraser profess to love their time with the 517th, even though Renton was not missed six times. (Because of double woundings on two occasions, he collected only four Purple Hearts.) Their attitudes undoubtedly reflect the sentiments expressed by Ludlow Gibbons, "Ninety-nine percent of all the excitement I have had in my life took place during the time I spent in combat. I believe it to be the ultimate test. I have never experienced anything close to it, before or since."

Indeed, asked why they volunteered for paratroop training, troopers commonly spoke in terms of testing themselves and of the prospect of excitement. At the time they could not have realized what their commitment would entail but nevertheless, the urge for this kind of experience was pervasive. The continued enthusiasm for their service with the 517th also bespeaks the phenomenon known as euphoric recall in which nostalgia screens out the negative experiences. In spite of the horrors he witnessed, Ben Sullivan now insists, "It was a great experience. It had a little bit of everything. I had no worry about finding my next meal, I lived the good life when not under combat conditions."

One consequence of the bonds forged over the thirty-three-month period and nurtured by that memory of the good times is the strength of the 517th's alumni association. While many military units formed such groups after World War II, the annual get-togethers of 517th graduates on both coasts plus the national reunion every two years draw a high percentage of the living.

On his own, Charlie Keen publishes a newsletter about B Company men. Barney Hekkala does the same for A Company. Charlie Keen also solicited members of the 1st Battalion to contribute money to help rebuild the church at St. Jacques and supply new gold candleholders for the altar. Serving as archivist, Clark Archer has diligently compiled accurate information on the

outfit's history. Tom Cross contributes a column about
members of the 517th to the *Static Line,* a newspaper
for the airborne. The alumni's concern for one another
stretched beyond reunions. Throughout his illustrious
career, Mel Zais, as he did for the retiring Nunnery, kept
an eye out for old 517th troopers. He was always delighted when a Tommy Thompson or Ludlow Gibbons
looked him up. In Vietnam, Zais made special arrangements just to shake the hand of Russel Brami's paratrooper son. Clark Archer corresponded with Lou Walsh
until the latter's death.

The aging vets have made pilgrimages to the battlefields of Europe where the grateful citizens of liberated
areas continue to welcome them and commemorate
their actions with plaques and monuments. A Belgian
battle marker at the Haid-Hits crossroads, for example,
celebrates the feats of the 1st Battalion between Soy and
Hotton. Markers at Wanne, Logbierme and St. Jacques
all name the 517th. Another tablet at Draguignan, created by the French, inscribes the 517th for participation
in ALBATROSS.

World War II, the last great conflict waged by a fully
united people, is long gone, succeeded by conflicts of
muted fame or inglorious controversy. The talk about
the U.S. military concerns its mission in a world without
a challenger of similar status, of downsizing, of the roles
of the draft, women and gays. The veterans of the
517th, for the most part stalwart believers in a strong
army, like the rest of America divide on the other issues.

In Shakespeare's *Henry V,* the young king rallies his
yeomen before the Battle of Agincourt with an appeal to
their sense of glory. What remains most vividly with the
former 517th troopers in their twilight years, are memories of their own Agincourts. Like those warriors from
Henry V, they too are entitled to say, "We few, we happy
few, we band of brothers."

INDEX

GERALD ASTOR is a World War II veteran and award-winning journalist and historian whose articles have appeared in *The New York Times, Playboy,* and *Esquire.* He is also the author of *A Blood-Dimmed Tide: The Battle of the Bulge by the Men Who Fought It* and *Operation Iceberg: The Invasion and Conquest of Okinawa in World War II.* He makes his home in Scarsdale, New York.

WAR

The glory, the horror, the excitement of men in combat—all captured in these unforgettable true stories